Using Experience to Develop Leadership Talent

The Professional Practice Series

The Professional Practice Series is sponsored by The Society for Industrial and Organizational Psychology, Inc. (SIOP). The series was launched in 1988 to provide industrial and organizational psychologists, organizational scientists and practitioners, human resources professionals, managers, executives, and those interested in organizational behavior and performance with volumes that are insightful, current, informative, and relevant to *organizational practice*. The volumes in the Professional Practice Series are guided by five tenets designed to enhance future organizational practice:

1. Focus on practice, but grounded in science
2. Translate organizational science into practice by generating guidelines, principles, and lessons learned that can shape and guide practice
3. Showcase the application of industrial and organizational psychology to solve problems
4. Document and demonstrate best industrial and organization-albased practices
5. Stimulate research needed to guide future organizational practice

The volumes seek to inform those interested in practice with guidance, insights, and advice on how to apply the concepts, findings, methods, and tools derived from industrial and organizational psychology to solve human-related organizational problems.

Previous Professional Practice Series volumes include:

Published by Jossey-Bass

Diversity at Work: The Practice of Inclusion
Bernardo M. Ferdman, Editor
Barbara R. Deane, Associate Editor

Developing and Enhancing Teamwork in Organizations: Evidence-Based Best Practices and Guidelines
Eduardo Salas, Scott I. Tannenbaum, Debra J. Cohen, Gary Latham, Editors

Managing Human Resources for Environmental Sustainability
Susan E. Jackson, Deniz S. Ones, Stephan Dilchert, Editors

Technology-Enhanced Assessment of Talent
Nancy T. Tippins, Seymour Adler, Editors

Advancing Executive Coaching: Setting the Course for Successful Leadership Coaching
Gina Hernez-Broom, Lisa A. Boyce, Editors

Going Global: Practical Applications and Recommendations for HR and OD Professionals in the Global Workplace
Kyle Lundby with Jeffrey Jolton

Strategy-Driven Talent Management: A Leadership Imperative
Rob Silzer, Ben E. Dowell, Editors

Performance Management: Putting Research into Practice
James W. Smither, Manuel London, Editors

Alternative Validation Strategies: Developing New and Leveraging Existing Validity Evidence
S. Morton McPhail, Editor

Getting Action from Organizational Surveys: New Concepts, Technologies, and Applications
Allen I. Kraut, Editor

Customer Service Delivery
Lawrence Fogli, Editor

Employment Discrimination Litigation
Frank J. Landy, Editor

The Brave New World of eHR
Hal G. Gueutal, Dianna L. Stone, Editors

Improving Learning Transfer in Organizations
Elwood F. Holton III, Timothy T. Baldwin, Editors

The Professional Practice Series

Using Experience to Develop Leadership Talent

How Organizations Leverage On-the-Job Development

Cynthia D. McCauley

Morgan W. McCall, Jr.

Editors

Foardswo by Allan I. Kraut, Moheet Nagrath, and Inge G. Thulin

JB JOSSEY-BASS™
A Wiley Brand

**Library of Congress Cataloging-in-Publication Data has been applied for and is on file with the
Library of Congress.**
ISBN 978-1-118-76783-2 (case); ISBN 978-1-118-76787-0 (ebk); ISBN 978-1-118-76796-2

Printed in the United States of America

FIRST EDITION

HB Printing   10   9   8   7   6   5   4   3   2   1

Contents

List of Figures, Tables, and Exhibits

Foreword
Series Editor

Many recent books in this Professional Practice Series focus on leadership, although they may use somewhat different phrases such as assessment and talent management. The search for good and better ways to select and develop leadership talent is of major interest to industrial-organizational psychologists and the organizations they help. It is our good fortune that the present book approaches the topic from a new angle and thus adds considerable value to our knowledge and practice.

I am reminded that some years ago, two of my well-established friends and colleagues (both became SIOP presidents) had a vigorous debate on whether selection or training was the best answer to getting better leaders. One had played a leading role in creating assessment centers, and he insisted that only selection mattered and that training added very little. The other disagreed. He was invested in management development training and felt that formal training could be of great value. These two viewpoints offer different ways to improve the level of leadership effectiveness. The debate continues about which of the two is more effective.

Now, fortunately, this book suggests a third viewpoint: the importance of experience, or on-the-job learning. Perhaps this approach can be considered as the third leg of a three-legged stool or as a Venn diagram with three overlapping circles. One of these is selection, a second is training, and the third is on-the-job experience. Job experience provides important development beyond formal classes, and success in doing one's job, in turn, becomes an important aspect of selection for further opportunities.

Some decades ago, as a fledgling member of IBM's newly formed Executive Resources Department, doing what would now be called succession planning and high-level talent management, I saw that all of these perspectives—selection, training, and experience—were recognized and noted. But they were not understood nor appreciated as parts of a coherent whole that could increase the level of leadership performance in the organization. It is exciting to see how the current volume ties together these different components and puts a long overdue emphasis on the value of on-the-job experience in developing leaders.

The editors of this book are in a rare position to observe these issues and to contribute to our understanding of them. Cynthia McCauley is a Senior Fellow and long-term staff member of the Center for Creative Leadership (CCL), perhaps the largest premier management development institution in the world. She is deeply involved in its offerings, including those custom-designed programs for specific companies. She also headed CCL's research and development division for many years and has co-edited three editions of *The Center for Creative Leadership Handbook of Leadership Development* (Van Velsor, McCauley, & Ruderman, 2010).

Morgan McCall has long written about the importance of job experience. His book *The Lessons of Experience* (McCall, Lombardo, & Morrison, 1988) is one of the all-time best-sellers in our field. And more recently, he extended those lessons based on his research in *Developing Global Leaders: The Lessons of International Experience* (McCall & Hollenbeck, 2002). As a former staff member of CCL, he was the leader of the team (with Michael Lombardo and David DeVries) that developed the Looking Glass Simulation, which has been used by tens of thousands of CCL management attendees to improve their leadership skills. As a professor of management and organization, McCall has also offered leadership courses to hundreds of MBAs attending classes at the Marshall School of Business at the University of Southern California. He and McCauley are deeply aware of the role of training and selection in addition to job experience as ways to build leadership talent.

I am especially pleased that this volume has materialized at all. I thank the book's editors, Cynthia McCauley and Morgan McCall, for agreeing to lead the development of this book. Both of them are extremely busy people, fully engaged in their professional lives, and it was generous of them to accept the burdens of time and energy that are required to produce a volume like this.

Of course, one of the benefits of being a book editor is that you can choose the contributors you would like to invite and shape the entire structure of the book to suit your vision of the field. McCauley and McCall have done so by enlisting the very best people on this topic, and working with them to produce chapters that will add to our knowledge and practice. The same label of "extremely busy people" also applies to the chapter contributors; their efforts are also much appreciated by me.

As even a brief look at the table of contents shows, they have done an extraordinary job here. The contents of the chapters represent a variety of viewpoints—from industry, consulting, and academia—but mostly from practitioners reporting a variety of innovative approaches. The book includes case studies from a dozen organizations, most of them global enterprises, and the chapter contributors come from Europe and India as well as from the United States—both of which highlight that leadership has become a global issue.

The chapters show diversity in how organizations accomplish three over-arching essential tasks:

- Making job experience a key part of the organization's talent development process
- Designing and/or choosing the job experiences that will enhance leadership development
- Ensuring that the learning from experience will be maximized.

Looking at the book in its entirety gives us a distinctive view of the importance of on-the-job experience, both in terms of its potential for assessing leaders as well as for strengthening the leadership bench in organizations. When job assignments intended to provide critical experiences are monitored and integrated with other aspects of talent management, they can be extraordinarily useful for raising the level of leadership performance in an organization. The various chapters in this book provide a range of perspectives and a nuanced understanding of how on-the-job experience can develop leadership capability of individuals and the firms in which they work.

In closing, I want to note what many readers of this series likely do not know: the editors and chapter contributors receive no payment nor do they share in the royalties of the book sales. These monies go to SIOP to encourage professional publications such as this. That means that the contributors are sharing their views and knowledge with us as a personal contribution to our profession. Their willingness to impart hard-won experience and knowledge is a gift to us, the readers. And for this I am genuinely grateful.

For their fine work, I want to acknowledge and thank the editors of this book and all of their distinguished chapter contributors. And to all of you readers, welcome to an intriguing and useful set of readings.

ALLEN I. KRAUT, Ph.D.
Series Editor
Rye, New York

References

McCall, M. W., Jr., Lombardo, M. M., & Morrison, A. M. (1988). *The lessons of experience: How successful executives develop on the job.* Lexington, MA: Lexington Books.

McCall, M. W., Jr., & Hollenbeck, G. P. (2002). *Developing global executives: The lessons of international experience.* Boston, MA: Harvard Business School Press.

Van Velsor, E., McCauley, C. D., & Ruderman, M. N. (2010). *The Center for Creative Leadership handbook of leadership development* (3rd ed.). San Francisco, CA: Jossey-Bass.

Foreword
A Senior HR Executive Perspective

*A mind that is stretched by new experience can never go
back to its old dimensions.*

OLIVER WENDELL HOLMES

Does all the effort, time, and investment poured into leadership
development really make a difference? The answer to this critical
question depends on how each organization chooses to measure
the success of the leaders it develops. Most of us recognize that
developing a robust and diverse pipeline of leaders who consistently deliver results is the lifeblood of any enterprise. It ensures
the sustainable growth of its business and its long-term survival in
volatile, continually changing markets around the world.

But how do organizations know whether all the activity directed
toward developing leaders is delivering a return on their investment? Unfortunately, it is not uncommon to see an absence of
business discipline in developing leaders. There is a real risk that
all the flurry of "feel good" activity is a distraction. It can create
an illusion that leaders are ready and capable of leading—often
leading to disruptions in the enterprise.

The most effective programs that develop leaders are strategically directed toward building a multi-generational cadre of talent
able to address emerging business challenges and take the business to a new level of performance. As a result, developing leaders
is a long-term activity. It plays out over time as individuals grow
through different experiences. And it requires a long view of the
strategic challenges of a business and the capabilities that are
necessary to win in the marketplace.

In the ultimate analysis, success of leadership development efforts is measured by the growth of the business and the

productivity of the organization. As an example, doubling business revenues in ten years with almost the same number of business leaders at the top two or three levels, most of them developed internally, clearly demonstrates a high level of effectiveness in developing leaders. Organizations that recognize this business imperative elevate the strategic value of developing the right leaders.

There is another compelling reason to elevate the importance and rigor in developing leaders. Long-term investors are influenced by the consistent quality of leadership in an enterprise—in addition to all the other earnings and industry related criteria they may consider. The reputation of the enterprise for the quality and depth of its leadership has a significant and meaningful impact on how investors and shareholders see the potential upside of the business. In fact, it is a governance responsibility to the shareholders and investors to ensure that the best-qualified leaders are developed and capable to lead the business. What better motivation to develop leaders than as a mission-critical business initiative?

There's a catch. The recognition that a systemic and enduring effort to develop current and future leaders is a source of competitive advantage can be brought to life only if the executive leadership of the enterprise sees it as an integral part of their responsibility. The "tone from the top" sends an all-pervasive message that influences the quality of leadership development efforts. Beyond exhortation, the real test of the importance of developing leaders shows up in the "smell of the place" and the amount of executive time invested and the resources allocated.

We know that business executives with a sustained track record of developing talent take voluntary accountability for identifying talent, coach and mentor potential leaders, actively engage in talent management forums to decide the best assignments to groom leaders, continually assess and provide feedback, and reward the best performers with the highest potential. As a consequence, the personal reputation that they acquire is a powerful magnet for high-achieving talent who want to work under their leadership. It is self-evident that leaders who develop leaders make all the difference. But how much attention do we pay to grooming, rewarding, and promoting these leaders?

There is an art, a science, and a technology to developing leaders. There is far too much at stake—the success and the future of an enterprise—to rely on amateur efforts, however well-intentioned and highly motivated. The systemic approach that integrates a wide range of developmental activities to build the required capability in leaders is a crucial and central work of experienced, professional experts. In essence, it is the balanced integration of three sets of activities that delivers results.

The first is an in-depth understanding of the business strategies and the challenges facing the enterprise. This in turn leads to identifying the leadership capabilities needed to win against the competition. The logical conclusion of this exercise is the design of experiences—such as assignments, roles, and projects—that, with the right amount of coaching and mentoring, will build the required capabilities.

Secondly, significant time and effort are appropriately spent on the identification of talent—finding the high achievers and those with the highest potential to grow. However, the pitfall here is that not all tools are effective in identifying talent. The most effective way is time-tested and a classic: watch your talent in action, over time, and in wide-ranging experiences.

No discussion about identifying talent and developing leaders can ever be complete without emphasizing the importance of diversity. The diversity of ideas and thinking that emerges from diversity of experiences and backgrounds simply cannot be replicated without a diverse talent pool. The most effective leadership development efforts embed the inclusion of diverse talent—in the broadest sense of the term—from the very early stages of developing leaders. There is no question that diversity is a success measure in a global economy. This is especially true when competitors can gain an edge by attracting and developing the best talent regardless of their thinking style and who they are as persons. Is this reflected in every organization's efforts to groom leaders?

The third set of activities is providing discontinuous experiences to accelerate the development of leaders. Exposing talented people to different kinds of experiences that develop them for specific destination roles is another time-tested classic. It is the most intuitive of all methods. Ask any leader what has influenced his or her personal growth and chances are it was an experience or exposure to another person. And yet providing these line experiences is the most challenging to implement in a systemic way. It involves the design and sequencing of experiences, coupled with catalysts that guide the individual to extract maximal learning. Inevitably, the availability of experiences is determined by the growth of the business, its scale and complexity, as well its organization structure.

Bringing these three sets of activities together—the business challenges, the talent, and the needed experiences—is the overarching strategy to develop leaders. In my experience, the ideas I have touched upon in this foreword are tested and they work. This book showcases the initiatives of a wide range of practitioners who recognize the strategic importance of experience-driven leadership development and have made the effort to convert ideas into practice. Their efforts can serve as a guide to others who seek to develop a leadership bench by making more effective use of experience. The emphasis on strategically relevant experiences and managing them with the rigor of a business is what distinguishes serious leader development from a hobby.

As they say, "hope is not a method." I believe that every organization deserves the leaders it develops.

Moheet Nagrath
Leadership Strategist
Leadership Architecture Worldwide LLC
(former Chief Human Resources Officer, Procter & Gamble)

Foreword
A Senior Line Executive Perspective

As a young hockey player in Sweden, I was fascinated by how coaches developed players—drawing the best from them and even pushing them beyond what they imagined possible to realize their full potential. These coaches understood that "ice time" is an essential part of becoming a top performer and a leader on the ice. There is no substitute for game experience.

As the CEO of 3M, developing our people is my top priority to ensure the future success of the company. Our approach to leadership development is centered on experience-based opportunities to give our people the "ice time" they need to build their strengths and become effective leaders. That's why I believe this book is so relevant and will help business leaders to build future leaders.

Using Experience to Develop Leadership Talent captures many diverse approaches to leadership development—all with an emphasis on experience-based learning. Chapter 3 more fully describes 3M's perspective on how leaders are shaped and how we weave together complementary human resources programs with real job experience. In addition, I offer these personal insights into developing leaders by affording them the right experiences in the right way:

- *Be intentional and strategic.* Planning out what developmental experiences are needed by an individual enables you to make choices that grow both people and businesses as situations arise. In other words, you need to plan to have the opportunity to be spontaneous.

- *Offer timely feedback to help people learn from experience.* Feedback is key to growth. It is best delivered immediately to be most effective and constructive. Focus on what is right for the business and do not make it personal.
- *Recognize and appreciate an individual's life experiences, in addition to business experiences, as people are shaped by both.* Take time to get to know people personally to better understand them and to gain insights into how to coach them.

At 3M, leadership development is an integral part of our business strategy. Ultimately, it is every leader's responsibility to develop talent. I believe what we have learned at 3M, along with the many companies in this book, can inspire others to use experience more effectively in developing their leaders. I hope this book encourages a broader dialogue among leaders to find new ways to continue to draw the best from their players.

INGE G. Thulin
Chairman of the Board, President, and CEO
3M

Acknowledgments

We would like to thank all of the authors of the chapters in this book who took valuable time, often from their personal lives, to share with us and with the larger professional community what they have learned from their experience. Thanks, too, to the organizations whose experiments are described in this book for allowing their stories to be told so that others may learn from and be inspired by their efforts. We also want to recognize Valerie Burns and Gloria Bader, whose innovative work has informed and encouraged us, even though it is not represented in this book.

We offer a special acknowledgment to Karen Paul, who not only contributed a chapter to the book and supported the research that went into another one, but also supported efforts to promote the book and was instrumental in convincing Inge Thulin to write a foreword. Speaking of which, we appreciate that both Inge Thulin and Moheet Nagrath believed enough in what we were doing to write forewords to the book.

Without the support, encouragement, and feedback from the members of the editorial board of the Society for Industrial and Organizational Psychology's Professional Practice Series (2011–2012), this book would never have happened. Our special thanks go to Allen Kraut who, as the series editor, commissioned this book and, with his inimitable charm, convinced the two of us to take it on. We appreciate his faith in us and his guidance as we struggled to put the pieces together.

The Editors

Cynthia D. McCauley is a senior fellow at the Center for Creative Leadership (CCL). With more than twenty-five years of experience, Cindy has been involved in many aspects of CCL's work: research, publications, product development, program evaluation, coaching, and management. Capitalizing on this broad experience, she has developed expertise in leader development methods, including developmental assignments and relationships, 360-degree feedback, and action learning. She co-developed two of CCL's assessment tools, Benchmarks and the Job Challenge Profile, and regularly coaches action learning teams. She has written numerous articles and book chapters for scholars, HR professionals, and practicing managers. She co-edited three editions of *The Center for Creative Leadership Handbook of Leadership Development* (Jossey-Bass, 1998, 2004, 2010). Cindy has a B.A. in psychology from King College and a Ph.D. in industrial-organizational psychology from the University of Georgia, and is a Fellow of the Society for Industrial and Organizational Psychology, the American Psychological Association, and the American Educational Research Association.

Morgan W. McCall, Jr., is a professor of management and organization in the Marshall School of Business at the University of Southern California. His research on the development and derailment of executives has appeared in numerous articles and books, including the trilogy *The Lessons of Experience* (Free Press, 1988), *High Flyers* (Harvard Business School Press, 1998), and *Developing*

Global Executives (Harvard Business School Press, 2002). He received the Distinguished Professional Contributions Award from the Society for Industrial and Organizational Psychology and the Executive Development Roundtable's Marion Gislason Award for Leadership in Executive Development. He has a B.S. degree with honors from Yale University and a Ph.D. from Cornell University, was director of research and a senior behavioral scientist at the Center for Creative Leadership, and is a Fellow of the Society for Industrial and Organizational Psychology. Morgan has applied his research findings on experience-based development of leadership talent in a number of companies, including Disney, Toyota, Eaton, Microsoft, and Procter & Gamble.

The Contributors

Nisha Advani, a senior principal in global talent management and development, Pharma Medicines, Roche, Inc., is responsible for designing and driving talent management strategies across the global pharma medicines division. Prior to this, as director of talent and organization development at Genentech, a member of the Roche group, she led a group of senior organization development, workforce analytics, and talent management consultants. In her more than fifteen-year corporate career in market-leading companies, including Genentech, Cisco, Anthem Electronics, and Intercontinental Hotels, Nisha has designed and implemented leadership development as well as a variety of organization development solutions. She is passionate about strategic talent development and applies social science principles to create business-relevant solutions for developing executive pipelines and effective human organizations. Nisha holds a Ph.D. in social-organizational psychology from Columbia University, a master's degree from Cornell, and an M.A. in social relations from The Johns Hopkins University.

Aditya Ahuja works at Tata Group Human Resources and is currently leading the TAS program. In this role he is responsible for identification of talent and talent development, with a view to create a leadership pipeline for the Tata Group. Aditya has diverse experience in the field of human resources spanning fourteen years, during which he has worked across companies in the energy, consumer goods, and industrial consumables sectors. He holds a master's degree in personnel management and is passionate about organization development. Aditya believes strongly in simple and efficient solutions to complex issues. In his spare time, he pursues hobbies that fire his creative side.

Asma Bagash has been a consultant in the talent acquisition team of Group HR, Tata Sons. In her seventeen-year career, she has worked in the area of human development across the education and corporate sectors. She began her career as a pre-primary teacher and later taught junior college students in India. She has been associated with the Tata Group since 2002, when she joined the Group HR team and was involved in talent management processes. She later moved to VSNL, the group's telecom company, where she managed the talent development and leadership development endeavors. A constant learner by nature, she believes in learning from experiences and using them to improve herself. She obtained her master's degree from the London School of Economics in industrial relations and human resource management.

Prakash V. Bhide served as group president, JK Organisation (Eastern Zone) for ten years until April 2012. He initiated and led the HR transformation at JK Organisation, which resulted in HR becoming a strategic partner with group businesses. In this role, he successfully conceptualized and implemented the Indian way of Krishna–Arjuna coaching and mentoring for six hundred high performer and high potential leaders and the Fire of Experience initiative for leadership development. He is also leading the Game Changing Innovation initiative in the JK Group. Prakash is a sought-after speaker and thought leader in the field of talent management, leadership development, 360-degree feedback, executive coaching and mentoring, building the leadership pipeline, and the differentiated workforce. He has a B. Tech (Mechanical) from the Indian Institute of Technology (Bombay, India) and a Ph.D. in leadership from XLRI (Jamshedpur, India) and the Academy of Human Resources. He has International Coaching Certification and has been honored with a Fellowship by the All India Management Association.

Brad Borland is senior director of global talent management and leadership development at Kelly Services, Inc. Brad is a lifelong learner and practitioner in the areas of human and organization development. He has a deep curiosity and interest in topics that include appreciative inquiry, experience-based leadership development, and client-driven organization change. In his current role, Brad is responsible for senior leadership development systems and practices, succession planning, executive coaching, and facilitating organization development interventions. He originally joined Kelly Services in 1995 as human resources development manager and returned to Kelly in 2007 as director of leadership development. Brad has worked in industries and organizations that include higher education, health care, and information solutions. He earned a B.S. from Ohio Northern University and an M.A. from Bowling Green State University in Ohio.

Steve Chapman is an independent change and creativity consultant who is fascinated as to how organizations *really* work as opposed to how they are *supposed* to work. Having spent more than twenty years in the corporate world, including as a senior learning and organization development director in a major blue-chip company, he brings a mix of experience and experimentation to his work. He has worked with a wide variety of clients in the pharmaceutical, FMCG, mobile telecoms, airlines, water, arts and culture, and charity sectors, helping them through times of change by developing their own creative and innovative spirit. He holds a M.Sc. with distinction in organizational change from Ashridge Business School, where he returns as visiting faculty to talk about change and improvisation. He is a speaker on change and creativity and writes a popular blog on the subject. His six-year-old daughter is his creative mentor and artistic director.

Dagmar Daubner works at HEINEKEN International, based in Amsterdam. She is currently responsible for the company's global diversity and inclusion strategy. Dagmar joined HEINEKEN in 2009 as an independent consultant, and in 2011 she was employed as a learning and development consultant. In this role, Dagmar was responsible for leadership development, in particular for HEINEKEN's global first-line manager development program (FLM-DP) and the international graduates' development. Dagmar is from Germany, where she previously worked in marketing and human resources roles in the white goods industry. She holds a bachelor's degree in business administration and an M.A. in organizational psychology. Dagmar is currently pursuing an external Ph.D. in organizational behavior at the VU University Amsterdam.

Vicki Flaherty helps individuals express their full potential and bring their best to their work. She is a leadership development consultant in IBM's talent organization. During her nearly fifteen years with IBM, she has led a variety of talent programs in the areas of on-boarding, leadership development, coaching, mentoring, learning, and career development. She is an IBM Corporate Service Corps alumnus, was a key member of the research team that developed IBM competencies, and has won awards for her work designing global career frameworks. She was instrumental in launching IBM's Storage Solutions certification portfolio and led various quality initiatives for the Professional Certification Program from IBM. She has consulted with companies across a variety of industries to transform their businesses via human performance and change management initiatives. She served on the board of directors for Green Building Certification Institute and as a commissioner for the Institute for Credentialing Excellence. Vicki received her doctorate from the University of Georgia.

J. Tim Galbraith retired as vice president of People Development for Yum! Brands, Inc., in 2012 after a twenty-seven-year career. His most recent areas of focus include leveraging organizational culture to drive business performance, facilitating leadership and executive development for breakthrough results, and partnering with Yum! Brand's chairman and CEO to deliver the chairman's signature leadership development program to executives around the world. Tim held various positions in management development and human resources at Frito-Lay, Inc., and led the training and development function for the U.S. and international businesses at Kentucky Fried Chicken. He played an instrumental role in structuring the new restaurant organization during the spinoff from PepsiCo and was named head of People Development for Yum! Brands. In this role he led all aspects of organization design, culture transformation, and executive and leadership development. Tim received a Ph.D. in industrial and organizational psychology from Bowling Green State University.

Terry Hauer is director of leadership development at Kelly Services, Inc., and a member of the organization's global talent management group. She led the cross-functional, global project team that completely revamped Kelly's performance management process. Terry also supports leadership selection, coaching, and executive assessment efforts, along with succession planning and strategic workforce planning. In Terry's previous roles with Kelly, she provided Kelly's branch operations and external customers with a variety of pre-employment tools and consultative support; and as a member of the HR development group, designed and facilitated development programs for people leaders. Terry has worked in industries and organizations that include public sector, consumer products, and HR consulting.

Randall W. Hill, Jr., is the executive director of the University of Southern California Institute for Creative Technologies (USC-ICT). A leader in understanding how classic storytelling and high-tech tools can create meaningful learning experiences, Randall steers the institute's exploration of the integration of virtual humans, mixed reality worlds, advanced computer graphics, dramatic films, social simulations, and educational videogames to augment more traditional methods for imparting lessons. He is a full research professor in the computer science department at the USC Viterbi School of Engineering. His research focuses on intelligent tutoring systems and virtual humans to create immersive learning environments. After graduating with a B.S. degree from the United States Military Academy, he served six years as a commissioned officer in the United States Army, with assignments in field artillery and military intelligence. He earned his M.S. and Ph.D. degrees in computer science from the University of Southern California.

Lori Homer, leadership development consultant, is a member of the Leadership Development Group at Microsoft, where she works with general managers and executives to promote increased leader and organizational effectiveness. Lori is responsible for Microsoft's most senior high potential development program, leadership assessment, and supporting leaders' and HR partners' ability to design high-performing organizations. Lori is passionate about supporting leader growth at work through increasing awareness and learning agility and about making good use of formal development time by creating space for leaders to learn from one another, explore different perspectives, and have conversations that matter. Lori contributes to growing leaders outside of work, including working with a local area girls' camp, Seattle University's Executive MBA program, and a local non-profit dedicated to building better community leaders. Before joining Microsoft in 2007, Lori was an independent consultant. Lori holds a bachelor's degree in economics with honors from Brigham Young University and a Ph.D. in management from the University of Washington's Foster School of Business.

Jim Howard is the director of learning and talent management at Disney Consumer Products, where he is responsible for building employee and organizational capability to execute on key business strategies, and for developing the leadership pipeline to ensure strong leadership bench-strength. He is also responsible for the Culture of Innovation initiative, designed to foster a culture of creativity and innovation. Prior to re-joining Disney, Jim was director of Yum! University at Yum Brands. While at Yum! Brands, Jim focused on re-branding, elevating, and aligning Yum! University with the business. One key element of that strategy was the recasting of the organization's leadership development strategy to integrate experience-based development into it and make development more accessible globally. Jim began his career at The Walt Disney Company, where he had a variety of training, organization development, and leadership development roles. Jim has a master's degree in higher education administration.

Cindy Johnson is director of leadership development for 3M. Her focus is on developing leadership talent across 3M, ensuring that

3M has the leadership talent to fill key positions, and helping 3M leaders ensure they have team members with the capability to execute business strategies. In her role, she is dedicated to helping 3M continue its track record of excellence in leadership development. Since 2003, *Fortune* magazine has ranked 3M as a Top Global Company for Leaders. Cindy has responsibility for setting the strategic direction and scope for global leadership development at 3M in support of global, regional, and local business goals, needs, and requirements. Her global team delivers programs to accelerate leadership development; assure a pipeline of leaders globally; align leadership development with 3M vision, strategies, and values; and build a high performing diverse global talent. She is a seasoned business leader with more than twenty-five years of experience in executive and global leadership development, employee development programs, and facility management.

Rajeev Kakkar is currently general manager, Corporate HRD, with the JK Organisation, New Delhi. In his twenty-nine-year career, he has worked in diverse industries in the areas of executive development and international marketing with Indian corporations. His areas of focus include learning and development, coaching and mentoring, leadership assessment, and development; his areas of interest include cross-cultural and international management. Rajeev completed his B.S. degree at San Francisco State University and his post-graduate in human resource management from XLRI (Jamshedpur, India) and in international management from International Management Institute (New Delhi, India).

Kathie Karls is the director of strategic workforce planning and talent acquisition for 3M. Her focus is to integrate the health of the organization, human capital planning, performance management, succession planning, and business analytics, along with recruitment and identification of high performing and diverse global talent. After two years of directing the workforce planning team, Kathie now has the responsibility for setting the tactical direction and scope for strategic workforce planning and talent acquisition at 3M. Both of her teams are delivering programs to ensure 3M's current and future success. Kathie is a seasoned leader with more than eighteen years of experience in the human resources field. She is a certified Six Sigma Black Belt, Facilitative Leader, and PDI coach. She has leadership training in organizational design and EEOC Charge of Discrimination Responder, as well as labor negotiations.

Elizabeth B. Kolmstetter, a member of the senior executive service, is the chief human capital officer at the U.S. Agency for International Development. Prior to joining USAID in 2013, she served on a joint duty leadership assignment in human resources at the Central Intelligence Agency (CIA), where, among other talent management initiatives, she managed the agency's joint duty program. She was on rotation from her position as the deputy associate director of national intelligence for human capital at the Office of the Director of National Intelligence (ODNI). Elizabeth has more than twenty years of public service in which she has pioneered numerous complex applied industrial-organizational programs across six agencies. She has worked in the private sector with BellSouth Corporation and in consulting with Westat, Inc. Elizabeth received her M.A. and Ph.D. in industrial-organizational psychology from Virginia Tech. She is a Fellow of the Society for Industrial and Organizational Psychology (SIOP), a recipient of SIOP's M. Scott Myers Award for Best Applied Research, and recipient of the National Intelligence Superior Service Medal for her leadership in human capital transformation, including the joint duty program.

Allen I. Kraut, series editor for the SIOP Professional Practices Series, is professor emeritus of management at Baruch College, City University of New York, which he joined in 1989. For much of his professional career, he worked at the IBM Corporation, where he held managerial posts in personnel research and management development. In 1995, he received the SIOP's Distinguished Professional Contributions Award, recognizing his work in advancing the usefulness of organizational surveys. In 1996, Jossey-Bass published *Organizational Surveys: Tools for Assessment and Change*, by Allen Kraut and Associates. His latest book, *Getting Action from Organizational Surveys: New Concepts, Technologies, and Applications*, is a 2006 publication by Jossey-Bass.

Kim Lafferty is head of learning and development at GlaxoSmith-Kline. She leads a team of experts within the talent, leadership, and organization development Center of Excellence at GSK. She is responsible for designing and implementing the global leadership development framework that forms the strategy for investing in people development. Kim designs and runs the Enterprise Leadership program for the most senior high potential executives and the CEO Forum hosted by Sir Andrew Witty. She also sits on the Enterprise Learning Council, which implements GSK's learning operating model. Prior to joining GSK, Kim worked at the Center for Creative Leadership. She has worked in learning and development for more than twenty years in various roles: in Academee (a collaborative e-learning start-up), Management Center Europe (a European training provider), Costain plc (an international civil engineering and construction company), and Waitrose ltd (a British food retailer). Kim holds a B.A. with honors in politics from York University, an M.A. in management learning from Lancaster University, and a Diploma in organization development from NTL.

Jeffrey J. McHenry is the founder and principal of Rainier Leadership Solutions and an adjunct professor of management at Georgetown University. Jeff's areas of expertise include leadership talent management, succession planning, executive coaching and assessment, leadership team building, and leadership and high potential development. He frequently speaks and delivers workshops at professional conferences, including the Conference Board, Linkage, and the Human Resource Planning Society. He has consulted with numerous clients, including Cigna, Juniper Networks, 3M, the Gates Foundation, Microsoft, and Panasonic. Previously, Jeff spent eighteen years at Microsoft Corporation, where he held a variety of HR and talent development roles based in both the U.S. and Europe. His last role at Microsoft was general manager, leadership development and recruiting, where he was responsible for executive recruiting and talent management, leadership and high potential development, and organization development for the entire corporation. Jeffrey has a Ph.D. in psychology from the University of Minnesota. He is a Fellow of the American Psychological Association and the Society for

Industrial-Organizational Psychology. He served as the society's president from 2006 to 2007.

Douglas McKenna is co-founder of The Oceanside Institute, which is located on Whidbey Island in Washington State. He works with young leaders, guiding their efforts to understand their context, refine their thinking, and improve their performance. In 1986, Doug found himself inside the door of Microsoft, a fledgling software company with four hundred employees, led by brilliant, aggressive young leaders whose strengths were decidedly more technical than managerial. Over the next sixteen years, first as a consultant and then as a general manager, Doug designed, built, and led Microsoft's leadership development effort—with invaluable assistance from Jeff McHenry. Throughout this process, Doug's core organizing principles were: (1) leaders grow primarily through digested experience and (2) Microsoft leaders must master the company's unique culture and context. Doug earned a Ph.D. in differential psychology at the University of Minnesota and stretched his understanding of the discipline of psychology by teaching courses ranging from experimental psychology to organizational psychology—all in a liberal arts context alongside philosophers, artists, and historians.

Dilep Misra currently serves as group president, human resources, with JK Organisation. His background spans more than twenty-five years of demonstrated achievement in human resources, organization learning and development, and strategic planning. Dilep's prior experience includes leadership assignments with leading-edge companies, where he earned a reputation for creating and implementing sustainable business solutions and developing leadership team and organizational capability. In addition, Dilep is a sought-after international speaker and International Coaching Federation certified coach. He has been invited to address events in Hong Kong, Singapore, Malaysia, the United States, the United Kingdom, and India. He was conferred with the award of Super Achiever in 2003 and Best Leader of the Year in 2004. Dilep is a past chapter president and life member of the National HRD Network (India). He is actively involved with SHRM, the Conference Board, and the International Coach

Federation (ICF), and on the governing board of the Management Institutes.

Moheet Nagrath is a leadership strategist with Leadership Architecture Worldwide and the former chief human resources officer for Procter & Gamble (P&G). In his thirty-year career with P&G, Moheet held senior-level positions in several businesses and senior corporate executive roles, making important contributions to a progressive, advanced, and fully integrated human resources organization. As CHRO, he was responsible for business-integrated strategic priorities and operational practices for all leadership, people, and organization aspects of the business. Moheet retired from P&G in 2013 to set up his own global consulting business and is bringing his competency in leading, designing, and orchestrating systemic change in global, strategic capabilities to other organizations. In addition, he is teaching, writing, and providing thought leadership in these areas of expertise.

Radhakrishnan Nair completed his post-graduate diploma in personnel management and industrial relations from Xavier's Labour Relations Institute, Jamshedpur, in 1984. In his career spanning more than twenty-seven years, he has worked in diverse industries from the automotive, metals, telecom, banking, and information technology sectors. Since 2002, Radha has been with the Tata Group and has worked on various assignments. Apart from the group HR assignments as vice president of learning and management development, he has been the head of HR of VSNL, the Tata Group's telecom sector. He has also been the head of HR for Tata Steel as well as the director of Tata Management Training Centre. Radha believes in a spiritually enriched life. His beliefs are an outcome of the learning he has had as a devotee of Bhagawan Sri Sathya Sai, believing in "Help Ever, Hurt Never" and "Love all, Serve all," a learning that has helped better his understanding of the role HR plays in organizations and employee development.

Mathian Osicki is a leadership development partner at IBM. She has been with IBM for twelve years in various roles, including senior employee climate researcher in global workforce research;

global manager of equity in executive compensation; two general-ists positions; lead climate analyst in Bangalore, India; a services contract sale in Cross River State, Nigeria; and most recently a leadership development role in the hardware business unit of IBM. Mathian received her Ph.D. in industrial-organizational psychology from the University of Tulsa. Mathian has attended school or worked in many parts of the world, including Canada, New Zealand, France, Poland, Japan, China, India, and most recently, Nigeria.

Karen B. Paul is responsible for leading the global measurement center of expertise at 3M. She has responsibility for the creation and execution of global strategy for executive assessment and coaching, testing, organizational survey research, engagement and retention, and employment brand. In her nineteen years with 3M, Karen has held numerous positions, including HR generalist and specialist assignments. Her chapter in *The Executive Guide to Integrated Talent Management*, published by ASTD, details the five year close collaboration within talent solutions at 3M that has resulted in numerous awards, including Best Practice by APQC for rewarding, engaging, and retaining key talent; HR Best Practices profiled in the SHRM video *Leadership Assessment, Succession and Development*; Top Companies for Leaders sponsored by the Hay Group; Best Companies for Leaders led by Hewitt and Associates; and the 2012 Best Companies for Leaders conducted by the Chally Group for *CEO* magazine. Karen received her Ph.D. in industrial-organizational psychology from Bowling Green State University and is a Society for Industrial and Organizational Psychology Fellow.

Mary Mannion Plunkett is the vice president of global talent management and development for Carlson, responsible for talent and performance management, resourcing, leadership development, and organizational capability. Previously, Mary worked abroad as the global director of people and organization development for HEINEKEN International, senior vice president of talent management for Lehman Brothers, and vice president, executive development, for BP. She has more than eighteen years of experience in the field of leadership and organization development, including roles with The Boeing Company, Ernst & Young, and McDonnell Douglas Aircraft Company. Mary also served as an adjunct professor in the organizational behavior department at Seattle Pacific University. She graduated from St. Louis University with a Ph.D. in industrial-organizational psychology. She has published numerous articles and co-authored *Real Time Leadership Development* (Wiley-Blackwell, 2009).

Laura Ann Preston-Dayne is a director in the talent management and leadership development group at Kelly Services, Inc. In this role she is responsible for creating and executing a global development strategy for Kelly's people managers. Laura Ann also provides leadership development support for workforce planning, talent segmentation, and succession planning. Prior to joining Kelly Services, she worked as a consultant for Personnel Decisions International, where she provided talent management, assessment, coaching, and development services to Fortune 500 clients. Laura Ann received both her M.A. and Ph.D. in industrial-organizational psychology from Central Michigan University, where she now serves as an adjunct faculty member. She has presented research on talent segmentation, multi-source feedback, high potential development, organizational restructuring and downsizing, and Six Sigma.

Inge G. Thulin is chairman of the board, president, and chief executive officer of 3M Company. A thirty-three-year veteran of 3M, he served as executive vice president and chief operating officer of 3M after having served as executive vice president, 3M International Operations. Inge joined 3M Sweden in 1979, working in sales and marketing, and subsequently assumed levels of greater responsibility. With hands-on experience building businesses in both developed and developing economies, he has a broad grasp of societal trends. For example, his business background and Nordic upbringing helped shape his view that the global trend toward sustainability presents tremendous opportunity for 3M to both improve the environment and 3M's business performance, simultaneously. He is also known for emphasizing teamwork, a concept he learned to value as a young hockey player in one of Sweden's top leagues. Inge earned degrees in economics and marketing from the University of Gothenburg, Sweden. He is a member of the Council on Foreign Relations, and Business Roundtable.

Connie Wayne, executive coach and leadership development consultant, has more than sixteen years of experience in the area of organization, leadership, and talent development. She has provided individual and organization development consulting in a variety of business models and has guided the implementation of numerous development processes, such as performance management, change management, and rotational development programs. Connie joined Eaton Corporation in 2000 as manager of organization development and was promoted to a new role as head of executive development. In this role, she was responsible for conducting assessments, on-boarding, coaching, development planning, and selection processes for the senior executive positions within Eaton. She was responsible for the design and facilitation of Eaton's executive development program, "In the Zone," and has been personally involved in the development and coaching of more than one thousand Eaton executives. Prior to joining Eaton, Connie spent fifteen years with Avery Dennison in sales, management, and leadership development. She holds a bachelor's degree in education, with a minor specialization in psychology from Ohio University.

Meena Surie Wilson is senior faculty with the Center for Creative Leadership and author of *Developing Tomorrow's Leaders Today: Insights from Corporate India* (Wiley, 2010). Her previous responsibilities include launching the CCL-Asia Pacific office (Singapore) in 2003 as interim managing director and directing the start-up of CCL's Asia Pacific research, innovation, and product development unit in 2006 to advance knowledge about leadership and leadership development in Asian countries. Meena's credits include book chapters, articles, keynote addresses, and workshops on learning from experience and cross-cultural leadership. Meena completed her undergraduate studies at Mills College in Oakland, California, holds an M.S. degree from Syracuse University in television-radio journalism, and a Ph.D. in adult and organization development from UNC-Chapel Hill. She is currently based in Jamshedpur, India.

Paul R. Yost is associate professor of industrial-organizational psychology at Seattle Pacific University. His current research and work focuses on three broad areas: strategic talent management, leadership development, and change management. Before teaching, Paul served as senior research specialist at Microsoft, with responsibilities in talent management, executive assessment, and leadership development. He also managed leadership research with The Boeing Company, where he focused on leadership training and development, training evaluation, and employee surveys. Previous experience includes work in assessment and selection, managerial training, and team effectiveness in positions at GEICO and Battelle Research. Paul received his Ph.D. in industrial-organizational psychology from the University of Maryland.

Section One

Introduction

CHAPTER ONE

Experience-Driven Leadership Development

Surveying the Terrain

Morgan W. McCall, Jr., and
Cynthia D. McCauley

> *You have to take the ones with the most potential and
> send them where the action is. That way you achieve two
> ends: You get the problem taken care of, and you get a
> manager who's grown through experience. Leaders are
> formed in the fire of experience. It's up to the head of the
> company to prepare a new generation and send them to
> hot spots as part of their training. He must prepare for a
> smooth transition by training people, guiding them,
> pushing them forward, but not too hard. Then, from
> among them, he must choose the successful ones, the
> future managers and directors, the ones he has confidence
> in, not because they're someone's protégé but because
> they've faced difficult tasks and accomplished them.*
>
> CARLOS GHOSN
> CHIEF EXECUTIVE OFFICER
> NISSAN AND RENAULT
> (GHOSN & RIES, 2005, PP. 152–153)

This isn't HR speak about development; this is the language
of a driven line executive facing a daunting challenge who recognizes that he needs to develop talented leaders if the company is
to be successful. If you are wondering what experience-driven
leadership development is, Ghosn's description provides a

starting point. Business success, he is saying, requires identifying people with potential, giving them challenging assignments, and holding them accountable for *both* results and growth. The process is driven by the senior leaders and, most importantly, by the chief executive. In other words, it's not the responsibility of human resources (although they have a crucial role to play); it's the responsibility of line managers. It's not about training or educational programs (although they can contribute value); it's about learning from job experience. And it's not about a process that is a nice extra benefit or a "human resource strategy," it's a part of the business strategy. Or, as Moheet Nagrath, former chief human resources officer at Procter & Gamble, put it, "Is leadership development a business necessity or a hobby?" (Nagrath, 2013)

That challenging experiences are central to developing leaders is what successful executives first told us almost three decades ago and we originally documented in *The Lessons of Experience* (McCall, Lombardo, & Morrison, 1988). It turns out that all "hot spots" and "fires" are not the same—experience comes in many shapes and sizes and its lessons are equally diverse. But the types of experiences that matter can be identified and are consistent across corporations and even across cultures (McCall & Hollenbeck, 2002). What differentiates experiences and at the same time makes them potent learning events are various kinds and degrees of adversity and challenge (McCauley, Ruderman, Ohlott, & Morrow, 1994). The specific lessons offered up by the different kinds of experiences are to some degree predictable and consistent (Lindsey, Homes, & McCall, 1987; McCall & Hollenbeck, 2002).

Knowing what experiences matter and what they potentially teach is a good beginning, but applying that knowledge requires answering additional questions. How do you identify who should have the relevant experiences? If the needed experience is across a boundary—say in another division or business or country—what mechanism can be put in place to move people in a safe and timely manner? Obviously, learning from experience is not automatic. Barbara Tuchman observed that, in politics at least, "learning from experience is a faculty almost never practiced" (1984, p. 383). So what can be done to increase the likelihood that the appropriate lessons will be learned? And finally, what does a successful leader look like in a particular organization, and how do the strategic business needs of the organization drive the use of experience to develop those leaders?

These questions led McCall (1998) to propose a framework to guide practice in more systematically using experience to develop leadership capacity. Simply put, the framework suggests that if people with potential are given the opportunity to engage in strategically relevant experiences, and something is done to ensure that they learn the lessons of those experiences, it increases the probability of having the leadership talent necessary to lead the business strategy. Each of the six elements—strategy, experience, talent, mechanisms for moving across boundaries, catalysts for promoting learning, and the resulting increased leadership ability ("the right stuff")—is a potential leverage point for improving the overall process of developing leadership talent (see Figure 1.1). For example, the ability to learn from experience is a key ingredient in identifying leadership potential (Spreitzer, McCall,

Figure 1.1. Examples of Leverage Points for Developing Leadership Talent

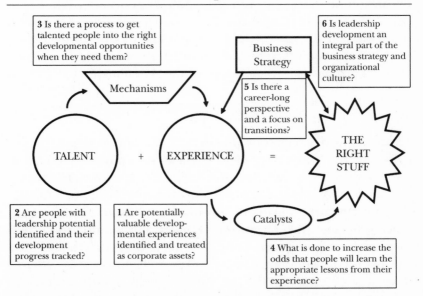

& Mahoney, 1997), so organizations can leverage that knowledge by finding ways to assess potential leaders on that dimension prior to giving them strategic experiences.

Putting Experience at the Heart of Development

Some organizations have worked to put experience at the heart of development, or at least to use it more effectively. At the request of the Society for Industrial and Organizational Psychology, we have gathered a number of contemporary efforts at doing so. Twelve of the eighteen chapters highlight a specific organization that is, in one way or another, using experience to develop leadership talent. Their efforts range from a focus on first-level management to very senior executives; from very specific programs to systemic interventions; from U.S.-based corporations to those based in India and Europe. The remaining chapters (excluding this introduction and the conclusions) dive into special topics: virtual reality experiences, everyday disciplines to enhance learning, bosses who are exceptional people-developers, and driving on-the-job development into the whole organization. While only some of the chapter authors have consciously used the McCall framework, it provides a guide to a number of the issues raised in the chapters and to the ways in which the organizations represented here have leveraged each of the six elements.

Driven by the Business Strategy

Most of the development practices described in this book are driven by the business strategy. For some it's a matter of growth and the need for more leaders with specific skills (e.g., JK Organisation and IBM). For others it is a matter of ensuring that leaders have the breadth to lead effectively across divisions, functions, or businesses (e.g., Tata Group, Genentech, and Eaton). Still others have leadership development deeply embedded in the core strategy and it is a core value of the CEO (e.g., GSK and 3M). Starting development early and finding ways to reach the large number of junior managers is a strategic thrust for some (e.g., HEINEKEN and Yum! Brands). The Intelligence Community, in contrast, is responding to a Congressional mandate to develop leaders who have crossed agency silo boundaries.

The importance of a direct and significant link to the business strategy cannot be over-emphasized. Access to specific job assignments, projects, bosses, and resources—the sine qua non of experience-based development—often depends on the business rationale and commitment of senior executives (so much so that Yost argues for getting rid of "HR speak" in favor of business language).

Focused on Experience

All of the chapters in this book deal with experience one way or another; it was one of the criteria for selection. It was interesting to observe how ever-present the "70–20–10" dictum has become as a rough guideline for the distribution of experience, other people, and courses. It has found its way into some companies' performance management processes, where an expectation might be for the development plan to contain 70 percent experience, 20 percent coaching or mentoring, and 10 percent training. Whether or not they follow the 70–20–10 rule of thumb, the chapters illustrate the variety of ways experience can be used and created. At Eaton, for example, an effort was made to systematically identify developmental jobs and experiences and then to build them into the career planning process. This resulted in a tailored set of experiences specific to the corporation, complete with the rationale for why they were important and what learning could be expected from them.

Several organizations designate particular assignments to be used for developmental purposes. For example, in the Intelligence Community, agencies have defined certain positions as "joint duty," meaning that they are permanently used as cross-boundary experiences. And two key assignments at Kelly Services (head of a global function and country general manager) are reserved for the further development of high-performing senior leaders. One of the most sophisticated uses of experience is at Tata Group, where newly hired high potential managers are given several cross-function, cross-company, cross-industry projects plus a community project in a year, followed by two two-year stints in a group company.

The most common kind of experience used comes in the form of projects of various kinds and degrees of sophistication. IBM and Microsoft both have programs that send talented managers to do good in developing parts of the world. At GSK you might spend six months in London exploring the future.

Among the more unusual uses of experience are JK Organisation's program aimed specifically at developing managers into better bosses, the Institute for Creative Technologies' (ICT) use of virtual humans to simulate interpersonal leadership situations, 3M's emphasis on community service, and Genentech's 10 percent of time for six to nine months in a different function.

In short, these organizations use special projects, cross-boundary assignments, programmed and time-limited postings, and other online experiences as developmental opportunities, and when those aren't available, create substitutes for them. Identification and use of assignments for development has been heavily exploited by these organizations.

Identifying Potential

While identifying and creating developmental experiences is common across these organizations, the same can't be said for the identification of leadership potential to decide who gets what experiences. For the most part the organizations described here rely on traditional assessment methods, mostly human judgment applied with varying degrees of rigor. Perhaps the most sophisticated approaches to assessment in this volume are found in our two Indian companies: JK Organisation combines assessment center data with intense evaluations by business leaders, while Tata Group uses a rigorous selection panel and puts candidates through a series of evaluations ("stage gating").

As a general practice, multiple assessors are used, but who they are varies. In some cases decisions are made by panels or boards consisting of human resources professionals, while in others both line managers and human resources are involved. In almost all cases in which the development processes are not available to all managers, nominees are chosen from a high potential pool or through some variation of a succession planning process or other nomination procedure. One exception is the IBM Corporate Service Corps (CSC), where managers apply for the opportunity to participate and top management prospects are selected by human resource review boards.

Few of the practices described in these chapters are consistent across organizations, and identification and selection of talent is no exception. There does seem to be a tendency, however, for increasingly serious involvement of line managers in assessment as more of the developmental experiences are real assignments with real performance expectations.

One particularly unique approach is used by Kelly Services. The recruitment process involves a rigorous assessment of each candidate's strengths and weaknesses, and that information is used to tailor a development plan for each of them.

While who does the evaluation of candidates and the process they go through in doing it are frequently spelled out, less often specified are the criteria used in evaluating candidates. Competency models of various sorts have stormed the corporate kingdom, so they, along with consideration of career goals or target jobs, often comprise the criteria for assessment discussions.

Mechanisms for Movement

It is often preferable and certainly less risky to develop people by reshaping or adding to their current jobs rather than by giving them new assignments. Sometimes, however, the business strategy requires that future leaders have broad exposure across organizational boundaries (e.g., see Eaton, 3M, Tata, and Genentech), or the experience a developing leader needs simply is not available in the current job.

For a variety of reasons, making cross-boundary moves can be problematic. To take just a few examples, managers may not be sanguine about giving up their most talented people, even for such a good cause as their development; people being "developed" may not want to leave their current geography, assignments, or units; the organization may not want to risk derailing one of its talented managers (crossing boundaries is one of the situational factors that can trigger derailment); or the recipient of the developee may not be comfortable taking on an unknown or lesser known quantity while simultaneously denying the position to one of its own (much less risk a decline in performance if the newcomer is not up to speed). Even in an organizational culture that supports cross-boundary moves, managers may not have sufficient knowledge about what experiences are available in various parts of the organization or why exposure to them might be important.

When significant resistance exists or knowledge of jobs is limited, there has to be some process in place to facilitate cross-boundary moves. We have labeled such processes "mechanisms," and they may be as simple as the hiring manager making the call or as complicated as a formal succession planning process starting at the bottom and working its way up to the senior management team. Organizations intent on using experience to develop leaders address the issue in a variety of ways. For example, at Kelly Services decisions are made at talent summits and accountability for follow-through is assigned. At IBM selection decisions for the Corporate Service Corps are made by a cross-agency board with representatives from relevant stakeholder groups. 3M uses executive resource committees, tier reviews, and succession plans that are reviewed by the CEO for their developmental implications.

Obviously, there are efficiencies when the same process that identifies or assesses talent also makes placement decisions, but whatever the actual mechanism there seem to be two critical ingredients: the deliberating body must have the authority to move people, even if there is resistance, and the deliberating body must have the knowledge to make informed decisions that take into account specific developmental needs of individuals and the risk to both business performance and to the individual's career. Both of these criteria suggest that accountability for developmental moves and their outcomes should reside in high-level executives (authority) from the various domains under consideration (knowledge).

Catalysts for Development

It seems obvious that experience does not come with guarantees. People can be amazingly immune to learning anything from their experiences and, with a little creativity, can even learn the wrong things. It is no surprise, then, that the organizations in this book add numerous catalysts to the potential-plus-experience mixture in hopes of precipitating the desired outcomes. These catalysts include a buffet of interventions for both the developee and the boss, including:

- Feedback from multiple sources, including senior management, coaches, 360 assessments, sponsors, mentors, bosses, panels, and peers. JK Organisation, for example, involves eight different stakeholders to provide feedback as well as a safety net. At 3M there are three distinct roles—mentors (all top executives serve as mentors), sponsors (who provide career guidance and advice), and champions (who nominate people for important projects).
- Accountability for development, for example, at Kelly Services, where bosses are held accountable for developing their people, or at Yum! Brands, where development is assessed in individual development plans and at people reviews.
- Online training and processes, such as Genentech's self-serve website and the extensive online processes Yum! Brands used to achieve global scale.
- Various forms of support and safety nets, such as the ongoing reviews at Tata.
- Workshops designed to provide tools and knowledge that could be applied immediately in the current assignment, like those at GSK to support teams working on a strategic project and at HEINEKEN for first-time supervisors.
- Workshops and programs designed to build networks and supplement or even replace job experience, like the programs at Microsoft and the leader-led sessions at 3M.
- Special attention to transition points, a part of career assessment at Kelly Services, and a focus at re-entry from a strategic assignment at GSK and from a joint duty assignment in the Intelligence Community.
- Developing a methodology for deliberate practice as part of leadership self-development, as described by McHenry & McKenna.
- Group sessions before, during, and after assignments, as in the intensive preparation for and debriefing after the projects in IBM's Corporate Service Corps and in HEINEKEN's continuous learning groups for first-line managers.

In addition, the chapter by Yost outlines a series of possible interventions from a human resources perspective, and McCall and McHenry report on a study of what exceptional bosses do that enhances learning from experience.

Organization of Chapters

The chapters are clustered according to their central emphasis. The chapters in Section II, "Putting Experience at the Center of Talent Development Systems," are the most comprehensive, emphasizing a systemic perspective linking business strategy and experience in a broader context of other organization practices. The second and third sections are more focused: Section III, "Designing Job Experiences for Leader Development," concentrates on identifying, using, or creating developmental experiences, while Section IV, "Maximizing Learning from Experience," pulls together chapters dealing with catalysts—helping make learning from experience intentional.

Although clustered together based on their general emphasis, the chapters in this book provide numerous examples for each of the elements of the development-from-experience framework described in Figure 1.1. To help readers find which chapters explore which of the elements with more depth or in a more novel way, we have created Table 1.1 as a rough guide to chapter content.

We should point out that diversity of approach is simultaneously the strength and weakness of an edited book. As editors we have made every effort to assure consistency in the quality of content and writing of each chapter, but celebrate and have taken great care to preserve the differences in perspective offered by each author. You will find, for example, that some chapters provide detailed examples of how to coach individuals as they choose and make sense of experience (e.g., chapters by Wayne and McHenry & McKenna). These chapters can be very helpful to line managers in their role of helping others (or themselves) navigate stretch experiences, and to others like business partners or coaches who provide such advice and counsel. Other chapters take you almost step-by-step through the design of an experience-based system (e.g. Yum! Brands) or program (e.g., Microsoft, ICT, and HEINEKEN), so can be valuable guides for human resource professionals who find themselves responsible for the development

Table 1.1. Guide to Chapter Content

	Strategy	Experience	Talent	Mechanisms	Catalysts	Right Stuff
Eaton	X	X		X	X	X
3M	X	X	X		X	X
Yum! Brands	X	X			X	X
Kelly Services		X		X	X	X
Yost	X	X			X	
Tata Group		X	X	X		
Intelligence Community	X	X		X		X
GlaxoSmithKline	X	X		X	X	X
IBM	X	X	X	X	X	X
Genentech		X		X	X	
JK Organisation		X	X	X	X	
ICT		X			X	
Microsoft	X	X	X		X	
HEINEKEN	X	X			X	X
McHenry & McKenna		X			X	X
McCall & McHenry		X			X	

Key

Strategy: Chapter contains at least moderate coverage of how the organization's particular business strategy or business challenges initiated or shaped the experience-driven development system or initiative.

Experience: Chapter contains an in-depth description of the experiences (on line or created) used for development.

Talent: Chapter contains a reasonably detailed description of how talent is identified for decisions about who to put into the experiences.

Mechanisms: Chapter provides at least moderate coverage of how people get moved into developmental assignments outside of their current jobs.

Catalysts: Chapter provides a detailed description of tactics for encouraging and supporting learning from the experience.

Right Stuff: Chapter either provides a framework of leadership ability that the experience-driven system or initiative is aiming to improve or reports in detail on the impact of the system or initiative on leadership ability.

of similar things. For those readers interested in high tech or high volume delivery, some chapters describe web-based and evolving technologies to achieve efficiencies and scale (e.g., ICT and Yum! Brands).

We make no pretense that the twelve organizations represented here are inclusive or representative of all organizations using experience in some systematic way to develop talent. While they include four of the world's most admired organizations (IBM, Microsoft, 3M, and Yum! Brands were in *Fortune*'s top 50 listing for 2013), we chose them based on personal contacts and word of mouth because they were doing interesting things and because we found someone who was willing to write about what they were up to. We have no doubt there are many others out there with still more to offer, but we are satisfied that the people and organizations in this book represent some of the best minds tackling the challenges of implementing experience-driven leadership development. Ironically, one of the oldest and most obvious approaches to leadership development ("of course leadership is learned from experience") turns out to be one of the most difficult things to actually implement systematically.

It seems that around every corner there is another paradox to resolve—short-term results versus long-term development, choosing the most qualified person for the job versus the person who could learn the most, assessing potential versus current performance, leadership development as a business necessity versus development as a hobby, and one set of leadership competencies versus many ways to lead successfully. It is our hope, and the hope of the authors, that the experiments recorded here will inspire others to take on the challenge of using experience to develop leadership talent. After all, it's when challenges push us outside of our comfort zones that we learn!

References

Ghosn, C., & Ries, P. (2005). *Shift*. New York, NY: Currency Doubleday.

Lindsey, E. H., Homes, V., & McCall, M. W., Jr. (1987). *Key events in executives' lives*. Greensboro, NC: Center for Creative Leadership.

McCall, M. W., Jr. (1998). *High flyers: Developing the next generation of leaders*. Boston, MA: Harvard Business School Press.

McCall, M. W., Jr., & Hollenbeck, G. P. (2002). *Developing global executives: The lessons of international experience.* Boston, MA: Harvard Business School Press.

McCall, M. W., Jr., Lombardo, M. M., & Morrison, A. M. (1988). *The lessons of experience: How successful executives develop on the job.* Lexington, MA: Lexington Books.

McCauley, C., Ruderman, M., Ohlott, P., & Morrow, J. (1994). Assessing the developmental components of managerial jobs. *Journal of Applied Psychology, 79,* 544–560.

Nagrath, M. (2013). Lecture to Management and Organization 571, Marshall School of Business, University of Southern California, April 15, 2013.

Spreitzer, G., McCall, M. W., Jr., & Mahoney, J. (1997). Early identification of international executive potential. *Journal of Applied Psychology, 82*(1), 6–29.

Tuchman, B. (1984). *The march of folly.* New York, NY: Ballantine.

Putting Experience at the Center of Talent Development Systems

CHAPTER TWO

Building Leadership Breadth at Eaton Corporation

Connie Wayne

If there is anything organizations have in common, it is the need to adapt to changes in the business environment. Change is everywhere, and great leaders learn to respond to the changes in their markets, to the needs of their customers, and to the increasing impact of global economies. These changes also affect how organizations approach leadership development, as the skills that have made leaders successful in the past will probably not sustain them for future success. As business strategies change, organizations must examine how they identify and communicate expectations of leadership: How does the model of successful leadership need to change to support the new business strategy? What new skills will leaders need? What skills are no longer relevant, or could actually be harmful to the achievement of business goals?

Such was the situation that Eaton Corporation found itself in in the late 1990s. A stalwart manufacturing company, Eaton was at that time approximately $7 billion in sales, headquartered in the mid-western city of Cleveland, Ohio, and solidly entrenched as a leader in components for the truck and automotive industry. Additional businesses included electrical, aerospace, hydraulics, and semi-conductor components.

Each of the businesses in Eaton's portfolio was largely autonomous, run by a strong, decentralized leadership team with its own business processes and practices. Few systems ran across the entire enterprise, and, in fact, there were multiple duplicate processes. For example, at one time there were at least four very different performance management systems in the organization, with variations in the assessment process and rating scales. If there was any interest in an employee moving to another business, there was no consistent way to address the employee's performance or potential for advancement. As a result, talent movement was typically vertical, up through the individual business rather than across the organization. Few, if any, leaders were moved across the enterprise or worked across the lines of business, and, if they were moved, it was usually within functional roles rather than into general management positions.

An additional factor resulting from this decentralized model was lack of interest in sharing best practices. Business leaders worked independently and felt they needed to solve their own problems rather than learn from peers in other parts of the company who had addressed similar issues, that no other part of the organization could have the same problems, and that they had nothing to learn from their peers. Leaders therefore spent a good deal of their time immersed in internal matters, redesigning the "plumbing" of their individual organizations rather than focusing on external factors—especially customers. Eaton did maintain a steady, if somewhat modest, growth rate over the years. Content to follow market projections and dedicated to the largest business, given its large North America market share, Eaton's success followed the truck organization's market cycle—up in some years, down in others.

The strategic changes that began in 2001 proved to be dramatic for Eaton. The driving factor in this transformation was a new chairman and CEO, Alexander Cutler, who was appointed in 2000. Cutler looked across the organization and saw the amount of time it was taking each business to "reinvent" what could be standard processes. He realized that this time could be better spent on growing the business with a focus on the customers and the products and services that would drive that growth. The first aspect of this transformation was to move away from a holding company model, where decentralization and a lack of standardization were the norm. Cutler and his leadership team recognized that achieving more aggressive growth targets would require a culture that spent less time focusing on the creation of unique internal processes and that avoided repeating mistakes across various business boundaries. The Eaton Business System was established as the foundation of an integrated operating model, driving standards and providing the organization with a series of processes and tools to enhance business and functional excellence. An additional aspect of this strategy was to change the mix of the business, placing less emphasis on short-cycle businesses such as truck and automotive. Through a series of acquisitions and divestures over a multiple-year time frame, Cutler set out to reposition the company.

Along with a reevaluation of the business with the intended goal of higher levels of sustainable market growth, he recognized the need for a new approach to learning. Systems and processes needed to be shared across the business so the organization could learn from past mistakes to prevent them from being repeated elsewhere. Silos needed to be torn down, and this required leaders to think and act differently.

Cutler also recognized the need for a different model for leadership development. The organization needed a development process that exposed leaders to the diverse portfolio of Eaton's different business models. Rather than having experts tied to a particular business, he wanted leaders who had breadth of experiences and could move into senior roles already understanding how to grow and manage an organization. He wanted leaders who had the opportunity to learn from multiple global business models and could apply what they had learned as they moved to other businesses across the enterprise—versus trying to reinvent the wheel each time they moved into a new role. He wanted more focus on external factors and less time spent on the "plumbing"—the internal factors of running the business.

As of this writing, with the completed acquisition of Cooper Industries, the corporation is approximately $22 billion in sales, with a large percentage of its 100,000+ employees located outside of the United States. Currently, about 80 percent of Eaton's sales come from the electrical, hydraulics, and aerospace segments, which is up about 60 percent from 2000. And about 55 percent of sales are generated in non-U.S. markets, with about 24 percent from emerging or developing markets. The truck and automotive businesses now make up less than 20 percent of the overall business enterprise.

Leadership Development to Support Business Strategy

To support the global, integrated operating company strategy, Eaton's leadership development process had to change as well. Traditionally, the fundamental philosophy of the company was to develop the major percentage of the leadership bench strength from within. While that remained, the concept of moving up vertically through a silo, with limited exposure to other markets, customers, or business models needed to change. Success required a specific plan—especially to change the mindset of ambitious leaders who were used to moving through salary levels or "bands" as an indicator of success. To drive the change, an additional aspect was added to the leadership development process to shift the mindset for growing leadership capabilities from attending leadership programs or moving through a series of salary bands to growing through strategically identified experiences, encouraging leaders to ask:

- What experiences have I had?
- What have I learned from those experiences, and how can I apply these lessons to other situations?
- What experiences do I need to broaden my perspective?

To facilitate this change, under sponsorship of the CEO, leaders from across the business and the globe were brought together in a program called "In the Zone"—a reference to the concept in sports when one is competing and producing at the highest level of capability. Although ostensibly a leadership development program, this gathering also took the role of a change enabler. A key objective of the program was to allow Cutler to discuss the new business strategy of an integrated operating company and to communicate to leaders that new knowledge and skills of leading would be required to make this approach work. Bringing leaders together would allow them to see how similar their challenges and experiences were and how they could learn from one another through collaboration and sharing of practices. It was also an opportunity to expose them to a new philosophy around development: that development really occurs through a variety of experiences and challenging assignments across differ-ent businesses or geographies. The intent was to break down the silo thinking around running the business and to open them up to movement across businesses to build a stronger, broader level of leadership ability.

I clearly recall the look on the faces of the attendees of the first session of this program. They were at very senior levels of the organization—many only two levels from the CEO. Most were running businesses of notable size ($550 million and up). Others were responsible for corporate-wide functions. We had asked a simple question. Perhaps it was too simple. Or perhaps, and more likely, they had never been asked to think or reflect on the topic. Whatever the reason, I knew what they were thinking—a pointless (and totally irrelevant) question from the program facilitator. The question was as follows: "Think about your greatest development or learning experience, one that has helped to make you the suc-cessful leader you are today. Describe it. What did you learn? How has it contributed to your success?"

We asked them to write down their answers, then to discuss their notes with partners. The discussions were lively, the anima-tion and noise level building as the stories progressed. After listening to a few examples with the entire group, the second and more important question was asked: "How many of your examples included a training program of some sort?"

Perhaps a hand or two went up. Then another question: "For how many of you was it a book or article that you read?" No hands this time. Then, the last question: "For how many of you was it a tough, challenging assignment or role?" A clear majority of hands were raised, and we knew we had them.

The point could be made, the mindset shifted. How do suc-cessful leaders develop? Through classroom-based activities? Through books and articles on the latest leadership notion? Their own experiences made the point for us—leaders develop by taking on challenging experiences, learning from those experiences, and applying those lessons in different situations. Sometimes those experiences and the related lessons come unexpectedly and spontaneously. Someone taps you on the shoulder and says he has a "once in a lifetime opportunity" for you. But what if, just perhaps, those experiences were carefully managed and arranged? What if they were based on the direction you wished your career would go? What if you had a roadmap of experiences that would help you build the capabilities to get there, and once there, be successful from the start?

We were then able to move to the more rational data (an important component given the engineering mentality of a manufacturing organization), having made the emotional point, by reviewing the research from *The Lessons of Experience* (McCall, Lombardo, & Morrison, 1988), showing the key experiences that leaders cited as best opportunities for learning. This research showed that the greatest, and most significant, learning came from challenging jobs and assignments, as opposed to the traditional approach of learning through a series of training programs. We continued by reviewing the specific assignments identified by the study that were shown to be the best for development, and because they fit into our philosophy for developing breadth, we made slight modifications to them to reflect specifics in Eaton (see Exhibit 2.1) and used them in the communication to our current and future leaders.

Exhibit 2.1. Thirteen Best Types of Experiences for Development at Eaton

- Fix it/turnaround
- Start-up
- Significant people demands
- Line-to-staff switch
- Staff-to-line switch
- International
- Heavy strategic demands
- Increase in scope
- Increase in scale
- Influence without authority
- Moves across different businesses
- Project/taskforce chair
- Project/taskforce member

It was interesting to see how, unprodded, the participants reviewed the list, counting up the different experiences they had had throughout their own careers, and perhaps silently identifying those they had not had, wondering what they had missed, or how this might affect their leadership capabilities—both in their current roles and in roles to come.

To supplement the philosophy introduced in the program, profiles were developed that identified the types of experiences leading to specific capabilities. Beginning with business leadership roles (those that would include P&L responsibilities), the CEO identified key experiences he believed would broaden the mindset and capabilities of those who aspired to these roles. The resulting profile (see Exhibit 2.2) was created to help those

---

Exhibit 2.2. Profile: Building a Career in General Management

A career path in general management is one opportunity for growth within Eaton. Consideration for advancement into leadership roles (general manager and above) will be based on development in the following areas:

Demonstrated Leadership Success

Regardless of position, individuals have the opportunity to demonstrate capabilities in the Eaton Leadership Model. In order to be considered for higher level positions, an individual must:

- Demonstrate success within all aspects of the Eaton Leadership Model: *Thinking and Acting Strategically, Getting Results, Building Organizational Capability, and Leadership Style* (rate 3 or higher on a scale of 1 to 5)
- Be an active leader of EBS initiatives
- Embody the principles and spirit of the Eaton Philosophy and Values

Commitment to Personal Development

Eaton values individuals who are continuously learning, sharing their learning with others to help them grow, and growing beyond the current requirements of their roles. Is the individual:

Continued

Exhibit 2.2 continued

- Teaching others?
- Representing Eaton outside of the company; serving on boards or leadership groups?
- Seeking and participating in a cross-group project?
- Maintaining an active, ongoing development plan, based on 360 feedback?

Breadth of Experience

Finally, Eaton values leaders who have breadth as well as depth. Breadth is all about being more effective in your role because of a variety of experiences and exposure to different approaches. Has the individual:

- Worked for different bosses, in different functions, in different cultures, in different companies/business groups within Eaton?
- Held a matrix assignment (*in a role or managing others where there is both a solid and dotted line reporting relationship*)?
- Held a position at a higher organization level (*e.g., group staff role before general manager role*)?

Experiences that will be valued and taken into consideration when identifying individuals for advancement include:

- Prior experience in managing others
- Involvement in a start-up or acquisition
- Involvement in a turnaround or fix-it situation
- Position or assignment in the front end of an organization (sales, marketing, business development)
- Position or assignment in the operations side of an organization (manufacturing, quality, supply chain)
- Line-to-staff move
- Staff-to-line move
- Cross-group assignment (worked in at least two groups)
- International assignment
- Certification in *and* application of the Eaton Business System

Creating a development plan for individuals interested in general management roles should evolve around providing opportunities in these areas, based on a realistic but achievable timeframe.

interested in these types of roles to create their own career development plans. This singular profile was quickly followed by similar profiles that outlined development for functional leadership roles, as well as a format for early talent development programs.

Leaders and those who aspire to leadership roles at Eaton are now grounded in the concept of "building breadth of experience" as they manage their career transitions. They are encouraged to have a variety of experiences and, more importantly, to acquire the unique set of lessons that each of the experiences offers. For each experience, key lessons that the organization holds as critical for success in leadership roles were identified (see Table 2.1). For instance, the experience of managing people provides opportunities to learn how to manage performance, provide feedback, motivate others, and get work done through others as opposed to doing it all yourself. In discussions between managers and employees around career development, these lessons are positioned as important to success. Those with a broader set of these lessons are the likely successors to leadership roles. Development discussions between a manager and direct reports during the performance management process are focused on what experiences an individual needs to have to be successful at the next level. During our succession planning process, each individual's breadth of experience is reviewed, and any significant gaps in key experiences are noted and become part of the individual career development plans. Our businesses and functions now hold regularly scheduled meetings called "Talent Reviews," where our high potentials are discussed from the perspective of what experiences they have had, what experiences they need, and what jobs or assignments in the organization will give them these experiences.

Ten years later, this very same concept continues as the core of our development philosophy at Eaton. For us, that philosophy has two major tenets: (a) leaders develop best by getting breadth of experiences and (b) building this breadth, since it takes time, should start early in a career and be managed both by the individual and the organization. We have made significant progress in communicating this approach as the core of our philosophy around development and have ingrained it in our human resource processes (i.e., performance management, succession planning, and career development). As a result those who aspire

Table 2.1. Developmental Experiences and Expected Lessons

Developmental Experience	Expected Lessons
Managing Others	• Upgrading the organization by raising the talent bar (better results = better people) • Providing performance and development feedback • Motivating others • Delegation skills
Start-Up or Acquisition	• Building or integrating a team • Setting and communicating priorities • Learning new content quickly • Working under time pressure
Turnaround or Fix-It	• Team building • Development and motivation of others • Working under time pressure • Dealing with emotionally charged situations
Front-End Assignment	• Ability to understand needs of markets, industries, and customers • Creating and communicating value propositions • Driving Voice of the Customer into the organization
Operations Assignment	• Ability to balance priorities, manage costs, and support growth • Implementing standard processes and controls
Line to Staff Assignment	• Influencing others • Role of functions in overall enterprise • Enhance ability to think strategically • Breadth of perspective
Cross-Business Assignment	• Broader understanding of Eaton's goals, strategy, and structures • Ability to align strategy and business models • Variety in leadership styles (working for different bosses)
International Assignment	• Developing an understanding of and appreciation for others • Ability to adapt to differences in surroundings, cultures, and people • Expanding thinking and decision making with a global mindset

to leadership roles in Eaton know how they can get these experiences, why we believe breadth of experience is important, and, perhaps most critical to the health of the organization, how to apply these principles to the development of future leaders.

Moving Across Boundaries

Frequently, when gathering specifications for open positions, hiring managers emphasize the need for in-depth industry experience. From their perspective, the successful candidates must be steeped in knowledge of the business that they will be joining, as each industry has unique characteristics that an "outsider" would not be able to understand and, more importantly, not be able to navigate. Without several years of specific industry experience, a potential candidate would not be considered.

Eaton has taken a broader approach in terms of the development of leaders for general management positions. This approach is, in part, supported by the fact that we are in an integrated operating company, made up of a variety of businesses that support power management. Our businesses provide products, solutions, and services for the distribution of electrical power, as well as ways to measure the quality of power supply. We also support the hydraulics industry, with products for the construction and agriculture markets, the aerospace industry, and the vehicle industry—in both automotive and truck markets. From a development perspective, this gives us a wide variety of business models to use to prepare our leaders. Each business is made up of a unique set of customers. Some businesses have a few, focused customers, while others have thousands of customers across a wide spectrum. Certain businesses use a variety of channels through which we go to market and are at different stages in the economic cycle—we have early, mid, and late cycle businesses.

For high performers who are interested in senior leadership positions in our organization, we believe that breadth of experience across these business models is a key to development. Learning how to lead in an early cycle business (one that builds strength in the beginning of the recovery from a downturn) helps to strengthen thinking about optimizing opportunities, making sure you are positioned to take advantage of them quickly. Late cycle businesses (ones that begin recovery later in the turnaround process) require patience, long-term planning, and program management. Our belief is that exposure to these and other scenarios helps a leader strengthen his or her capabilities and be ready to face any situation or problem. It also brings creative application of approaches that leaders might not have thought of if only exposed to one scenario. Each year we review our leadership bench strength in our succession planning process and discuss the potential of our high-performing talent for moving to higher levels in the organization. Have they demonstrated the core capabilities of leadership—the ability to get results, to think strategically, to build an organization's capability through the selection, management, and development of talent? Finally, but most importantly, do they behave in a way that is consistent with our values? If individuals have the potential to move higher in the organization, and if they are motivated to do so, then we create specific development plans intended to make sure they gain the breadth we believe is critical for success.

To see how this has been applied to the development of specific individuals, I will share several real situations in four different scenarios: moving across businesses, moving from line to staff positions, moving across geographic regions, and moving across functions.

Cross-Business Experience

Dev Chavan (all names have been changed) is a high-performing individual who has worked at Eaton for nine years. He came to Eaton after spending six years in a business that designed and manufactured suspension systems for the heavy-duty truck market. Looking for opportunities to work toward his goal of running a business, he joined the company as a participant in a rotational development program. Upon completion of this program, he accepted a role in our truck business helping to evolve emerging technologies. His next role, also considered a staff assignment, was manager of business operations, responsible for driving standard processes and measurements across the truck organization. In both of these assignments, Dev was located in the headquarters building of the business, which gave him access to several levels of leadership and to functional expertise. Dev's experiences, as well as his educational background, are captured in a tool that we use as part of our succession planning process. It documents each of the roles that the employee has had, both within Eaton and with other organizations, and aids us in identifying possible gaps in experience that might need to be addressed.

Early in 2010, as part of my role as a coach and advisor to our high potential talent, I received a call from Dev. He was interested in talking with me about the next step in his career plan. Due to his strong performance, as well as his interest and potential to advance to higher level positions, he had been offered a move to the next level. Accepting it might have been an easy decision, except that Dev had three very different promotion opportunities that he could pursue. He wanted to talk them through with me so that he could make sure he was thinking strategically about his development. The three roles were

- *Director of Quality:* leading the quality function and strategy for the North America truck business,
- *Director of a Market Segment:* managing the manufacturing, distribution, and pricing strategy of a global product line, and
- *Plant Manager:* leading a manufacturing facility.

Each role presented Dev with an opportunity to learn and grow. The key question was which one would help him broaden his perspective and challenge him in areas that, although uncomfortable, would stretch him the most. As I asked for more information, Dev explained that the first two opportunities would provide expansion of his strategic thinking and scope, something that he was very interested in doing because he liked strategy and business development. But both were staff assignments and thus a continuation of what he had been doing since joining the truck organization. Furthermore, they both were in his current location, and one was even reporting to a manager he had worked with previously.

As we continued our conversation—and I clearly heard his excitement about the strategic focus—we shifted to discussing the plant manager role. Dev had had little experience in a manufacturing environment, but given his engineering degree and his other roles he knew the importance of understanding and implementing processes and of managing costs. From his perspective, what was unique about the role was exposure to another business within Eaton—the electrical organization. Dev was excited about "the opportunity to work in the electrical sector." He went on to say, "I also like working with people and working as a plant manager provides you plenty of opportunity from that perspective. You get to see the results of the decisions you make in a very short time, and there is something about instant gratification which excites me. Every day you can feel that you have been able to achieve something."

He was certainly intrigued by the opportunity to learn another part of the company, but expressed more than once that his entire career with Eaton to date had been in the truck organization. He had deep knowledge of that market, which allowed him to think strategically about its future and the possibilities to serve that customer base. I reminded him of the "Building a Career in General Management" profile and the fact that experience in multiple businesses was highly desired. We discussed what he could learn from moving to another business—the fact that the electrical business had a very different channel to market, a much larger customer base, and a different economic cycle. Could having these new and different experiences possibly help him in the future? We also talked about the experience level of the staff that would report to him. They were all strong in their areas and had been at the plant for a good amount of time. He could rely on them when expertise was needed. As Dev stated, "I had heard that it was a strong team at the plant and this would be an opportunity to work with a strong team that has managed the cyclicality in the business well." The last point that we discussed was the location of the facility. It was in Lincoln, Illinois, isolated from any other Eaton facility and far from his boss's office. Dev quickly realized the challenge and opportunity that would give him; he would not be able to stop by his manager's office to run something by him. He would be the senior leader at the facility, and therefore would be the one the organization looked to for motivation and decisiveness. How would it feel not to be co-located with the boss?

Dev reviewed the three opportunities and the lessons that each would provide him: clearly the plant manager role was the greatest stretch for him. In retrospect he told me, "I had been with the truck/vehicle group for eight years, and I had established a fairly good network. On the electrical side I did not have the same type of network established. I was a little apprehensive about moving into a new organization. I was also concerned about taking a plant role, and I had never worked in the plant before, though I had roles previous to joining Eaton where I implemented projects in the plant and worked very closely with them. The previous experience of working with the plants definitely came in handy."

Our markets and business conditions have expanded far more globally than we have perhaps expected. Our leaders need to have far broader perspectives to be able to plan and react in these conditions, so leadership development must take this into consideration. Giving our leaders the encouragement and opportunity to leave a comfortable standing in one business, and moving them into a business with different customer needs and market trends, can only help prepare them for more variation and change. As Dev states, "I have learned a lot, and it has been a challenging role—managing the operation which is seeing double-digit growth year over year after going through some real tough times with the downturn. There has been a shift in the strategy from growth to more focus on profitability. Making a positive impact on improving profitability has been a very good experience. It is definitely a turnaround situation. All this has definitely resulted in broadening my perspective and further enhancing my business acumen."

Crossing from Line to Staff

Nothing creates more trepidation than to tell a high potential leader that you would like him or her to take on a staff assignment, such as leading a corporate function. In a line or direct business role they make the decisions, set the strategy, and deal directly with customers and employees. In contrast, in a staff role the pace of work is different, the customers feel far away, and the ability to make an individual decision and implement it changes to a more collaborative, consensus-based mode.

This is exactly why the senior leaders of Eaton wanted John Krasny to move into a corporate staff role. As customer director in our automotive business, John had been successful in the market with the most demanding customers, and he had dealt with them with a high level of professionalism. His ability to acknowledge and address their needs while communicating our needs as a business helped both organizations grow in challenging market conditions. When discussing the future with him, John was asked whether he had ever considered running a business. He seemed surprised; not only had he not thought about that option, but no one had ever brought it up before. As John stated, "When I first joined Eaton, I initially thought that I would be in sales the rest of my career. I had been very successful in sales with my prior employer, having progressed from an account manager to a senior director in a very short time. I believed that I could continue this progression within Eaton and move to a vice president or executive within sales in a short period of time. Honestly, I first started thinking about a role outside of sales when I participated in Eaton's executive development program. The program was the first in-depth opportunity I had to better understand the Eaton corporation—how it was organized, the importance of functional and line roles, and the immense opportunities that were available to employees who were willing to go across businesses or functions, or accept a corporate role." The CEO saw leadership traits in John that could be transformed in another direction and wanted to pursue that in his development. The development challenge was how best to prepare John for an eventual move into a business leader role. It was decided that an interim role to help broaden his perspective and help him learn more about growth and strategic thinking would be the best position.

John was offered the job of corporate vice president of sales and marketing. "I was initially very surprised and didn't think it would be a good fit for me. Throughout my career I had worked in multiple different functions—engineering, marketing, program management, and sales—and really enjoyed how fast-paced they were and seeing the impact I had on the business on a daily basis. Based on my initial understanding of the corporate VP of sales and marketing position, I thought it would focus on employee training and be mostly academic."

Staying in his area of expertise would allow him to continue producing results and adding value based on his knowledge and past experience. So when suggesting such a dramatic move to an individual used to performing at a high level, it was important to allow him some level of comfort that he could actually get results in the new role and add value. John would be able to do this as he would be in his functional specialty. So what would be the learning for John? A staff role offers the strongest opportunity that I can think of to develop the ability to influence others. Rarely does a staff role allow a person to force decisions around strategies or priorities. It requires building buy-in and support, and in John's case, it would mean gaining that support and buy-in from very senior leaders of the businesses. He would have to learn about and address the different issues faced by each business, beyond what he knew in the automotive space. This would broaden his knowledge and perspectives about the businesses, exposing him to those with a larger customer base and longer product design and launch times. Where could approaches and processes add value if standardized? Where did they need to remain unique due to customer requirements? The role also offered John the opportunity to be involved in multiple growth strategies—new technologies, global expansion, acquisitions—all useful in managing a business.

John spent three years in the corporate role, establishing market strategies for growth opportunities that cross more than one of our businesses. As part of the development process, John and I would meet every few weeks to discuss the assignment and review the lessons he was learning as a result of having the experience. "There were many things I liked about the role once I was in it for a while. Given that I had been in the automotive business for eighteen years, it was great to gain exposure to Eaton's four other businesses and really learn about each of them. It was fantastic to work with the CEO and senior leadership team and gain insights into how the corporation was run, to improve my strategic thinking skills, and to exchange ideas with a very bright group of leaders. I also liked having the opportunity to have a major impact on the corporation through identifying key strategic programs that were implemented across the businesses. In terms of dislikes, I think the first six to nine months in a corporate role is extremely challenging. When you move from a very fast-paced environment where you see results every day or every hour, it was very difficult at first to see what real impact I could have within the businesses in a corporate role. It was also difficult to go from an environment where people were calling every day for help or asking me to make a decision to one in which nobody was initially calling or asking me to make tough business decisions."

Armed with broader business perspectives around growth, enhanced strategic thinking, and stronger influencing skills, John's next move was to general management—his first role directly managing a P&L—and he is poised to move to roles with larger scope and scale. The self-admitted "sales guy," who thought that would be his path for his career, has a different road to follow. "I learned many things from being in the corporate role. First of all, I have a much better and broader understanding of what Eaton does in each of our businesses and how the corporation is run. I also have a much better appreciation and understanding of the role of the corporate office and how change can be implemented effectively across a large organization. This is extremely beneficial, as I meet with customers and employees and describe to them everything that Eaton does and how everything is connected through our power management strategy. Many employees do not have a complete awareness of what Eaton supplies to our industries and the impact we have on the world. The relationships I developed while in corporate are also very beneficial and help me get to the right people quickly when needed. I also learned how to effectively influence others who don't directly report to me. This skill has been very helpful as I work with other VPs and general managers to implement programs and strategies. I also learned the importance of implementing strategic objectives and approaching the implementation in a manner that is similar to meeting short-term operating results. As an example, we are currently working on four key strategic objectives within the business that will take three to five years to implement, but we are reviewing status and progress regularly in my monthly staff meetings. I am attempting to make sure that our long-term objectives receive the same level of attention and regular measurement to performance as our short-term objectives do."

Cross-Regional Moves

It comes as no surprise that any global company needs to develop leaders who can manage in a global economy. For Eaton, as it expanded into emerging markets and geographies, it became very clear more leaders were needed who had the experience of living and leading outside of the United States. Prior to Sandy Cutler becoming CEO, the organization was largely focused on the North American automotive and truck markets. For the last twelve years, under Cutler's leadership, Eaton focused on building resources and infrastructure in the emerging markets in Asia Pacific, Europe, the Middle East, and Africa. The dilemma was that many of Eaton's leaders had spent their entire careers in the U.S., and, while they had knowledge of doing business outside of the U.S., few had the actual experience of living in these emerging growth countries. Willingness to lead outside of the home country became a cornerstone of our leadership development model. Leaders need to be close to the markets and customers in these emerging areas in order to clearly understand their needs. They also need to understand how to select and motivate talent in other cultures.

Nilos Korba joined Eaton after several years in multiple roles with a large, multinational, and diverse manufacturer. When he came to Eaton, he took over as chief technology officer, leading Eaton's global engineering organization. In his four years in that role, he helped to build the organization by designing systems and processes that became the standard across all businesses, and by focusing on upgrading the talent in the function.

When Eaton decided to support its global growth strategies by enhancing the role of regional leadership, regional presidents took on a bigger responsibility for expanding the company's presence within their areas. They would work with leaders of the businesses within the region to promote Eaton's products and services, build brand recognition, and learn how to succeed in multiple cultures and economies. Eaton also hoped to provide development opportunities for leaders by allowing them time to lead outside of the U.S.

Nilos was tapped to become the president of Europe, Middle East, and Africa. Greek by birth, Nilos had spent most of his life in the U.S. and worked for U.S.-based companies. As CTO his focus on growth, his approach to building talent, and his personal interest in getting closer to business decisions made him a perfect choice to take this expanded role. "I had spent most of my career as a technology person, and wanted a change into a totally different role—a role that would position me toward running a P&L, stretch me in a number of different ways by having to learn new items, get good in new areas."

The organization was gaining a leader who had honed a strong business perspective in a variety of technical roles. He knew the products and services and could speak to them as Eaton tried to spread its message across the region. For his personal development, Nilos was learning how to work and collaborate across a number of different cultures and how to deal with the variation in governmental, social, and economic influences. As his abilities as a global leader grew, Eaton gained a leader with more global perspective. When asked what he was learning in the role, Nilos responded "influence, influence, influence—the ability to put yourself in other people's shoes, see things from their own perspective, and not to judge them too quickly; the interrelationships and influences of so many diverse items that affect good business judgment."

Cross-Functional Moves

As a final example of learning through experiences, I will examine the concept of moving across functions to support development. Most people begin their careers in one functional area and progress for a time building expertise in that area. At some point, if they make a commitment to a higher level leadership role, that expertise becomes less relevant, and developing a new kind of expertise in leadership becomes the predominant factor.

For one such high performer, a move across functional lines helped to broaden her capabilities. Lenda Odili started her career with Eaton as quality manager in a manufacturing site. As a part of a talent review process, Lenda was identified as a strong learner. Her solid performance and capabilities in her function helped the site leaders recognize her potential for higher level leadership roles. If she wanted to move to higher level positions, what were the gaps in her experience and how could the organization provide the needed experience? In reviewing the "Building a Career in General Management" profile, one of Lenda's development gaps centered on coaching and developing others and building her ability to influence higher up in the organization. Much to her surprise, it was a role in human resources that would provide both.

As mentioned earlier, Eaton has a rotational development program with the objective of building an early talent pipeline for leadership positions. Participants in the program have graduate degrees and five to seven years of work experience, so are not only on the mature side but also very focused on their career plans. The manager of this program needs to be able to coach and guide the participants, frequently pushing back on their assumptions or expectations around career moves. The manager also needs to work with the business leaders to promote and market the program, find challenging assignments for the participants, and maintain the right guidelines to ensure sustainability. It is a perfect development role for someone to learn how to influence, guide, and manage an enterprise-wide initiative.

Lenda accepted the program manager position and in her first year focused on improving analytical processes to help the organization evaluate the effectiveness of the program. This was a natural fit to her skill sets from her previous role. In addition, she assumed responsibility for facilitating the board of governors for the program—a governance committee made up of very successful and highly opinionated senior leaders representing the various businesses across Eaton. The group was tasked with providing guidelines and direction for the program.

During Lenda's time in her role, she learned how each member thought about development and how each one required a different approach when she needed him or her to agree to or support an initiative. As a member of this board, I was able to watch her over time as her confidence grew, and she became capable of pushing back effectively against those more senior than she. It was very clear that she was able to move into this new function by applying some of the skills (e.g., critical thinking, analysis) that she had used in previous roles, but that this experience also allowed her to develop skills in areas she had yet to master. Her next promotion moved her to customer service manager in the aerospace organization. She is now a manager of people, and uses her newly crafted skill of influence on a regular basis.

Conclusion

As someone who has spent over ten years in a role supporting the development of others, I have seen, and even created, a variety of methodologies for development—classroom training, online training, integrated curricula—to name a few. All have their place and time and can add value if connected with the business strategy. I have also seen the power of an organization committing to providing learning through experience and how powerful and sustainable that can be for both the individual and the organization. If the world, and therefore business, is becoming more complex, doesn't it follow that those who have had more variety of experience will be able to navigate through this complexity with a bit more ease and confidence? If you ask your leaders or your high potentials when they have learned the most, I have little doubt that they will tell you it was through an experience or assignment where they were challenged to learn something new or to apply already acquired skills to a new situation. Why then not make that the core of your development approach?

If you chose this approach, here are some key things to consider:

- What are the important skills and capabilities that your leaders will need to learn in order to help the organization achieve its strategic goals? As an example, given Eaton's integrated operating company, more leaders were needed who could exert influence across the organization. Influencing and collaborating across boundaries became a key part of the leadership model.
- What are the jobs or assignments within your organization that will provide these lessons? We have identified a series of positions that provide the opportunity to learn and practice key leadership skills. Staff roles are the place to practice influencing; regional roles provide the opportunity to learn new cultures; cross-business opportunities within a function allow employees to learn about different models.
- How will you communicate throughout the organization what the needed leadership skills are and what experiences can teach them? Eaton's profiles and models around key lessons

are tools used by employees and managers alike in discussions of career development.

- How will you manage the movement of talent in your organization? Many of Eaton's leadership teams discuss talent as a part of their regularly scheduled staff meetings. They have recognized that the best plans and strategies require great talent to make them happen, so why would they not discuss their people capabilities and bench strength as seriously as the numbers or the project plan? Talent reviews can help identify the high performers with potential to move to higher roles. They can foster discussions around open positions: What types of experiences and lessons do these openings provide? Who would benefit most by having these experiences?

In support of its structure as an integrated operating company, Eaton recognized the importance of building a strong leadership pool—one that was populated with talent that could move across a variety of industries and business models. As leaders broaden their experience base with assignments across the various businesses, they increase their skills and broaden their perspectives, making them ready to adapt to today's changing environment. As such, they are more capable and confident leaders. As Eaton continues to grow and expand globally, it will have the leaders with the experience to take on roles of greater scope and scale, and position the company for future success.

Reference

McCall, M. W., Jr., Lombardo, M. M., & Morrison, A. M. (1988). *The lessons of experience: How successful executives develop on the job.* Lexington, MA: Lexington Books.

CHAPTER THREE

Developing a Pipeline of Internal Leadership Talent at 3M

Karen B. Paul, Cindy Johnson, and Kathie Karls

In Stockholm, Sweden, a young man is called to his boss's office. A suggestion of concern briefly flits across his face as he mentally reviews what might have brought him this level of attention from the boss. He knows he has done a really good job with his group. No real problems he can think of come to mind. He is actually slightly perturbed to be taken away from the press of the day. He wonders how long this interaction will take because he still has many calls to make and a long day in front of him. His team is depending on him. Still, it was unusual to be called in . . . and his boss was a very reasonable man. He has learned a great deal from this man so he knew it must be important.

What the young man doesn't yet know is that he is about to receive his first large business (and developmental) assignment and that the path he is about to embark on will eventually lead him to the highest post, that of CEO, of this very same corporation. The year was 1987, the company, 3M, and the man, Inge Thulin. At the time, Thulin had not considered the possibility that he would still be working for the company more than twenty-five years later. "Being a CEO wasn't even on my radar at the time," he says. "All I was thinking about then was how to do a good job and best support my little growing family."

Inge Thulin was appointed president, CEO, and chairman of the board in 2012. As of this writing 3M has over 85,000 employees in more than seventy countries with over $29 billion in revenue. Thulin himself is a product of this well-established company widely known for its innovation and leadership development. Yet, never one to be content with the status quo, this was not enough for Thulin. An innovator and developmental leader at heart, Thulin, within a week of his appointment as CEO, announced a new vision for the company and six major business strategies, one of which was aimed directly at raising the bar even higher for "building diverse and global talent" at 3M. Certainly, many companies *think* leadership effectiveness at all levels is critical to driving an aggressive growth strategy. Yet, Thulin has operationalized this, making leadership development a core business strategy.

So how was this young man developed and groomed in order to become the head of this global company frequently cited by *Fortune* magazine as one of the Top 20 Most Admired Companies and repeatedly named as one of the Best Companies for Leaders? How is 3M planning to continue raising the bar on its own successful approaches to leadership development? To understand where 3M is going, it is essential to first review the developmental philosophy, essential culture, and foundational programs currently in place, and on which it is building for the future.

The Role of Learning in an Innovation Culture

3M has a well-established reputation for breakthrough innovation and for consistently bringing radically new products to the market. What few people realize is that 3M currently has more than 55,000 different products (Gunther, 2010). Many of 3M's products are extremely well known worldwide, from Post-it Notes® to Scotch Tape® to Ace® bandages. However, what isn't known is that most of 3M's products are embedded in other products such as automobiles, factories, planes, boats, homes, and offices. These products are in diverse markets such as aerospace (restoring an army helicopter window in ten minutes without having to remove the window from the aircraft), dentistry (computerized teeth scans to produce dental appliances), security (biometrics such as iris and facial recognition), optical films (to enhance viewing of flat screen TVs or provide private viewing of computer monitors), and even fire-blocking foams for building construction.

3M supports forty-six different technological platforms that it leverages in product creation and development. These cutting-edge technological platforms include acoustic control, micro-replication, nano-technology, light management, and microbial detection and control, as well as more well-known but nonetheless cutting-edge technologies such as abrasives. An indication of 3M's prevalence is that in most industrialized countries, in a typical day, consumers come into contact with more than one hundred products made by 3M, often without knowing it (3M, 2011).

Since its inception, 3M has had a developmentally oriented, coaching-based approach and philosophy with employees. This makes sense given 3M's continual quest for innovation as a competitive advantage. How could an organization continue to innovate, adapt, learn, and grow unless the culture places a premium on individual learning and development? Stated another way, it is impossible to support innovation without a heavy emphasis on and support of learning. Experiential learning (or learning by doing) for innovation and professional growth grew to be synonymous at 3M due to many cultural mechanisms that reinforce and support innovation. Individual initiative and innovation were encouraged through the institutionalization of cultural hallmarks such as an internal venture capital fund (to help people explore by funding new ideas), the Technical Forum (where 3Mers present technical papers and exchange ideas with each other to encourage cross-pollination of ideas, technologies, and people) to the famed 15 percent rule, as well as numerous other practices.

Scientists at 3M like to remind outsiders that the principle of "15 percent time" goes back to the firm's beginnings as a mining and manufacturing firm in Minnesota in the first years of the 20th century, and has become one of the pillars of the company's corporate culture. "In business, the first principle is the promotion of entrepreneurship and insistence upon freedom in the workplace to pursue innovative ideas," wrote William L. McKnight, 3M's president in the 1920s. Accordingly, 3M allows scientists to use up to 15 percent of their working time to pursue pet projects, reflect on consumer needs and "tinker" to create new products based on technological breakthroughs. Their track record of creating breakthrough technology leading to new products and new markets has been a distinctive feature of 3M's continuing success as a major Fortune 100 company.

It is the invention machine whose methods were celebrated in the influential 1994 best-seller *Built to Last* by Jim Collins and Jerry Porras. A more comprehensive treatment of the many cultural mechanisms reinforcing innovation and learning can be found in Ernest Gundling's (2000) book on *The 3M Way to Innovation*. The heavy emphasis on learning through innovation built many a career, as 3Mers who successfully grow a new product or idea could receive the opportunity to run it as their own project, department, or division (depending on sales levels of products), providing a mutually reinforcing loop of learning and doing. Thulin himself entered this culture and early on distinguished himself by building 3M's health care business in Europe. According to Thulin, "One of my first bosses at 3M taught me that placing people into challenging and new situations provides one of the best vehicles for leadership learning and development and business growth."

The roots of learning in 3M's culture can be traced back to the early days of the corporation. William L. McKnight was 3M's president from 1929 to 1949 and became 3M's chairman of the board from 1949 to 1966. Many believe McKnight's greatest contribution was as a business philosopher because he created a corporate culture that encourages employee initiative and innovation through challenge and freedom to develop. His basic rule of management was laid out in 1948:

> As our business grows, it becomes increasingly necessary to delegate responsibility and to encourage men and women to exercise their initiative. This requires considerable tolerance. Those men and women, to whom we delegate authority and responsibility, if they are good people, are going to want to do their jobs in their own way. Mistakes will be made. But if a person is essentially right, the mistakes he or she makes are not as serious in the long run as the mistakes management will make if it undertakes to tell those in authority exactly how they must do their jobs. Management that is destructively critical when mistakes are made kills initiative. And it's essential that we have many people with initiative if we are to continue to grow. (3M, 2002, p. 9)

In the book, *Our Story So Far* (3M, 1977), 3M discusses that "perhaps the greatest reward for a person's work is not what a person gets for it, but what that person becomes by it" (p. 118). 3M encourages its people to "become" through formal and informal training, experience, and personal initiative.

This can also be seen in 3M HR principles, which are

- Respects the dignity and worth of individuals, by encouraging their highest level of performance in a fair, challenging, objective, and cooperative work environment. Individual rights are respected. Timely and open communication to and from employees is encouraged. Supervisors and managers are accountable for the performance and development of the employees assigned to them.
- Encourages the initiative of each employee by providing both direction and the freedom to work creatively. Risk taking and innovation are requirements for growth. Both are to be encouraged and supported in an atmosphere of integrity and mutual respect.
- Challenges individual capabilities through proper placement, orientation, and development. Responsibility for development is shared by the employee, by supervisors and managers, and by the company.
- Provides equal opportunity for development and equitably rewards good performance. Performance is evaluated against objective, job-related criteria and rewarded with appropriate recognition and compensation.

As important as these values and principles are and have been, learning has been central to the organization in other ways. 3M, a leader in supporting employee development as early as the 1960s, provided tuition reimbursement to employees seeking to develop through additional education.

Leaders Teaching Leaders

Learning from experiences and from others is core to the 3M experience. In 2000, this was also reified under the cornerstone tenet of "Leaders Teaching Leaders," which is a concept funda-mental to all of 3M's leadership development programs. Senior executives teach other executives; leaders share with other leaders their own individual business experiences and their success and failure stories. In conjunction with "Leaders Teaching Leaders," 3M has also instituted "action learning" as another key compo-nent of 3M's leadership development programs. In action learning, participants are charged with a business problem to solve with a group of other participants. Typically, each group is given about ten days to solve its problem. Conclusions of the projects are reported back and debriefed in front of the CEO and his direct reports as part of the last day of the experience. The CEO also sets an example by teaching in 3M's Leadership Devel-opment Institute. This modeling by example has led 3M senior executives to take their roles very seriously as teachers in 3M leadership programs. Typically, Thulin spends about one-fifth of his time as CEO on talent, for example, teaching in leadership programs such as the Accelerated Leadership Development Program (ALDP) and by directing pipeline development (dis-cussed later in this chapter).

In the nine years that 3M has offered ALDP, seventy-one action learning projects were successfully completed across twenty-three sessions. Participants and experts outside the company have rec-ognized the program as highly successful on a number of fronts. Typically, an ALDP team has sixty to seventy hours to develop and recommend a solution to the CEO, operations committee, and sponsors. If appropriate, the sponsor resources and implements the plan. In 2010, changes were made to join the efforts of ALDP with another 3M leadership program, the Emerging Leaders Program (ELP), to enhance both by making learning and busi-ness results more prominent. Each action learning project now has an economic goal of making at least $25 million in new sales without reducing existing international growth plans or division strategic plans. Now ALDP participants create the solution, global direction, and strategic intent for their projects. The projects are reviewed in front of the CEO and with executive sponsors and the results become the starting point for a second wave of action learning projects in the ELP, which addresses regional implemen-tation specifically.

ELP is designed to address how to maximize 3M capability worldwide. The participants are given fifty to sixty hours of action learning time in which to build a plan to implement or alter the ALDP project recommendations in their regions or countries. Those plans are then reviewed for resource approval by the area vice presidents. After the program, the participants are expected to spend approximately 15 percent of their time over the following twelve months implementing their plans. There are typically two or three review meetings in which an emerging leader's group reports its learning and results to its executive sponsors. The action learning project recommendations subsequently are implemented by subsidiary operations in growing economies.

These programs help cultivate a growth mindset and, at the same time, help achieve the leadership development objectives of the company. Developmental objectives for participants include collaboration, strategy, execution, and relationship management. The monetary goal has created a very exciting and challenging learning experience and raised the stakes for senior executives and participants alike by putting experience at the center of formal training. Action learning projects are now enjoying their highest ratings since their inception in 2001. Commentary from leaders participating and teaching also reflects a high level of engagement (with class scores moving from 4.68 to 4.82 on a five-point scale, with 5 being the highest score possible). Thulin has been both an active participant and for the last several years one of the core faculty members—a leader more committed to development would be hard to find.

"Leaders Teaching Leaders" is now part of 3M's cultural fabric from the classroom to the cubical. This ensures that leaders are themselves learning by teaching, and are modeling learning and good developmental practices to the next generation. In effect, time spent on development is not a task to be managed, but an important and ongoing part of the role. A philosophic approach such as "Leaders Teaching Leaders" is key to helping embed developmentally oriented behaviors into the culture of the organization. The many individual day-to-day practices add up over time—having candid, regular performance reviews and creating a rhythm and regular schedule for talent reviews—that embeds development into the culture of a company.

Mentors, Sponsors, and Champions

Getting the most development out of experience often requires the help of a third party. One of 3M's most passionate supporters of people development is Giuseppe Castaldi, vice president of Central East Europe. When asked to describe what he did to be named by so many people as an excellent people developer, he replied, "It is very easy . . . you just need to learn to find time to talk to people . . . and not ONLY about financials. . . . I always make some time to talk to our best people . . . informally . . . over breakfast or while going to see a customer, and I ask people about themselves, their ambitions and goals . . . their family. I want to get to know them!" His approach and personal involvement help illustrate the substantial effect that leaders can have on an individual's development. Three roles at 3M that leaders play to assist in people's development and innovation are mentor, sponsor, and champion. Each role can be formal or informal, depending on the specific situation, and some leaders can play one or all roles for an individual.

Mentoring

Mentoring is probably the best understood role. People, usually in the same profession or field, typically "self-select" each other informally to form a one-on-one relationship. The mentor is a good listener, teacher, and guide. Relationships may be short and episodic or last for years. Mentoring typically revolves around professional development in an area that is outside a mentee's area of experience. Relationships are personal—a mentor provides both professional and personal support. Mentors typically say that they gain as much—if not more—from the relationship as they give. Mentors can provide a sounding board for mentees, but more commonly mentors help individuals discover for themselves the types of questions they should be asking or thinking about, often by helping the person to reframe thoughts or providing context or a broader perspective. Successful people in business can nearly always cite at least one mentor (and often more) who helped them.

3M practices both informal and formal mentoring. Thulin himself is an active mentor and has all top executives serve as mentors in a formal program. In the formal mentoring program at 3M, each top executive works with two mentees for a one-year period. Mentoring as a development activity demands time and personal excellence from the mentor. "Mentoring," said Sandy Tokach, vice president of HR Talent Solutions, "requires a lot of personal rapport." It is not surprising that people in leadership roles are expected to serve in supporting roles. "One of the criteria used in assessing a technical career is whether that person engaged in mentoring," said Tokach, whose own mentor was Al Pocis, corporate scientist. "I saw how successful he was in getting his research out into the commercial arena," said Tokach. "That takes so much skill—not just technical talent, but people skills."

Sponsorship

Sponsorship at 3M goes beyond mentoring by having someone take informal or formal responsibility to assure that an employee's career is on the right track. Sponsors advocate on an employee's behalf and actively help both the organization and the individual identify the right business opportunities to maximize the individual's talents. For example, if a 3M employee goes on a global assignment, he or she is assigned a "re-entry sponsor." When employees return to Moscow or Shanghai, on home leave from a global assignment, they meet with their sponsors. "In this case, it's a formal relationship and people take it seriously," said Marlene McGrath, senior vice president of HR and a re-entry sponsor herself.

The sponsor wants to make sure that the person in the global assignment is making the most of that opportunity and, after the individual returns, the sponsor helps identify the best opportunities available for the person. "A sponsor is someone who helps ensure you get the right developmental opportunities," said Thulin. "It's someone who talks to you about your future. I've sponsored a lot of people in my life; it's an important part of being a manager and a good leader. I was lucky someone took a risk on me early on and I also learned early on it is part of my responsibility to do it for others."

Champions

New ideas and new business ventures create opportunities for both business and individual development. Champions have strong credibility within 3M and they are persuasive "lobbyists" for company investments in new ideas or products, thus creating experiences that can develop others. For example, Ernie Moffet, retired group vice president, Consumer Business, was the consumer champion when 3M still thought of itself as strictly an industrial company. He provided the space and support for others to develop the area.

H.C. Shin, executive vice president of International, was the champion for Tracy Anderson while Anderson was advocating for pulling together the strong technology base and product portfolio that was distributed across the company for Renewable Energy customers and proposing it as a business. At the time Anderson had responsibility for the High Capacity Conductor business (overhead power cables) and had a broad understanding of the energy industry and experience in building new businesses within 3M. He began to investigate renewable energy opportunities and, instead of limiting his thinking to the products within his own division, he recognized the broader opportunity for 3M and the value to the customer of bringing it all together. With Shin's support and guidance, he started advocating for the creation of a new division within 3M. Part of the champion role is to provide guidance and some measure of protection for individuals as they are challenged by and develop through the experience of running a project. As a result, champions aid in leadership development by providing a supportive environment for individuals as they work on a business project in "uncharted waters."

The three roles a leader can play correspond to common developmental needs. Individuals often need help developing or broadening in their current jobs (mentor), assessing which next opportunities or roles would help them to learn more (sponsor), and having some specific guidance on work and/or support as new skills are practiced in the business environment (champion). Sometimes the three roles come together and are played by one leader for a person, but more often the roles play out over time and with a variety of individuals.

Talent Reviews

A key element in individual and system-wide change is measuring progress and providing feedback about movement toward goals. Evaluation and feedback facilitate learning and development. 3M collects and uses feedback in a number of different ways, starting with assessment of the attributes that define and guide best practice leadership within the corporation. 3M's leadership attributes serve as the common thread aligning HR processes and practices and emphasize the importance of development in the company. The 3M leadership attributes are

- Thinks from the outside in
- Drives innovation and growth
- Develops, teaches, and engages others
- Makes courageous decisions
- Leads with energy, passion, and urgency
- Lives 3M values

A 360 process is available to all salaried employees that provides feedback on the leadership attributes and advice/guidance for a development plan based on the scores. The leadership attributes also serve as the foundation for all of 3M's upper-level leadership development courses in which leaders receive 360-degree feedback and coaching.

3M's talent process uses management team reviews (MTRs) to identify high potential or "top talent" leaders within each business. An MTR is a consensus meeting of a management team to review individuals as part of the performance management cycle. Prior to these meetings, individuals self-define their contributions in terms of what they delivered versus what they committed to deliver. All employees are evaluated not only on meeting their commitments but also on the extent to which they exhibited the leadership attributes in that year. This dual emphasis ensures that leaders and the corporation pay attention not only to *what* was accomplished, but *how.*

In order to get a cross-sectional look at talent, 3M instituted functional (or tier) talent reviews. In a tier review, a segment of employees belonging to a *functional* grouping (e.g., manufacturing, R&D) are reviewed regardless of the business in which they reside. This results in a functional perspective on talent and provides a consensus built on a coordinated view (functional and business) of individual development needs. The MTRs and tier reviews roll up into the "health of the organization" (HOO) process, during which the CEO personally reviews each business's talent pipeline and discusses with the executives how they are developing talent. All of the information from these reviews feeds into succession planning.

HOO is a subset of 3M's approach to succession planning. HOO focuses on the talent pipeline for a specific business/market, while succession planning ensures the cross-business and enterprise level of talent development and placement. Overall, Thulin reviews more than one hundred executive positions, discussing first what additional experiences each individual in the current role may need to be prepared for future roles, and second, discussing what potential successors for the role will need to accomplish to be ready to take on the role. In addition, the HOO process captures planning for more than five hundred global positions. The entire approach is driven corporately with leadership accountability at the most senior executive levels.

Experiences Matter

According to McCall (2010), "To the extent that leadership is learned, it is learned through experience." Given that experiences drive learning, placement (to gain those experiences) is critical. Researchers and practitioners alike have known for a long time that formal classroom learning provides a relatively small component of our professional development. "Working the three-dimensional chess-board is really key to developing leaders," says McGrath. "Three-dimensional is a good description of the nexus of how our matrix works. At 3M, we have diversity of geographies, markets, and business models that intertwine to collaborate, which helps develop our talent. Making sure people have roles in different aspects of the matrix is key."

"In fact, 3M is one of the few places you can have multiple careers and never have to leave the company," according to Donald Chang, regional managing director, Southeast Asia, and managing director, 3M Singapore. Dawn McGinley, director, HR communications, elaborates by saying, "You can have a technical role in an adhesives laboratory in our Industrial Adhesives and Tape division, then switch to applying that same technology in our Aerospace or Drug Delivery division or switch over to the business side in any of those divisions." McGrath adds, "At 3M, you can go deep or you can go broad. There are as many ways to be successful here as there are people. We don't believe in a single model for success, because for innovation to thrive, many people doing many different things are required, and you never know what and who will develop based on what is needed and what is yet to be."

While there are no rigid, cookie-cutter, step-by-step placements, 3M does have several types of placement opportunities that contribute to leadership development. According to Jon Ruppel, vice president of international HR, "We know a variety of situations really allow people to get better at handling the demands and challenges of leadership here, and first-hand experience in very different situations is how mastery is built." For example, a Six Sigma leadership role is considered quite prestigious and is much sought after as a broadening experience. In addition, it requires learning influencing skills.

3M also has a dual ladder career system so that individual technical professionals can continue to grow their careers and gain needed experiences in two ways, both of which provide opportunities for promotion. One path is immersion in research; the other is the path toward management. The highest position on the technical side of the ladder is corporate scientist, the same rank as an upper level director on the managerial side of the ladder. This allows individuals to stay in the laboratories if they wish and creates an independent promotion track for talented scientists who choose not to become line managers. Some individuals cross to the other portion of the ladder at different points in their careers, creating opportunities for different experiences and understanding on both sides of the ladder.

Even the CEO's direct reports are not exempt from expectations for development: each is encouraged to serve on an external public board of directors (Donlon, 2009). This helps to broaden people's outlooks and exposes them to valuable outside perspectives. In fact, opportunities to be part of the non-profit board of directors are open to all leaders and routinely advertised by 3M Community Affairs. Nina Ylagen Pedro, manager of 3M's Asia Pacific Talent Solutions Center of Expertise, explains, "We see talent development as a series of individually planful experiences."

McGrath is also quick to add, "At 3M, global assignments are critically important. By the time Inge was named CEO, he had worked in so many different parts of the company—both in the United States and internationally—that he seems to understand 3M intuitively." Global experience is key to 3M's leadership development and Thulin sets the standard. Thulin has been at 3M for more than thirty years, speaks five languages—English, Swedish, German, French, and Dutch—and has had responsibility for seventy countries and has personally lived in five different countries. "We want and need to continue to develop global transformational leaders. We need leaders with a truly global mindset in order for the company to be successful," said Thulin. In fact, his leadership team is comprised of people who were born in eleven different countries, with each having lived, on average, in three other countries.

Frank Little, vice president and general manager of 3M's Occupational Health and Environmental Safety division, believes the business development and project manager roles are key for helping leaders to develop broadly. Others such as Joaquin Delgado, executive vice president of 3M's electro and communications business, believe "The TD or technical director role is one of the hardest in the company, requiring a balance of both technical expertise and business acumen." All agree that having experience on all sides of the 3M matrix, from a functional leadership role to running a division to running a country subsidiary, are key experiences for some of the more complex leadership roles at 3M. Mario Mascolo, managing director of 3M Italy, sums it up by saying, "Most companies have one major technology or have one or two geographic regions or serve one market, which simplifies the leadership development task. 3M has multiple technological bases, serving vastly different markets from health care to fast-moving consumer goods to high-tech electronics and in every region of the globe. We need to develop everyone we can."

"We are very good at placement, both for individual development and fulfilling critical business roles with changing needs. You might say it is a core competency here. We collectively work hard to know our people and fit them to the right opportunities," said Chris Holmes, executive vice president of 3M's industrial and transportation business. It is a 3M practice that the business owns the responsibility for talent development up to a certain point in people's careers; then they become corporate assets. Corporate assets are reviewed and moved into roles based on the needs of the company and the needs of the individuals, resulting in more rapid development of both. As part of the HOO review process (described earlier), key talent is profiled in terms of strengths and weaknesses, which yields important developmental needs that are captured both for development planning and also for succession planning purposes.

A detailed portfolio on each individual is amassed as people are considered for senior level positions. As a position opens, people are evaluated based on the business requirements of the role and the needs of the individual. The experience of the team around the individual is also considered. For example, does the role require a high-stakes quick turnaround scenario? How high is the risk of not turning around the business quickly? Does this same business have a newly appointed controller or human resource manager? All are considerations as the task is also about risk assessment. If the stakes are high and there are already several people new in their roles and levels on the leadership team, then this is not an ideal situation for someone as a huge stretch assignment to turn around this business. However, this might be a great developmental experience for someone who had sufficient turnaround experience but needs exposure to a different business model or market within 3M. Analogously, an acquisition or turnaround situation might be the perfect opportunity for someone needing to learn to make tough decisions and to develop the tenacity to manage through complex situations. Balancing business demands for talent and opportunities to successfully stretch individual leadership capabilities is an art form.

Job assignments for development are carefully planned and just as carefully adjusted by the executive resource committee (ERC). An example of one particular lab manager illustrates how the process works. This technical person had a very carefully choreographed series of experiences and was first placed in a Master Black Belt role to learn influencing and negotiations skills. Having successfully navigated the role, the person reentered the business as a technical director, and following that role was asked to lead a small subsidiary where he could learn how to navigate 3M's internal matrix from an international perspective. Next, the person was brought back to the U.S. to run one of 3M's businesses.

Each step was done in sequence and could have changed had lessons not been mastered, but the overall plan was already discussed and laid out before the first move to Master Black Belt was made. This is the same way Thulin was carefully developed and can be seen through his trajectory of roles within a country to an assignment working across a region to running countries to running divisions to running a region to running International to CEO.

Pamela K. Martyn, retired director of succession and workforce planning at 3M, summarizes the process of matching individual and organizational needs by saying, "We look at the amount of time available for a learning curve for the role and align it with an individual's ability to come up to speed . . . if the job has (little or) no time for someone to get his feet under him we will most likely need someone more experienced . . . other roles may have a bit more flexibility around the learning curve due to factors such as strong people around the person that mitigates the risk." Before any appointments are made, all candidate slates for director and above positions are reviewed and discussed at the monthly ERC headed by the CEO. Brian Ronningen, director of HR corporate staff services, points out, "Doing our human capital planning in connection with our business strategic planning has really given us an edge in terms of knowing what is coming up."

Individual Assessment

3M believes in using psychological assessment to provide both individual participating executives and 3M leadership with an additional independent view of an executive's strengths, potential blind spots, and developmental opportunities. Two assessment processes exist for these purposes, one for external executives (seeking to become part of the company) and one for current internal executives (for developmental guidance as well as to provide information for succession planning).

The external executive assessment process is a professionally developed assessment used to evaluate top candidates being considered from outside 3M for high-level leadership positions (i.e., director and above). The objective is to provide an independent view of an individual's fit with the company as well as to help fast-track developmental planning should the person be hired. The process uses multiple methods to gather information and create a holistic view of a person and his or her capabilities. These methods include interviews, cognitive ability tests, personality measures, and work simulations.

The internal executive assessment process, which is known as the executive assessment and development process, also uses multiple methods, including business simulations, standardized testing, and in-depth interviews with peers, subordinates, and the executive's boss. As part of the process, participating executives are expected to generate individualized development plans to share with their bosses based on the results of this assessment. Finalized development plans are subsequently filed with human resources to assist with implementation and aid in identifying trends. The participant's boss and corresponding HR director are charged with following up to ensure the development plan is implemented. Currently, there are written development plans on 87 percent of the top 110 leaders in the corporation, with plans in place to complete the remaining new appointments. Results across participants are examined for commonalities that suggest needed leadership development programming.

Thulin also participated in this process, and, in fact, this process was integral to the succession process used by the board to select Thulin as CEO (Kristie, 2009). This process is also highlighted as a best practice in the Society for Human Resource Management Foundation's video: *Seeing Forward: Succession Planning at 3M* (2008). Finally, plans are in place to create another assessment process, complementary to the two outlined above, that will assess individuals earlier in their careers.

Leaders Developing Leaders

Thulin wants to take building diverse, global leaders to a new level at 3M. As part of this strategic direction, HR, under the leadership of McGrath, has undertaken development of an initiative entitled "Leaders Developing Leaders." While this arena has always been important, this new initiative is aimed specifically at further strengthening 3M's pipeline of internal talent to meet business needs as identified in the human capital planning process. A variety of activities are currently underway for this initiative, from educational to structural process changes.

First, in a desire to bring more focus on developmental planning, 3M is decoupling its employee contribution and development process (EC&DP). Starting in 2013, employees will have individual developmental planning discussions with their managers separate from their performance appraisals (Meyer, Kay, & French, 1965). A variety of educational and system tools have been rolled out in support of this change. 3M is also instituting new definitions of high potential to increase the focus on specific pools of leadership talent and on identification of leadership talent earlier in people's careers. In moving to four high potential codes reflecting both the current job level of the employee and the person's leadership potential to reach the next significant transition, the company hopes to have a more specific, detailed, and broader view of its talent pools. For example, to receive an "M1" code an entry-level employee must demonstrate the leadership potential to reach the manager level or equivalent on the technical ladder, as judged by a consensus of his or her leadership team.

Second, a half-day learning module has been developed and integrated globally into supervisory and management training. The purpose of the module is to increase supervisors' effectiveness at developing their people. A ten-minute video on "coaching" has also been developed as an awareness and skill-building tool for supervisors and managers. A longer video-based learning session on coaching and career development is also being created. A new career and development portal recently was launched to bring up-to-date tools and education to all employees. From a social media perspective, a "Career Development Community" was launched in connection with the portal, which contains career-related blogs, wikis, forums, and resources. 3M distributes an e-newsletter to all employees with career-related news, options and resources, and links to the career community of interest. 3M is also establishing geographical centers for learning and development that will enable more regional self-sufficiency by accelerating the development of employees.

Third, in an attempt to provide global experiences earlier in people's careers, 3M redesigned its global mobility program to provide more experience-based opportunities through international work. Options include extended business trips (three to twelve months), global project-based assignments (twelve to twenty-four months), and global temporary assignments (twenty-four to sixty months). These changes are viewed positively because data shows that the desire to live internationally is highest among those early in their careers. Ensuring that development opportunities with international experience are available to junior employees helps fulfill their personal life objectives and also helps drive the needed experiential learning that will aid them and 3M in the long run. Such early international opportunities also effectively help to retain top talent by providing desired developmental experiences.

Fourth, 3M is participating in a major leadership study with Microsoft, Infosys, Disney/ABC Television Group, and P&G, led by Dr. Morgan McCall of the University of Southern California and Dr. Jeff McHenry of Rainier Leadership Solutions. The study focuses on senior leaders who are outstanding developers of high potential future leaders and what they do (critical behaviors they use) to help their high potentials learn from experience (see Chapter 17). This research will be used at 3M to shape both formal leadership education and job assignments. Participation in this study required 3M to select its top people developers (within three layers of the CEO) to be interviewed. This required coming up with a common definition and way of measuring "great people developers." While the 3M leadership attribute "develops, teaches, and engages others" provided some insights, it was insufficient for identifying the very best of the best. A combination of methodologies was used to identify the top twenty people developers, including:

- Nominations by human resource generalists based on their observations
- Best-in-class scores on the employee opinion survey completed by all employees in their organization, with particular emphasis on high scores on the topics of "employee development" and "careers"
- A compilation of write-in nominations by leaders
- Vetting with the chief human resource officer and director of succession planning

As a double-check, a nominee had to have at least two documented high-profile success stories of developing high potential talent to be included on the list. The mere process of examining and defining who was good at developing people allowed for greater clarity in 3M's own program development. While a complete review of the results of this study is beyond the scope of this chapter, several key insights and lessons learned provide a nice summary of 3M's continuing tinkering with its development pipeline of internal leadership talent.

Lessons Learned

Below are some reflections on what 3M has learned about successful internal pipeline development of talent from discussions around this chapter among the authors and 3M leadership.

Link all talent decisions to the strategy of the business. Development needs to be an integral part of the business strategy or it loses focus, attention, and impact. If the approach is to be enduring, it needs to address strategic business problems. During the late 1990s, due to cost-cutting, 3M forgot this rule and was lucky to have two external CEOs who understood and brought this lesson back to the forefront of talent development at the company.

The CEO owns the talent agenda. According to the 776 top executives from around the world who responded to The Conference Board CEO Challenge 2012 survey (Mitchell, Ray, & Van Ark, 2012), human capital—including acquisition, leadership, employee development, training, and engagement—is the second most "important" challenge that organizations face, second only to innovation. The CEO owns the talent agenda. HR can provide tools and processes, but the CEO is the de facto leader of the talent agenda, whether he or she wants to be or not.

Find a way to identify who is better at developing leaders. Coming up with a process for identifying the best talent developers and what they do forces the development of metrics and tools that can help everyone improve. More importantly, it starts a dialogue within the leadership team on *what* is important for developing leadership talent and *how* talent is developed within the culture to meet the strategic business needs of the company. A secondary benefit is the possibility of identifying "hotspots" of talent development by area, leader, or location from which a disproportionate number of leaders emerge. This sort of study can be used formally or informally as part of developmental practice or to bring organizational knowledge to the forefront.

Allow people to learn in their own way, but hold them accountable. People need some guidance along the way, but they learn and develop in their own way. Refraining from telling people how to do the work is simple, but not easy. Not surprisingly, several 3M leaders remarked how difficult it was to hold one's tongue and allow people to learn things the way that they needed to learn them.

Discussing learning increases the developmental impact of experience. The McCall and McHenry (2012) study of top developers found that top people developers at 3M discussed with people what skills they needed to develop and could learn in and from an assignment, and why learning these things was important. Protégés of the developers (who were also interviewed) confirmed that this type of discussion made a difference in their learning. In fact, the person who was considered the very best at following up on what was to be learned was also considered by independent criteria to be the top people developer in the company. This person is known for following up and asking people both what they did and what they learned. Shortly after the interview segment of the study was completed, the top people developer in 3M was also named CEO.

References

3M. (1977). *Our story so far: Notes from the first 75 years of the 3M Company.* Saint Paul, MN: Author.

3M. (2002). *A century of innovation: The 3M story.* Saint Paul, MN: Author.

3M. (2011). *3M: The story of our brand.* Saint Paul, MN: Author.

Collins, J. C., & Porras, J. I. (1994). *Built to last.* New York, NY: Harper Business.

Donlon, J. P. (2009, January 31). 20 best companies for leaders: How George Buckley's 3M shot to the top. *Chief Executive Magazine*, p. 40.

Gundling, E. (2000). *The 3M way to innovation.* Tokyo, Japan: Kodansha International.

Gunther, M. (2010, September 27). 3M's innovation revival. *Fortune International* (Asia), p. 37–40.

Kristie, J. (2009). A strengthening nexus: Boards and the CHRO. *Directors & Boards, 34*(1), 24–26.

McCall, M. W., Jr. (2010). Recasting leadership development. *Industrial and Organizational Psychology: Perspectives on Science and Practice, 3*(1), 3–19.

McCall, M. W., Jr., & McHenry, J. J. (2012). Preliminary results to stakeholders: How the best senior leaders develop their high-potentials. Personal communications to participants.

Meyer, H. H., Kay, E., & French, J.R.P., Jr. (1965). Split roles in performance appraisal. *Harvard Business Review, 43*(1), 123–129.

Mitchell, C., Ray, R. L., & Van Ark, B. (2012). *The Conference Board CEO Challenge® 2012 survey: Risky business—focusing on innovation and talent in a volatile world (Report No. R-1491–12-RR).* New York, NY: The Conference Board.

SHRM Foundation (Producer). (2008). *Seeing forward: Succession planning at 3M* [DVD]. Available from www.shrm.org/about/foundation/products/pages/seeingforwarddvd.aspx.

CHAPTER FOUR

Developing Leaders at All Levels at Yum! Brands

J. Tim Galbraith and Jim Howard

In 2008, Yum! Brands, Inc., began its second decade as an organization, having spun off as a separate company from PepsiCo in 1997. By all measures, the first decade had been very successful, having added more than seven thousand restaurants, grown operating profits by 9 percent CAGR, improved ROIC from 8 to 20 percent, paid down almost $3 billion in debt, and increased our stock price by 500 percent. It would have been very easy for us to sit back and say, "Let's keep doing what we've been doing and hope the next ten years are just as successful!" But our CEO, aware of the dangers of complacency, challenged the organization to begin a "second set" in which we would look at everything we were doing and ask ourselves how we could drive improvements that would increase our performance as an organization even further. A particular concern he had was around talent and leadership development. To accelerate our growth and achieve even greater success, we would need more, better prepared leaders at all levels of the organization, from restaurant managers to division presidents. What could we do to significantly improve the results of our leadership development efforts to ensure we would have the leaders we would need to be successful in our second decade?

To begin to answer that question, we launched an internal survey asking people at every level what they felt was working and not working with regard to our current approach to developing leadership capabilities. At the same time, we reached out to and interviewed our leadership development counterparts at seven

Exhibit 4.1. Results of Internal and External Research

We already do a lot of great things to develop leaders:

- We provide on-the-job, experience-based development. The size and scope of our jobs provide unique opportunities to develop breadth and depth of leadership capability.
- Our culture is powerful in creating a fun, engaging work environment, driven by recognition with a "breakthrough results" focus.
- We provide development opportunities for all because we expect everyone to be a leader and make a difference no matter his or her level or role.
- Our leaders teach. They are committed to growing and developing people.
- We use coaching and formal training and development to enhance on-the-job development.

How can we improve our efforts?

- First, make sure we stick with what we already are doing. Don't walk away from current practices.
- Add even greater emphasis on accountability:
  - For walking the talk of our culture
  - For owning your own development
  - For learning from on-the-job experiences
  - For coaching and developing your people
- And provide focused support tools to maximize learning, growth, and development.

of the top companies on Fortune's 2009 "Best Companies for Leaders" list (GE, PepsiCo, IBM, Capital One, MasterCard, Southwest Airlines, and General Mills). The output of that research highlighted for us the current practices we felt were working well for us, as well as pointing us to some additional best-company practices that could greatly enhance our efforts (see Exhibit 4.1).

With our research in hand, we convened a design summit with the objective of crafting a leadership development strategy to span all our businesses and geographies that would build on and enhance our current efforts. We invited internal human resource

Exhibit 4.2. Key Principles Guiding Our Design Efforts

- Since our biggest investment in people is the salary we pay them to do their jobs, we must make on-the-job, experience-based development the centerpiece of our approach.
- Success at any level in our organization is dependent on living the Yum! values (as defined by our "How We Win Together Culture" principles), so a formal culture-building experience must be a part of the framework.
- All development efforts must be focused against the needs of our business strategy.
- Everyone owns his or her own development and must be held accountable for learning and growing his or her capabilities.
- Every supervisor, manager, and leader is a coach; every coach is expected to grow talent and must be held accountable for it.
- Focused (that is, few but powerful) support tools must be provided to help increase the probability of success in current and future positions.
- Organization systems and processes must reinforce and support individual and supervisor accountabilities for growth and development.
- The strategy must be global in scope, universally applicable, and impact everyone from entry-level/individual contributor all the way through senior leaders.

leaders, learning and development leaders, and several business leaders from our businesses around the world, along with several carefully selected external experts. We started with a set of key principles gleaned from our research that were to guide our effort, shown in Exhibit 4.2. The framework that we crafted in this two-day session integrated these key principles and provided a roadmap for developing the key components that would bring it to life across the organization.

Design of the Leadership Development Framework

We laid our Leadership Development Framework (see Figure 4.1) against four distinct career stages (the horizontal layers in the

Figure 4.1. Leadership Development Framework

Our Leadership Development Framework

	Culture	Own Your Own Development	70% of Development Occurs On-the-Job	Leadership Development	Filling in the Gaps
Senior Coach					
Broader Coach	- Introduction to HWWT2 - Understanding the Yum! Dynasty	- Everyone's a Leader - Learning from Experience	Experiences	LD3: Taking People with You	Electives
First-Level Coach				LD2: Leading Others for Breakthrough	
Individual Contributor				LD1: Leading Self for Breakthrough	
	Everyone (First 30 days)	Everyone (First 6 months)	Everyone (Ongoing)	Role Specific	

Organizational Process to Drive ACCOUNTABILITY

framework: Individual Contributor, First-Level Coach, Broader Coach, and Senior Coach). We should note here that Yum! long ago adopted the term "coach" as the preferred title for anyone with supervisory or managerial responsibilities. The thought was that this term better described the expected role of everyone within Yum! who had the privilege of managing and leading others.

Following our key principles, we put "learning from experience" at the center of our framework (the middle pillar in Figure 4.1), thereby identifying it clearly as the primary vehicle for developing leadership capabilities for everyone. Our objective was to shift mindsets away from development as "something that happens in the classroom when I can take the time" toward fully leveraging day-to-day work experiences as powerful development opportunities. We surrounded this pillar with focused learning programs and tools meant to teach skills and processes to help people be more successful in making the most of their on-the-job experiences, as well as develop consistent leadership skills important at each distinct career stage.

Everyone in the organization was expected to complete the Culture and Own Your Own Development programs. Individuals in each career stage were expected to complete the role-specific learning path designed for their level in the organization. For example, every individual contributor would be expected to complete the LD1 learning experience, entitled Leading Self for Breakthrough, while first-level coaches would be expected to complete the LD2 learning experience, Leading Others for Breakthrough (we describe these programs below). Additional programs and tools would be available as electives on an as-needed basis to address identified developmental needs and gaps. We reinforced the framework by embedding stronger accountability measures into all of our key organizational processes such as performance management, individual development plans, and people plan reviews. Finally, because of our global scale, we committed to a full technology-enabled and supported learning process in multiple languages. This was critical in order to make the entire process accessible and affordable to all sixteen business units and our learners around the globe.

With the framework drafted, we engaged in an alignment process with our CEO and senior leadership teams. This involved walking them through the progress to date, explaining the framework and its components, taking their input and gaining their commitment to support and drive the framework going forward. This process, while time-consuming, was essential in helping to make sure we kept all content tightly focused on the most important needs of the businesses and built support for the eventual phase-in of the entire approach. Before the design of this new leadership development strategy, we did have consistent people processes in place around the world, but our formal development efforts were inconsistent and not always connected across the organization.

Development of Framework Elements

With leadership alignment around the framework, we established five global development squads, each focused on a piece of the framework, with a central coordinating body in place actively working to ensure consistency and alignment across all the squads.

Each squad was comprised of human resource generalists and training and development professionals representing the majority of our business units. We asked each squad member to identify and maintain a group of non-HR professionals within their business unit for periodic input and review of materials. The squad role was in addition to their regular accountabilities.

Experience-Based Development

The broadest and most critical squad was our Experience-Based Development group, which was tasked with bringing the centerpiece of the model to life. To guide our efforts here, the squad adapted McCall's (1998) general model for developing executive talent (see Figure 4.2) that he presented during a People Development gathering at Yum! Brands.

This model provides a simplified illustration of the basic formula underlying an experience-based development process: identifying the right talent and giving them the right experiences builds the expertise needed to deliver results. Making sure that the experiences are tied to the business strategy, having the right

Figure 4.2. A General Model for Developing Executive Talent

Experience-Based Development

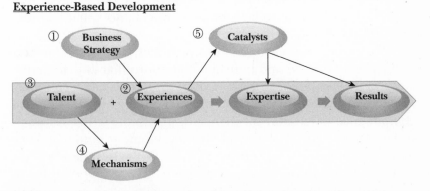

Adapted and reprinted with permission from *High Flyers: Developing the Next Generation of Leaders* by Morgan W. McCall, Jr. Harvard Business Press, 1998. Copyright © 1998 by Harvard Business Publishing; all rights reserved.

mechanisms to appropriately match talent with experiences, and leveraging organizational catalysts to ensure follow-through and accountability support and reinforce the model. For each of the key input components, we developed questions we thought would need to be answered from both the organization and the individual perspective in order to bring the formula to life (see Table 4.1).

Starting with our current Yum! business strategy documents, this squad compiled an initial list of key challenges, capabilities, and perspectives that we thought would be called for by the strategy. We reviewed this list with our CEO and other senior leaders, targeting those with significant international accountability (e.g., China, India, and Middle East). The output of this effort was the input and alignment of our senior decision-makers on the critical core capabilities required by the strategy and therefore needed by our next generation of leaders.

With this list in hand, the team developed an interview protocol to be used with a broader group of leaders. The purpose of the interview was to gather a list of available experiences that would help build the capabilities called for by the business strategy. Specifically, we asked more than eighty leaders around the world for their thoughts on the aligned list of critical capabilities and any additional ones they thought were missing. Then we asked them what specific on-the-job experiences they were aware of or could think of that could be used to help develop those capabilities. Finally, we asked for their ideas about catalysts that we could put in place to help improve the chances that learning from experience actually occurred.

The output of these interviews provided us with the answers to the organizational and individual questions that we had generated for the business strategy, experience, and catalyst components of our talent development model. For the remaining two components, talent and mechanisms, we conducted a thorough review of our current assessment, development, and feedback tools and processes and compared them to the best practices we had discovered in our external research. We developed a list of ways to improve our current tools and processes to better support and enable our experience-based development approach and build greater accountability into our organizational processes. We

Table 4.1. Key Questions

	Organization Perspective	*Individual Perspective*
1. Business Strategy	What are the key challenges for the success of Yum! going forward? What experiences, skills, and capabilities will leaders of the future need in order to be successful?	What are the skills and capabilities I need going forward to build a successful career with Yum!?
2. Experiences	What are the experiences that are available today to help prepare talent for the challenges of tomorrow?	What are the experiences that can help me build the skills and capabilities for a successful career with Yum!?
3. Talent	What are people's long-term career goals? What are their strengths? What are their gaps (experience, skills, knowledge)? What is their growth potential? What is their derailment potential?	How do I know which skills and capabilities I should be working on? How do I know which experiences are right for me?
4. Mechanisms	How best to match individual needs with the appropriate experiences?	How can I be sure that I am doing the right things that will help me grow?
5. Catalysts	How to hold individuals accountable for learning? How to hold coaches accountable for developing their people?	How will I be held accountable for my own development? How will my coach be held accountable?

involved the chief people officer and the global human resources leadership team in refining and finalizing changes.

Most of the changes were related to our mid-year individual development planning (IDP) process, where everyone receives 360-degree feedback and has the opportunity to discuss the results with his or her coach on an annual basis. The output of that discussion is an aligned plan that is used throughout the year to guide the development efforts of the individual. To enable and reinforce a greater use of on-the-job development strategies in those plans, we:

- Re-crafted the instructions for creating a compelling development plan to focus more on the power of on-the-job experiences and provide tips on how to get the most out of them (see Exhibit 4.3, "Preparing Your Individual Development Plan").
- Included a "self-goading checklist" with instructions that help employees assess the quality of their plans and ascertain the likelihood that it will make a difference in their growth and career. If someone scores low on this self-scoring checklist, he or she is encouraged to revisit his or her IDP and strengthen it (see Exhibit 4.4, "Individual Development Plan Checklist").
- Included a "how has this person grown over the last year" section on the development plan itself to help emphasize the value we place on learning and growth.
- Introduced an on-the-job experiences guide of available experiences gleaned from our interviews with Yum! leaders. Experiences were organized around the critical core capabilities identified in our review of the business strategy and were offered as real-world examples to be used as is or as thought starters to spur additional ideas (for examples related to Restaurant/Operations Experience see Exhibit 4.5, "On-the-Job Experiences Guide").
- Developed an instruction page for coaches focusing on their accountability for helping every person on their team realize his or her potential. This again reinforced the power of on-the-job developmental experiences and the coach's role in making them as powerful and meaningful as possible.

Exhibit 4.3. Preparing Your Individual Development Plan (IDP)

At Yum!, we believe *everyone* has the potential to make a difference, regardless of level or role. Living up to that potential is all of our responsibility. This means knowing what experiences, know-how, and skills you need in order to meet the challenges of your current role and/or future roles, and making sure you find ways to strengthen or acquire them.

The Individual Development Plan (IDP) is a key tool that allows you to take charge of your own development. Work with your coach to put together a plan that can truly help to maximize your potential. Here are some guidelines to help you:

- With your coach, identify the one or two most significant experiences, know-how, or skills you need to strengthen or acquire in the next twelve months to continue growing *and* delivering breakthrough results. Remember to build on current strengths as well as acquiring new skills. The 360-degree feedback process is a great way to increase your self-awareness about your needs.
- Focus your development plan on those one or two big things.
- Seventy percent of personal development happens on the job, so identify experiences that you can have on the job that will help build the know-how or skills you need.
- Good developmental experiences have one or more of these kinds of challenges:
  - Involve unfamiliar responsibilities
  - Success and failure are possible and will be obvious
  - Requires "take charge" leadership
  - Involves working with new people, a lot of people, or both
  - Creates pressure, such as deadlines or high stakes
  - Requires influencing people you don't have direct control over

True development happens when you are stretching yourself beyond your "comfort zone." If you are not a little nervous about your plan, then it is probably not as developmental as it could be. Refer to "Examples of Developmental Experiences" at HRonline for ideas. Use the Individual Development Plan Checklist (Exhibit 4.4) as a "self-goading" mechanism to ensure your plan is as strong as it can be. Review this checklist with your coach as you align with your final plan.

Exhibit 4.4. Individual Development Plan Checklist

Use this checklist as a "self-goading" tool to ensure your plan is as strong as it can be. Put a check next to the statements that are true, and then add up the number of checkmarks. A scoring key is provided at the end.

Build a Strong Development Plan
❑ My development plan will help develop the skills and know-how I need to continue growing *and* delivering breakthrough results.
❑ I am strengthening or acquiring experiences, know-how, and skills that will be in demand three to five years from now.
❑ At least 70 percent of my development plan is comprised of experiences and assignments that can currently exist or could be incorporated into my current role.
❑ The experiences and assignments I have planned have at least one of these challenges:
  ▪ Involves unfamiliar responsibilities
  ▪ Success and failure are possible and will be obvious
  ▪ Requires "take charge" leadership
  ▪ Involves working with new people, a lot of people, or both
  ▪ Creates pressure such as deadlines or high stakes
  ▪ Requires influencing people I don't have direct control over
❑ My plan focuses as much energy on developing my strengths as it does on improving weaknesses.
❑ This development plan will push me to the edge of my comfort zone.

Hold Yourself Accountable
❑ For each development goal, I have included a metric to assess whether the goal has been reached.
❑ I have plans and methods in place to hold myself accountable for my development plan (e.g., a calendar entry that reminds me to reflect on what I'm learning and how to apply it to my role).
❑ I have transferred my development goals to my Goals and Objectives form to increase my ownership of my development.
❑ I commit to review my development progress with my coach on a monthly basis.

Your Score	What It Means
0 to 4	You are in danger of finishing the year no more capable than when you began. Schedule thinking time over the next two weeks when you can seriously focus on your development and discuss it with your coach. Your future is worth it!
5 to 7	You have a good development plan, but it needs some work. Look at the items you did not check and strengthen your plan accordingly.
8 to 10	You have created a strong development plan that will provide the experiences you need to better meet the challenges of your current role and position you for future career growth.

Use formal training and development programs to "fill in gaps" or build skills that will help ensure you are successful in the experiences you identify (see https://yu.yum.com for a listing of current Yum! University offerings).

Keep your IDP alive all year:
- Schedule a monthly 1:1 with your coach to actively revisit your IDP and consider your progress.
- Be sure to reflect after key events, meetings, or milestones.

Ask yourself:

- What am I learning?
- How am I applying what I've learned?
- Transfer your IDP development goal(s) to your Goals and Objectives form to help hold yourself accountable.

Adapted and used with permission from *Real Time Leadership Development* by Paul R. Yost and Mary M. Plunkett. Wiley-Blackwell, 2009.

Exhibit 4.5. On-the-Job Experiences Guide

The most important factors in your success at Yum! are the extent
to which you walk the talk of our HWWT2 culture *and* the results
you achieve along the way. These should be first and foremost in
your mind as you think about continuing to grow and develop in
Yum!

From a longer-term career standpoint, there are also some key
perspectives that will play a role in your success at Yum! These
perspectives are reflected in our Yum! Dynasty Growth Model
and are tied directly to the unique nature of our business and
organization:

- Growth Orientation
- Restaurant/Operations
- Brand Building
- Customer Mania/Insight
- Global Business
- Franchise/One-System Sensitivity

As you put together your individual development plan, consider
in which of these perspectives you may have gaps. Think about how
you might begin to close those gaps through assignments and projects you can take on in your current role to challenge yourself, add
value to our business, and acquire critical learnings that will help
enable your success in the future.

On the following pages you will find real-world on-the-job experiences collected from our leaders around the globe. You may be
able to incorporate these exact experiences into your IDP or you
may choose to use them as thought starters for your own IDP or
those of your direct reports. Not all of these experiences will be
viable choices for all employees, but they should cause you to think
of experiences that can be viable.

Remember, the best developmental experiences have one or
more of the following challenges:

- Involve unfamiliar responsibilities
- Success and failure are possible and will be obvious
- Require "take charge" leadership
- Involve working with new people, a lot of people, or both
- Create pressure, such as deadlines or high stakes
- Require influencing people you don't have direct control over

As you work with your coach or your direct reports, make sure to create meaningful on-the-job experiences that have specific purpose and help expand the person's capability. Both the person and our organization will benefit.

Restaurant/Operations Experiences
- Complete an industry study focused specifically on restaurant operations.
- Build your know-how by looking specifically at operating models (drive thru, counter service, BOH processes, technology), ownership models (franchise, company, sole proprietor, mixed models), or talent models (attraction, retention, engagement, the employee value proposition).
- Before beginning the work, get sponsorship from a key operations leader in your business—agreeing on what you will study and why and the desired outcomes for your work.
- Present your findings, including recommendations for your division, to your coach and your operations leader sponsor.
- Complete restaurant general manager training as if you were a manager hired from a competitor.
- Attend team member training and all management training modules before practicing your new skills as the restaurant manager for at least three months, being held fully accountable for all aspects of restaurant operations.
- When your experience in-restaurant is complete, present your learning to your coach and provide recommendations for your brand based on your experience. This experience may take up to six months.
- Lead or fully participate in an operations project. Lead or fully participate in a project that is important to the brand, to the brand's customers, and to team members. This may be current work your brand is doing, or it may a new idea. It may be an operations improvement project, a customer satisfaction project, or a restaurant people capability improvement project. The ideas are endless! The key is to serve as the leader or on the team for the life of the project and bring recommendations to your leadership team. Debrief your learning with your coach.
- Serve on a brand franchise board. Most brands have various committees or boards, many with franchisee and company

Continued

Exhibit 4.5 continued

representation that exists for different purposes. Join one of
these boards for a minimum of a year. While serving, focus on
learning both the company and franchise perspectives on the
issues the board faces. Do field visits with some of the
franchisees on the board, building relationships and learning
more about their businesses.

- Complete multiple field visits with operations leaders in your
  brand. The goal is to gain a broad operations perspective, so
  complete visits with leaders at different levels (COO, head
  coach, region coach, area coach) and different functions
  (Operations, Finance, HR, Development). This is good to
  complete over six to twelve months and in different regions of
  the country so you can gain a broad perspective of the business,
  including different marketing windows, different restaurant
  volumes, varying customer and team member profiles, etc.
  Share your learning with your coach and the COO.

- Move into an operations or operations support role. This could
  be directly in an operations leadership role (area coach, region
  coach), an operations support role (Finance, HR,
  Development) or in the restaurant excellence team of your
  brand. Moving into a new role will give you full accountability
  for a piece of operations and build your know-how very quickly.
  This is a multi-year commitment, designed to fully build your
  capability in operations.

- Complete team member training for multiple brands. Team
  member training typically take two weeks to complete in each
  brand. Once training is complete, work as a team member in a
  restaurant for at least one week. This experience will give you a
  deep understanding of "how a restaurant works" and the
  culture of a restaurant from a team member perspective. It will
  also teach you how to satisfy our customers and how to resolve
  issues our customers experience. Debrief your experiences with
  your coach, including recommendations for the brand based
  on your experiences.

- Learn your brand's customer satisfaction measurement system,
  analyze the current results, and make a recommendation to the
  COO for improving customer satisfaction. The project could
  include a deep analysis of the current data (including both ops
  and marketing customer data), a root cause analysis of poor

results, and interviews with customers, restaurant managers, and team members. It may also include you completing the customer satisfaction measurement process (customer based or vendor based, standards based or experience based) in multiple restaurants and in multiple regions.

Other Thought Starters
- Conduct and present a competitive restaurant analysis and provide recommendations.
- Conduct and present an internal cross-brand/cross-division analysis of best demonstrated practices (BDPs).
- Adopt a profit and loss statement (P&L) for a restaurant, an area, or a market.
- Conduct an in-depth study of a process control approach and how it could apply to your restaurants.
- Develop a year-long peer mentoring relationship with a seasoned operator to see the business through his or her eyes.

Having defined the centerpiece of our Leadership Development Framework, we turned to developing the supporting programs.

Culture

Although we are a widespread global entity operating in over 116 countries, Yum! has a consistent organizational culture across all our businesses and markets—from the restaurants to the restaurant support centers that enable them. This culture is based on a set of behaviors we call our "How We Win Together" principles. These principles, shown in Exhibit 4.6, were created at the time of our spinoff and have been deeply embedded into every aspect of our business, from restaurant employee orientation to senior management meetings. Everyone in the organization is expected to practice these behaviors on a daily basis, and there is among all senior management the belief that only through doing business according to these principles will we all "win together."

Since living the culture is such a critical part of success at Yum!, we developed a core cultural learning experience as the

Exhibit 4.6. Yum!'s How We Win Together Principles

Believe in *All* People

We trust in positive intentions and believe everyone has the potential to make a difference.
We actively seek diversity in others to expand our thinking and make the best decision.
We coach and support every individual to grow to his full capability.

Be Restaurant and Customer Maniacs . . . *Now!*

We love running great restaurants, and our customers rule. We act with urgency to ensure that every customer sees it and feels it in every restaurant. We make sure we have great RGMs who build great teams. We are maniacal about rigorous execution of our core processes to deliver our Brand Standards as our number 1 brand-building initiative. It's the foundation for making customer mania come alive.

Go for Breakthrough

We begin by asking ourselves, "What can I do *now* to get breakthrough results in my piece of Yum!?" Our intentionality drives step-change thinking. We imagine how big something can be and work future back, going full out with positive energy and personal accountability to make it happen.

Build Know-How

We grow by being avid learners, pursuing knowledge and best practices inside and outside our company. We seek truth over harmony every step of the way. We consistently drive outstanding execution by scaling our learnings into process and tools around what matters most. Breakthroughs come when we get people with knowledge thinking creatively.

"Take the Hill" Teamwork

We team together to drive action versus activity. We discuss the undiscussable, always promoting healthy debate and healthy decisions. Our relationships allow us to ask the earth of each other. We make specific verbal contracts to get big things done with urgency and excellence.

Recognize! Recognize! Recognize!

We attract and retain the best people and inspire greatness by being world famous for recognition. We love celebrating the achievement of others and have lots of fun doing it!

first requirement of all new employees. This was designed to ensure that everyone coming into the organization would receive an in-depth understanding of what the culture is all about, as well as how they would be expected to walk the talk and reinforce the culture in their day-to-day jobs. This was developed as a series of nine online modules covering the How We Win Together principles that were to be completed within the first thirty days of employment.

The series starts with a video message from our chairman talking about the importance of the Yum! culture in our success and the expectation for each and every person to walk the talk of the culture every day. Each module in the series then covers one of the How We Win Together principles by showing scenarios of how that principle shows up in day-to-day interactions and asking the learners how they might react in each situation. Each scenario is then followed by current employees at all levels across the organization, including senior leaders, sharing their perspectives about that principle. At the end of each module the learners record their insights and questions about how that principle might be demonstrated in their jobs and are asked to discuss what they recorded with their coaches in their next one-on-one. This approach of receiving content, applying it to the workplace, and receiving supervisor support was a key design feature of all of our programs.

Leadership Development 1: Leading Self for Breakthrough

The second key supporting element of our framework is focused on helping individuals learn how to maximize their personal growth and impact as leaders at Yum! Although we had always stated that everyone owns his own development, we had not provided any training to help individuals understand how to do that. With the added emphasis we were placing on learning from experience in our new framework, we felt it was critical to help prepare everyone for the experience-based development approach and to provide them with the foundational tools for growing their leadership capabilities.

LD1 was designed as a twelve-week blended learning experience that introduces content, models, and skills that a learner then incorporates into her day-to-day job. After applying and gaining experience with applying the concepts on the job, a virtual classroom follows in which learners on the same learning path discuss successes and challenges and learn additional strategies to apply to successfully transfer the learning and integrate it into their day-to-day lives. All new employees are to complete this program within their first six to nine months with Yum! This learning path includes a variety of assessments, and content is introduced through several e-learning modules and a half-day instructor-led workshop.

The content of this program focuses on five foundational areas to help individual contributors build core leadership skills important at Yum!:

- *Everyone's a Leader:* Teaches what we believe about leadership at Yum!: Everyone's a leader no matter your level; you have to own your own career; you have to be personally accountable to get results; and you have to get results the right way (that is, by "walking the talk" of the culture).
- *Learning from Experience:* Introduces the learner to a development model that suggests that 70 percent of how we learn is through experiences, 20 percent through feedback and relationships, and 10 percent through formal training. The module highlights key steps for maximizing learning from experience by introducing practices useful before, during, and after the experience. Learners are introduced to methods such as how to establish learning goals, how to reflect, and how to ensure accountability and intentionality throughout the experience. Learners have access to job aids and tools that help them put these steps into action back on

their jobs. One such tool requires them to assess their own skills and attributes against best practices and behaviors associated with continuous learning (e.g., continuously seeking know-how, openness to feedback, and reflection) and to compare their self-assessments with their supervisors' assessments of them.

- *Breakthrough Performance:* Teaches a coaching model that learners at any level can use to coach themselves to break through barriers and achieve a high level of performance and results.
- *Emotional Intelligence:* Highlights the importance of emotional intelligence and its link to high performance, leadership, collaboration, and culture in the Yum! environment.
- *Shadow of a Leader:* Helps learners discover their leadership shadows (personal brand) and the impact they have on others and on the results that they get. The module guides learners to develop action plans to increase their value to the organization and to strengthen their leadership shadows to become more effective for long-term career growth.

When designing the e-learning to accompany this learning track, as well as the learning track for supervisors, we developed a story-based approach and created a set of characters that reflect the diverse, global environment of our restaurants, while also using stories that acknowledge our business and reinforce our culture. Since Yum! has restaurants in more than 116 markets, with restaurant support centers in sixteen countries, we wanted this initiative to truly feel global. Since the squads that were involved in designing these learning tracks represented many parts of our global business and brands, we had the right people to collaborate in developing story lines and situations that would help ensure the characters and the learnings resonated cross-culturally. And, because of our global approach, we were able to test concepts—and make changes early in the design phase—just by involving our squad early and in every step of the process. Because of this collaborative approach, little additional localization was needed beyond the translation of all the content and collateral material because the development approach was so global from the beginning.

Training assignment, status tracking, and reporting for this and all programs are completed via our internal learning management system. Coaches in the field have continuous access to status reports, while coaches in the restaurant support centers receive quarterly reports detailing the progress of individuals within their groups. In addition, coaches throughout the organization receive regular email updates and notices regarding their responsibilities for debriefing and discussing learners' experiences in the programs.

Leadership Development 2: Leading Others for Breakthrough

The third key supporting element of our framework is focused specifically on the unique role of the coach (again, within Yum!, coach is synonymous with supervisor or manager), and especially new coaches. Its purpose was to build the capability of new coaches in a just-in-time approach to lead their teams in achieving breakthrough results in the Yum! culture. The design approach matched that of the LD1 program: blending e-learning, classroom, on-the-job application, and supervisor support components into a year-long learning experience.

To ensure we consistently communicate what it means to be a leader and how to maximize on-the-job experience, this track starts with the Foundations of Leadership offered in LD1, comprised of Everyone's a Leader and Learning from Experience, and then dives into the unique challenges of managing others within the Yum! culture:

- *Transitioning from Individual Contributor to Coach:* Highlights the challenges of moving from individual contributor to coach and how to make an effective transition utilizing Arthur M. Freedman's Let Go-Preserve-Add On model (Freedman, 1998).
- *Mindset of the Yum! Leader:* Focuses on the role of coach in the Yum! culture and the expectations that go along with the role. Provides learners with tools that help them understand the critical roles of the coach, gives them opportunities to

practice those roles, and shows them how to effectively build trust with their new teams.

- *Breakthrough Coaching:* Because a key component of the coach's role is the development and performance of team members, this module provides a tool and process that helps the coach break through barriers and achieve a high level of performance and results with the team.
- *Building People Capability:* These just-in-time modules provide coaches with an in-depth understanding of our annual Building People Capability cycle, including goal setting at the beginning of the year, mid-year development planning, and end-of-year performance achievement processes. The emphasis is on preparing coaches to fulfill their critical responsibilities during each of these processes to maximize the performance and personal growth of their team members.

The online portions of this program use the same set of global characters introduced in LD1, thus providing continuity and familiarity for learners as they progress through the leadership development framework. All new coaches are to complete this program during their first year in their new roles.

Leadership Development 3: Taking People with You

The fourth key supporting program of our framework focused on the responsibilities of more senior coaches across Yum! This three-day classroom experience is led by the Yum! chairman and CEO, David Novak, and provides an approach for motivating and aligning teams to achieve results together, faster, and with greater ownership. It is based on the chairman's personal journey of leadership development and reinforces again the power of learning from experience. For example, in the program he relates his early experiences in marketing to how he approaches the leadership of people. In marketing he learned to understand the needs and desires of his target audience so he could be successful as a marketer of products. In leading people, he realized it's the same concept—to get people truly aligned and motivated you have to understand and address their needs and desires. So in leading any effort, he first identifies who he needs to affect, influence, or take with him to be successful. Then, he works to identify the perceptions, habits, or beliefs those people have that he needs to build, change, or reinforce in order to accomplish the goal. This marketing "insight-driven" approach to leading people is a direct outgrowth of his early marketing experiences.

In the program, he presents a set of thirteen leadership principles and actions that he has found to be most effective in understanding and addressing the perceptions, habits, and beliefs of the people on any given project or leadership team. For every principle, he relates one or more specific experience that he had that led him to include that principle in his repertoire of leadership behaviors. Put together, it is a powerful roadmap for achieving success in any size leadership endeavor.

This program has recently been developed into a book, *Taking People with You: The Only Way to Make BIG Things Happen* (Novak, 2012) as well as a set of online learning modules to allow restaurant general managers in the Yum! system to learn and apply these leadership lessons on the job in the restaurant.

Organizational Processes

The final component of the framework was making sure that all key organizational processes were supporting and reinforcing the experience-based approach and were driving accountability at all levels. Changes to the mid-year development process were described above and shown in the exhibits in this chapter. Additional changes to ongoing processes included:

- *Recruiting and On-Boarding Materials:* Includes a copy and description of the framework and its components so that everyone knew from day 1 what their learning and development responsibilities would be.
- *People Planning Discussions:* Includes the key questions of "How has this person grown over the past year?", "What is his/her key development challenge in the coming year?" and "What is his/her next best move or experience that will help address his/her development challenge?" in all mid-year people planning and succession planning discussions. In those

discussions, all coaches are required to review the answers to these questions for the people on their teams with the next level of coach. The answers to these questions play a large role in promotional decisions throughout the organization.

- *Internal Staffing Process:* Ensures questions were in place to facilitate person-job matches based on both the needs of the job and the development needs of the individual. While this doesn't always work perfectly (i.e., the needs of the job still often outweigh the development needs of the individual), just having the questions in place as part of the decision-making process ensures that the development needs of the individual are part of the conversation.
- *Performance Management:* Includes sections on the end-of-year performance achievement forms that required everyone to answer: "How have you grown and developed this past year?" and for coaches to respond to: "Who have you developed this year?" These questions were meant to reinforce and raise the accountability for ongoing, on-the-job development. To support these additions, we created an online module that walks individuals through the process, provides tips on how to complete it, and gives well-written examples of how to do this well. In addition, all completed performance achievement forms are reviewed and followed up on by human resource generalists.

Launch Strategy

Throughout the entire content development process, the development teams were reviewing and gathering feedback from their review teams back in the business units. This helped ensure that content going into each program was right for our target audiences. Additionally, we "soft launched" various components of the framework with target audiences in business units around the world—specifically, Dubai, Singapore, Australia, and the U.S.—as we neared our global launch date. We felt this soft launch was critical to help road test and modify the programs and tools prior to a global cascade and prior to translation and localization efforts.

Although the target audience for many of the supporting programs would be new employees or coaches going forward, our launch strategy was to have all current employees experience the relevant portions of the framework. This was to ensure that we embedded the learning-from-experience approach across the organization right away and that everyone had a common understanding of the concepts and tools included in the Culture, LD1, and LD2 programs.

For the actual launch we developed a comprehensive branding and communication strategy that included:

- Marketing-style promotional materials and teaser communications leveraging the globally diverse characters from our online modules.
- An introductory video from the chairman and CEO reinforcing the concepts of everyone is a leader, owning your own development, and taking advantage of the significant learning opportunities present in every assignment.
- Specific communications from each senior business leader introducing the framework and supporting programs and laying out the launch plans within their business units.
- Testimonials from individuals who had experienced the programs during our soft launches.
- Detailed resource guides for the training and development teams in each business unit.
- Detailed, step-by-step instructions for learners and coaches to help them navigate each learning experience.

All program registrations, communications, materials distribution, and execution were launched through our internal learning management system. The entire launch process took almost two years as each business unit incorporated the launch into its ongoing business flow.

Initial Research on Effectiveness

We conducted initial research on the effectiveness of the various programs and tools one year into the launch. As expected, we found lots of things to be excited about and lots of things that needed additional support and refinement. The biggest positive was that the core concepts of "owning your own development" and "learning on the job" (our 70–20–10 approach) were heard loudly and clearly throughout the organization, and that attitudes and behaviors were positively changed. Comments like these were commonplace:

- "I had assumed that my supervisor was the leader and it was his responsibility to drive my career development. However, I learned that it is my responsibility. . . . Since taking the course, conversations with my supervisor have been going well, he has been asking me for more ideas, and I feel now that I am a leader and have ownership of my development and need to be thinking about and providing ideas."
- "It made me start thinking (and now I ask myself regularly), 'What have I learned from this project or meeting?' Never before had I taken the time to reflect on what I have learned on the job."

The biggest opportunities we uncovered were in the area of communications, specifically related to introducing so much at once. Learners and coaches reported being confused and at times overwhelmed by the multitude of components being introduced, leading to less-than-expected completion rates. We discuss our lessons learned in the next section.

Lessons Learned

With any large-scale initiative or project such as this, there is great opportunity to reflect, identify lessons learned, and apply what we learned to future endeavors and experiences. This notion of learning from experience applies as much to us now as it does for the learners to whom we were directing this entire initiative.

The following observations are some of our key takeaways that, if we were to take on a similar project, we would want to keep top of mind and thoughtfully work through. We offer them as guideposts for others undertaking large-scale development initiatives such as the one we've described.

Whether an enterprise is large or small, there is great value in having a clear and simple leadership development framework that can be communicated, reinforced, and supported. It helps establish consistent vocabulary, skills, and models across the organization. As you craft these, simultaneously challenge yourself to be as simple as possible so that everything you create—from the framework itself to programs and tools to communications—is understandable, clear, and easy to execute. Looking back, there are opportunities for us to have been even simpler, especially in our communications and launch materials. Never assume that you sound too simple!

A holistic leadership development framework that supports and reinforces itself helps make the model operate as more of a system than simply a collection of parts. Additionally, being system-driven helps integrate the model and tools and makes them part of the fabric and culture of the organization. As you develop all the pieces of the framework, acknowledge the capacity of the organization to absorb and integrate all the changes that you're introducing so that it's more measured. In a matter of just over a year, we introduced a new leadership development framework, new processes, multiple learning paths and programs, and tools within those paths to start applying. This was massive change being generated from just one area of human resources within a large, complex operating environment. Looking back, a more sequenced and measured introduction of all this change would certainly have contributed to it being absorbed and integrated more fully in all parts of the organization and allowed us the requisite time, focus, and support to help employees at all levels integrate it into their day-to-day work. For example, spending more time up-front road-testing and explaining the framework itself, then following up with the rollout of one program at a time, would have helped maximize the integration of the whole effort into the day-to-day operations of the businesses.

It is helpful to give the launch and implementation of an initiative like this as much time, effort, and focus as you'd give to a complex, large-scale change initiative, versus just as a communications effort. We didn't fully appreciate the amount of change and support that this initiative really required as we began, and we would have benefitted from developing deeper understanding and broader ownership among all the leadership teams. At times, we delegated to members beyond the core team the responsibility of creating awareness and ownership with senior leaders in our various business units. But because this project wasn't their first or only priority, those non-core members sometimes had difficulty in creating the deep level of understanding and senior ownership that are critical in a project such as this. As the core team, we should have assumed primary responsibility for gaining that senior leadership support and sponsorship in every business unit.

Identify ways to fully educate and develop ambassadors and supporters of the initiative within the HR and leadership community prior to, during, and long after the initiative launches. This will help ensure local understanding, and create local champions who can support learners on-site. Make your HR partners and program alumni your "black belts" of the process and empower them to help bring the model to life.

Measure not only the overall impact and effectiveness of the initiative, but also identify shorter-term metrics to help create a feedback loop to guide and gauge how the implementation is going so that you can adjust as necessary to ensure a successful launch and implementation. For example, build in early and ongoing survey feedback from your audience group to ensure that your communications and marketing materials are as clear and instructive as possible.

Although employees are introduced to different tools, models, or skills when going through the learning paths, be sure to provide support following the program—both short- and long-term. Support is needed to help employees transfer learning to their current jobs and to make sure the tools introduced during the programs are available outside the programs so that learners can access, use, and re-use over time. Even better, embed the additional tools in the process itself, such as our including the self-goading checklist within the IDP form itself.

Focus on educating coaches (i.e., supervisors and managers) about the framework and their role in supporting their employees directly, and remember that they have many competing priorities. Determine how to sustain this support post-launch, knowing that new coaches are coming into the organization over time and your communication efforts need to account for that dynamic.

e-Learning and development of online tools not only help make the effort scalable and more consistent, but provide 24/7 accessibility to the learning resources across the organization. This is important in organizations that are large, multi-site, and operate across multiple geographies. We used a global approach in developing content to reduce market-level localization requirements (beyond language), and we centrally funded all development efforts—including pilots—to help remove cost as a barrier to implementation across the entire organization.

When developing blended learning, be sure to understand the capabilities of your internal learning management system (LMS) so that the design of any learning paths can be executed simply, leveraging the existing functionality of the LMS. Also, consider how to support and motivate learners to persist through the entire track, especially if they are not familiar with a blended approach that combines multiple elements (e.g., e-learning, virtual classroom, instructor-led classroom). While the majority of our learners had attended instructor-led training or completed e-learning in the past, very few had ever experienced an extended, blended path that combined different media over time.

To help employees better manage their careers and own their own development, identify not only experiences unique to your business, but also more generic experiences and skills that one should acquire or build at different levels. This menu of level-based experiences makes experiences more accessible and serves as a compass so that employees know what experiences they should acquire at different stages of their careers to help prepare them for success within or outside your company. Integrate these experiences into your individual development planning and succession planning processes to help ensure that experiences are owned by the individual. By tying requisite experiences (and the expected lessons learned from them) to individual development goals and succession planning outcomes, you drive home the importance of experiences for growth, development, and future success.

References

Freedman, A. M. (1998). Pathways and crossroads to institutional leadership. *Consulting Psychology Journal, 50*(3), 131–151.

McCall, M. W., Jr. (1998). *High flyers: Developing the next generation of leaders.* Boston, MA: Harvard Business School Press.

Yost, P. R., & Plunkett, M. M. (2009). *Real time leadership development.* London: Wiley-Blackwell.

CHAPTER FIVE

Experienced-Based Development
Building a Foundation at Kelly Services
Brad Borland, Terry Hauer, and Laura Ann Preston-Dayne

The Talent Management and Leadership Development group at Kelly Services was founded in 2007 with distinct goals: ensure people managers have the leadership skills necessary to be successful; drive enhanced job performance; shorten the time-to-productivity learning curve; heighten employee engagement and retention; guide goal-oriented career development; facilitate workforce planning, development, and succession decisions; and produce an expanded pipeline of diverse leadership talent. Five years later, each of these objectives continues to guide our work. This chapter describes how we have incorporated experience-based development into our foundational leadership development practices across the organization to positively influence talent outcomes.

Foundational Enablers

We introduced three foundational frameworks into the organization to create a shared understanding of leadership development and to lay the groundwork for embedding experience-based development into our talent management processes: the employee lifecycle, our Leadership Blueprint, and a learning and coaching framework (PARR).

Figure 5.1. Kelly Service's Employee Lifecycle

Defining the Employee Lifecycle

Unlike many Fortune 500 companies, Kelly did not have a longstanding talent management or leadership development function. Rather, the organization operated as a loosely coupled federation of businesses with varied human capital practices and few shared tools. As a start-up function, it was imperative for us to "respect the wisdom of the past" by taking inventory of all existing practices, processes, tools, and approaches to determine what was available for use and what was working well that could be leveraged in the future. To organize our findings, we created the employee lifecycle, a visual depiction of the recurring stages of an employee's career with corresponding human resource practices (see Figure 5.1). After conducting in-depth interviews with senior leaders, their human resources (HR) support partners, and members of Kelly's learning organization, we identified existing practices upon which we could build a leadership development strategy.

To support our efforts, we collected a variety of existing Kelly competency models that were being used in various functions. Additionally, there was a corporate performance management process that had been altered several times yet was still regarded by employees and leaders as a bureaucratic annual exercise. Numerous live, virtual, and self-paced courses and learning modules were available through our internal learning portal. The rich library of technical and functional training provided full-time and temporary Kelly staff access to the tools necessary to perform in their current roles.

Defining Leadership

It became apparent that before we could focus our efforts on driving development and improving the leadership pipeline, we

Figure 5.2. Kelly Service's Leadership Blueprint

think the unexpected

Respect the wisdom of our past.
Take intelligent risks for our future.
Challenge conventional thinking.
Commit to innovation and change
leadership.
Know the global implications.

deliver breakthrough
results

Execute our strategy.
Accept personal responsibility for
achieving Kelly's goals.
Demand excellence from yourself
and others.
Make decisions with results in mind.
Create competitive advantage.
Act with urgency.

leadership

champion your **people**

Engage your team's energy, talent,
and intelligence.
Establish guard rails and remove
barriers.
Communicate with clarity and impact.
Embrace and practice collaboration.
Discover unique talents and nourish
potential.

make it **personal**

Role model Kelly's character and
values.
Initiate courageous conversations.
Commit to Kelly before team, and
team before self.
Project passion and positive energy.
Champion diversity and inclusion.
Never stop learning.

needed a common organizational understanding of desired leadership capabilities. We facilitated conversations and workshops with board members, senior leaders, and HR to outline the competencies necessary to be a successful leader at Kelly. The result was Kelly's Leadership Blueprint. It outlines the kind of leaders we want to be and be known for and acknowledges that all employees—managers and non-managers alike—have the opportunity to demonstrate leadership behaviors (see Figure 5.2).

The blueprint is aspirational—leaders are not expected to excel in each and every area of the blueprint today, but there is an expectation that all leaders continue to grow and develop in these critical areas. Although it is applicable to all Kelly employees across the employee lifecycle, it also provides a balanced framework for evaluating a leader's success.

As the blueprint was utilized and eventually ingrained in the language of the organization, it became clear that leaders were using the terms "learning" and "development" synonymously (i.e., development occurs as a result of participating in a formal training type activity). In order to broaden the concept of development to include experience, we needed to introduce a new approach to development that would encourage leaders to leverage opportunities in their daily interactions—in short, making learning part of their work instead of taking time away from work to learn. Once leaders began acknowledging that going to a class, reading a book, or checking a box on their performance management plan was not sufficient to drive individual and organizational growth, we began introducing the concept of experience-based development.

Defining a Shared Framework for Experience-Based Development

To reinforce the behaviors within the "champion your people" quadrant of the Leadership Blueprint and to support the performance management process, we began offering a one-day Leader as Coach workshop for senior leaders across the organization. This program focused on providing leaders with practical coaching tools, techniques, and strategies to help participants understand the expectations Kelly has for its leaders; achieve higher levels of performance from their employees; select and execute meaningful development for themselves and others; and drive employee engagement and retention.

We identified an interesting development paradox during these workshops. When we asked leaders to describe the most impactful development experience in their careers, we inevitably heard things like working in a turnaround situation, coaching or mentoring from a trusted leader, joining a strategic project team, and managing an expansion or downsizing—all experience-based development opportunities. Yet when we asked these same leaders to discuss which development methods were being used by their staff and which development activities they typically suggested, they described sending individuals to training programs, asking them to read books or whitepapers, or providing

Figure 5.3. The PARR Model: A Framework for Experience-Based Development

	PREPARE ⚙	ACT !	REFLECT ?	REVIEW 🔍
Learning Model for Managers and Leaders	"What is the competency I must acquire?"	"What are the activities I should engage in?"	"What did I learn from my experiences?"	"What learnings can I share with my manager and peers?"
Coaching Model for Direct Managers and Manager-Advisors	"How can I help contextualize the competency he or she must develop?"	"What suggestions can I provide him or her based on my personal experience?"	"What questions should I ask to help him or her reflect on his or her learning?"	"What questions should I ask to help him or her explore his or her learning?"

little to no specific guidance at all. As a result, we incorporated the IBM Parallel Learning and Coaching Model, PARR (IBM Corporation, 2005), into the live training to provide an interactive format for sharing experience-based development as a philosophy and to remind senior leaders that as "keepers of the culture," their actions would either reinforce or negate the importance of development.

PARR as depicted in Figure 5.3 is a four-step approach (prepare, act, reflect, review) that helps employees select, execute, and transfer learning from development opportunities, and helps managers support employee development through questioning, encouraging reflection, and supporting the transfer of knowledge back to the job (Corporate Executive Board, 2009). Note that the model is divided into upper and lower sections, depicting the shared responsibility between an employee and his or her manager for development. Highlighting the role each individual plays in development (e.g., employees should not wait for managers to "develop" them and leaders should not just be "sending" employees off to develop) was a critical step in moving the concept of experience-based development forward.

In the model, *Prepare* ensures the employees know where they are headed and what competencies it will take to get there. Findings from the performance management process indicated that managers and employees rarely discussed professional development, so managers often assumed that their employees knew what was expected. In turn, managers were unpleasantly surprised when employees' development efforts were not focused in the areas they thought were important. We began emphasizing the importance of launching the development process with a clear understanding of the end goal: clearly identifying the results to be achieved and what success will look like.

In many cases, choosing what to do (*Act*) in order to achieve development goals is a challenge for leaders and employees alike. After all, if you know you are not good at doing something, then how can you know how to improve? We found that, when unsure of how to develop in a particular area, most employees defaulted to the same solutions—taking a training class, reading a book, or asking someone else what steps he or she took to improve. In order for development to truly occur, employees need to identify multiple viable methods of development and then choose the best ones for the situation. The fact that not all development is created equal became a key teaching point for leaders and employees. We began educating leaders on the impact associated with different methods of development using Bersin's Enterprise Learning Framework depicted in Figure 5.4 (Bersin & Mallon, 2009). In

Figure 5.4. The Impact of Various Learning Methods in the Modern Learning Age

Formal	Informal		
	On-Demand	Social	On-the-Job
Instructor-Led Training	e-learning	Wikis, Blogs, Forums	Performance Support
Virtual Classroom	Search	Expert Directories	Feedback
Games	Books and Articles	Social Networks	Rotational Assignments
Simulations	Videos	Communities of Practice	After-Action Reviews
Testing and Evaluation	Podcasts	Conferences	Development Planning
e-Learning	Learning/Knowledge Portals	Coaching and Mentoring	
20%	80%		

particular, we emphasized that the majority of development occurs through doing one's job, and development plans should reflect this (e.g., look for daily opportunities to refine existing or grow new skills, understand different perspectives, or build partnerships).

Reflect and *Review* are focused on transferring learning from development activities back to the employee's work. In order to maximize experience-based learning, it is critical that the employee go beyond just completing the designated action (commonly seen at Kelly by dutifully checking the completion box) to reflect on one's learnings during the process. Leaders often only engage in thoughtful reflection when something has gone wrong (e.g., What happened and why? What could I have done differently?), yet we wanted them to understand that just as much knowledge can be gained by thinking about what one is learning from engaging in the identified activities (e.g., What insights have I gained that I need to apply going forward in my work? What useful skills am I developing?).

Managers can help maximize transfer of learning by facilitating ongoing dialogue about development progress and regularly asking what employees have learned. This also helps drive accountability for sustained development throughout the year versus the mad dash to "complete" development before performance management conversations. Finally, to complete the PARR cycle, employees were strongly encouraged to review with others what they had learned. Through sharing and teaching, employees are able to solidify their own learning, provide insights to others, and reinforce the usefulness of experiences to drive development. In many cases, this application of learning then turns into another opportunity for experience-based development.

Embedding Experience-Based Development in Key Processes

Once we defined the recurring stages of an employee's career, leadership competencies, and the framework for experience-based development, we were ready to grow awareness of and foster engagement in experience-based development. We chose to focus our efforts on the elements of the employee lifecycle that best aligned with leadership development: selection, performance, development, succession, and transition.

Selection

As a key front-end element in the employee lifecycle, selection is vital to create, perpetuate, and enhance a healthy leadership bench. In many organizations, selection is done quickly and reactively as roles open, usually via a hit-or-miss interview process, with the primary decision being made by the hiring manager. We were no different. As a result, we launched a cross-functional effort to enhance selection. Our "Hire the Best" program created refined emphasis or outright change within our selection practices, including:

- Placing a greater and regular focus on competency-based selection
- Creating a bank of competency-aligned interview questions that tied directly to specific key elements of the open role
- Distinguishing selection competencies between those involving organizational fit and those involving skills and abilities
- Introducing team-based selection via a consensus process
- Identifying post-selection development needs
- Planning post-selection development
- Creating a fluid handoff to a leader transition support process

Combined, all of these changes made a significant and fairly rapid impact. However, like most any other change, it was met with resistance.

From an experience-based development standpoint, the post-selection development elements above are most worthy of further discussion. Identifying post-selection development needs was tied directly to both the use of competency-based selection and the use of a consensus selection process. We found that even though the consensus process produced more thoughtful decision making (and pre-start candidate endorsement), no candidate is perfect; each had obvious development needs beyond simple orientation.

Post-selection development planning was done while the selection data were fresh. We took the unusual next step to intentionally engage selection team members in the identification of development needs, rather than simply thanking and disbanding them. The prime beneficiaries of this practice included the hiring manager and the newly hired or internally selected leader. It also drew notable positive reaction from team members, many of whom commented that they "wish that had been done for me." Early results also were impressive. For the selected leaders, there was a sense of customized development interest that helped affirm their decision to join or stay with Kelly. Hiring managers were able to identify development needs earlier.

A much more targeted development plan was created when development was identified early. Most development with transitioning leaders had been restricted to a series of one-on-one, meet-and-greet sessions with enterprise-wide stakeholders. Although the time spent together enhanced relationship building, it did very little to boost specific skills. Armed with specific development targets, the hiring manager, HR generalist, and transitioning employee were able to select experiences (e.g., facilitate a sales loss or win post-mortem) to accelerate and improve relevant development.

An important lesson learned for us was that simple ideas can have big impact. We were sitting on a mountain of valuable development data, yet never used it to drive development. We stopped prematurely by using the data only for its primary intended use in the selection process. The expanded use created a more seamless flow right into leader transition support. We also learned that thoughtful selection and development of both external and internal employees created benefit for both Kelly and the chosen, developing leader.

Performance Management

My Career is the term Kelly Services uses for its performance management process. Although performance management has undergone a lot of change at Kelly, the My Career process was transformed in 2008 when we elected to eliminate performance ratings. This major change was undertaken to steer the emphasis from ratings to a more meaningful discussion on performance feedback and coaching for development.

In the past, we placed equal emphasis on business and development goals as discussion topics throughout the My Career process. But we knew the conversations typically focused on business goals, since these goals are generally metrics-driven, making them more objective and easier to discuss. It became clear through focus groups and other communication channels that employees were eager to have more intentional, structured conversations about their development. In addition, our focus group participants—primarily the people-leaders—confessed that they were struggling with the development conversations, and they asked for help.

Although we had training for our people-leaders, we determined it would be beneficial to add a complementary resource to the training. As a result, we created one-page scripts or discussion guides. The discussion guides are purposefully designed to gather information about experience-based activities to date and help guide these same types of activities going forward. Sample questions include:

- What actions did you complete (e.g., on-the-job development)?
- Did you find ways to apply your new behavior in more challenging circumstances?
- How might you leverage your new learning in different situations?
- What do you plan to do differently as a result of your new learning?
- Why did you select this particular development goal?
- What do you want to achieve as a result of accomplishing this goal?
- What will be different when you achieve this goal?

In addition, we created a document for employees to help them prepare answers for the questions they would be covering during their My Career discussion.

Since implementing these documents, employees have reported that they have a better understanding of what they need to do differently after their performance reviews. They also report having plans for making the intended changes. In fact, a random audit of employee development plans revealed that, in many cases, they include experience-based development in their action steps.

Although our leadership training was well established and highly regarded, additional resources were needed to augment our performance management process and help our people-leaders and their employees improve their development conversations. As one of our people-leaders said, "Even if I don't use all the questions, it's a jumping-off point for me and helps me get the conversation going."

Assessment

Kelly Services uses two assessments as part of our leadership development program to provide leaders with in-depth insight into their development opportunities. The first is a 360; the second measures leadership experiences and accelerators such as career goals and career preferences, which might include individual contributor versus people-leader aspirations. Leaders receive individualized output reports along with one-on-one interpretation from a trained, internal HR feedback provider.

The leadership experiences and accelerators assessment includes an entire section that gathers quantitative information concerning the leader's experiences. For example, a leader might indicate that he has been involved in a merger or acquisition activity and, perhaps, took a support role in the activity. That same individual may have been moved into a role leading a team that is struggling to meet business goals. Regardless of the experiences, the overall results of the assessment allow us to clearly determine where the leader requires more experience-based development and the activities and roles that should be included in the development.

Leaders use the information from the assessments, along with that of the feedback provider, to create a robust development plan. We first encourage leaders to look at development from a different perspective. The default is to view development as a discrete event or task—just one more thing to add to an already full plate. We help leaders understand that development can and should be woven into the work they are already performing. For example, we push leaders to move out of their comfort zones and think about how they might approach a particular task or project with the goal of enhancing a current skill. We might ask them how they would plan to take a new approach to an old issue or apply an old skill in a new way.

Regardless of the competencies the leader has elected to develop, our backdrop is the 70–20–10 model. Where we see leaders defaulting to training programs or reading books, we reduce the quantity they have chosen. For those programs or books they retain in their plans, we ask for clear action steps that describe how they will use this newly acquired learning on-the-job.

We also encourage leaders to build reflection and ongoing feedback into their plans. We want them to take stock of what has happened and course-correct if needed. Development plans are refreshed on an annual basis or at critical milestones. At these times, we ask leaders to outline the actions they have taken to reach their goals and describe any feedback they have received or changes they have observed as a result of reaching their goals. To ensure a continued focus on experience-based development, we ask them to consider how they might use their new behaviors in support of other development goals.

Our feedback providers find that they most frequently coach leaders in two areas:

1. *Clearly describing goal achievement in terms of what success would look like.* Often, leaders tried to describe success in terms of business outcomes versus development outcomes.
2. *Transferring behavioral action steps into experience-based development activities.* Leaders lamented over adding "something else to my already overflowing plate," versus recognizing that experience-based development could simply be a re-framing of their approach to the work they were already performing.

Development

The development area of the employee lifecycle was rich with opportunities to embed experience-based development. As a result, we focused our experience-based development efforts on two Kelly audiences: selected senior leaders and the company at large.

Senior Leaders: Development Roles and Assignments

For the first time, we identified two key development roles that were reserved for high-performing senior leaders who were viewed as potential successor candidates: head of a global function and country general manager. The thoughtful selection of people for these roles was important. We wanted to select people who:

- Were perceived widely as high performers
- Had a career aspiration to lead a large operation or function
- Had a penchant for development via new experiences
- Were willing to accept an assignment without any specific post-assignment promise

The first few role-holders were successful enough to warrant the ongoing use of this experience-based development tactic. In fact, each of the first two role-holders was promoted to other, more strategically significant roles, in large part due to the skills and perspective developed and performance attained while in the new development role.

Two key elements of this process included clarification of the role assignment and ongoing support as the individual transitioned roles. For the country general manager role, plans were made to return the individual to the corporate offices on a regular basis. This added assurance was necessary to address any concerns about no longer being at corporate headquarters and whether an "out of sight, out of mind" career derailer could possibly emerge. Although regular planned trips to corporate headquarters were helpful, we also arranged ongoing, high-touch leadership transition support meetings, including ongoing coaching.

Although the country general manager role itself was a terrific development opportunity, we learned that it is important to plan with real precision the targeted development that is anticipated to be the most game-changing. Taking a new job and doing it the same as the former job was insufficient and tempting. Articulating the targeted development (e.g., managing managers globally) makes the new job actually developmental. Another lesson is that development and good performance in the role both matter. One without the other is insufficient.

We also experimented with development assignments for senior leaders. Different from a role, an assignment is shorter term and specific to an organizational need (e.g., grow account base in region Z) and the leader's development need (e.g., learning to influence and lead change in a cross-border, multi-culturally complex environment), while likely also being a one-time occurrence. Again, these development assignments are reserved for senior leaders expected to move up in the organization. We used similar selection criteria and development support described for development roles, and to date believe this is ripe for more regular use.

Company at Large: Talent Summits

Beyond succession planning, developing and sustaining a leadership bench is always a priority. Talent summits were created to both refine and broaden our leadership bench. A talent summit is an organized, leader-led, person-by-person review of select talent, including both people managers and individual contributors. Summits were convened initially to launch and create greater:

- Organization-wide understanding of the talent needed to achieve our strategy
- Awareness of our cross-functional and geographic talent
- Accountability for the development and deployment of talent

The third bullet point in particular is most relevant to our experience-based development discussion. An important aspect of the talent summit is for leaders to arrive prepared to tell a talent story for each person being discussed. The talent story includes, among other things, identifying and discussing a person's strengths, development needs, and career aspirations. In the first year of talent storytelling, the development methods most commonly cited were training, coaching, mentoring, and time in role.

Time in role actually was useful to further the promotion of experience-based development as a viable, high-impact development practice. As development strengths or needs were presented, we noticed that leaders really struggled to meaningfully identify how robust development was actually going to occur. Leaders tended to equate formal learning events with development and then wondered why they were not seeing post-course behavioral changes. During the summits and in real time, we began offering leaders development guidance that included identification of development-focused, tangible experiences (e.g., making sales calls, turning around a struggling market). Time in role assertions also allowed us to ask, "What, specifically, will you be expecting a person to experience and be able to do differently?" This ignited a useful exchange to underscore that time alone—void of targeted development—had no intentional impact. The time in role assertion also created a chance to ask leaders what, specifically, more time would provide developmentally. Moreover, not all responses reflected specific action steps, but rather some highlighted the outcomes of experience, including "living with the result of your decisions" and "gaining credibility and confidence."

The unanticipated next step was the need to create accountability and follow-through. Asking the talent presenters about the development commitments they were making was instrumental in fostering accountability. The lesson was that people struggle to plan and execute their own development in addition to struggling with knowing how to best assist in the development of their direct reports or other talent.

Fitness Challenge

We wanted to drive a greater awareness and understanding of the impact of experience-based development and ease of use throughout the organization. Recall that many of our employees saw development as a discrete event that happened away from their "real jobs," and though they wanted professional development, there was perceived to be no time for it. In response, we created the Leadership Fitness Challenge in 2011. Using our internal social networking platform, employees around the world were invited to join the leadership development team in "exercising" their leadership muscle over a thirty-day window.

The Leadership Fitness Challenge was designed to be a simple way for employees to access experience-based development activities that took no more than five to ten minutes to complete. Each daily challenge reinforced the Leadership Blueprint competencies and provided practical insight into the wide range of skills people leaders and individual contributors need to work successfully in a matrixed environment (e.g., influence, collaboration, communication, change leadership). To keep things interesting, we focused on a finite activity each day and included weekly videos from topical experts, how-to worksheets, popular leadership articles and blogs, and best practice discussions. Finally, to support the use of the PARR model, we dedicated each Friday to reflecting and reviewing. Participants were given specific instructions to think about the past week and information on how to transfer the learning into their daily routine. Exhibit 5.1 provides a sample of the daily Fitness Challenge activities.

Exhibit 5.1. Sample Leadership Fitness Challenge Activities

- **Day 1:** Kick off the Fitness Challenge by crafting a personal leadership vision statement describing who you want to be as a leader and what you want to be known for. This will help guide you through the next thirty days. To get started, consider this brief video from Dan Pink, renowned motivation expert.
- **Day 7:** There always appears to be more work to do than time in the day, but are you effectively leveraging the brief touch points you have with others each day? Create an elevator speech using the attached worksheet to grab people's attention, showcase the value of your work, and create advocates for your efforts.
- **Day 15:** Another week has passed and you were likely moving rapidly from one thing to the next. Take a moment to think about how well you listened to others this week (*when you really listened with a deep "seek to understand" desire*). What did you learn about the other person? His or her point of view? Yourself as a person who can engage others through listening?
- **Day 17:** Review the Q2 financial report and identify one action you can take this quarter to help Kelly meet its financial targets by 2013.
- **Day 28:** Plan and execute spontaneous recognition. Go out of your way to express appreciation today in an unexpected or unfamiliar way. To begin, take a look at the following link for fifty No/Low Cost Recognition Ideas.

The daily structure of the Fitness Challenge allowed people to partake at their own pace because activities did not build upon each other, and the social media platform captured the daily updates as to what had or had not been completed. In total, we had nearly three hundred participants globally, representing all levels of the organization—far exceeding our original expectations for a voluntary development initiative.

After the close of the Fitness Challenge, we conducted a focus group with our most active participants to learn what they liked about the program and determine whether we would run the event again. Brevity and variety were cited most often when asked what made the program successful. Everyone noted that this event made them stop and think about how they were behaving as leaders—formally or informally—and many requested worksheets and takeaway materials that they could use on the job. On the flip side, technology challenges (e.g., logging into the system, accessing videos) limited our ability to fully engage participants from our field organization. We have been working with our technology partners to improve the speed and capabilities of the internal social networking platform. Based on the overwhelming positive feedback, we are currently incorporating focus group improvements and preparing for the second annual Leadership Fitness Challenge.

Succession

Succession planning, as in many organizations, had primarily focused on the identification of capable senior leader successor candidates. Although a typical output of the succession planning process is a thoughtful and informed list of candidates, it seemed incomplete.

The opportunity to enhance the process, and in particular the executive profile created for senior leaders, presented itself when natural curiosity arose about whether successor candidates, from one year to the next, had become more ready to take on a new role. Too often, the answer was unclear. Since scant attention had been paid to ensuring that named candidates were participating in role-relevant development, we decided to add a development focus to the executive profile. The emerging emphasis on development launched innocuously by simply adding a section called "development focus."

In each successive year, we continued to adapt the executive profile to become increasingly focused on development, which included identifying preparation needed for the next role. Year-over-year profile additions beyond development focus included:

- Each successor candidate's current leadership strengths
- Development needs
- A corresponding development plan
- Development achieved
- Development impact attained

These combined changes caused greater and sustained focus on development in general and experience-based development in particular. At the start, development plans used a mix of typical development tactics that proved fairly ineffective. The opportunity to more legitimately emphasize experience-based development included:

- A growing realization that little development was actually occurring using traditional means
- Interest in knowing how to make development stick
- A development reference point, presented under the guise of the actual role(s) for which a successor was considered

These together allowed us to look at a person's development differently. Armed now with a specific career goal (discovered via the My Career process), roles, and leadership assessment data, we were able to focus on both the leader's strengths as well as qualities most needed to prepare to excel in the next role, whether it was a vertical or horizontal move. We began to consultatively work with the successor candidate and his or her manager to identify targeted experiences that would accelerate both development and next-role readiness. The appetite to explore and utilize experience-based development was enhanced by asking a few questions when planning development. When meeting with the employee and/or manager, we regularly asked:

- When you think back over your career, what really drove significant development?

The answer always was a significant experience, which led naturally to the second question:

• What is your high-priority development focus (limit to one to three), and what work opportunity do you have now, or need to have, to ensure that development occurs?

A challenge in the use of role-focused experience-based development was the organization's unwillingness to transparently share with successor candidates the specific role(s) for which they were being considered. This was a speed bump rather than an experience-based development deal breaker. Our modest solution was to make general references to "career development" while rightfully working to avoid any misunderstanding or "implied promise" issues. When envisioning development through use of a future-focused career lens, leaders naturally felt more valued and engaged, and thus more likely to stay.

Transition

The days of easing slowly into a role are long gone. Given how difficult transitions can be, we drew on the work of Watkins (2003) and Charan, Drotter, and Noel (2001) to craft an early and intentional process to support the leader's accelerated assimilation into the role and his or her ability to contribute sooner. Since transition is a time of both excitement and vulnerability, most leaders express a ready willingness to engage in their own transition planning as a means to help guide their success.

Not all aspects of a new job are equally new, challenging, or important. Within the transition process, we help the leaders identify new outcomes for which they are accountable. This guides thoughtful selection of development opportunities.

The prime experience-based development challenge while in transition, because the pace has hastened, is actually slowing down long enough to reflect and learn. The PARR model described earlier is a key enabler. In some ways, transitioning leaders have a developmental advantage compared to other experience-based development opportunities, as so much of the work is new and ripe for real development.

Few leaders instinctively know about or value transition support. Once explained, it was usually enthusiastically embraced.

Somewhat surprisingly, there was resistance or ambivalence to also offering transition support to internal leaders changing roles. Internal leaders were rightly believed to have an advantage in that they likely knew aspects of the culture, had formed relationships, and understood the business model. Those alone, although foundationally useful, were not enough to ensure a smooth or successful role change.

Conclusion

Kelly Services uses the employee lifecycle to communicate to employees and leaders alike that development occurs throughout the employment experience and that "never stop learning" does not apply only to those who are in new roles (see Exhibit 5.2). We believe that development is a critical way to engage our employees throughout their careers and ultimately retain them. Whether you use the techniques in this chapter or your own, it is important to

Exhibit 5.2. Summary of Experience-Based Development Opportunities Within the Employee Lifecycle

Selection	Embed and conclude the selection process with the creation of an experience rich, targeted development plan.
Performance Management	Use the performance management process as a recurring opportunity to discuss, plan, and utilize experience-based development.
Development	Place disproportionate emphasis on the use of experience-based development; it's not innately understood as a planned aspect of development.
Succession	Insist on experience-heavy development of successor candidates as a tried and true means to build individual capability and a broader bench.
Transition	Pay attention to role transitions as an incredibly fertile time to work closely with leaders to plan, reflect, review, and grow while engaging in a new job.

build foundationally firm practices that enable experience-based development throughout the recurring stages of an employee's career. And treat the introduction of experience-based development into the organization like any other change: create and execute a change leadership plan that includes clear goals (e.g., drive accelerated development and performance, build bench) and roles (e.g., developing leader, leader's manager, HR generalist).

References

Bersin, J., & Mallon, D. (2009). *The enterprise learning framework: A modern approach to corporate training.* Retrieved from www.bersin.com/uploadedFiles/Bersin/Website_(Pages)/Resources/Linda/Enterprise_Learning_Framework.pdf

Charan, R., Drotter, S., & Noel, J. (2001). *The leadership pipeline: How to build the corporate leadership-powered company.* San Francisco, CA: Jossey-Bass.

Corporate Executive Board. (2009). *Developing senior leaders who build the next generation of talent: An overview of the roundtable's resources on leader-led development.* Washington, DC: Authors.

IBM Corporation, IBM Center for Advanced Learning. (2005). *On-demand learning: A new era for learning in business.* Cambridge, MA: Author.

Watkins, M. (2003). *The first 90 days.* Boston, MA: Harvard Business School Press.

CHAPTER SIX

Leading from Where You Are

Driving On-the-Job Development into the Whole Organization

Paul R. Yost

One of the hot topics in organizations today is integrated talent management. Unfortunately, more often than not this topic is transformed into one of three practices: (1) a company-wide competency model that ignores the importance of experience, (2) a top-down approach that inevitably leads to the quagmire, "Before we do anything, let's make sure it is all integrated," or (3) a perfect plan that fails to survive the next company reorganization.

Unfortunately, organizations today seldom stay still long enough to integrate anything. We live in an age of highly complex, dynamic organizations where change is the rule rather than the exception; what some have christened VUCA environments (Volatile, Uncertain, Complex, Ambiguous; Johansen, 2009). The market changes, technology changes, a new CEO is hired, a new vice president of human resources is appointed, or a new business strategy is launched. Suddenly, the grand plans for an integrated talent management process have to be scrapped and the work has to start over.

In addition to a dynamic environment, most industrial-organizational (I-O) psychologists and human resource (HR) professionals have to lead from the middle. The majority of on-the-job development initiatives are likely to be launched within a single HR process (e.g., succession planning, performance management, leadership training programs) and often within a specific geography, business unit, or a targeted employee group (e.g., first-level managers).

The purpose of this chapter is to explore how I-O and HR professionals can build on-the-job development initiatives that start in one place but are crafted in a way that promotes the adoption and spread of experience-based development throughout the whole organization. Rather than waiting to build on-the-job development into the organization from the top down, a more effective strategy in a dynamic organization is to build experience-based development initiatives that thrive in these kinds of environments. The secret is to create programs that are designed as catalysts, promoting experience-based development throughout the organization. Leading from where you are means building on-the-job development initiatives in a way that can "go viral" and "infect" the talent management processes and systems throughout the organization. The first half of the chapter will explore five design factors that are likely to increase the spread and sustainability of on-the-job development initiatives. The second half of the chapter will illustrate how the five factors can be applied within three HR systems: succession planning, performance management, and relationship-based development processes such as communities of practice.

Five Design Characteristics for Viral On-the-Job Development Initiatives

I-O and HR professionals are influenced by several fields that tend to emphasize a top-down approach: strategic human resources (Becker & Huslid, 2006; Lawler, 2003; Ulrich & Brockbank, 2005), project management (Westerveld, 2003; White & Fortune, 2002), and change management (Cummings & Worley, 2008; Kotter, 1995). All three often begin by talking about the importance of starting at the top—enlisting senior management support—and then cascading the initiatives down through the organization. But relying on a top-down approach can be counter-productive in today's organizations, where change is often the rule, not the exception. The external environment can change, the organization's priorities can change, and the people at the "top" can change. CEO tenure has decreased in recent years, with 40 percent of CEOs leaving their jobs after only 1.8 years (Gottfredson, Schaubert, & Saenz, 2008). This is not necessarily a new trend. Ciampa and Watkins (1999) tracked the success rates of ninety-four COOs who were brought in to eventually move into the senior role. Five years later, twenty-two had left the company and 75 percent had not made it to the top as expected. Top management is only one example of the typical obstacles and dynamic changes that interventions are likely to face externally (e.g., the entry of new competitors, markets getting worse, markets getting better, and technology changes) and internally (e.g., corporate reorganizations, changes in HR leadership, time pressures, and competing priorities).

Furthermore, approaches that start at the top often underestimate the role of people in the middle of the organization. Historically, civil rights movements across the globe would not have happened if people waited for "top management support." Minority voices and groups can create change if they are confident, consistent, and sustained (Hogg, 2010; Sharp, 2010; Wood, Lundgren, Ouellette, Busceme, & Blackstone, 1994). Recent work has begun to identify the factors that predict the adoption, adaptability, and sustainability of organizational innovations (Ansari, Fiss, & Zajac, 2010; Kossek, 1987, 1989; Som, 2007; Wolfe, 1995; Yost, McLellan, Ecker, Chang, Hereford, Roenicke, et al., 2011).

To drive change from the middle, HR professionals need a different approach and a different set of tools. The person who leads from the middle needs to think of himself or herself as a catalyst for change. This is all the more true in today's highly networked and dynamic environment where how ideas and processes are crafted are good predictors of which ones will be the most likely to gain traction over time (Heath & Heath, 2007; Weick, 1984).

Furthermore, organizational changes are often iterative and incremental, but can still be significant over time (Bellman, 1992; Frohman, 1997; Reay, Golden-Biddle, & Bermann, 2006). Iterative changes can also fail. They need to be designed in a way that will increase adaptation and growth over time (Weick,

1984; Yost et al., 2011). Five design characteristics are particularly important:

- *Strategic*: Does the on-the-job development initiative align with and support the business strategy?
- *Simple*: Are the processes and tools simple and easy to use? Do they make the manager's job easier? Do they make the end-user's job easier? Do they avoid "HR speak"?
- *Sneeze-able*: Are the process and tools "sticky" (i.e., do people *want* to use them?) and are they sneeze-able (i.e., do people want to *pass them on*)?
- *Systemic*: Are the processes and tools designed so they can be easily integrated into other HR processes in the organization? That is, are they crafted in a way that complements and enhances other talent management processes within the organization? Will other business and HR systems be able to easily integrate them?
- *Sustainable*: Are the processes and tools built in a way that is sustainable? That is, do they require continued investment and energy or are they self-sustaining, able to adapt to changing conditions in the organization?

Other characteristics are, of course, also important to consider when crafting and implementing on-the-job development interventions (e.g., cost, execution, resources), but these five characteristics play a particularly important role in building on-the-job development initiatives that will be self-sustaining and are likely to grow and spread.

An Executive On-Boarding Program That Is Strategic, Simple, Sneeze-able, Systemic, and Sustainable

Let's begin with an example. Imagine an HR generalist who is charged with the task of building a process to help new executives who are joining the business unit. From research, we know that transitions are ideal times for leaders to learn how to leverage experiences and build a set of learning capabilities that will increase their capacity to capture the lessons of experience in future challenges. For example, leaders can learn how to take on and navigate through stretch assignments, the importance of seeking feedback, reflection to capture the lessons, and the importance of developmental relationships.

Imagine that one of the tools created is an executive on-boarding checklist. A very specific process can be designed for these leaders, but the impact is likely to be limited to one group of employees in one business unit. However, the processes and tools in the executive on-boarding intervention could alternatively be crafted in a way that is more likely to be picked up and integrated into other HR processes within the organization (e.g., a new employee orientation, new manager training, leadership development programs).

Exhibit 6.1 provides of an example of how this information might be turned into a checklist that the new executives could

---

Exhibit 6.1. Executive On-Boarding Transition Checklist

My Transition Checklist

My Manager
I have met with my manager, and we have done the following:
❑ Discussed my goals for the coming year and how my success will be measured.
❑ Identified the key stakeholders who will be critical to my success.
❑ Discussed the challenges and barriers that I will face and my manager's ideas on how I might address them.
❑ Identified the resources that I will need to be successful.
❑ Noted the small wins I will accomplish in the first thirty to ninety days.
❑ Discussed the ways that I want to develop in the coming year and my long-term career aspirations.

My Direct Reports (if in a supervisory position)
❑ I have set up meetings with my team to discuss:
  ▪ Their thoughts about the team's strengths and areas for improvement.

- Their individual jobs and performance goals for the coming year.
- Their long-term development goals.

❏ I have scheduled regular 1:1 meetings with each of my direct reports.

My Network

❏ I have identified the key stakeholders in this new role (e.g., senior leaders, thought leaders, peers, key people in other departments, customers, suppliers) and have scheduled times to meet with each of them.

❏ I have identified the people I need to meet with regularly in this job and set up ongoing meetings with each of them.

❏ I have met with at least two other executives who have recently joined the company.

Feedback and Reflection

❏ I have identified some natural places during the day and throughout the year to reflect on how I'm doing, what's working and what's not, and where I want to go from there.

❏ I have asked my boss and at least two other people to give me feedback if they see me start to veer off course. I have reminders on my calendar to ask for feedback every two weeks.

use to ensure they are setting themselves up for success in their new jobs. The checklist is designed in a way that is useful for the targeted initiative and the five design characteristics have been incorporated in a way that should increase the adoption and spread of the tool.

Strategic. Both scholars and practitioners have noted that HR processes—and experience-based development initiatives by extension—are significantly more likely to be accepted when they are closely aligned with the business strategy (Becker & Huslid, 2006; Lawler, 2003; Lengnick-Hall, Lengnick-Hall, Andrade, & Drake, 2009; McCall, 2010). Based on this principle, experience-based leadership development is more likely to be picked up when it is discussed in the context of organizational goals and what leaders will need to meet future strategic challenges. Leadership development becomes a fully integrated and fundamental part of achieving the business strategy (McCall, 2010). Leaders are developed when they are put in roles where they can execute the business strategy and develop themselves *at exactly the same time* (Yost & Plunkett, 2009, 2010).

In the case of an executive on-boarding program, the on-boarding process should be seen as good business, not as another HR process. The guidance and support materials should be crafted with this same strategic focus. The checklist should be perceived as a tool that senior executives can use to start driving results as soon as possible. The materials should use business language and be based on the factors that research has found are critical to successful on-boarding. For example, in our field, we know that it is critical for new leader to set goals, to identify and connect with key stakeholders, and to seek feedback from other people. All of these should be part of the checklist. However, the way they are discussed and positioned will often determine whether the guidance is used. For example, the transition checklist should probably not talk about "setting performance goals," but instead should use the language of executives, such as "determine how your success will be measured in this job." Similarly, the checklist should probably avoid using language that states the executive should "identify his or her developmental network" and instead direct the leader to "identify and meet with the key stakeholders who will be critical to your success." The differences are subtle, but important.

Simple. On-the-job development processes and tools should be simple and easy to use. Are they concrete with clear actions that the leader can take? Do they make the leader's job easier? This is not to say they should be simplistic. Any process or tool might include significant complexity behind the scenes, but the user interface that the person sees should be simple and easy to understand—think Apple products.

For example, the executive transition checklist should ideally be no more than a page. Of course, there are countless activities that an executive needs to consider to succeed in a new job, but a longer checklist is unlikely to be read. The on-boarding checklist is only one piece of information in the deluge of other priorities that will compete for the executive's attention. A short checklist will be used.

Sneeze-able. Are the on-the-job development processes and tools "sticky" (Gladwell, 2000; Heath & Heath, 2007); that is, do people want to use them? Are they tools that you would want to use? The on-the-job development processes and tools should be so compelling that leaders would be stupid not to use them. Beyond just sticky, the on-the-job development processes and tools also should be "sneeze-able" (Godin, 2001); that is, the experience-based development systems and tools should be so compelling that people want to pass them on to others. Sneeze-able processes and tools are self-contained, that is, standalone tools that don't require the user to understand a larger context (e.g., a leader doesn't need to reference other information to understand and use them). They should also be designed to promote interactions with others to encourage their proliferation into the larger system. For example, a transition checklist could include a suggestion to connect with other new executives who have recently joined the company.

Continuing with the transition checklist as the example, a sneeze-able checklist will be able to stand on its own and does not require the user to consult any other materials. The temptation will be to make the checklist part of a larger on-boarding process, which will naturally draw the person crafting it to reference the other elements of the process. The checklist should be written in a way that complements other processes, but it should be designed as a standalone tool (see also the discussion about building systemic processes below). As you build the tool, consider using first person—focus on what the user wants. Build a checklist with items that one would be crazy to ignore (e.g., Why wouldn't a leader want to talk to his or her manager to identify a list of the key stakeholders in his or her new job?). A great indicator of the transitions "sneeze-ability" is if leaders do, in fact, pass it on to colleagues and new members who join their teams. When you are done, ask yourself, "Is this a checklist that I would want to use as I begin my next job? Will I really use it?"

To further illustrate, consider the following additional sneeze-able development tool examples. In a former company, I was part of an executive assessment process that required senior leaders to perform card sorts with the leadership competencies and derailment factors for leaders in the company. At the end of the meetings, leaders often asked whether they could "get a set of those cards" for their own use. In another company, colleagues and I created a one-page *"Reader's Digest"* quiz called "Development Plans That Aren't a Waste of Time" with items that were in people's self-interest (e.g., I am developing skills that will be in demand three to five years from now; I get excited when I look at my development plan). When people finished the quiz, they looked up what their score indicated. People who scored toward the lower end of the scale received the rather draconian statement: "You are likely to finish the year less employable than you started it." The quiz went viral because it was personal and simple to pass on to others. In the following weeks, we discovered that several managers were forwarding a link to the quiz to their employees during the performance management cycle, asking employees to use the checklist as they put their development plans together.

Systemic. Even though the on-the-job development processes and tools should stand on their own, they should be designed in a way that will complement and enhance other talent management processes in the organization. Integrated talent management systems do not need to be complex, top-down hierarchical systems; other organizational models are available (e.g., Kates, 2006; McKenna & Wright, 1992; Vosburgh, 2007). The World Wide Web might be a better metaphor—separate entities that complement, combine, and sometimes compete with each other. Or think Legos™ or hamster Habitrail components that can exist as standalone products but can be combined with other components. In a dynamic and connected ecosystem, the challenge is to create a process that complements and is easy to attach to other processes.

Taking the executive on-boarding checklist as an example, as it is being crafted, the secret is to identify the other talent management processes where it might be used and build the checklist so it will be picked up by other processes. For example, could the checklist be written in a way that could be used in the organization's employee orientation process? Could it be used in a manager training program for new supervisors? As you build the checklist, use language that would apply to leaders at multiple leadership levels and in multiple locations in the organization.

Sustainable. To maximize the sustainability of on-the-job development interventions, they should be designed in a way that will require as little ongoing energy and as few resources as possible. New priorities and new work will always threaten to overwhelm ongoing work. Ideally, the intervention should be built so it will be self-sustaining and self-adapting to emerging business realities. The critical question becomes: "Did I build the on-the-job development intervention in a way that will outlast me?" In a series of critical incident interviews, Yost and colleagues (2011) interviewed sixteen senior I-O and HR professionals, asking them to identify HR interventions that had lasted for ten or more years and then describe the organizational, intervention, and change leader characteristics that allowed the intervention to survive. One of the interesting findings was that some of the top-down factors emerged, but the initiative leaders emphasized the role that they played in proactively making them happen. For example, the change leaders talked about the importance of proactively involving key stakeholders and end-users in the process, recruiting sponsors from key business units, and engaging top management when opportunities arise. The top-down factors were important, but they were often led from the middle. The classic example is the HR professional, who in a conversation with a senior leader, plants an idea that eventually becomes the leader's idea.

On-the-job development interventions that will have organization-wide impact need to be built not only to survive, but also built to thrive in environments where the future is unknown and often unknowable. Weick (1984) proposed that the best strategy in an environment where sensemaking is limited may be to focus on building small wins. He proposed that optimal small wins are discrete, self-contained actions with a high probability of success that can serve as stable building blocks for future actions. The small wins allow successes to build on one another, learning what works and what doesn't, and iteratively using this information to adapt to new emerging challenges.

Going back to the executive on-boarding transition example, the transition checklist could serve as one of the discrete building blocks in introducing on-the-job development into an organization. Other building blocks might include creating a peer mentoring process whereby new executives can meet to discuss challenges and lessons learned, or providing guidance on common derailers and how to avoid them. The executives who utilize the transition process also represent potential building blocks as they advocate for and model the importance of on-the-job development strategies in working with others. How the process and tools are crafted will also impact the sustainability. Are the processes and tools built so they can be modified and adapted over time? Have key stakeholder groups been engaged in the rollout (e.g., the HR generalists who support the leaders)? Can you conduct a pilot project in the business unit of a senior leader who is recognized for developing others? How can you use the pilot to increase the visibility of on-the-job development and create a "pull" in other areas of the organization? Remember that the ultimate goal is to build a process that is scalable and will outlast you.

Building On-the-Job Development into Organizational Talent Management Systems

The five design characteristics provide a framework for building on-the-job development initiatives that are more likely to have a broad, deep, and long-term impact within an organization. In the following section, strategies for integrating on-the-job development into three talent management processes are reviewed: succession planning, performance management, and communities of practice. Each section begins with specific ideas on how on-the-job development can be integrated into the process and then explores how the five design characteristics can be used to broaden the impact of the interventions into the larger organization.

Succession Management

Because of its high visibility, succession management is an ideal place for an organization to begin building experience-based development into an organization's DNA. At its best, succession management is about experience-based development—strategically placing aspiring leaders in assignments that will stretch and develop them for more senior roles. The succession planning process is a natural place for the critical leadership experiences to be defined and to then become a platform to spread them to other leaders in the organization. Regrettably, most succession planning processes focus the preponderance of their attention on candidate selection and relatively less attention on development (Karaevli & Hall, 2003). This is unfortunate, since there is a natural pull for other leaders to look to the succession planning process to discover the experiences that are most valued in the organization and use the information to chart their own development. Several corporations—PepsiCo (Church & Waclawski, 2010), Microsoft (Yost, 2010), and HEINEKEN (Plunkett, 2013) among others—have explicitly included developmental experiences in their succession planning processes.

There are a variety of ways that on-the-job development can be built into the succession planning process. Key developmental experiences can be built into the succession candidate profiles, for example, rating candidates on the extent to which they have had key leadership experiences such as leading a start-up, turning a business around, global assignments, and key business unit or functional experience. (See Yost and Plunkett, 2010, for suggestions on how to identify critical experiences in an organization and build them into an organization's succession planning processes.) Beyond identifying the experiences, the succession planning process also serves as a signal for the leadership behaviors that are rewarded in the organization (e.g., Are leaders promoted for performance or for performance and developing the people in their organization?).

Despite the potential, many organizations fail to use the succession management process to spark on-the-job development in the larger organization. The five design principles discussed above provide guidance on ways to leverage on-the-job development initiatives in the succession planning process to plant seeds in the larger organization. For example, as senior executives discuss the future challenges that the organization is facing, they can also discuss the leadership experiences and competencies that will be needed (strategic). A description of the key leadership experiences that are assessed in the succession process could be created and made more broadly available in the organization (simple, sneeze-able).

As the experiences are being created, the developers should define the experiences broadly enough that they also apply at lower leadership levels. For example, what does a start-up experience look like for senior leaders and for first-level managers (e.g., starting up a new division versus building a team from scratch)? The broader definitions will enhance the capacity for and likelihood that the leadership experiences will be integrated into other processes such as employee development plans (systemic). A matrix could be created mapping the key experiences to the competencies and lessons that are most likely to be learned in the experience (see Figure 6.1; simple, sneeze-able). Put the experiences and other tools on the company intranet so everyone can access them and so they can easily be linked into other talent management processes.

Performance Management

Employee development plans are the talent management process that will touch the broadest range of employees and an obvious place where on-the-job-development should be highlighted. Unfortunately, the development planning process "required by HR" can also be one of the most maligned and underutilized talent management processes within organizations. Employee development plans are often a box that appears at the bottom of the goal-setting form, a place to put the training classes that you want the company to pay for, or the paperwork that HR requires everybody to fill out every year. The typical instructions that accompany the forms don't help, often reading like a tax form (see Exhibit 6.2 on pages 128–129).

How can the performance management process be used to encourage on-the-job development? Sometimes all that managers and employees need is a list of on-the-job development ideas. Exhibit 6.3 provides an example of how simple the lists can be. Several sources are available with a variety of on-the-job development examples that can be adapted and tailored to match the language used in different organizations (e.g., Lombardo & Eichinger, 1988; McCauley, 2006; Simons, 2005). Alternatively,

Figure 6.1. Experience by Lessons Matrix

	1. Running the Business	Thinking Strategically	Innovative Problem Solving	Learning How the Business Works	Understanding the Customer	Shouldering Full Responsibility	2. Managing People	Engaging and Directing Others	Building a Team That Works Together	Relying on Others' Talents and Expertise	Developing Others	Understanding Others' Perspectives	Managing Through Multiple Levels	3. Working Across the Business	Collaboration and Cooperation	Dealing with Conflict	Political Savvy	Working with Senior Leaders	Strategies of Negotiation
1. Setting the Stage																			
Early Work Experience	O	◆	◆	O	◆			O	O			◆	◆		◆	◆			
First Supervisory Experience	◆		O					◆	◆	◆	O	◆			◆	◆			
2. Leading on the Line																			
Starting Something from Scratch	◆	O	◆					O	O										
Turning a Business Around	O			◆				◆	◆	◆	O	◆				◆			
External Relations	O	◆		◆				◆	O						◆	◆			◆
Global Experience				◆				O	O			◆	◆		◆			◆	
3. Leading by Persuasion																			
Project/Task Force Assignment	◆	O						O	◆						◆			◆	
Functional/Staff Role	O	O						O			◆						O		O
Intergration Role	◆		O					O					O						
4. Other																			
Good & Bad Role Models	O						O												
~~eer Hardships																			
…uration		O	O																

organizations might define the key challenges or experiences at different proficiency levels so leaders and employees can easily adapt them to their own job situations (see Exhibit 6.4).

Including simple instructions at the beginning of a development plan can often make a significant difference in what people include as development activities. For example, the development plan instructions could refer to the ubiquitous "70–20–10 Rule" for development (70 percent of development occurs on the job, 20 percent from other people, and 10 percent in training) to encourage employees to include more on-the-job activities in

Exhibit 6.2. HR Tools at Their Worst

Employee Development Plans at Company X

Instructions in Brief: Your ongoing development and improvement to your time at Company X. Every year employees are asked to complete an Employee Development and Performance Plan (EDPP). Prior to the actual feedback session, the supervisor schedules a time to discuss with the employee the Employee Development and Performance Plan (EDPP), as itemized below. The amount of time between the Preview Session and the Feedback Session should be reasonable and adequate to allow appropriate preparation of the EDPP.

1. Carefully review the EDPP Instructions as well as any specific agency policies or procedures.
2. Ensure a mutual understanding of the process and timing that will be followed.
3. Review the position description (classification questionnaire) to ensure accuracy of stated duties and responsibilities. . . ."

Exhibit 6.3. List of Developmental Activities

Turning a Business Around
- Volunteer to take on and work with one of the department's most dissatisfied customers.
- Lead a cost-cutting initiative.
- Champion a change your group has been resisting.
- Lead a quality improvement project for a product or process.
- Take over a project that hasn't succeeded in the past.
- Take over a failing business unit.

Starting a Project from Scratch
- Volunteer to lead a project that requires building a new process.
- Find work that is currently "falling through the cracks" in your organization and volunteer to solve it.
- Take on a project that requires you to build the team and make it successful.

- Visit a customer's site.
- Find ways to work with customers and clients in new markets.
- Work on a strategic plan for a non-profit organization.
- Lead a business that is entering a new market.

Leading Without Authority
- Organize a networking group to study a "hot" topic in your organization.
- Take on projects that will require you to influence other departments without any formal authority.
- Ask your boss to delegate the leadership of one of the team's tasks to you.
- Lead a cross-company initiative that requires you to work across multiple departments and/or business units.
- Lead a virtual team.
- Take on a staffing or corporate role that requires building processes and systems across multiple organizations.

Learning from Other People
- Find a mentor and meet with him or her monthly.
- Volunteer to serve on a team that is functionally or globally diverse.
- Become a mentor for someone else.
- Identify three people who can provide feedback in an area you are trying to develop.
- Create an informal working group to discuss new trends and challenges facing people in your business.

their development plans. (Interestingly, research suggests that these percentages do not necessarily hold for women and minorities, who report that other people play a greater role in their development [Douglas, 2003; Van Velsor & Hughes-James, 1990]).

Combining the instructions with specific examples can also serve as a powerful catalyst to promote a stronger focus on experience-based development (e.g., "As you plan for your development in the coming year, remember that the best development comes from on-the-job assignments that stretch you in the areas you have targeted for development. For example, volunteer to

Exhibit 6.4. Managing External Relations

Definition: Representing the organization with external organizations such as working with customers, representing the company in a professional group, serving on a standards board, working with the media, or serving as a government liaison.

Limited Experience: Representing the organization with external customers or organizations through attendance or presentations. Attending meetings with external groups, but the position doesn't include a leadership role or serving as an official representative of the company. The experience doesn't include the development and nurturing of ongoing relationships. The experience is short-term (e.g., lasts less than one year).

Moderate Experience: Ongoing interaction with one or more external groups as a representative of the organization with the goal of building ongoing relationships. The relationship is important to the organization's success and includes specific outcomes to be achieved. The experience lasts more than a year.

Deep Experience: Serving as primary point of contact responsible for building ongoing relationships with key external groups (e.g., customers, government agencies). The position directly impacts organizational strategy and investment decisions. The position lasts for three or more years.

lead a project team, manage the budget for your team, or launch a new product."). Encourage managers to hold two separate conversations with their employees—one focused on performance goals for the year and a second focusing on development goals. Ideally, these should occur at different points in the year; but at a minimum, encourage managers to schedule two separate meetings (perhaps even noting that devoting one hour a year to an employee's development is a pretty small investment considering the potential payoff for the employee and the organization).

All of these ideas are good, but are unlikely to lead to an organization-wide impact if they fail to incorporate the design principles discussed earlier. For example, the list of on-the-job development ideas should be a self-contained tool and readily accessible to all employees (e.g., on a web page or as an Adobe .pdf file that is posted online) so that it is easy for people to access and pass on to others (simple, sneeze-able). Once created, the tools can be pushed so they appear "just in time" when leaders and employees need them, such as live links in the development plan instructions (systemic). Managers should have easy access to the ideas as they are preparing for development planning discussions with their employees (systemic). URL links to the tools should be provided in the development planning tools on the pages where they are needed. The developmental assignments should be in business language, not HR language (simple) and with actions that combine doing the job and developing oneself at the same time (strategic).

People, Networks, and Learning Communities

People in a leader's network play a critical role in his or her development. They serve as role models, mentors, peer coaches, and feedback sources and provide social support. Leadership by its very nature requires getting things done through other people, managing diversity, and influencing others. Much of the development via other people happens informally. For example, in a study asking people to identify key career conversations, Kidd, Hirsh, and Jackson (2004) found that only 7 percent took place in the performance management or development planning process and only 21 percent were with a boss. Mentoring research suggests a similar finding: informal mentoring relationships are often more effective than formal ones (Chao, Walz, & Gardner, 1992; Ragins & Cotton, 1999). The challenge then becomes how to launch formal systems that incorporate the characteristics of informal mentoring relationships (Allen, Finkelstein, & Poteet, 2009; Ragins & Kram, 2007).

Strategies might include creating a pool of mentors so mentees can choose who they want, building peer coaching into training programs, linking new employees with experienced peers who can serve as mentors, sponsoring affinity groups that address gaps in employee development (e.g., women in leadership), or creating organizationally sponsored communities of practice composed of people who share common interests that meet regularly to share ideas and best practices. All of these are good ideas, but the challenge is building the relationship interventions so they are sustainable and build energy over time.

Communities of practice serve as a prime example. Defined as "groups of people informally bound together by shared expertise and passion for joint enterprise" (Wenger & Snyder, 2000, p. 139), they can exist inside one organization or span multiple organizations. Their primary purpose is to stimulate personal development and help organizations harness informal networks (McDermott & Archibald, 2010). However, like any other intervention, communities of practice are not guaranteed to accomplish their anticipated goals (Kirkman, Mathieu, Cordery, Rosen, & Kukenberger, 2011; Roberts, 2006). Several conditions are necessary to build sustainable communities of practice (Kirkman, Mathieu, Cordery, Rosen, & Kukenberger, 2011; McDermott & Archibald, 2010; Wenger, McDermott, & Snyder, 2002). A substantial number of them fall within the five design characteristics discussed thus far. For example, communities are more likely to survive when senior leaders serve as sponsors of the practice communities (strategy).

Pilot groups can be sponsored and used as models for other groups just getting started (simple, sneeze-able, systemic). Communities of practice can be encouraged to build structures that are self-sustaining, with shared leadership, ongoing activities to engage active participants (sustainable), and easy on-boarding opportunities for outsiders to join the communities (sneeze-able). Taken together, this paints a picture of system-wide people development. The process might start with one initiative or one community, but it has the potential to gain momentum and grow because of how it is designed.

Conclusion

The field has come a long way since *Lessons of Experience* (McCall, Lombardo, & Morrison, 1988) was published twenty-five years ago. I-O and HR professionals are much more cognizant of the critical role that experience plays in the development of leaders. In some corners, 70–20–10 development has become a buzzword. Some talent management processes, such as succession management, are based on the idea of experience-based development, even though in many companies it continues to be more role-based than experience-based.

The next frontier for the field is to make experience-based development as much of an integrating element in talent management systems as competency models are today. The key message is that, in today's organizations, on-the-job development initiatives will only meet this challenge if I-O and HR professionals are able to find ways to take advantage of the dynamic, highly networked organizations that will be typical of the 21st century to craft on-the-job development interventions that gain energy over time.

References

Allen, T. D., Finkelstein, L. M., & Poteet, M. L. (2009). *Designing workplace mentoring programs: An evidence-based approach.* London, UK: Wiley-Blackwell.

Ansari, S. M., Fiss, P. C., & Zajac, E. J. (2010). Made to fit: How practices vary as they diffuse. *The Academy of Management Review, 35,* 67–92.

Becker, B. E., & Huslid, M. A. (2006). Strategic human resource management: Where do we go from here? *Journal of Management, 32,* 898–925.

Bellman, G. M. (1992). *Getting things done when you are not in charge.* San Francisco, CA: Berrett-Koehler.

Chao, G. T., Walz, P. M., & Gardner, P. D. (1992). Formal and informal mentorships: A comparison on mentoring functions and contrast with nonmentored counterparts. *Personnel Psychology, 45,* 619–636.

Church, A. H., & Waclawski, J. (2010). Take the Pepsi challenge: Talent development at PepsiCo. In R. Silzer & B. Dowell (Eds.), *Strategy driven talent management: A leadership imperative* (pp. 617–640). San Francisco, CA: Jossey-Bass.

Ciampa, D., & Watkins, M. (1999). The successor's dilemma. *Harvard Business Review, 77*(6), 160–168.

Cummings, T. G., & Worley, C. G. (2008). *Essentials of organization development and change.* Cincinnati, OH: South-Western College Publishing.

Douglas, C. A. (2003). *Key events and lessons for managers in a diverse workforce: A report on research and findings.* Greensboro, NC: Center for Creative Leadership.

Frohman, A. L. (1997). Igniting organizational change from below: The power of personal initiative. *Organizational Dynamics, 25,* 39–53.

Gladwell, M. (2000). *The tipping point: How little things can make a big difference.* Boston, MA: Little, Brown.

Godin, S. (2001). *Unleashing the idea virus.* New York, NY: Hyperion.

Gottfredson, M., Schaubert, S., & Saenz, H. (2008). The new leader's guide to diagnosing the business. *Harvard Business Review, 86*(2), 62–73.

Heath, C., & Heath, D. (2007). *Made to stick: Why some ideas survive and others die.* New York, NY: Random House.

Hogg, M. A. (2010). Influence and leadership. In S. T. Fiske., D. T. Gilbert, & G. Lindzey (Eds.), *Handbook of social psychology, Vol. 2* (5th ed.; pp. 1166–1207). Hoboken, NJ: John Wiley & Sons.

Johansen, B. (2009). *Leaders make the future: Ten new leadership skills for an uncertain world.* San Francisco, CA: Berrett-Koehler.

Karaevli, A., & Hall, D. T. (2003). Growing leaders for turbulent times: Is succession planning up to the challenge? *Organizational Dynamics, 32,* 62–79.

Kates, A. (2006). (Re)designing the HR organization. *Human Resource Planning, 29*(2), 23–30.

Kidd, J. M., Hirsh, W., & Jackson, C. (2004). Straight talking: The nature of effective career discussions at work. *Journal of Career Development, 30,* 231–45.

Kirkman, B. L., Mathieu, J. E., Cordery, J. L., Rosen, B., & Kukenberger, M. (2011). Managing a new collaborative entity in business organizations: Understanding organizational communities of practice effectiveness. *Journal of Applied Psychology, 96,* 1234–1245.

Kossek, E. E. (1987). Human resources management innovation. *Human Resource Management, 26*(1), 71–92.

Kossek, E. E. (1989). The acceptance of human resource innovation by multiple constituencies. *Personnel Psychology, 42,* 263–281.

Kotter, J. P. (1995, March/April). Leading change: Why transformation efforts fail. *Harvard Business Review, 73*(2), 59–67.

Lawler, E. E., III. (2003). From human resource management to organizational effectiveness. *Human Resource Management, 44,* 165–169.

Lengnick-Hall, M. L., Lengnick-Hall, C. A., Andrade, L. S., & Drake, B. (2009). Strategic human resource management: The evolution of the field. *Human Resource Management Review, 19,* 64–85.

Lombardo, M. M., & Eichinger, R. W. (1988). *Eighty-eight assignments for development in place.* Greensboro, NC: Center for Creative Leadership.

McCall, M. W., Jr. (2010). Recasting leadership development. *Industrial and Organizational Psychology: Perspectives on Science and Practice, 3,* 3–19.

McCall, M. W., Jr., Lombardo, M. M., & Morrison, A. M. (1988). *The lessons of experience: How successful executives develop on the job.* New York, NY: The Free Press.

McCauley, C. D. (2006). *Developmental assignments: Creating learning experiences without changing jobs.* Greensboro, NC: Center for Creative Leadership.

McDermott, R., & Archibald, D. (2010). Harnessing your staff's informal networks. *Harvard Business Review, 88*(3), 82–89.

McKenna, D. D., & Wright, P. M. (1992). Alternative metaphors for organization design. In M. D. Dunnette & L. M. Hough (Eds.), *Handbook of industrial and organizational psychology* (2nd ed., Vol. 3, pp. 901–960). Palo Alto, CA: Consulting Psychologists Press.

Plunkett, M. M. (2013). Succession planning: Developing general managers through experience. In C. D. McCauley, D. S. DeRue, P. R. Yost, & S. Taylor, *Experience-driven leader development: Models, tools, best practices, and advice for on-the-job development* (pp. 445–450). Hoboken, NJ: John Wiley & Sons.

Ragins, B. R., & Cotton, J. L. (1999). Mentor functions and outcomes: A comparison of men and women in formal and informal mentoring relationships. *Journal of Applied Psychology, 84,* 529–550.

Ragins, B. R., & Kram, K. E. (2007). *The handbook of mentoring at work: Theory, research, and practice.* Thousand Oaks, CA: Sage.

Reay, T., Golden-Biddle, K., & Bermann, K. (2006). Legitimizing a new role: Small wins and microprocesses of change. *Academy of Management Journal, 49,* 977–998.

Roberts, J. (2006). Limits to communities of practice. *Journal of Management Studies, 43,* 623–639.

Sharp, G. (2010). *From dictatorship to democracy: A conceptual framework for liberation* (4th ed.). Boston, MA: Albert Einstein Institute.

Simons, R. (2005). Designing high-performance jobs. *Harvard Business Review, 83*(7/8), 54–62.

Som, A. (2007). What drives adoption of innovative SHRM practices in Indian organizations? *The International Journal of Human Resource Management, 18,* 808–828.

Ulrich, D., & Brockbank, W. (2005). *The HR value proposition.* Boston, MA: Harvard Business School Press.

Van Velsor, E., & Hughes-James, M. W. (1990). *Gender differences in the development of managers: How women managers learn from experience.* Greensboro, NC: Center for Creative Leadership.

Vosburgh, R. M. (2007). The evolution of HR: Developing HR as an internal consulting organization. *Human Resource Planning, 30*(3), 11–23.

Watkins, M. (2003). *The first 90 days: Critical success strategies for new leaders at all levels.* Boston, MA: Harvard Business School Press.

Weick, K. E. (1984). Small wins: Redefining the scale of social problems. *American Psychologist, 39,* 40–49.

Wenger, E. C., McDermott, R., & Snyder, W. M. (2002). *Cultivating communities of practice: A guide to managing knowledge.* Boston, MA: Harvard Business School Press.

Wenger, E. C., & Snyder, W. M. (2000). Communities of practice: The organizational frontier. *Harvard Business Review, 78*(1), 139–145.

Westerveld, E. (2003). The Project Excellence Model: Linking success criteria and critical success factors. *International Journal of Project Management, 21,* 411–418.

White, D., & Fortune, J. (2002). Current practice in project management— an empirical study. *International Journal of Project Management, 20,* 1–11.

Wolfe, R. A. (1995). Human resource management innovations: Determinants of their adoption and implementation. *Human Resource Management, 34,* 313–327.

Wood, W., Lundgren, S., Ouellette, J. A., Busceme, S., & Blackstone, T. (1994). Minority influence: A meta-analytic review of social influence processes. *Psychological Bulletin, 115,* 323–345.

Yost, P. R. (2010). Integrated talent management at Microsoft. In R. Silzer & B. Dowell (Eds.), *Strategy driven talent management: A leadership imperative* (pp. 641–654). San Francisco, CA: Jossey-Bass.

Yost, P. R., McLellan, J., Ecker, D., Chang, G. C., Hereford, J., Roenicke, C., Town, J., & Winberg, Y. (2011). HR interventions that go viral. *Journal of Business and Psychology, 26,* 233–239.

Yost, P. R., & Plunkett, M. M. (2009). *Real time leadership development.* London: Wiley-Blackwell.

Designing Job Experiences for Leader Development

CHAPTER SEVEN

A Project-Based Approach to Developing High-Potential Talent in the Tata Group

Aditya Ahuja, Radhakrishnan Nair,
and Asma Bagash

TAS (formerly known as Tata Administrative Service) is the flagship leadership program for entry-level talent for the Tata Group, which includes more than one hundred operating companies. TAS is a unique group-level talent identification and development program that develops a cohort through project-based exposure, experiences, and learning. The TAS recruits are considered a group resource, and for the first five years of their careers with the group they are under the aegis of the group office. The first five years are segmented into three parts: one year of induction and projects followed by up to two two-year job assignments.

To understand the TAS program, it is necessary to understand the ethos and expanse of the Tata Group, the genesis and ethos of TAS, and the process of recruiting young talent into TAS. The partnership with group companies is essential to making the program a success and to continually improving the program to match current and future requirements of leadership.

Note: The authors thank the past and the current TAS managers for their contribution toward the chapter. The authors also appreciate the support and guidance provided by Meena S. Wilson during the writing of the chapter.

Tata Group Ethos and Expanse

Humata, Hukhta, Hvarshta (*Good Thoughts, Good Words, Good Deeds*), the basic tenets of faith, are the seeds on which the Tata ethos was grown. These words not only grace the emblem of the Tata Group but have been imbibed into its values, culture, and work methodology. From this core philosophy springs the uniqueness of the group, where faith, goodness in business dealings, and social responsibility are equally as important as profitability and the growth of business.

The Tata Group, India's leading industrial house, was founded by Jamsetji Nusserwanji Tata in 1868. Tata's early years were inspired by the spirit of nationalism, industrial growth, and economic self-sufficiency. The Tata name has been respected in India for 140 years for its adherence to strong values and business ethics. "Trust" is attached to the name of Tata and evoked in the minds of Indians whenever the name is mentioned. This reputation, with which the group is honored in India, is now being recognized globally.

The more than one hundred Tata Group companies operate in seven business sectors: communications and information technology, engineering, materials, services, energy, consumer products, and chemicals. The group runs operations in more than eighty countries across six continents, and its companies export products and services to eighty-five countries.

The total revenue of Tata companies, taken together, was $100.09 billion in 2011–2012, with 58 percent of this coming from business outside India. Tata companies employ more than 456,000 people worldwide. Every Tata company or enterprise operates independently. Each of these companies has its own board of directors and shareholders to whom it is answerable. There are thirty-one publicly listed Tata enterprises, and they had a combined market capitalization of about $88.02 billion (as of August 2013), and a shareholder base of 3.9 million. The major Tata companies are Tata Steel, Tata Motors, Tata Consultancy Services, Tata Power, Tata Chemicals, Tata Global Beverages, Tata Teleservices, Titan, Tata Communications, and Indian Hotels.

The group has pioneered several industries of national importance in India, including steel, power, hospitality, and airlines. In more recent times, its pioneering spirit has been showcased by companies such as TCS, founded in 1968, which pioneered the IT services industry in India, and Tata Motors, which made India's first indigenously developed car, the Indica, in 1998 and recently unveiled the world's lowest-cost car, the Tata Nano.

In tandem with the increasing international footprint of Tata companies, the Tata brand is also gaining international recognition. Brand Finance, a UK-based consultancy firm, valued the Tata brand at $15.75 billion in 2011 and ranked it forty-first among the world's one hundred most valuable brands (Haigh, McDonald, & Yoxon (2012). *Business Week* magazine ranked Tata seventeenth on its "50 Most Innovative Companies" list (Arndt & Einhorn, 2010).

A healthy pipeline of leaders is essential for running such a large and highly diversified conglomerate. The principle of "Unity in Diversity and Diversity in Unity" is a fundamental tenet when developing leaders for the group. While there is unity in the cultural values and beliefs and convergent behavior among Tata leaders, the needs of each business across the conglomerate vary greatly. Tata leaders, however, must be capable of running any of the businesses. Hence, it is imperative that leaders grow from within the group. TAS becomes the primary vehicle for this endeavor.

TAS: A Vehicle for Leadership Development

TAS was conceived by JRD Tata, the late chairman of the Tata Group. He realized the importance of creating leaders by recruiting young talent and then developing them for leadership roles. He aimed to create a talent pipeline of leaders who would steer the group companies and make them stronger—fortifying the Tata Group as well as contributing to nation building. JRD Tata foresaw that this pool of talent would become a group resource—one that could be tapped by companies across the Tata organization.

With these intentions, the first cohort was recruited in 1956. Entry-level and junior-level managers, depending on their performance and capability, are generally on a fast track of career growth and leadership development. TAS provides them with career experiences across functions, industries, and geographies. The program enables managers by giving them the right exposure, in terms of quality of tenure within various Tata companies, opportunities for professional growth, and lifelong career mobility. Their perspectives and prospects are broadened by interacting with top leadership, and this second kind of exposure molds their minds toward the distinctive Tata approach to leadership and fosters loyalty to the Tata values and culture.

The first year of the TAS program is comprised of a comprehensive induction to the group, followed by several short-term project assignments in different group companies. This is followed by a full-time assignment in a carefully chosen role at the start of the second year. TAS managers are expected to stay in this role for two or three years, following which moving to alternate roles is examined, keeping in mind the career plan and organizational requirements.

In the initial years, the career development of this cohort aims to sharpen their ability to lead, through special assignments and interventions. The entire process is co-owned by the Tata companies, ensuring that selection and development activities are carefully implemented.

TAS creates perhaps the only cadre of its sort in Indian business. The TAS manager has, as his or her career canvas, India's largest business house. The program consciously imparts that macro view of business critical in preparing young professionals for general management. Over the years, the TAS program has morphed to suit the business environment. However, the essence has remained the same—*to identify and hone talent for leadership roles in the group by providing varied exposure and experiences.*

Recruitment and Selection: In Search of Top Talent

In its many years of existence, the TAS program has recruited from diverse candidate pools across different disciplines. In recent years, recruitment has been focused more from within the Tata group, where young and talented employees of group companies are carefully selected, as well as through a campus recruitment program at premier business schools in India.

Overview of Recruitment and Selection

The recruitment and selection process is extremely competitive and rigorous with the three major aspects of the process being: selection criteria; selection panel; and stage-gated selection. The thoroughness of all three aspects ensures that the various facets of the applicant's personality and potential are assessed comprehensively before candidates are finally selected to join the TAS program.

The Selection Criteria. A set of competencies, based on Tata's leadership practices, are uniformly used to observe the behaviors of all applicants. Individuals who show a bright spark and are seen as able to make a maximum difference are carefully identified in the selection pool.

The Selection Panel. Business leaders and senior executives from across the group are panelists in the selection process. Panelists are identified with the help of human resources (HR) heads of the Tata Group companies based on their track record in selecting and developing people. Their participation in selection underscores the importance of senior leaders identifying future leaders.

Stage-Gated Selection. Even though the program has been running for six decades, the number of graduates of TAS is small, as the combination of potential with capability and alignment to the Tata values and ethos is rare. The multi-stage recruitment and selection process as it happens on campuses is described below.

Successful recruitment is grounded in vigilant brand building and constant focus on connections and relationships. The effort to promote awareness of the program is continual and includes regular road shows and presentations with the candidate pools during the year. This outreach highlights importance and the career options available to TAS managers. The objective of these efforts is to position the program appropriately and secure the best quality of applicants.

Once the recruitment process is set into motion, applicants are short listed for the selection process based on their academic and extracurricular achievements. These candidates are then subjected to various assessment tools, such as scenario-based group discussions, case studies, personal interviews, and psychometrics, before the final selection decision is made.

The overall success of the recruitment and selection drive depends on several factors: Tata's brand as a preferred employer; the involvement of the Tata Group's top leaders as interviewers and panelists; and most of all, the partnership with group companies, which are completely involved with branding activities and the selection process.

TAS Leadership Program

From its inception, *exposure* and *experience* have been the mainstays of TAS leadership development. The exposure is to the various facets of the group's businesses and to its senior leaders in order that probationers learn about the breadth of the Tata enterprise and company culture and values. The experience is of different challenges and roles, which is considered the core of development.

The top-most leaders of the Tata Group are often closely involved through this first year, during the induction and the projects. This is now an institutionalized practice. The quality of talent the cohorts bring, and the importance of retaining and developing this talent, make their involvement imperative. Furthermore, this is an opportunity for the leaders to gauge the talent and showcase their commitment to the development of the group's leadership pipeline. The exposure through induction and projects presents an opportunity to the probationers to interact with group chairmen and business leaders. They learn the science and art of business organizations—both business strategies and business behaviors. Through its history, the Tata Group top leaders have exemplified professional and ethical business behavior, and this is what the young professionals are able to observe, learn, and imbibe.

Induction

The induction program includes a mix of classroom sessions and site visits to various group companies. During the company interactions, managing directors and top-level executives intro-duce inductees to businesses, financials, and business development strategies in various industry sectors. Sensitization to the Tata work culture and workforce is an important aspect. Since this is a first job for a majority of the probationers, sessions on work ethics in an organization and on how work life is different from educational life are also provided.

Probationers travel to the factories and plants of various com-panies and meet with executives and operations teams. They directly see and understand the workings of a plant and how prod-ucts are manufactured. The probationers are shown not only the large companies but also the medium-size companies of the group. These extensive visits enable the probationers to gain a first-hand experience of the size and scale of the Tata Group operations.

Probationers also visit corporate office facilities, where senior executives present overviews of the business, strategies, future plans, and challenges. Their questions are answered to enable a better understanding of the company.

The induction program is entirely designed and implemented by the TAS office. Well in advance, the TAS office liaisons with company HR and business heads for the planning and rollout.

These classroom and on-site visits have the complete involve-ment of the group companies, since it gives them the opportunity to showcase themselves to the TAS probationers. To attract talent, all the companies involved in the induction program put their best foot forward.

For the probationers, the exposure to the reality of the group's expanse, capability, and potential for growth impacts their think-ing, making them proud to be associated with this prestigious business house. They begin to realize that all the information and insights they obtain will help them immensely as they embark on their projects and careers. There are serendipitous benefits, too. Probationers get to know and bond with others in their cohort, bonds that often last across long years of divergent career paths.

Projects

Project-based development has been a cornerstone, and "learning through exposure" is its mantra. Since its inception in 1956, the first year has been entirely project-based. The wisdom behind the project-based training is to give the probationers exposure to fields about which they know very little, and where they have to perform and deliver. The assumption is that, when the TAS probationers are assigned to projects in areas to which they have not been exposed previously, they will step up, learn, and deliver their best.

The TAS office works with the group companies to select projects that are time-bound, complex, and challenging. Further, they must address unique problems, include an analysis of business plans, and involve creating processes for large initiatives. Projects are selected if they open up unfamiliar ground, widen their perspective, and create opportunities for functional and people learning.

The profile of the probationer and his or her career aspirations are factored in to match projects with probationers and provide them with well-rounded exposure. For example, the projects must rotate the probationer through at least two functions and three companies in two different industry sectors. The probationer's initial projects may not always be within his or her area of specialization. There is also a mix of assignments to line and staff roles and to projects that address both strategic and operational issues.

A project guide helps the probationer and assesses the quality of his or her deliverables. From providing a brief of the project, to being there for support, giving advice as needed, and showing various possibilities to the probationer, the project guide plays a key role. Assessment and a performance discussion between the project guide and the probationer take place toward the end of each project.

Given that the assigned projects would normally be undertaken by an employee with at least four to five years of experience, probationers are naturally stretched beyond their current capabilities. They undergo a feeling of discomfort that is created by a combination of excitement and fear. When the pressures of performance are overlaid on this discomfort, probationers learn. Their talents and best abilities come to the fore. Thus begins the inductees' career with the Tata Group.

. The learning from this broad exposure within their first year has a profound impact. They become aware of the various facets of business and management and leadership behaviors through their interactions with executives and employees at various levels. This enables their holistic development as leaders.

The First Year Project Cycle: An Illustration

The following example of the fictitious probationer Gopal Jaiswal illustrates how leadership capabilities can develop during the first year's project cycle.

Project One. After his group induction, Gopal was assigned to his first project at a high-end technology and industrial design company where the employees are primarily engineers and innovation is a major component of the work. In a market facing a slowdown, the project assigned to Gopal was focused on people issues: increase the level of employee engagement and retention.

To deal with this ambiguous situation and come up with unique methods to solve the problem, Gopal had to meet with employees and understand why they felt disengaged and bored. He created an "ideation platform" for employees to experiment with various ideas and showcase those ideas to the management. He proposed and formed a team that would work toward making the ideas of the employees into practices in the organization. He then created processes to make the initiative sustainable. His idea was institutionalized and is regarded as an HR excellence process.

Gopal was sensitized to people and learned various facets of human relations in his work environment. He needed out-of-the-box thinking to create a sustainable endeavor. Senior management was well aware of the reasons for employee disengagement; so Gopal's cross-functional team knew that they had to brainstorm options and create processes to improve the work environment. The team used various tools to plan a companywide interactive process.

Project Two. Gopal's second project was in the area of operations at a consumer goods manufacturing plant. The plant, which was based in rural India, was running at a loss, and Gopal's assignment was to study the problem and suggest how to turn around the situation and make it profitable. There was a gamut of issues to deal with: financials, people interactions, and the supply chain process. Gopal had to deal with vendors, labor issues, and management perspectives. He came up with an innovative idea: create a client-relations hub. This would be the place that export clients could come to for seeing samples and checking quality without going to the rural location of the factory.

Gopal was dealing with ambiguous situations at the factory on a daily basis. He had to understand the constraints in the supply chain that led to delays and how to overcome them by streamlining processes ranging from vendor management to storage. One of his major lessons had to do with bringing people on board to his viewpoint. He became results-oriented and understood that complex issues require that various facets be considered.

Project Three. Gopal's third assignment was a corporate social responsibility (CSR) project in a rural area. His project dealt with the livelihood enhancement of a rural community through various interventions. He had to live in the village for three months, contribute to development activities, streamline development processes, conduct analysis of anecdotal and statistical data, and come up with innovative ideas to make a difference. Gopal's project required that he liaise with various stakeholders—the village headman, the community, the NGOs, and the government administration and authorities. Essentially, he had to learn to manage a socially oriented rural start-up—conceptualizing and implementing a small-scale business using social and rural business models.

The CSR assignments have met with enthusiasm from probationers and participating non-governmental organizations (NGOs). The TAS office works with the Tata Trusts (to be described momentarily), to source projects from the NGOs it is associated with, especially the ones that are implementing projects in rural India. These projects could be new initiatives or ongoing endeavors. The projects are varied, ranging from health care to setting up or improving rural industries to rural economic advancement.

The ownership structure of the Tata Group is internationally unique, with the Tata Trusts holding nearly 66 percent of the equity of Tata Sons, the Tata promoter holding company. The Tata Trusts are philanthropic trusts, and the wealth that accrues from this asset supports an assortment of causes, institutions, and individuals in a wide variety of areas like education, health care, rural and urban livelihoods, and natural resource management, to name a few.

Working with the underprivileged, understanding their situations, and liaising with the NGOs and government officials for implementing the project creates an experience that is unique and wholesome. As voiced by one trainee, project activities are "a leveler of sorts"—whatever the probationers' socioeconomic background, this experience is humbling and yet very fulfilling. Probationers become aware first-hand of the daily life issues faced by nearly 70 percent of India's population; they are emotionally sensitized to the problems of the deprived.

Rural-based projects aim at exposing the TAS probationers to the corporate social responsibility activities of the group and helping them realize the ethos of the group—serving the community. By participating in projects that are funded by one of the Tata Group's many foundations and trusts, the probationer connects with the societal purpose of Tata's business ventures. The rural project aims to open the probationer's eyes, making him or her mindful of others and imparting wholesomeness of character.

Review Mechanisms

The mandate of the project guides is to assess the probationer on his or her performance vis-à-vis project deliverables as well as displayed behaviors. Assessments are noted on a performance appraisal form. The appraisals are used as inputs for two major reviews during the first year, which are conducted at the group level and have elements that are similar to the initial campus stage-gated selection process.

Reviews are organized during the first year, during which senior HR executives and business leaders listen to presentations made by the probationers concerning their deliverables, challenges, and methods used to achieve goals. During the presentations, probationers are asked to share their functional, strategic, and people learning.

This review mechanism creates an opportunity to help probationers to course correct by providing appropriate feedback. The feedback is aimed at discerning whether learning opportunities have been fully utilized, with lessons appropriately captured and understood. The reviews aid the individuals to recapitulate what they have undergone, identify gaps in their learning, and sort out how these gaps can be bridged. This can be through classroom-based skill building or via their next assignment, with the TAS office monitoring to ensure that the required learning happens.

Reviews generate important metrics. The probationers and the TAS office gain insights about the quality of learning absorbed. Assessment data is a mechanism of course correction not only for the individual but also for the TAS office.

Embarking on a Career with the Tata Group

Equipped with skills learned during their first year as probationers, and with the potential to achieve much more, the fledgling TAS managers are given their next challenge: a full-time assignment in a group company. The assignment is given based on available opportunities, their preferences, and aspirations.

Being a part of the TAS program puts pressure on the TAS managers to perform and deliver more than the expected. With this awareness, the TAS managers take on their first major career roles in life.

The First Assignment: Understanding the Work Environment and Self

The TAS manager's first assignment continues to be an accelerated learning and development experience. His or her role is substantial and impacts company performance. Typically, he or she works directly under the guidance of the business leader. The objective is to aid TAS managers in understanding their roles and themselves, in the context of a work environment; and to continue to develop their understanding of business, people relationships, and how work gets done. Two examples (with fictional names) follow.

Bhasker was assigned a sales role in an automobile company on his first job as a TAS manager. He was responsible for mapping the company-wide sales and dealership processes. The end in mind was for him to re-engineer processes to achieve uniformity and efficiency across customer touch points and a leap forward in customer experience.

Bhasker led an eight-member task force to roll out the re-engineered processes to thirty-six dealerships. The improvements were documented in the "Sales Manual," which all dealerships must follow now. Thus, in his very first role, Bhasker experienced a new job challenge, managed a team, and delivered a significant outcome. This opportunity made it possible for him to be an "all-rounder" in the areas of business, people, and results.

Sneha was assigned to a business development role with a realty development company. She was tasked with identifying new real estate business opportunities and scoping out each opportunity for feasibility, revenue potential, scalability, and strategic fit. She was also responsible for creating a business case to present the multiple sources of competitive advantage that acting on the opportunity would bring and an implementation plan.

Sneha worked with a three-member team and focused on understanding the business, its vision, and its plans for strategic growth. She met with people from contractors to executives from leading financial institutions. As typical of such projects, Sneha managed the successful and profitable execution of a job that would normally be assigned to an employee with five to seven years of experience. The leadership learning designed into this role was for her to deal with ambiguity and learn to think strategically.

To help the TAS managers further develop their personal skills, continuous education and learning programs (CELP) are conducted by the TAS office. The focus of CELP programs is on introspection and understanding oneself.

The Second Assignment: Managing Self and Others

After spending a few years in the first assignment, TAS managers may move into subsequent higher-order roles, where they learn to be leaders of small teams and realize that the final onus of delivery is on them. The lessons to be learned are on taking ownership of the work, and yet walking with the team.

In his second stint, Gautam was given the role of a product manager in an automotive company. He had to interact with the operations and field teams to develop a product that would fill a niche in the market. His job responsibilities encompassed branding activities for the product, such as launch events, product displays on brochures and websites, and so forth. Of course, exhaustive research was necessary to determine in advance how the product launch had to be handled in different markets. Then there was the challenge of delivering sales revenues by meeting with corporate clients, doing product presentations, and training field teams to do the same.

This example illustrates that TAS managers typically take on huge responsibilities at an early career stage, and that their performance and behaviors continue to be scrutinized through their fifth year with the Tata Group.

On the Threshold of Leadership

Going further, individual TAS managers make planned career moves from time to time aligned to their preferences and aspirations. Individuals may wish to continue in the same organization or switch to another one. But without doubt, as TAS managers stand on the threshold of their leadership journeys, they are well-equipped to handle whatever challenges come their way. The initial years help them to find the career paths on which they want to forge ahead on the landscape of the Tata Group and define the contributions they can make. The speed of his or her career growth is the responsibility of the TAS manager. Albeit in the background, the TAS office and the leadership of the group are there to support these managers in their endeavors. The TAS program gives wings to people who aspire to fly high in their careers and think they can.

Conclusion

The history, design, depth, and range of the TAS program make it an institution. Further, the trust, interest, and effort of the leaders in this institution have fostered its growth for more than five decades. The main achievement of the program is that it has delivered high-quality leadership. Its graduates work with an ethos more than a century old and envision the future, too. The challenge for TAS is to be holistic in enabling leaders to think, act, and deliver beyond the boundaries of individual business domains, geographies, and cultures.

Currently, the group HR team at Tata Sons is involved in a rigorous process of reconstructing key elements of the TAS program. Prime among these is a more comprehensive employee lifecycle approach to developing, mentoring, and managing the career of every TAS manager.

References

Arndt, M., & Einhorn, B. (2010, April 15). The 50 most innovative companies. *Bloomberg BusinessWeek*. Retrieved from www.businessweek .com/magazine/content/10_17/b4175034779697.htm?chan= magazine+channel_special+report

Haigh, D., McDonald, M., & Yoxon, R. (2012). *Brand Finance Global 500: The annual report of the world's most valuable brands*. London, UK: Brand Finance Plc.

CHAPTER EIGHT

Collaborative Leadership in the Intelligence Community

Joint Duty Program

Elizabeth B. Kolmstetter

There is no greater demand for extraordinary leadership than in the national security and defense arenas. The global security situation has created unprecedented complexity and uncertainty. Consider the impact of just some of the trends such as changing world demographics, emerging patterns of globalization, shifting economic patterns, increasing energy technologies and demands, unpredictable effects of natural disasters, capability of hostile states to develop weapons of mass destruction, emergence of transnational terrorist organizations, and conflict in the cyber and space domains (Army Training and Doctrine Command, 2009; National Defense Authorization Act, 2013; Office of the Director of National Intelligence, 2008b, 2009). The U.S. Intelligence Community's revolutionary joint duty program requires

Note: All statements of fact, opinion, or analysis expressed are those of the author and do not reflect the official positions or views of the Office of Director of National Intelligence (ODNI) or any other U.S. government agency. Nothing in the contents should be construed as asserting or implying U.S. government authentication or information or Agency endorsement of the author's views. This material has been reviewed by the ODNI and CIA to prevent the disclosure of classified information.

intelligence professionals to complete rotational assignments outside their home agency as a prerequisite to senior executive promotion. The program's goal is as compelling as it is straightforward: the development of a collaborative intelligence community workforce with an enterprise-wide focus rather than an agency-centric one, to fight the intelligence wars of the 21st century as a single, integrated force.

This innovation has its antecedents in the tragedy of 9/11, and one need look no further than the 9/11 Commission's report on the intelligence community's failure to understand the complexity it faced. The commission identified significant institutional, cultural, and organizational factors that had prevented the components of the U.S. Intelligence Community (a group of sixteen agencies and the Office of the Director of National Intelligence that work separately and together to engage in intelligence activities for the protection of the national security of the United States*) from operating in an effective and collaborative manner. For example, they found that no single intelligence activity or organization had all the keys to the terrorist attack or the ability to "connect the dots" that may have ultimately revealed it. Prior to 9/11, secrecy had become the norm, so ingrained that sharing information or collaborating with others (not just across agencies, but even within the same agency) was actively discouraged. Legacies of the Cold War, these very patterns of behavior impeded sharing and collaboration that are essential to fighting and winning the global war on terrorism.

It was expected that the needed large scale culture change would be driven, in part, by a mandatory rotation program, known as "joint duty," that would build collaborative leadership and enterprise perspective. The joint duty program requires thousands of the best and brightest professionals to complete extended inter-agency (i.e., joint) assignments as a mandatory requirement to senior leadership responsibility. By working in another intelligence agency—literally, by "walking a mile in their shoes"—these future leaders will begin to build the collaborative social networks and new behavioral norms necessary to share the most secretive

---

*See www.ODNI.gov for a complete history and description of the Intelligence Community and its agencies.

and sensitive information, and in so doing, help the community give the nation's policy-makers the "ground-truth" as free from institutional or political bias as humanly possible.

Origin

Congress concluded that the intelligence community needed to create a civilian joint duty program modeled after military reforms mandated by the historic Goldwater-Nichols Department of Defense Reorganization Act of 1986. *Goldwater-Nichols* required that military officers complete a "joint" assignment in order to be promoted to general or flag officer. From a historical perspective, it is important to note that when *Goldwater-Nichols* was enacted, a similar call for cultural change was at its core—a need to move the Department of Defense away from its service parochialisms toward inter-service cooperation and coordination to ensure that its leaders would be prepared to plan, support, and conduct joint, or multi-service, operations. Senator Goldwater and Representative Nichols gave examples going back to World War II that demonstrated the military services did not work well together, a problem that continued to be seen in more recent operations of the time, including the failed hostage rescue mission in Iran and the invasion of Grenada. The resultant military joint duty program is widely regarded today as a great success that has resulted in a common military culture that brings together all branches of service, while still allowing each military branch to remain distinct.

The President and Congress commissioned a number of reviews following the 9/11 terrorist attacks, including the 9/11 Commission and Weapons of Mass Destruction (WMD) Commission reports. These reports identified significant institutional, cultural, and organizational factors that had prevented the components of the intelligence community from operating in an effective and collaborative manner. In short, there was an immediate call for fundamental changes in the scope, authorities, organization, and activities of the community. Specifically, in one report the commission concluded that the intelligence community had failed to encourage joint personnel assignments that could break down cultural barriers and foster collaboration among intelligence components (WMD, 2005).

In 2004, Congress enacted the Intelligence Reform and Terrorism Prevention Act (IRTPA), which created the Office of the Director of National Intelligence (ODNI) and required this new agency to prescribe mechanisms to facilitate the rotation of employees to other community agencies during their careers, in order to obtain the widest possible understanding of the range of requirements, methods, users, and capabilities throughout the intelligence enterprise (IRTPA, 2004). It was expected that this large scale culture change would be driven, in part, by a mandatory rotation program, known as joint duty, that would build collaborative leadership and enterprise perspective.

On May 16, 2006, the new joint duty directive was issued—one of the very first policy documents signed by the new director of national intelligence (DNI). Developing the implementing guidance proved to be controversial and a first step in the new era of collaboration. The director was finally able to broker an agreement, and on June 25, 2007, with the support of the leaders of the six major intelligence departments and the Central Intelligence Agency (CIA), the DNI signed the joint duty policy guidance, making joint duty a prerequisite for promotion to senior executive rank within the intelligence community. This policy set a firm standard that—for the first time—reinforces and rewards an enterprise-minded culture. This is all about what then director Mike McConnell called "creating a culture of collaboration." The joint duty program has faced a number of unprecedented challenges, all stemming from the fact that its target population is exclusively civilian (with a completely different social contract than military officers) and spread across multiple departments and agencies with no single organizational chain of command. It will continue to take strong leadership to drive this transformation throughout the community over the years.

Joint Duty Program

Joint duty as a mandatory prerequisite for promotion to senior executive was implemented between 2007 and 2010, at which time it became mandatory for promotion to all senior executive levels in all seventeen agencies. The goal of the program is "to ensure that, at a minimum, intelligence community professionals, managers, and executives come to know first-hand, through one or more joint duty rotational assignments, the intelligence 'enterprise' and their interagency responsibilities in executing its missions" (Sanders, April 2009).

The requirements for joint duty credit are

- Assignment must be at least twelve months in length and at the General Schedule 11** (GS11) and above (or equivalent) in another intelligence agency (or approved external position);
- Assignment must be approved by the employee's first-level supervisor and second-level manager, in coordination with the employee's career service or career program (where applicable);
- Assignment must have duties and responsibilities that require the employee to acquire and apply substantial practical knowledge and understanding of the organization to which assigned, including its mission, structure, key personnel, and culture;
- Assignment must be consistent with the employee's career development plan(s);
- Assignment must be consistent with applicable competency requirements and career path(s) established by the individual's professional community; and
- Employee must receive a satisfactory performance evaluation while on rotation.

The policy allows for employees to gain joint experience in traditional interagency rotations, joint operation centers, national security and presidential councils, and other joint initiatives. Credit can also be achieved through qualifying assignments in a designated combat zone and even sometimes in non-intelligence

---

** See www.OPM.gov for a description of the government's General Schedule (GS) that has fifteen pay grade levels, plus a senior executive level, associated with levels of work The original joint duty program included officers between GS13 and GS15; in February 2013, the ODNI expanded the program to include GS11 and GS12 officers through GS15.

government agencies, private sector organizations, and academic or educational institutions.

In addition, many of the agencies offer professional training and education courses to personnel who are on, or have completed, one or more joint duty assignments. Participants from across the enterprise take these courses in mixed agency cohorts. All intelligence agencies provide a comprehensive suite of leadership training courses and it is common for officers who are on or have completed a joint assignment to attend them.

Figure 8.1 provides a summary of how the joint duty program arrays against the design spectrum for job rotation programs (Partnership for Public Service and McKinsey & Company, 2012).

Figure 8.1. Joint Duty (JD) Program as Arrayed on the Senior Mobility Design Spectrum

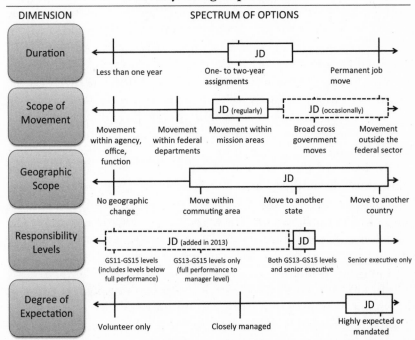

Adapted and reprinted with permission from "Mission-Driven Mobility: Strengthening Our Government Through a Mobile Leadership Corps." Copyright© 2012 by Partnership for Public Service and McKinsey & Company. All rights reserved.

Selection for Joint Duty Assignments

The program is open to every officer at GS11 (or equivalent) and above. This comprises the vast majority of intelligence professionals. There are just over one thousand senior executive level positions across the community, and being promoted to executive rank is a highly competitive process. Selection for a joint assignment is very competitive and both the home agency (i.e., permanent employment agency) and the gaining agency (i.e., temporary employment agency while on rotation) must determine that a candidate is qualified for a specific assignment.

Agencies routinely identify positions to advertise as joint duty assignments. The ODNI hosts a website on which openings are posted. Officers can review assignments by agency, by location, by occupation, by grade, and by key words. Agencies have designated some positions as permanently joint duty positions so employees know these particular assignments will continue to be available for their career planning. Many positions are also located within joint operation centers on an ongoing basis such as at the ODNI's National Counter Terrorism Center, the National Counter Proliferation Center, Federal Bureau of Investigation's (FBI) National Security Branch, and CIA's Counter Terrorism Center.

Individual managers may also determine that they would like to broaden their internal applicant pool by posting specific vacant positions for both internal agency *and* joint duty applicants. These positions may or may not be posted in the future for joint duty, depending on the needs at that time. In some cases "exchanges" are arranged between offices of different agencies with similar occupations. These exchange assignments have the advantage of ensuring that no lapse in work occurs while taking the time to backfill a position vacated by an employee who rotates to a joint assignment.

To ease the application process, the community has adopted a common application form so employees do not have to complete multiple forms if they elect to apply for multiple opportunities (although a completed application form is submitted to each specific opening). Figure 8.2 depicts the typical process for joint duty.

Some positions *internal* to each agency have been approved by the DNI for joint duty credit. Agency employees who encumber

Figure 8.2. Process for Joint Duty Rotations

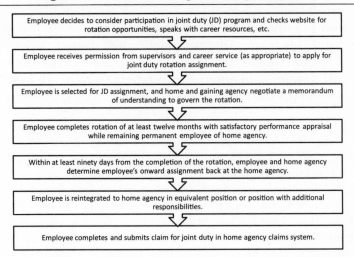

those specific positions are allowed to stay at their home agency and still receive joint duty credit upon completion. To qualify, these internal positions must involve significant policy, program, managerial, operational, liaison, tasking, or coordinating responsibility for resources, programs, policies, or operations that are carried out by the employee's agency in conjunction with one or more other agencies or organizations. These positions are considered "joint" experiences due to the nature and responsibilities associated with them. For example, a leadership position for a joint operation, joint center, joint terrorism task force, or serving as the intelligence community executive agent (i.e., running programs and making decisions for the entire community) are often granted credit as "internal" joint positions. For these positions, employees do not have to leave their home agencies to earn joint duty credit, but they must meet the rest of the completion requirements.

Jointness as a Strategy

Each of the directors of national intelligence (DNI) has taken important steps to tie joint duty to the very planning and success of the intelligence mission. There have been four DNIs since the creation of the agency in 2005: John Negroponte, Michael

McConnell, Dennis Blair, and James Clapper; each one has publicly and strongly endorsed the joint duty program.

As an example of explicitly tying the program to the intelligence strategic plan, Director McConnell issued *Vision 2015* (ODNI, 2008b) for the intelligence community. In it he made clear that collaboration and enterprise-mindedness were critical to the future success of the intelligence and national security mission:

> Risks are often unforeseen and threats are hidden and agile, making the job of intelligence professionals more critical and more challenging. Our national security depends on anticipating risks and out-maneuvering our adversaries, not just out-muscling them. Therefore, intelligence is more critical than ever. We must address these risks and threats by integrating all elements of national power—defense, homeland security, diplomacy, development, and intelligence. However, the Intelligence Community is still largely structured, staffed, and operated around a design optimized for a different era. Adapting the community to this new environment is our fundamental challenge. (p. 1)
>
> Our leaders will need to transcend the traditional independent, agency-centric orientation, and move toward a leadership style based on cross-agency collaboration and interdisciplinary experience. In particular, this will require leadership that can build coalitions across agencies and cultures, bound by a shared purpose and unity of action to achieve mission objectives. We will need leadership development programs, performance evaluation systems, and an incentive structure that span the Intelligence Enterprise. [Joint Duty] policy sets a firm standard that—for the first time—rewards Enterprise-minded culture. (p. 15)

Director Blair issued the *National Intelligence Strategy* (ODNI, 2009) requiring an integrated enterprise. In congressional testimony, then associate director for national intelligence for human capital, Dr. Ron Sanders, summarized it well in his Congressional testimony:

> The success of the National Intelligence Strategy depends on our people; it requires nothing less than a unified corps of dedicated intelligence professionals that is bold and innovative, focused on results and on the future, collaborative and self-evaluating, and led by senior officers who understand and leverage the capabilities of the entire U.S. intelligence enterprise. The Joint Duty Program

is a cornerstone of our efforts to achieve that vision. (Sanders, April 30, 2009)

Tying the relevance of the program to the desired performance outcomes, and then to the very accomplishment of the mission, has been a necessary and powerful driver. Agency heads and senior leaders highlight the program-to-mission connection in strategy documents, briefings, presentations, orientations, and training courses, which has helped tremendously in building the credibility of the joint duty requirement for promotion to senior ranks across the community.

Jointness as Leadership Development

Nick Petrie (2011) captured it well: the leadership development challenge of today is "how to grow bigger minds." According to research by Petrie and his colleagues at the Center for Creative Leadership, managers will increasingly be required to engage in strategic thinking, collaboration, systems thinking, leading change, adaptive thinking, and comfort with ambiguity. However, according to research, less than 8 percent of leaders have reached that level of thinking (Fisher, Rooke, & Torbert, 2000). Petrie describes the new concept of leadership development as both horizontal and vertical. Horizontal development means developing more competencies and can be taught and learned from experts. Vertical development, on the other hand, is the equivalent to human development stages that must be experienced, earned, and accomplished for oneself. McGuire and Rhodes (2009) suggest that when an individual is confronted with increased complexity and challenge that can't be met with what he or she already knows and can do, that individual is "pulled" to take the next step. At this next developmental step the individual is required to understand that new ways of doing things are possible, should recognize that old assumptions may be challenged, and, finally, must successfully implement new ideas, thus advancing him or her to the next stage. Petrie challenges organizations to accelerate the vertical development of leaders (and leadership cultures) by creating processes and experiences that embed these principles into the workplace. We have found that the joint duty program does just that.

The intent of the program certainly can be described as expecting employees to have the equivalent of an "out of body experience" by working in a completely different agency, under different policies and processes, using different systems and techniques, and building new networks. In the best-case scenario, these officers are reaching a new level in their vertical development while on rotation. They have to successfully manage in new ways under different rules, experience first-hand broadening activities that challenge what they have known and done, and gain a new perspective on the intelligence enterprise. They come to realize there are new ways to collaborate and lead across and within the enterprise. At a minimum (i.e., worst-case scenario), these officers are at least being exposed to a different part of the enterprise and gain an awareness of the differences and similarities that exist. Over time, the interagency experience of the leaders should result in greater cohesion among agencies and employees, further enabling the goal of breaking down structural and cultural barriers that inhibit the community.

Regardless of whether an organization is private or public, for-profit or non-profit, domestic or international, small or large, it is clear that all leaders will be required to excel in the competencies of collaboration, integration, and big picture thinking. As Dennis Blair, former director of national intelligence, noted, "When the next generation of intelligence leaders moves into the top jobs, their experience will make them better joint leaders. They will instinctively pool their skills and capabilities. My most important job as DNI is to force-feed them, to speed up this process so they arrive sooner, rather than later" (April 6, 2010).

Augmenting Leader Development While on Rotation

Joint duty program managers and participants have found augmenting the rotational experience with other leader development programs to be highly beneficial (U.S. Government Accountability Office, 2012b). Supplemental development programs include:

- Utilizing an executive coach (certified consultants);
- Receiving 360 feedback for development;
- Attending leadership seminars and roundtables with senior leaders from various agencies;

- Participating in leadership "field" trips (i.e., visit to Congress, attend the Gettysburg Leadership Experience);
- Shadowing (i.e., spending a day with a senior leader at the host agency); and
- Joining networking sessions.

These programs are being used to enhance the experience of an agency's officers who are out on joint assignments as well as host agencies for officers on rotations into their organizations. The ODNI has piloted several programs employing some of these practices with cohorts of their own senior officers who are out on joint assignments across the community. This additional support and development was viewed as extremely positive and impactful for the participants. Most officers found that these programs enhanced their joint experience because they: (1) provided objective, differing perspectives on the participant's leadership skills; (2) encouraged participants to "push and stretch yourself" in the assignment not just "do another job somewhere else"; (3) enabled participants to be more reflective about their new experience and its application to self-development; and (4) allowed for peer mentoring and networking among the cohort.

Implementation

The next section covers a series of important attributes and activities that have been worked through during the ongoing implementation of the program. Each one has been approached with scientifically based, thoughtful, and practical solutions. Perhaps the most significant obstacle to implementation has been the organization-centric cultures that exist throughout the community. In each of the program areas described, you will find implicit and explicit culture change initiatives that have aided in the program sustainability. Specific agency examples have also been included to highlight some community best practices.

Program Visibility

Agencies have found that it is important to continuously market, promote, and communicate the program and its benefits. Even if officers do not yet know whether they want to become senior executives, the benefits of a joint duty assignment are career enhancing and personally rewarding. The community has been promoting a culture of "leadership at all levels," including the need for continuous learning. To that end, joint duty is marketed as a program for all officers at the GS11, or equivalent, grade level or above, regardless of whether they aspire currently to reach executive rank. Although some assignments are arranged by managers to fill or develop specific skills and capability needs (i.e., for a specific task force or agency initiative), every effort is made to openly complete rotational opportunities. The ODNI hosts a joint duty website that includes a blog, streaming video of senior leaders underscoring the importance of joint duty, timely articles about joint duty, and frequently asked questions about the program. In addition to the ODNI-sponsored website, many agencies have developed internal websites to improve access to program information, application forms, agency points of contact for assistance, internal positions that qualify for credit, and frequently asked questions and answers. In-person joint duty fairs have also been highly successful for officers within the Washington, D.C., commuting area.

The ODNI program office established a joint duty community of practice made up of representatives, typically joint duty program managers, from all intelligence agencies. This working group meets on a monthly basis to share best practices, review and analyze program metrics and studies, and improve program implementation. This group facilitates joint duty "fairs" at different locations in order to promote available assignments. For example, in 2012, the ODNI and CIA joint duty program offices co-hosted two Joint Duty Information Exchanges (i.e., "fairs"). The event was designed to increase awareness of rotational assignments available across the community that offer opportunities for leadership and career development. Nearly all agencies participated in the fair-like setting, with booths full of information and representatives ready to answer questions about various assignments.

In addition to the Information Exchange, one event featured a panel discussion with five joint duty participants, each representing a different agency. The panelists stressed the positive impact their assignments had on their careers and leadership development, and also some of the practical challenges to being on rotation. This event alone served an in-person audience of several hundred officers at the panel session (and more through video on demand), provided over three hours of continuous information at the booths, and resulted in a spike of thousands of hits on the joint duty website during the week following the event.

Orientation

Orientation programs can generally be categorized in two group-ings: (1) those designed for brand new employees with basic infor-mation (i.e., salary structure, benefits explanations and form completion, vacation rules) or (2) those designed specifically for senior, highly experienced executives in whom the organization is making a significant and long-term investment (i.e., year-long executive on-boarding programs). Agencies have excellent new employee orientation programs that are commonly combined with various training and education courses required for specific occupations. For senior executive ranks, on-boarding programs have been established as a means to orient them to the highest priorities and challenges of the mission, quickly build their inter-nal networks, and ensure their connectedness to all facets of the organization. It appears that employees on rotational assignments *do* need some form of orientation to learn critical organizational information that accelerates their understanding of the host agency, allowing them to more quickly become effective in their new assignments. I have concluded that a compromise, something in the middle between new hire orientation and a senior on-boarding program, is beneficial for our rotational employees.

Agencies across the community are now developing the best way to orient joint duty officers. Some have custom designed an orientation session, while others have created a hybrid from their current orientation and on-boarding programs. Taking only relevant portions of the new employee orientation program, com-bining it with a few modules from a senior on-boarding program, and creating a new module that addresses specific rotational issues can achieve an applicable orientation for rotational employees.

An example is the CIA's joint duty orientation program designed specifically for officers on joint duty from other agencies. This customized program provides an overview of the agency, its mission, and its leadership. In addition, the orientation covers some of the informational programs, training courses, and benefits (i.e., family day, medical services, fitness facilities and programs) that officers can take advantage of while they are on assignment. Officers are also provided with an overview of the agency's joint duty website and useful contacts. Invitations are sent to these officers for special programs throughout each year, such as senior leadership seminars, career development day, and community information exchange events.

Taking a slightly different, but equally helpful, approach, the Federal Bureau of Investigation (FBI) implemented a mandatory "out-briefing" class for all employees being assigned temporarily to other organizations, including joint duty participants. The class covers issues that employees face when they move from their home agency to a gaining agency, such as how to handle their time and attendance, how and when to complete mandatory training, the need to familiarize themselves with the host agency's emergency procedures, and how the reintegration process works.

Amount of Structure

The current joint duty program is not very structured. Each agency develops and implements its own program and processes. There is no requirement to be designated "high potential" or even likely to be promoted to a senior executive in order to participate. Employees work with their managers and mentors to find a good fit for their joint duty assignments or even multiple joint duty assignments throughout their careers. While there are now thousands of employees with joint duty credit, it is too early to tell whether enough senior level employees have joint duty credit for the bench strength needed for current and future senior executive openings. Some agencies, such as the National Security Agency (NSA), have already integrated this mobility program into their succession planning activities. Other agencies, like the CIA, have incorporated discussions of joint duty assignments into their career development programs.

Perhaps the most structured program to date is at the National Geospatial-Intelligence Agency (NGA). Employees who wish to be considered for joint duty assignments must apply for consideration (available quarterly) and be approved by the directorate's leadership. The process ensures that officers are high performing, will serve as excellent representatives of NGA, are likely to benefit personally from the rotation, and are prepared to return to a more responsible position following the rotation. NGA also has a very structured and successful reintegration program that is described later in this chapter. The U.S. Marine Corps has also implemented a structured pre-approval process for employees who wish to be considered for joint duty assignments.

Reintegration

One of the program's greatest challenges continues to be the reintegration of officers back into their home agency after their rotations (Burke, Ericson, Fillman, Graber, Jones, Mitchell, Rodgers, et al., 2012; U.S. Government Accountability Office, 2012; Partnership for Public Service and McKinsey & Company, 2012). On a personal level, officers fear being "out of sight and out of mind" and left out of consideration for highly desirable or senior leadership openings. On an organizational level, it can be unwieldy to keep track of all officers out on rotation, when they are returning, and the timing between the end of their assignments and the opening of appropriate follow on assignments. In some cases, joint duty officers are even offered permanent positions at the gaining agency and elect to convert to a permanent employee of that agency. While this type of conversion is viewed as positive for the intelligence community writ large, it can result in added complexity for the home agency's onward assignment planning and succession management.

The NGA uses a structured process for reintegration. It begins six months prior to the completion of the assignment and offers all joint duty participants up to three assignment preferences when they return. A senior panel reviews upcoming openings for opportunities that will put an officer's new skills to use. Each officer is offered a return assignment and must have this decision finalized at least sixty days prior to returning to NGA. This model allows for the agency to better manage which officers are coming back from rotation and when, what additional skills are being developed by their officers, and to plan for how the organization can best benefit from the rotational experiences. The CIA uses its career services infrastructure (personnel management by occupations) to ensure that returning officers have an onward assignment upon their return. In some cases, officers may serve on a special project or task force until a more permanent position is available.

Performance Management and Recognition

Intelligence agencies have different personnel systems; six different department or special authorities regulate these personnel policies and systems. Adding to this complexity, some components of the intelligence community come from one specific organizational division that is part of a much bigger agency or department. For example, only one division in the FBI, the National Security Branch, is part of the intelligence community. The rest of the FBI is not part of the intelligence community and the Department of Justice (DOJ) governs the entire FBI. As such, FBI employees can fall under personnel requirements from the FBI, DOJ, and/or the Intelligence Community directives (mandated by the ODNI). Prior to and during the launch of the program it was imperative to review and resolve similarities and differences in performance management system requirements across the community. For example, processes were developed to establish and ensure employees were receiving appropriate and timely performance appraisals (in some cases, employees receive an appraisal from their gaining *and* home agencies), were being considered for appropriate monetary and non-monetary awards, and were granted salary increases if applicable.

Salary increases for officers on rotation remain within the purview of the home agency. The majority of employees are covered under the general schedule pay rules (referenced earlier). In these cases, home agencies must continue to monitor when each employee is eligible for a within-grade ("step") increase, which is dependent on employment anniversary date, years of tenure, and successful performance (these often occur at times other than the official end-of-year performance evaluation).

However, NGA employees are on pay bands and perform under a pay for performance system that is different from the general schedule system. It was imperative to work out the pay implications for NGA officers going to other agencies for rotation (so they were not left out of reviews for annual pay increases) and for other officers going to the NGA for rotation (to receive their within-grade increases and any bonus as appropriate). It was also important to ensure that officers from NGA on assignment to other agencies receive performance appraisals on the NGA schedule, not on the host agency's performance appraisal schedule, so they would not be disadvantaged when time came for consideration for annual pay increases.

Performance bonus systems also vary across the community. The terms for bonuses are contained in the memorandum of understanding that officers and both the gaining and home agencies sign so that it is understood what conditions will apply for that officer. Because rotations do not begin and end at predictable, standard points in the year, officers often perform part of the year in their home agencies and part of the year in a gaining agency. In such cases, these officers end up being considered for a bonus in the home agency and in the gaining agency—but without the benefit of a complete performance year to demonstrate achievement and impact in either. The joint duty program managers have developed an end-of-year reconciliation process through which every officer on joint duty is accounted for; the gaining agency determines the performance rating and applicable bonus after consultation with the home agency. This extensive and painstaking process ensures that officers are not missed and any necessary arrangements are made to reconcile bonus decisions.

Expanding to Junior Employees

In February 2013, the ODNI formally expanded the joint duty program from starting with GS13 level officers to now include GS11 and GS12 level officers. The intent of this expansion to more junior officers is to expose them to the broader community earlier in their careers. It is believed that if officers are exposed to the broader community earlier in their careers, they will be more able and willing to collaborate, share information, and think of ways to work across the agencies to achieve mission. Although the intelligence community currently has a low attrition rate and is consistently rated as one of the best places to work in government (Partnership for Public Service, 2012), leadership believes that expanding the program would be viewed as enhancing career development and future retention.

Rotational assignments at junior levels will likely be in technical positions. Having an "out of body experience" as a junior employee is much different than "being dropped on Mars and having to lead your way to success" (as one participant described it). The intent of the original joint duty program was to have a *leadership* experience—to have to make decisions, lead under different rules and policies, collaborate with other senior officers, and figure out how to drive results in another part of the enterprise. Opening the program to more junior employees, by definition those who have not yet reached full performance levels, will likely require that agencies first ensure that these junior, or developmental level, officers have an appropriate level of depth in understanding their specific "tradecraft" as well as the mission of their home agencies.

Tradecraft has historically meant clandestine techniques applied to the activity of intelligence but is now used more widely to describe a skill acquired through knowledge and experience in a particular occupation. For most intelligence occupations, it takes about five years to become fully proficient in the tradecraft for a specific occupation in a particular mission set of an agency. The community of practice continues to explore ways to ensure junior officers are ready to participate in the program. Examples of criteria being examined are having served in multiple offices within an agency before applying for a rotational assignment between agencies, being fully credentialed in one's occupation (successfully completed all training and education, met proficiency standards), and being certified out of any probationary or trial period of employment.

Support for Mobility

In the public sector, specifically the intelligence community, agency performance systems are still designed to promote and reward those who deliver excellent results and produce high impact. Managers themselves are incentivized and rewarded for producing results. Even if managers support the premise of rotational assignments, the performance management system simply makes it hard for them to send their best employees not only away from their teams, but also out of their organizations. With shrinking budgets, personnel and contractor cuts, tight deadlines, and increasing mission demands, managers are concerned with allowing their top performers, often in fairly senior roles, to leave on a joint assignment. Likewise, some leaders have described being wary of incoming rotational employees who may not have the right technical skills, organizational knowledge, or internal network to quickly achieve results and not make mistakes in a high-risk environment. As in any program that requires a change in culture, it will continue to gain support as managers have positive experiences with incoming rotational employees and see the organizational benefit in officers who have returned from a successful joint assignment.

The Department of State has introduced an interesting requirement that should positively impact support for the program. They now require all returning employees to complete presentations and brief co-workers through "Trade Craft" presentations as a forum for sharing knowledge and insights gained during the rotation. Throughout the implementation of the joint program, communicating and publicizing success stories through vehicles such as website postings, firsthand presentations at leadership courses, and having vocal "mobility champions" who raise program awareness have been paramount to building necessary support.

Evaluation and Insights

As described earlier in this chapter, joint duty has been more than a collaborative leadership development program; it has been a large scale culture change effort. As such, it is even more critical to have a continuous evaluation and improvement initiative to ensure that the program reaches its full potential. A number of formal evaluations have taken place by third-party reviewers alongside many agency-specific feedback and review efforts.

Across all of these efforts a number of best practices and lessons learned have been gleaned, and focus areas for program improvement have been identified and are summarized in this section.

External validation and praise for the program came in 2008 when the Intelligence Community Joint Duty Program was awarded the Innovations in American Government Award from the Ash Institute for Democratic Governance and Innovation at the Harvard Kennedy School. This recognition served to highlight the importance and early successes of the program. The citation recognized the program's ability to build collaborative, inter-agency information-sharing networks at the same time as having its officers gain a deeper and broader knowledge of the inner workings of American intelligence (ODNI, 2008a).

Several comprehensive, objective studies have provided extensive evaluation of the program (i.e., Burke et al, 2012; U.S. Government Accountability Office, 2012a). Across these studies, senior officials and participants have agreed that the program enhances collaboration, increases networking, results in a better understanding of the community as a whole, and offers a new opportunity to develop professionally. In 2009, nearly three thousand employees were on some type of joint duty assignment (Sanders, 2009). In 2011, over 50 percent of the GS15-level employees were reported to have joint duty credit, and of the hundreds of officers promoted to executive rank across the intelligence community that year, all but one officer had joint duty credit (GAO #12–679, page 25; policy allows the DNI to grant waivers for unique circumstances).

Another indication that these rotation programs are having a positive impact on leadership in the government and national security arenas comes from the recent passage of the National Defense Authorization Act of Fiscal Year 2013, signed on January 2, 2013, by President Obama. This act includes §1107, Interagency Personnel Rotations, in which Congress seeks to foster greater interagency experience among executive branch personnel on national security matters by encouraging rotational assignments and providing for preference during selection to senior-level positions within an interagency community of interest to individuals who have performed interagency rotational service within that community of interest. The fundamental premise of this strategy was based on their conclusion that interagency rotational assignments significantly improved the individual's overall functional area knowledge and understanding of the larger scope of development and employment of integrated federal government capabilities required to meet current and future challenges to the nation's security.

Table 8.1 provides a summary of conclusions and suggestions across several studies. Agencies are working independently and also together through the community of practice working group to address and make improvements in needed areas.

Practice Pointers for Developing Rotational Assignment Programs

Mobility and rotational assignment programs are on the rise. Public and private organizations with overseas offices and departments often require high potentials and leaders to serve outside of the United States in order to gain breadth of experience. In addition, some private sector, and even public sector, organizations are setting specific percentage goals for senior leadership teams to come from another part of the organization, another organization altogether, or even a different market sector in order to bring innovation, challenge the current traditions and culture, and keep operations "fresh." These are all trends and practices demonstrating the increase and more organized approach to providing mobility and breadth of experience for leaders.

Voluntary vs. Mandatory. Perhaps one of the most frequent questions about designing rotational programs, at least in the government, is around whether to make them voluntary or mandatory. I do not believe that the joint duty program would have reached its current level of participation and success if it had been completely voluntary and left to individual organizations to implement. In fact, Congress' expectation for the government's senior executive service (SES) when established in 1978 was that the men and women who hold the senior most jobs in the federal government would be "a mobile resource, bringing managerial excellence to a variety of roles and ideally, to a variety of government institutions" (www.opm.gov/ses/about_ses). However, a recent study by the Partnership for Public Service and McKinsey & Company (2012)

Table 8.1. Summary of Findings from Program Evaluations

Working Well

Area/Issue	Insight/Actions Underway
Efforts to achieve common performance rating and evaluation components to appraisals; employees are now evaluated on a common set of performance competencies and under appraisals with common core elements.	Rotational assignments are better managed and easier to evaluate when agencies adopt a common performance appraisal system.
Promotion panels evaluate candidates' enterprise thinking, broadening experiences, and ability to lead change as part of the executive competencies and qualifications to being promoted to senior executive rank.	Competencies strengthened during joint experiences are part of the executive promotion criteria and demonstrate the linkage to candidates of their importance; officers view joint experiences as improving their competitiveness for promotion.
ODNI instituted the quarterly National Intelligence Awards program to recognize outstanding individual and team achievement across the enterprise; award criteria include behaviors expected of intelligence officers in the areas of collaboration, cross-agency integration, and teamwork; one award is specifically given for joint leadership.	Reinforces the culture movement toward "jointness" and its importance to achieving mission; adds positive visibility to many officers on joint rotations and/or leading joint teams.
Policy and process in place to ensure that the gaining agency reviews and considers rotational employees for appropriate award and bonuses available.	Program managers convene and reconcile employees on rotation for annual bonus and award recognition.
Agencies report program metrics to the ODNI on an annual basis.	ODNI completes an annual review of program metrics.

Table 8.1. Continued

Working Well

Area/Issue	Insight/Actions Underway
Officers report positive experiences in joint assignments such as gaining unique knowledge of other agencies and mission areas and having leadership role experiences they would not otherwise have obtained at their home agency.	Participants are being well-integrated within their gaining agency and given meaningful assignments.

Areas for Improvement

Area/Issue	Insight/Actions Underway
Mechanisms for communication and contact between an employee and his/her home agency while on rotation.	Provide clear responsibility and means for officers to "reach back" to their home agencies and improve mechanisms for home agencies to stay in touch with officers on rotation.
Comprehensive and timely communications about the program, including guidelines, success stories, personal experiences, special opportunities, articles, town hall meetings, brown bag seminars, and marketing tools.	Joint duty website is undergoing updates and the community of practice is developing marketing tools and hosting more frequent events.
Improved reintegration process, timeline, and follow-on assignment assistance for employees returning to their home agencies.	Agencies are implementing more preparation and processes for follow-on assignments.
Difficult to maintain long-term relationships with contacts made during rotation assignment.	Seeking ways to offer cross-agency social networking sites and more inter-agency communities of practice.

Compiled from GAO, 2013; Partnership for Public Service and McKinsey & Company, 2012; Burke et al., 2012; Sanders, 2009; Intelligence Community Directives 650, 651, 655, 656, and 660; and Intelligence Community Policy Guidance 601.1.

of personnel data from the Office of Personnel Management found that only 8 percent of the 2011 SES members government-wide had ever changed agencies and only 11 percent had changed subcomponents within an agency. Further demonstrating the lack of voluntary mobility among today's senior executives in the government, the data showed that nearly half (48 percent) of today's executives have *never* changed positions since being promoted to the senior executive service.

While the joint duty program is mandatory for employees who wish to be considered for promotion to senior executive, there is also a voluntary aspect to the program. Officers can and do participate on joint assignments without knowing for sure that they aspire to be, or have what it takes to be, a senior executive. For example, many officers take joint assignments because they like the idea of experiencing work in another agency, seek variety in their career development, or wish to work under the leadership of a particular person and/or division. In addition, with the expansion of the program to include GS11 and GS12 officers, it is anticipated that employees will be taking more than one joint assignment over their careers (e.g., an assignment as a GS11 and a very different assignment as a GS15).

In developing the joint duty program, extra care was taken to look for ways to ensure that the requirement did not disadvantage or preclude any employee qualified to participate. Some of these measures include:

- Approving some internal positions that meet specific "joint" criteria allowing officers to earn credit without leaving their home agency;
- Allowing officers to take a rotational assignment any time between the equivalent of three pay grades, GS13 to GS15 (this was expanded to five pay grades from GS11 to GS15 in 2013);
- Defining rotational assignments broadly, allowing for some to be outside the intelligence community;
- Allowing employees to accumulate joint credit by completing multiple rotations (i.e., two six-month assignments that are separated with time back at the home agency); and

- Allowing for the DNI to grant waivers to the joint duty requirement for special circumstances (i.e., highly specialized jobs with relatively few positions or opportunities across the community such as medical doctors).

Table 8.2 summarizes some additional practical tips for developing a rotational or mobility program.

Pitfalls and How to Avoid Them

Over-generalizations from a bad experience, or negativism that is reflective of current cultural attributes, can spread through social networks, harming any organizational change effort. I found it important to listen carefully to "nay-sayers" who were critical of joint duty, and of rotational programs in general, or those who really had bad experiences during their joint duty assignments. Heading these off early during implementation and communications planning will be important for success. Tips for avoiding eight such pitfalls are suggested in the list below.

- *Out of sight, out of mind.* Many positive employment actions, formal and informal, are tied to visibility, face time with senior leaders, longevity of achievements, and a track record of success. So be sure not to leave out employees who are on rotation, find ways to keep them in touch with the home agency, and encourage them to take on the responsibility to actively seek ways to visit and stay informed.
- *Re-integration will be easy, especially for senior leaders.* While senior, well-connected leaders may make it look easy, there are usually fewer positions to return to or to go to as leaders become more senior. So be super-organized and planful about the next assignment for those out on rotation.
- *Check the box mentality.* Some employees might view mandatory rotation programs as just "get it done as soon as possible," rather than working hard at finding the *right fit* for the rotational experience that will benefit them and the organization. Be sure the rotation experience is good for both the organization and the employee.

Table 8.2. Checklist for Designing Rotational Programs

The What	The How
Clarify program intent	Implement clear, consistent, and frequent communications regarding the intent and purpose of the rotational program
Link to organizational priorities and plans	Create a clear line of sight from the use of rotational assignments, which will develop and strengthen stated leadership capabilities, to the organization's mission success
	Develop a specific objective in the human capital plan that addresses the need for essential leadership competencies which are developed through rotational assignments
Integrate with talent management system	Ensure there is appropriate orientation for employees in the rotational program and for managers about the benefits of the program and how to manage rotational employees
	Ensure that rotational assignments are rewarded, reinforced, and integrated with other career advancing initiatives, including incentivizing managers to take in rotational employees
	Ensure there is a smooth process for returning employees into their next assignments
Identify and remove barriers (real and perceived)	Identify real and perceived barriers for employees to participate in rotational assignments (some of these might be cultural)
	Review, revise, clarify, and/or establish human resource policies and processes to support rotational assignments
Reward and recognize participants	Seek ways to reward and recognize those who take rotational assignments
	Recognize that it is harder to go on a rotational assignment than to stay in the familiar home office or organization

Build supporting infrastructure, including access badges, computer systems and tools access, office space, parking, medical and security clearances, emergency preparedness	Build the necessary infrastructure for effective rotational assignments (this will probably be harder than you think); be patient as you work through the implementation details Consider identifying points of contact in each applicable division (i.e., HR, security, IT, facilities, medical, travel) who can help navigate infrastructure issues that will be faced by rotational employees
Develop an implementation plan	Convene a cross-organization working group to develop the implementation plan; determine whether your program should begin with a pilot group or proof-of-concept (i.e., in a specific division, for a specific job level, for specific occupations) before going organization-wide Ensure there is a comprehensive communications plan and easily accessible information about the program
Establish and then refresh a group of senior champions	Have a plan for identifying senior champions and then refreshing your champion pool with new members Invite rotational assignment "alumni" to be champions and recruit others to take rotational assignments; request that successful alumni visibly promote and endorse the benefits of the program; capture their stories on video if possible to be used on websites, in training, and for presentations
Capture and communicate success stories	As with most change efforts, find ways to highlight and publicize early program successes; this can be done with early adopters, role models, and rotation stories Nominate your program for internal and external awards and recognition which can validate the credibility, success, and purpose of the program

- *Any manager can advise employees about rotations.* Managers need training on how to advise subordinates about rotation assignment choices, optimal timing, what to expect, how to prepare, and how to be successful—especially if not all managers have had rotational assignments themselves. Be sure to provide training, talking points, and coaching on how to advise employees to take rotational assignments and why.
- *I can't let my best employee leave.* Managers may want to hoard their top talent to ensure the team or office achieves their results; managers need to be recognized and reinforced for allowing top talent to go on rotational assignments. Put in place a "backfilling plan" and allow for overlap and knowledge transfer before the rotation begins whenever possible.
- *Single champion syndrome.* Sometimes large scale organizational change efforts are associated with a single leader. While this can be beneficial in getting the program off the ground, the long-term sustainability of the program will need to be tied to organizational success, multiple leaders' visions, and specific goals and values everyone believes are worthy. The risk is high that the program will die (or be killed off) if there is only one visible champion and that leader departs (or falls out of favor).   .
- *Rotational assignments don't fit our culture.* Most top leaders and highly successful organizations now realize that, to remain competitive, they must build continuous learning and broadening experiences into their leadership cultures. Encourage and ensure top leaders are vocal about how rotational assignments made them better leaders.
- *Passing of the deadwood.* Some managers may be tempted to pass off low performers or problem employees by sending them on a rotational assignment just to move them out of a current position. This will harm the reputation of your rotational program. Review the performance of those on rotational assignments against similar groups to ensure that the program is not improperly used to pass off underperforming employees, seek feedback from gaining divisions/organizations about the performance and

contribution of the rotational employees, and allow gaining offices to return employees who really don't work out short of fulfilling the rotational assignment.

Conclusion

Just as it took over twenty years for Goldwater-Nichols and the Department of Defense to realize a change in culture of the U.S. military, the ODNI and joint duty program are challenging and changing the intelligence community culture at its core. There is no question that rotational assignments, or "out of body" experiences, are broadening for the individual and are contributing to improved collaboration and integration at the team and organizational levels. Employees report improved collaboration and information sharing skills, an expanded network, and improved knowledge of the intelligence mission of another component of the community.

Has the intelligence community achieved our mandate to build collaborative leadership, to break down traditional stovepipes preventing integration, and to operate as an effective enterprise? For certain, progress and real change has begun. It took approximately twelve months to negotiate the implementation of joint duty in 2006–2007, to get the Secretaries of State, Defense, Treasury, Energy, and Homeland Security, plus the Attorney General and Director of the CIA, to agree to give up their most talented managers to the agencies of the community so that they could complete a one- to three-year joint duty rotation and thereby meet the joint qualification for senior executive. Such a lengthy inter-agency assignment as a prerequisite for senior service had been unheard of outside of the military. There are now many thousands of employees with joint duty credit, thousands of employees on a rotational assignment in any given year, and there has been over three years of the mandatory joint duty requirement for promotion to senior executive rank. The nation can be very optimistic about the prospects for collaborative leadership as this generation moves into the senior manager and executive ranks over the next decade.

Perhaps the most significant recognition of the community's progress was shared on May 20, 2011, at CIA Headquarters when Director of National Intelligence James Clapper, then Director of the Central Intelligence Agency Leon Panetta, and President Barack Obama (White House, 2011) together addressed the workforce. Each leader made it clear that the successful takedown of Osama bin Laden, who was responsible for the 9/11 terrorist attack, was *only* possible because of cross-agency collaboration and integration of the intelligence community:

> [Thanks] . . . To the men and women in the intelligence community who contributed directly—notably, from CIA, NSA, NGA, NRO, and NCTC—and many others from intelligence organizations who contributed indirectly, taken together are a magnificent example of teamwork and intelligence integration.
>
> DIRECTOR OF NATIONAL INTELLIGENCE JAMES CLAPPER
>
> I think it's fair to say that we've never had a closer, more effective working relationship, both within our community and across the national security sector of our government. We thank all of you—all of you—for the team effort that was involved in the operation to go after bin Laden. It would not have happened without your full cooperation. Jim Clapper deserves a lot of credit for his leadership in bringing the intelligence community together.
>
> CIA DIRECTOR LEON PANETTA
>
> This is one of the few times when all these leaders and organizations have the occasion to appear together publicly. And so I thank all of you for coming—because I think it's so important for the American people to see all of you here today. No one piece of information and no one agency made this possible. You did it together—CIA, NSA, NRO, NGA, everyone at ODNI and the National Counterterrorism Center. And that's exactly how our intelligence community is supposed to work, using every capability—human, technical—collecting, analyzing, sharing, integrating intelligence, and then acting on it. That's what made this one of the greatest intelligence successes in American history, and that's why intelligence professionals are going to study and be inspired by your achievement for generations to come.
>
> PRESIDENT BARACK OBAMA

I am personally convinced that mobility and breadth of experience are critical (necessary but not sufficient) for any senior leader to be effective in today's world. I encourage all organizations, private and public, to develop robust leadership development programs that ensure that such experiential learning takes place— even making such assignments mandatory if the current culture is not in place to support it. I look forward to seeing the joint duty program expand to more junior officers earlier in their careers and finding more ways to encourage officers to take multiple joint duty assignments throughout their careers—expanding the use of rotational programs throughout the government. Nothing in the development of this program has been easy. I commend my colleagues in the ODNI Office of Human Capital who led the development of the joint duty program, the chief human capital officers from across the community who persisted in the implementation of the program, the community senior leaders who visibly role model jointness, and all officers who are active participants in the program and are redefining the culture every day. It is a privilege to work with the extraordinary talent and dedicated leadership of the intelligence community in this journey. Real change has begun and I could not be more excited about the next generation of leadership for whom collaboration, integration, and enterprise thinking is the norm.

References

Burke, J., Ericson, P., Fillman, K., Graber, J., Jones, E., Mitchell, C., Rodgers, R., Wilson, N., & Sievert, R. (2012). *Implementation of the joint duty program at CIA: Analysis and recommendations. A project commissioned by the Center for the Study of Intelligence in coordination with the George Bush School of Government and Public Service.* College Station, TX: Texas A&M University.

Fisher, D., Rooke, D., & Torbert, B. (2000). *Personal and organizational transformations through action inquiry.* Boston, MA: Edge\Work Press.

Goldwater-Nichols Department of Defense Reorganization Act, Public Law No. 99–433 (1986).

Intelligence Community Directives 601, 650, 651, 655, 656, and 660; Intelligence Community Policy Guidance 601.0. Retrieved from www.dni.gov/index.php/intelligence-community/ic-policies -reports/intelligence-community-directives

Intelligence Reform and Terrorism Prevention Act, Public Law No. 108–458, § 1011 (2004).

McGuire, J. B., & Rhodes, G. B. (2009). *Transforming your leadership culture.* San Francisco, CA: Jossey-Bass.

National Defense Authorization Act for Fiscal Year 2013. H.R. 4310 112th Congress. Washington, DC.

Office of the Director of National Intelligence. (2008a). Intelligence community civilian joint duty program honored as Innovations in American Government Award Winner. Press release retrieved from www.reuters.com/article/2008/09/10/idUS19596+10-Sep-2008+BW20080910

Office of the Director of National Intelligence. (2008b). Vision 2015: A globally networked and integrated intelligence enterprise. Washington, DC: Author.

Office of the Director of National Intelligence. (2009). National intelligence strategy. Washington, DC: Author.

Partnership for Public Service. (2012). Best places to work in the federal government. Retrieved from http://bestplacestowork.org/BPTW/index.php.

Partnership for Public Service and McKinsey & Company. (2012). *Mission-driven mobility: Strengthening our government through a mobile leadership corps.* Washington, DC: Authors.

Petrie, N. (2011). *Future trends in leadership development.* Greensboro, NC: Center for Creative Leadership.

Sanders, R. P. (2009, April 30). National security reform: Implementing a national security service workforce: Statement for the record before the Senate Subcommittee on Oversight of Government Management, the Federal Workforce, and the District of Columbia. Washington, DC.

The Commission on the Intelligence Capabilities of the United States regarding Weapons of Mass Destruction. (2005, March 31). Report to the President of the United States. Washington, DC: Commission on Intelligence Capabilities.

U.S. Army Training and Doctrine Command. (2009, December). The U.S. Army Capstone Concept (TRADOC 525-3-0). Retrieved from www.tradoc.army.mil/tpubs/pamndx.htm

U.S. Government Accountability Office. (2012a, March). Interagency collaboration: State and army personnel rotation programs can build on positive results with additional preparation and evaluation (GAO-12–386). Washington, DC: Author.

U.S. Government Accountability Office. (2012b, June). Intelligence community personnel: Strategic approach and training requirements needed to guide joint duty program (GAO-12–679). Washington, DC: Author.

White House. (2011, May 20). President Barack Obama's remarks to the Intelligence Community at CIA headquarters. Press release retrieved from www.whitehouse.gov.

CHAPTER NINE

Advancing Strategic Work and Accelerating Leadership Talent at GlaxoSmithKline

Kim Lafferty and Steve Chapman

GlaxoSmithKline's (GSK) leadership strategy is closely aligned with the future strategic requirements of its global business. The strategy focuses on ensuring that GSK has the leadership needed to deliver on the organization's growth ambitions. Leadership development is a key element of the strategy, contributing to the creation and maintenance of a high-quality supply of leaders at all levels of the pipeline—leaders with the capability, capacity, and confidence to lead the organization in the face of a demanding business environment.

Historically, GSK has always invested significantly in formal training, coaching, and work-based secondments, but these have tended to happen in isolation from each other, rather than as part of a deliberate approach aimed at accelerating a leader's development. This makes it difficult for the rich learning insights to be fully integrated into the day-to-day process of leading the business. In 2010, GSK implemented the concept, popularized by Lominger, of 70–20–10: 70 percent of adult learning takes places on the job, 20 percent in developmental relationships, and 10 percent in formal training and development activities. Since then, significant work has been undertaken to experiment with different combinations of learning methodologies to ascertain what works most effectively. One of our conclusions is that the Future Strategy Group (FSG) represents an innovative and impactful approach to work-based learning.

This chapter outlines how FSG blends organizational problem solving and leader development within the business context into one integrated, intense experience. It illustrates how the organization is becoming increasingly sophisticated about how it develops leaders over time and how it accelerates them into critical roles with the appropriate capabilities and mindsets to succeed.

The CEO's Future Strategy Group

The CEO's Future Strategy Group is an accelerated talent development offering that was initiated in 2010 by Sir Andrew Witty, CEO of GlaxoSmithKline. Between 2010 and 2012, sixty leaders from twenty-eight countries participated in FSG. The offering was created in response to organizational challenges in two key areas. First, there were critical, ongoing organizational issues that the Corporate Executive Team were identifying and needed to explore and resolve. Second, there was a strong sense that GSK needed to strengthen its leadership capability in innovative thinking, collaboration across the businesses, and exposure to the external environment.

The unique feature of FSG is that it is both a *think tank* to advance strategic work and a *development chamber* to accelerate mid-career talent. The CEO and the Corporate Executive Team agree on the program's agenda, and FSG is managed out of the Strategy Office—both of which give it significant prestige and power. This arrangement also distinguishes it from the vast majority of action learning in organizations that is initiated from HR and then invites participants to search for projects that may be beneficial to the organization.

The purpose of FSG is twofold: (1) to diagnose, analyze, and make a set of recommendations to deal with organizational issues identified by the Corporate Executive Team as critical to GSK's transformation agenda and (2) to accelerate the development of key emerging, mid-career talent across GSK and give them visibility to senior executives.

There have been four cohorts of participants in the 2010–2012 timeframe. Each cohort consists of twelve to eighteen leaders who have been identified as emerging talent, and they work in groups of three to four. They are drawn from across GSK's business units, geographies, and functions.

Origins of FSG

Sir Andrew Witty created FSG as a vehicle for accomplishing multiple agendas that the organization was dealing with. Having taken over as CEO in 2008, he initiated a transformation agenda that required a number of significant changes to how GSK worked globally. FSG was designed to bring new, fresh thinking to business problems that exist across GSK businesses. The idea is that leaders who are not intimately involved in these issues on a day-to-day basis will look at the problems and opportunities from different perspectives. FSG was also designed to identify issues that GSK, as a whole, has energy for and wants to move forward on. It offers the possibility of giving visibility, priority, and velocity to internal discussions by producing a set of recommendations to the Corporate Executive Team that can be debated and acted upon. The Corporate Executive Team is the only cross-enterprise strategic decision-making group, and thus FSG was, in effect, invited to act as their thought partner.

Selection Criteria

To ensure that the objective of accelerating the development of key, emerging mid-career talent is met, the selection criteria are of critical importance and have evolved over time. While the earliest cohort of participants was selected based on intuition and gut feel, a more tangible, specific set of selection criteria has emerged over time and become a core element of the program. The key criteria for selection into FSG are leaders who:

• Have the potential to be successful in a more senior role as identified through the GSK integrated talent management process as well as through on-the-job observation

- Have a strong development focus, a high level of learning agility, and can articulate how FSG will support their careers and personal development plans
- Have an ability to actively drive their own development in the future beyond the program
- Are currently in a director-level role
- Can relocate to London for six months, with or without their families
- Can be released from their full-time roles for six months

Structure of the Experience

The experience is designed to be a six-month, continuous assignment with a focus on one project for the duration. Participants are located in West London at the corporate headquarters of GSK in a dedicated part of the building. The twelve to eighteen individuals are split into groups of three to four, and each group is given a project. There is no choice of who one works with or what topic one tackles, although in several cases expertise is required to be on a particular team. Cohorts begin in March and September of each year. While a process of continuous improvement over the life cycle of a cohort means that each cohort has had a slightly modified experience, the core components of the experience remain the same and include the following learning resources:

- A dedicated GSK coach
- Workshops from the Accelerated Delivery Program (ADP), GSK's internal change consultancy, to help improve skills of lean thinking, project management, and change management
- Lessons in innovation and creative thinking by an external expert organization
- Feedback from peers and senior leaders
- Resources, in the form of external contacts and money, for whatever the projects require to deliver world class research and recommendations
- Access to anyone in GSK
- A sponsor from the Corporate Executive Team

The ten projects that have been worked on over the two-year period are quite varied in scope and nature. They reflect the subjects that GSK is wrestling with. Topics include ones that are more internal to GSK (e.g., shaping GSK's 2020 environmental sustainability strategy) and those that are external (e.g., exploring how to create access to medicines for patients at the "bottom of the social hierarchy" in emerging markets and Asia Pacific).

The work of the project includes (1) comprehensive qualitative and quantitative research from multiple sources, including academic literature, best practices in other organizations, consultations with thought leaders, and internal data gathered from stakeholders and subject-matter experts on the current state of play and (2) a set of recommendations that addresses the topic in a systemic and strategic way. The intention is for the recommendations to be implementable once the project is concluded, although it is rare for the participants who completed the project to then implement them. The lack of accountability for implementation is thought to encourage innovation and more edgy ideas.

During the six months that the project is in progress, the project's sponsor acts as a sounding board to the team. The sponsor connects the team with internal and external experts, challenges their thinking, and encourages them to propose imaginative, bold, and pragmatic recommendations.

Career Progression for Participants

Although one of the selection criteria is the participant's potential for bigger and more senior roles, changing roles is not an explicit promise made to participants. In reality, role changes are often a consequence of the participants having been out of the business for six months, and on their return, finding that organizational changes had happened during their secondment, which prompts them to look for new opportunities. Given the personal growth that participants experience, they have usually outgrown their original roles and so the move to a new assignment is positive. The critical component is a thoughtful talent plan that identifies a suitable role in a timely way to avoid any concern on the part of participants that they do not have a route back to an appropriate permanent position. One of GSK's talent strategies is to facilitate

Table 9.1. Role Changes Made by FSG Participants

Role Change	Number of Participants
Moved to a new role in the same function	14
Moved to a new role in a different function	7
Promoted into a new role in the same function	12
Promoted to new role in a different function	2
Returned to original role	13
Currently on projects	12

more cross-business moves, and FSG may hold the potential to naturally encourage this movement. Table 9.1 shows the number and types of role changes made by FSG participants.

A Researched Review of FSG

Following the evolution and visible successes of the first two years of the FSG, we wanted to explore what it was delivering from the perspective of its various stakeholders. This work was prompted by a new vice president taking over the day-to-day running of the group with a fresh perspective on its value and potential role.

As part of our effort to understand the success of FSG and how its impact could be further enhanced, we interviewed twelve participants drawn from each of the four cohorts of the program. We also interviewed key stakeholders who were involved in establishing and running FSG. In this section of the chapter, we summarize observations about the key elements of the program. Verbatim quotes from the participants we interviewed are shown in Table 9.2 to help paint a richer picture of our findings.

Joining the FSG

The process of joining FSG was similar for all participants, in spite of the fact that they were in different parts of the world, doing varied roles, and working in different businesses. Typically, they had a discussion with a senior line manager about their careers. Then they received a phone call from the CEO Strategy Office

Table 9.2. The Voice of Participants

Findings from FSG Review	Participant Statements
Joining FSG held surprises.	"I thought we would spend more time and focus on project work, but by the second or third week when we were coached in open forums, we realized the focus on development was true."
Learning from experience was influenced by the context and content of FSG and by the social dynamics of the situation.	"There was no way for me to get through our project without stretching my skill set and capabilities in these areas (strategic thinking and enterprise thinking) . . . That was fantastic. The other piece was senior stakeholder management and being exposed to this at a global level."
	"The development was self-driven with a clear message that 'we will support you'. I felt very supported."
	"We had some really tough conversations. For the first time, we had someone who told us what he thought of us. It was undiluted . . . we were all on a journey."
Participants deepened their awareness of self, the business, a culture.	"The self-reflection and coaching that [my coach] gave me really helped me identify my self-limiting beliefs."
	"I learned that emotional intelligence is key."
	"I picked up confidence and became more courageous."
	"I got a valuable bird's eye view of the company."
	"I developed a much stronger awareness of different cultures and how to adapt, flex, and be more sensitive in these areas."

Table 9.2. Continued

Findings from FSG Review	Participant Statements
Home country, career stage, and re-entry expectations influenced participants' experiences.	"The language barrier made it difficult to express my emotions and feelings." "The relocation was a real culture shock." "I feel this would have provided me with more opportunities to change tracks if this had been earlier in my career." "Delegates should be mature enough to get benefit and young enough to give it back." "It has been very hard going back—we are missing the energy, the buzz, and the fundamental challenge to nail a project in 5.5 months with no wiggle room." "Having had to raise your game for six months, it [returning to my job] feels distinctly underwhelming."

inviting them to take part in an interview. This interview was chaired by a member of Sir Andrew Witty's team and a global talent business leader from HR. The call briefly described the opportunity that FSG presented and asked questions about their learning and career ambitions. The majority signed up and felt privileged to be invited to join the group because of the title of the program and the explicit promise to work at the most senior level in GSK. In most cases, the details of what this meant, the learning it would provoke, and the opportunities it would create, were not fully known or understood. Nonetheless, participants expressed excitement and anticipation about what the six months would provide, and although specific outcomes were not always known at the beginning, they expressed a huge level of satisfaction and gratitude at the end.

The FSG Developmental Experience

The head office location, project work, feedback-rich environment, proximity to power, and small working group are some of the critical components that make FSG such a potent and intense experience. Almost every participant interviewed spoke of his or her surprise at the development all received during their time within the FSG. This surprise arose for a number of reasons: a belief that FSG was simply about the delivery of projects, a belief that the 50 percent focus on personal development was simply "spin," and unexpected experiences during the program, such as receiving feedback in the moment and in public.

Key Influences on the Learning Experience

Participants' comments on the key elements that influenced their learning from the experience fell into two arenas: (1) the context and content of their work and (2) the social dynamics of the situation. Important aspects of the context and content of their work included the significance of being in "the center of the universe" (i.e., GSK House in London); the opportunity to work in the U.K.; working in the corporate center, which encouraged enterprise thinking; the strategic nature of the project; the six-month timeframe that culminated in a set of recommendations; the external perspective and ability to speak to a wide range of leaders, academics, and others from different organizations or disciplines; and the Accelerated Delivery Program (ADP), which brought discipline, rigor, and new language in lean thinking, project management, and change management.

Important social dynamics of the experience included new and different relationships with leaders from different businesses, geographies, and specialties; access to senior GSK leaders; the personal development, which most of them underestimated, which came from feedback from their peers, the VP who led the program, and their coach; and small and large group dynamics. The combination of these factors created a unique and incredibly rich learning experience that some participants described as life changing.

An important note is the influence of the formal training element embedded in the experience. Every participant spoke of how integral training in the ADP fundamentals was to their development, bringing some simple, practical, and methodical tools to their work. What was striking about the way in which participants spoke of ADP was that they hadn't simply introjected the tools in their entirety but were taking a personal and practical approach to selecting what they found helpful on a day-to-day basis. Participants spoke of improvements in the ADP delivery process between FSG cohorts and, particularly in cohort 1, how the training delivery had moved from a top-down "this is how you do it" approach to a more inclusive and engaging one.

Learning and Development Outcomes

The impact of the experience was varied. Everyone seemed to have a special set of takeaways, depending on the starting point for his or her journey. However, commonly cited learning outcomes from the experience were

- Efficient ways of working that enabled participants to be more time-efficient when they returned to the business
- A global mindset and enterprise thinking
- What it means to be a great leader of people, especially the role of coaching and feedback
- A model for problem solving—one participant mentioned that he created a mini-FSG to solve a business problem in his area

Moreover, participants reported developing deeper awareness in three arenas: self, the business, and culture. Participants pointed to a deepening of their self-awareness from a combination of the 360-feedback report they received at the start of the program, the in-the-moment and very public feedback during the experience, and the ongoing coaching they received. The combination of interventions created significant personal "developmental heat" that not only challenged their capabilities and competencies but their beliefs about themselves and others. The deliberate and intense focus on developing deeper self-awareness provided a valuable counterpoint to the norms of leadership development that they had been exposed to and created an internal shift that lasted well beyond their time on FSG.

Second to self-awareness, many participants spoke of how valuable it was to develop a broader, more enterprise awareness of GSK. This awareness was stimulated by the projects they were assigned and from working with senior sponsors, but also through being located at GSK House. One of the greatest gifts that the FSG experience appears to have given its participants is context. The boundaries of their experience were stretched by being exposed to different parts of GSK, different parts of the world, and different organizations and sectors. This has meant that, while still focusing on the local task at hand, their actions and decisions have become more informed by a broader, more sys-temic world view.

Finally, a number of participants, in particular those from the U.S., spoke about how much the FSG experience deepened their cultural awareness. Exposure to difference was another key factor that contributed to the developmental heat of the experience, and exposure to a culture that is different to the participant's norms was an intense learning experience. And although the challenge was of a different degree of intensity, even participants from the U.K. spoke of the different cultural norms and habits that they experienced working in a head office environment around the most senior leaders in the organization.

The Impact of Individual Characteristics on the Learning Experience

As we conducted the interviews, it became apparent that, although there were some universal experiences, there were some key indi-vidual characteristics that affected the participants' experience, including:

- *Home country.* Delegates who relocated to London from another country for the period of their FSG assignment had an extra level of learning and intensity layered over and above the project and development work. Living in a different country, often away from family and friends, provided a rich source of learning and self-discovery, combined with a source of strain and a drain on personal resilience. Delegates spoke of the challenge of staying connected with their family and friends, the difficulties the language barrier presented, and concerns over what awaited them on their return.
- *Age and time in career.* During the interviews, we explored with delegates the question of when in somebody's career the FSG

experience would be most valuable. Although there was some variation in responses, the general theme was to continue to maintain the rich diversity of the group but to ideally target individuals early in their careers while they still have a strong learning agility that has not been too "contaminated" through many years in senior positions at GSK.

- *Returning to the business.* As with a number of experiential development programs at GSK, the experience of returning to the business proves as challenging and insightful as the experience itself. For example, GSK's PULSE program gives employees the opportunity to apply their skills in an NGO in the developed or developing world for six months on full pay, and participants experience a similar issue with re-entry. These experiences provide participants with an opportunity to step back and witness their organization from a distance in an environment that is supportive of their learning and at the same time challenging enough to engender a balanced mix of excitement and anxiety—which they suddenly realize is missing in their day-to-day roles when they return.

A key factor affecting re-entry is the expectations that were set (or implied, or imagined) by the participants at the start of their experience. These expectations appear to have shifted and evolved with each subsequent cohort hearing stories from the previous cohort. The first cohort had very few expectations as to what would happen on leaving the program, and the majority of those we interviewed went on to new roles in which they were able to maintain the excitement and developmental heat that they had experienced within FSG. Those who were part of later waves spoke of their expectations that a different role or opportunity would await them at the end of their experience. No participants spoke of specific conversations in which they were told that the purpose of the FSG was to change roles, so it seems that expectations are set through a combination of success stories from previous cohorts that self-perpetuate within the current cohorts throughout their experience. These stories both fuel expectation during the FSG experience and cause an artificial sense of disappointment or even failure on returning to the business. This pattern is amplified with each subsequent cohort as additional success stories are written and fewer big new role opportunities exist within the business compared to the early days.

A second factor affecting re-entry is the bias created by the FSG experience toward external stimuli as the triggers for developmental heat. The majority of the stretch during FSG was created through an external stimulus (e.g., in-the-moment feedback, direct contact with senior leaders). An unintended consequence of the way in which participants develop during the FSG experience may be that they become over-reliant on external stimuli to generate the challenge, excitement, and personal resilience they have become used to and subsequently find lacking back in the business.

Recommendations and Questions Going Forward

The interview process yielded rich qualitative data and themes on the strengths and potential areas for enhancement of the FSG. Initial high-level recommendations are summarized below as areas for further discussion and inquiry.

Professionalism of the Process

The "form" of FSG has successfully evolved from some rather informal beginnings. Significant work has been done to formalize the components of the six-month program experience. However, there is still curiosity and mystique around the FSG that would benefit from standardizing specific elements of the processes to increase clarity and transparency. These include:

- Positioning with line managers
- Published selection criteria
- Induction process
- Training early in the process on how to learn from experience
- Ending elegantly
- Feedback on the project report quality, recommendations, and ability to implement
- Feedback on the delegates' performance and input into their development plans

- Enhanced involvement and contact with line managers before, during, and after the experience—with clear expectations regarding their roles and accountabilities
- Career management discussions

Organizational Value

Every participant had a rich personal learning experience as a result of a combination of the project, the relocation, and their peer group. However, there is an opportunity to bring a greater focus on the value of the experience to the organization by:

- Quantifying the quality of project recommendations and their value to GSK,
- Monitoring and tracking the impact of recommendations that were implemented,
- Gathering views of the individual by HR professionals,
- Monitoring and tracking the performance of individuals post-FSG, and
- Sustaining the FSG alumni network and deploying them strategically (e.g., to conferences, think tanks, specific projects, mentoring).

Role of the CEO, Corporate Executive Board, and Strategy Office

The origins and the title of the FSG set an expectation that groups would work in close proximity with the CEO and the Corporate Executive Board on strategically important projects. Although this is often the case, the evolution of the group, range of the projects, and internal structuring of the FSG have evolved over time. It would be valuable to take a step back and appraise the appropriateness of the title "CEO's Future Strategy Group," the impact of internal restructuring and ownership of FSG, and the selection criteria of projects that are assigned to FSG participants.

Setting Balanced and Overt Expectations

As noted earlier, the expectations of participants joining the FSG have evolved over time based on the stories passed on by previous participants. Although participants will always carry a certain amount of expectation by virtue of being invited to participate in the program, paying attention to the messaging early on and throughout the experience will help maximize both the learning experience and the participants' impact on their return to the business. Potential improvements include:

- Continuing the balance between 50 percent project and 50 percent personal development, but focusing personal development around developing leadership skills and abilities that will benefit participants in their next roles.
- Being overt early on about how participants will succeed in the FSG experience, and addressing the covert question of "competition or collaboration" through explicit conversations.
- Being open and transparent regarding the stories of previous delegates, their experiences, and the roles they returned to.
- Shifting the focus of FSG to be a developmental experience, as opposed to an intense interview for promotion.

Developing a Challenger Spirit

The whole premise of FSG is that an internal group of talented leaders is able to challenge the status quo and bring new thinking in from the outside to address problems and opportunities in GSK. As suggested in the title of the book by Dehnugara and Breeze (2011) on this subject, we think of this as nurturing a "challenger spirit" that encourages the participants to be agitators for change and to challenge conventional wisdom and existing orthodoxies. One area that was explored during the interviews was how effective internal leaders can really be, given that they are part of the system that they are trying to change. There was a certain sense that recommendations may be modified to fit the corporate environment. Looking at factors that inhibit this ability to challenge both organizationally and individually will further enhance the impact of the FSG. This includes:

- Reviewing the project-selection criteria and creating a bias toward projects that actively challenge the established norms of GSK or contain green field opportunities.
- Conducting a review of previous final reports in detail to ascertain whether the basis on which certain

recommendations were accepted or rejected was challenged too much or too little.

- Amplifying participants' learning by including developmental experiences that increase their ability to challenge the status quo and developing the personal resilience required to do so. This work would not only increase the impact of the participants during their projects, but would enhance their ability to appropriately challenge the organization when returning to the business.
- Enhancing participants' ability to self-generate developmental heat outside of the FSG experience to reduce a potential over-reliance on external stimuli.
- Being intentional about enhancing the development of learning agility, flexible thinking, developing others, innovation mindset, and enterprise thinking.

Applying "Developmental Heat" Principles

The concept of *developmental heat* refers to a rich learning state that arises out of experience. Lombardo and Eichinger (1989) identified eleven common challenges in successful experiential learning (see Exhibit 9.1) of which five must typically be present for developmental heat to occur. We may think of these as environmental or outer stimuli for learning. Appraising and enhancing the FSG participants' experience against these stimuli will strengthen the impact more consistently for both delegates and the business.

In addition to environmental stimuli, we believe that a certain amount of internal developmental heat is required to ensure that participants are altered by their experiences in a way that enables them to bring their new selves to their old roles. We think of this as the "inner work" required for learning. Further work is needed to develop this concept and the criteria for stretch and challenge in the inner work of personal growth and transformation.

Conclusion

FSG is an impactful, edgy, state-of-the-art leadership development program that has evolved during its two-year existence. Our

---

Exhibit 9.1. Common Challenges in Successful Experiential Learning

1. Success and failure are possible and visible to others.
2. Requires aggressive "take charge" leadership.
3. Involves working with new people, lots of people, or both.
4. Creates additional personal pressure.
5. Requires influencing people, activities, and factors over which one has no direct authority or control.
6. Involves a high degree of variety.
7. Will be closely watched by people whose opinions count.
8. Requires building a team, starting something from scratch, or fixing and turning around a team, an operation, or a project in trouble.
9. Has a major strategic component and is intellectually challenging.
10. Involves interacting with an exceptionally good or bad boss.
11. Something important is missing, such as top management support, key skills or technical knowledge, or credentials and credibility.

Adapted and reprinted with permission from *Eighty-Eight Assignments for Development in Place* by M. M. Lombardo & R. W. Eichinger. Copyright © 1989 by Center for Creative Leadership. All rights reserved.

---

recommendations reflect a desire to maximize its potential and position in GSK's differentiated development landscape. The ambition is to create a systemic offering that guarantees a potent participant experience, ensures a professional transition into and out of the program, and maximizes the short- and long-term value for participants, stakeholders, and the business.

References

Dehnugara, K., & Breeze, C. G. (2011). *The challenger spirit: Organisations that disturb the status quo.* London: LID Publishing.

Lombardo, M. M., & Eichinger, R. W. (1989). *Eighty-eight assignments for development in place.* Greensboro, NC: Center for Creative Leadership.

CHAPTER TEN

Developing IBM Leaders Through Socially Responsible Services Projects

Vicki L. Flaherty and Mathian Osicki

IBM's Corporate Service Corps (CSC), launched in 2008, uses international volunteering as a springboard for developing its next generation of leaders in a socially responsible manner while expanding business knowledge and opportunities in emerging markets. The CSC experience involves global teams of IBM employees working for one month in disadvantaged, developing, or emerging parts of the world to perform pro bono work for the public and private sectors that would not typically be aware of or immediately afford IBM services. The program provides a triple benefit: IBM gains more loyal leaders with a deeper and broader range of skills who can function in a global context. Participants gain a unique set of leadership opportunities and development experiences and view their employer in a more positive light. Communities in emerging market countries obtain IBM's best problem-solving skills, talent, and capabilities.

This multifaceted positive impact is the foundation for a program with a clear corporate social responsibility (CSR) focus. That is, the program represents a "context specific organizational action or policy that takes into account stakeholders' expectations and the triple bottom line of economic, social, and environmental performance" (Aguinis, 2011). Other labels, in addition to CSR, that might be used to describe this aspect of the program include organizational responsibility, corporate philanthropy, corporate citizenship, corporate sustainability, and environmental stewardship, which all have an underpinning of doing business in a socially responsibly manner (Aguinis, 2011).

The IBM Corporate Service Corps has been described as a "living laboratory for experiments in leadership development, market expansion, and social engagement at a time when organizations are under incredible pressure to change the way they operate in this, the first truly global century" (IBM, 2011a). Indeed, CSC reflects a new, very powerful model of leadership development with a socially responsible twist. CSC provides the future leaders of the corporation with a once-in-a-lifetime problem-solving exercise in a developing world. The program's sponsor, Stanley Litow, IBM's vice president of corporate citizenship and corporate affairs and president of IBM's International Foundation, says, "The CSC helps high potential employees develop smarter leadership skills while engaging organizations in emerging markets and helping them grow their business. Not only do participants learn first-hand how business is done in local communities, but they share what they know with colleagues back home and gain a personal understanding of what it means to be a global citizen" (IBM, 2009a). In today's globally integrated economy, successful leaders need to be effective global citizens and able to collaborate with people from a wide range of backgrounds and perspectives.

The Corporate Service Corps is one of the most successful talent development experiments conducted at IBM in recent years. Four years after its inception, the CSC has deployed two thousand IBM employees across more than 160 teams on assignments to nearly thirty countries, including Brazil, Cambodia, Chile, China, Egypt, Ghana, India, Indonesia, Kazakhstan, Kenya, Malaysia, Morocco, Nigeria, the Philippines, Romania, Russia, South Africa, Sri Lanka, Tanzania, Thailand, Turkey, and Vietnam. The program has expanded and will continue to expand to new locations each year. The CSC participants have come from over fifty countries.

The Corporate Service Corps has sponsored more than six hundred pro bono projects that have helped local businesses, non-profit organizations, and governmental institutions become more successful. Participants have worked on community-driven economic development initiatives such as developing growth strategies for the African Wildlife Foundation, improving school conditions in Ghana, helping female entrepreneurs in Romania, and providing operational expertise to micro businesses. When one team leaves, a second group may pick up the threads of their work, with the goal of sustainable improvements. The program includes partnerships with nongovernmental organizations, which play a critical role by handling on-site logistics, identifying the small businesses and organizations that utilize the skills of IBMers. The aim is to establish projects that challenge the teams to meet the goals of their project in locations where resource challenges force them to be nimble and creative.

How It Started

Employee volunteerism is not new to major corporations (Mirvis, Thompson, & Gohring, 2012). For years companies have been supporting their employees by providing time off to volunteer and hosting all-staff community service days. For example, at IBM, in 2003 the On Demand Community was launched to enable employees and retirees to find volunteer activities online that are aligned with their skills and interests, and by June 2010 more than ten million service hours had been logged by more than 150,000 participants. In 2011, during IBM's centennial year, the company hosted a worldwide Celebration of Service, and more than three million volunteer service hours were logged, primarily in human services, community and economic development, and K–12 education. More recently, companies have focused on matching the needs of organizations in the emerging markets with their company and employees' expertise in order to serve their corporate social responsibility and business strategy objectives. In addition to IBM, companies such as HSBC, Starbucks, Mars, and others have offered variations on this approach, but have not scaled their programs to the degree IBM has (Mirvis, Thompson, & Gohring, 2012).

IBM's chief executive officer in 2006, Sam Palmisano, introduced the notion of "The Globally Integrated Enterprise" in an essay for *Foreign Affairs*, where he contrasted the future organization against the traditional multinational firm. As the company focused on developing business in fast-growing emerging markets, it would need managers adept at working in a global environment. There was a realization that the company could not go to market in the way it had for mature economies; rather, it would be critical to address social issues impacting economic development in emerging markets (IBM, 2011a). The vision for IBM as a globally integrated enterprise was, in part, the impetus for the creation of a program that supported development of global acumen for IBM's top talent and future leaders. The idea for the program evolved from elements of other existing programs, including the Peace Corps and the National Outdoor Leadership School (Thompson, 2012). From the Peace Corps came the idea of helping underprivileged portions of the population. From the National Outdoor Leadership School came the central focus on making a difference through teaming. The program is very much aligned with IBM's heritage of improving the world and a belief in the importance of giving communities the tools, tactics, strategies, and resources for self-sufficiency to help themselves.

Who Goes on Assignment

Thousands of IBM's employees (of which there were well over 400,000 in 2012) apply each year for just a few hundred CSC assignments, making CSC one of the most competitive employee programs ever created at IBM. From its inception the program exceeded expectations; in 2008, IBM expected five hundred applications and received 5,500. The number of applicants has grown each year as awareness of the program across the company has increased and efforts have been made to integrate the program more deeply into IBM's talent management system. According to Mirvis, Thompson, and Gohring (2012), it may be easier to be admitted into an elite business school than into IBM's CSC program.

Employees from all strata of the population are interested in the program, including younger employees with a strong service orientation, mid-career managers seeking something new in their work, employees with many years of service who want to give back, and individuals interested in honing their multi-cultural and global leadership skills. IBM selects top management prospects for the assignments. Teams are formed from IBMers from across the business with diverse backgrounds, skills, and expertise. Employees are drawn from different job families, business units, geographical areas, and generational groups. The goal is to form teams of emerging leaders who bring unique perspectives and to expose IBMers to different areas of the business. Initially, the program focused on growing the leadership pipeline to the executive ranks; however, because of the program's success with strengthening the leadership capability of top individual contributors, CSC was expanded in 2010 to include executive-level leaders. These leaders also embed themselves in communities for about one month as part of diverse teams; however, they tend to focus on urban areas in more industrialized and developed geographies and provide more strategic counsel.

The application process opens each spring for approximately four weeks. Applicants complete an application form, which includes several short essays uniquely crafted for each application cycle. Participants are selected by country HR boards based on a variety of criteria such as tenure (e.g., must have two years with the company) and performance (e.g., must have strong performance evaluation ratings over the past several years). Some of the key factors considered during the selection process include, for example, having a service orientation, being a flexible problem solver, interest in increasing cultural awareness, adaptability to change, and ability to communicate effectively in a variety of situations. Because employees must be away from their jobs for a month, applicants must have the support of management in order to take an assignment. Also, when making assignments, staff builds in extra flexibility for the deployment timing, allowing for delays of weeks or even months if a manager needs an employee for a crucial period. Assignments to particular locations are based primarily on applicants' geographical preferences and the skills required for the planned in-country projects (IBM, 2011a).

Key to handling the application process is a decentralized approach to participant selection (Marquis & Kanter, 2009). Management authority was distributed by forming application review boards in eight regions around the world based on employee population density. The boards, which are located in India, the United States, Japan, two regions across Europe, and three regions across the Asia Pacific, are overseen by a team member and given a designated number of applications to accept for the region. This distributed approach supports scalability of the program.

How It Works

Selected applicants are grouped in teams of up to fifteen individuals, representing diverse countries, business units, and job roles (across disciplines such as technology, consulting, research, human resources, sales, marketing, and finance). An important design objective for the program is to provide high performing employees the chance to build networks with people with whom they might never otherwise interact. This also enables employees to bring different perspectives and expertise to solving problems and encourages interaction with people from different cultural backgrounds and traditions.

Teamwork is an essential part of the CSC experience (IBM, 2011a). These teams of top performers are given the opportunity to experience working as part of a leaderless group. The structure of the preparation encourages team members to take ownership of the experience and determine how they can best lead and contribute to the team. Christopher Marquis, who uses the Corporate Service Corps as a case study in a course he teaches at Harvard (Marquis & Kanter, 2009), indicates that the combination of strategic teaming and service learning in a business community makes the program worthy of study.

IBM relies on its non-government organization (NGO) partners to identify potential assignments with local organizations. IBM works with three NGOs, selected via a competitive process: CDC Development Solutions based in the United States, Digital Opportunity Trust based in Canada, and Australian Business Volunteers. The NGOs specialize in placing corporate employees in volunteer situations globally. They are critical partners, taking responsibility for all of the program logistics, which includes opportunity identification, project scoping and agreements, travel arrangements, and local logistics (e.g., accommodations and transportation). These partners are key to IBM's ability to make a difference in local communities, and they ensure IBM has reach around the globe.

A senior advisory structure was created to govern the program. This sponsoring group, which includes key leaders such as executives from human resources, marketing and communications, corporate finance, and key country general managers, provides recommendations and oversight. The program is funded through the IBM Foundation and is non-revenue-generating. The company invests roughly $5 million per year to run the program (Tergesen, 2012).

Team Preparation

Prior to departure, the teams engage in three months of preparatory work to learn about global teaming, cultural adaptability, corporate social responsibility, project goals, and the socioeconomic and political realities of their destination countries. Teams are guided through the preparation phase by a facilitator who is a CSC alumnus. Another CSC alumnus from the country to which the team will be deployed also supports the team by answering questions and by sharing his or her understanding of the culture, lessons learned, practical tips, and other insights.

Several of the preparation activities encourage self-reflection and self-insight, including reaching clarity about personal and professional goals for the assignment and understanding one's individual learning styles and strengths, for example. A robust curriculum was developed and has been enhanced since the program's inception. The learning focuses on developing useful problem statements, applying a consultative approach, participating in effective negotiation, team building, and, among other topics, understanding the customs, language, and work culture of the host country. There are also learning modules and team discussion related to corporate social responsibility and international development. Employees use conference calls, along with a variety of online tools including blogs, wikis, and data repositories, to complete their preparation virtually. They move through a structured learning plan that is delivered via a learning management system.

Goodman (2012) indicates that exposure to other cultures is insufficient to glean benefits such as increased creativity and innovation; proper training, understanding, and appreciation of fundamental cultural differences and values are essential because they impact workplace relationships. Through IBM's cultural preparation, employees become familiar with some of the cultural differences that Goodman says are key to building working relationships: attitude toward hierarchy, attitude toward time and relationships, future/past orientation, preference for risk taking, direct/indirect communication styles, preference for group/ individual behavior and recognition, attitudes toward fairness of applying rules to all people equally, and action versus being orientation.

On Assignment

Teams are on assignment in-country for four weeks. On location, the teams work with local governments, universities, and business groups on a variety of initiatives, engaged in projects that intersect business, technology, and society. CSC volunteers join together to improve the lives of the world's citizens by working on projects that target disaster recovery, infrastructure improvements, economic development, business processes, information and communication technologies, or one of the many other issues vital to healthy businesses and communities. Participants have worked on projects that range from building strategy to developing new technologies in support of growing tourism, promoting digital entrepreneurship, preventing violence, improving public water quality, and alleviating poverty. Exhibit 10.1 provides three examples of CSC team projects.

Teams usually begin their on-site work by building relationships with their clients and clarifying the scope of their projects. During the first two weeks, team members gather information by interviewing a wide variety of stakeholders. During the second two weeks, they develop plans and proposals for their clients. During their work, the team may research best practices and consult with IBM experts. The final days are usually spent developing client recommendations, culminating in a final meeting and presentation of ideas.

Typically, larger teams are divided into sub-teams to focus on specific projects. The sub-teams work in parallel on distinct, perhaps related, projects and take advantage of the opportunity

Exhibit 10.1. Sample CSC Team Projects

Recife, Brazil

Team	Fifteen individuals from eleven countries, including Australia, Austria, Canada, Germany, Ireland, Japan, Singapore, Switzerland, Romania, United Kingdom, and the United States.
Client	Participants worked with a total of five NGO partners on a variety of projects with work scope ranging from data management to organization development to international business.
Projects	Create a cloud-based portal solution for an NGO that uses architect groups to design childcare centers around the country.
	Develop a strategic roadmap to achieve a 2020 vision for a business incubator at a state university.
	Create a collaboration platform to improve communication and engage volunteers for an NGO that monitors indicators of sustainable development in Recife.
	Design a data management system for a youth-focused NGO that links students to job opportunities in the marketplace.
	Develop a strategy for micro and small enterprises to engage in international business.

Accra, Ghana

Team	Twelve individuals from the following countries: Australia, Brazil, China, Germany, India, Ireland, Singapore, and the United States.
Client	This was the first full team to fall under the umbrella of the Center for Excellence in International Corporate Volunteerism (CEICV), a partnership between the U.S. Agency for International Development (USAID) and IBM, with CDC Development Solutions as the implementing partner. The team completed work to support the Ministry of Health in developing a five-year supply chain master plan.

Continued

Exhibit 10.1 continued

Projects   Develop a roadmap for an information system that supports health commodity requirements for the public sector health system.

Develop a cost model for a proposed supply chain management unit.

Develop a risk management and mitigation strategy for the supply chain management unit and draft an intervention strategy for the supply chain master plan.

Novosibirsk, Russia

Team   Ten individuals from six different countries, including Brazil, China, India, Mexico, Slovakia, and the United States.

Client   The team collaborated with several organizations, including a technical university, the Ministry of Education, and an organization focused on democratic development.

Projects Develop a marketing strategy for a regional civil society organization.

Develop a system for evaluation of innovation activities at higher education institutions for the regional administration.

Design an Information Society portal for the city administration.

Conduct a SWOT analysis of a technical university's research and innovation activities.

to collaborate collectively, to leverage the broad expertise of the full team. Often there are opportunities for the full team to come together to make presentations at local schools, colleges, or businesses (for example, focused on careers). In some instances, a team or sub-team's work in country may extend from the work of a previously deployed CSC team.

Although it is impossible to quantify the full value the CSC teams deliver for clients, IBM (2011a) indicates that, in billable hour terms, the average team of ten provides roughly $250,000 in high-quality IT and business consulting.

Post-Assignment Give-Back

After their in-country service, employees share their experiences in their home communities and with the company. During the two months after completing an assignment, employees are asked to harvest insights from their experiences. This phase of the assignment is unstructured, with participants identifying opportunities to share their experiences. They pass their insights and learning about the culture and context of working in emerging markets to their teams, businesses, and communities inside and outside of the company. Often alumni want to continue their experience in some way and give back in more structured ways, including participating as team facilitators, guiding other teams through the three-month preparation process, or acting as a mentor to teams preparing for their assignments. Alumni are sometimes also invited to contribute to the program, for example, by participating in the application review process or helping with program enhancements. Returning teams are also responsible for placing team project documents on a central website where the material is available for others.

Program Impact

IBM Corporate Services Corps experiences have been shared in newspapers, magazines, periodicals, radio broadcasts, YouTube, and a variety of other media, including blogs and social media shared by CSC (visit ibm.com/corporateservice corps). When reading or listening to the personal accounts, you will clearly see that the CSC experience has a huge impact on the individual IBMer as well as a positive impact on IBM and the local community served.

Impact on Participants

Since the inception of CSC, three studies have been conducted that provide insight into the value of the experience

Exhibit 10.2. Key Learning Areas During the CSC Experiences

- Engage with varied working styles and cultures.
- Follow local business rules of engagement that are different from own.
- Be empathic and respect others' views.
- Embrace openness and share one's own experiences.
- Find common ground and mutually agreeable ways forward.
- Consider others' objectives, aspirations, constraints, and cultures.
- Take responsibility and follow through on commitments.
- Be honest and share own perspectives and differences of opinion.
- Spend social time together.
- Appreciate the value of listening.
- Look at situations from different perspectives.
- Adapt to varied clients and situations.
- Discover own potential and gain self-insight.
- Gain clearer appreciation of own priorities and ways to make a difference.
- Boost the desire to complete career with company.
- Increase understanding of the company's role in the developing world.
- Learn about industries and job functions different from one's own.
- Understand working styles and preferences of different generational groups.
- Develop mentoring relationships and enduring friendships.
- Build a strong global network.

for participants, especially related to leadership development opportunities. Exhibit 10.2 highlights some of the key areas where employees developed as a result of their experiences.

First, Christopher Marquis, assistant professor at Harvard Business School, conducted a program evaluation study to examine the impact and outcomes after CSC was initially launched (IBM, 2009b). One of the main purposes of the evaluation, which involved surveying program participants, was to understand how the program affected individual CSC participants. Key areas where the program was found to have an impact included global leadership skills (using open-ended questions for establishing ties with others when there are language and cultural differences, dealing with ambiguity and lack of control, and building "resilience" or the ability to deal with adversity and challenges), cultural intelligence and global awareness (having heightened understanding of global differences and how to work in different business climates and cultures), and intrapersonal growth (feeling changed as a person as a result of being exposed to the culture of an assignment and spending significant time with a diverse team).

A survey conducted by IBM CSC staff in 2011 included 575 CSC respondents (60 percent response rate). This research found that a majority of participants expanded their cultural awareness, increased their understanding of IBM's role in the developing world, and received a boost to their desire to complete their business careers at IBM. Also, Marquis showed that alumni of the program come back from their assignments invigorated and clearer about their priorities and ways they can make a difference (IBM, 2009b). In fact, Hewlett (2012) points to such programs as great ways for individuals to inject excitement into their jobs, see their employers in a kinder light, and discover meaning in their careers. In line with Greening and Turban's (2000) Social Identity Theory research, which found that employees have a higher self-image when working for a company that is perceived as socially responsible, participants indicate that the program has a positive impact on their perceptions of themselves as individuals. Logically, doing the right thing for an underprivileged part of the world for a few weeks is bound to have a positive impact on those who participate.

A survey was administered to all of the approximately 1,500 IBM CSC alumni in March 2012 in order to gain a richer understanding of how the CSC experience helps IBMers grow their leadership competencies. The 483 survey participants (approximately 30 percent response rate) came from across IBM's business units, represented all of IBM's job families, and were spread across the globe. The study was specifically focused on leadership as defined by IBM's competency model (see Table 10.1 for a list of the nine leadership competencies).

Table 10.1. Extent to Which IBM CSC Experience Helped Develop Competencies

Competency	Percent of participants reporting "to a large or extremely large extent"
Collaborate globally	95.2%
Embrace challenge	95.2%
Build mutual trust	89.7%
Communicate for impact	87.6%
Influence through expertise	87.5%
Partner for clients' success	82.8%
Help IBMers succeed	78.3%
Continuously transform	76.9%
Act with a systemic perspective	72.8%

Over 95 percent of the survey respondents indicated that the IBM CSC experience is better than most or one of the best leadership development programs for building IBM competencies, with 77 percent reporting the IBM CSC experience as one of the best leadership development approaches and another 18 percent indicating the CSC experience is better than most. These results are in alignment with previous survey data gathered by CSC program staff in 2011 that reported 93 percent of respondents felt that the CSC experience was the best or one of the best leadership experiences in IBM and 88 percent felt that their experience helped them develop their leadership skills.

The 2012 survey found that survey respondents consider the CSC experience to be helpful in developing all nine of the IBM competencies, with Collaborate Globally, Embrace Challenge, and Build Mutual Trust topping the list. For example, 95 percent of respondents indicated that their IBM CSC experience helped them develop the Collaborate Globally and Embrace Challenge competencies to a large or extremely large extent. Refer to Table 10.1 for how each of the competencies measured up.

Collaborate Globally

Given that global collaboration is the very essence of the CSC program, it is no surprise that collaborate globally was identified as a top competency developed through the CSC experience. For some IBMers, their CSC experience was their first opportunity to participate on a global team with colleagues from around the world. Some IBMers work with international teams as a part of their jobs but interact with their colleagues virtually; these individuals found that the on-the-ground, in-person engagement of the teams deepened their understanding of what it means to work together across boundaries.

Individuals repeatedly pointed out that they had been able to learn as much from their team members as they did from being abroad for a month. A key benefit was learning about the working styles and cultures of their team members, not just their host country and client. Their team experiences also enabled them to learn about industries and job functions different from their own, as well as working with peers from different generational groups. Marquis and Kanter (2009) found teaming was a key variable underlying many of the positive program impacts, with most CSC participants seeing the opportunity to work on a diverse team as one of the most beneficial parts of their assignments.

In the 2012 research, many participants noted that they built strong relationships with their teammates during their CSC experience, some describing enduring or life-long friendships. The team building on assignment sets the foundation for informal mentoring relationships and ad-hoc collaboration that continues after the in-country experience. Alumni return to their jobs with a stronger global network. They know IBMers doing different kinds of work located in different parts of the world and have a web of relationships that serves them and IBM in the future.

Collaborating globally also took the form of learning to understand local business rules of engagement, different sensibilities driven by cultural norms, and varied approaches and styles for addressing challenges. The challenges inherent in collaborating with people from different cultures provided opportunities to be empathic and respect others' views as well as embrace openness and share one's own experiences. Even with the differences among global team members, some survey respondents noted that IBMers have a common set of shared values related to clients, trust, and collaboration—as well as similar approaches and methods—that support engaging quickly together to create value. Shared values enabled the teams to find common ground and mutually agreeable ways forward, and they work through differences to present a united, "One IBM" front to the client.

Build Mutual Trust

Participants clearly saw relationship building as the heart of creating mutual trust, according to the 2012 survey comments. Participants learned to find common ground with others who had different objectives, aspirations, constraints, and cultures. They did this on two levels: with their IBM team and with their client. Written survey comments indicated that the three-month preparation time was important for beginning the trust-building process. One of the factors identified as crucial to team trust was taking responsibility and following through on commitments because team members need to know their colleagues will come through for them, especially given the collaborative nature of the work. Another important factor was being honest and sharing perspectives and differences of opinion for the greater success of the team and the client, within a context of shared goals. There was recognition that personal trust forms the foundation for professional trust, and participants found that spending time together engaged in social activities as a team and with their clients was key to their reaching a point at which their clients could appreciate the expertise they brought to the situation.

Embrace Challenge

In response to the 2012 survey, IBMers reported that their assignments challenged them to get out of their comfort zones and embrace challenge in a variety of ways. For example, survey respondents identified the following types of challenges: having unclear and changing work scope, working on a project outside their normal area of expertise, performing with limited resources, delivering value within a limited timeframe, working in unique and sometimes difficult living situations, dealing with many new and different things at once, and varied demands of communication—with team members, clients, and stakeholders as diverse as farmers to political officials. The payoff for being open and "going with the flow" through the challenges was personal learning that included appreciating the importance of listening, looking at situations from different perspectives, adapting to clients and situations, and learning about different cultures and work styles.

Impact for IBM

IBM benefits in a variety of ways from the program. In addition to helping IBM fulfill its commitment to being a socially responsible organization, the CSC strengthens IBM's ability to attract and retain top talent, develops more knowledgeable staff, enhances the company's reputation, positively impacts financial performance, and creates a strong pipeline of leaders.

Studies have shown a link between CSR activities such as CSC and a strengthened ability to attract top talent, engage current employees, and increase commitment to the organization (Weiner, 2013). For example, within Person-Organization Fit Theory, where fit is "the congruence between the norms and values of organizations and the values of a person" (Chatman, 1989), applicants or employees who value CSR will be attracted to companies that practice CSR (Judge & Cable, 1997), and in turn, will create an organization of global citizens.

Staff who have been on assignment develop qualities that contribute to innovation and market creation, including greater knowledge of countries that are important to business expansion, greater sensitivity to individuals working in different parts of the world, and broadened networks of professional colleagues around the world. Additionally, having an enhanced reputation in the countries where programs are implemented ultimately contributes to the company's ability to win new business. For example, the company credits generation of about $5 million to date, including a contract awarded in April 2010 to manage two public service programs for Nigeria's Cross River State (Tergesen, 2012).

Beyond obvious financial benefits such as tax incentives for participating in philanthropic activities, the investment community is more likely to support a company that acts responsibly. A company that thinks about the future is also likely to outperform competitors over the long term. In the United States, responsible investing is worth more than $2 trillion, while in the UK—Europe's largest market—it is valued at £25 billion (Regester & Larkin, 2008). IBM also benefits from the linkages between the firm's financial performance and organizational citizenship behavior. Data linking the bottom line and corporate philanthropy generally show a positive or nonexistent relationship. In a cross-industry and -context meta-analysis aggregating data across fifty-two studies, Orlitzky, Schmidt, and Rynes (2003) found a positive relationship between corporate social/environmental performance and financial performance. In other studies, there are extraneous variables such as shareholder perceptions, value placed on philanthropy, and perceptions of genuine help, for example, which influence the relationship. Additionally, there are methodological challenges such as small sample sizes. While the mixed results may not convince some organizations of the financial benefit of participating in CSR activities, IBM is committed to its program and has been leading the way. There is an embracing of a philosophy proposed by Sara Weiner (2013): If it does no harm, why not participate?

McGill Murphy (2011) indicates that leadership is the single largest determinant of competitiveness in business. Creating a strong pipeline of emerging business leaders is essential for developing a strong leadership brand and critical to helping organizations sustain business performance. Kowitt and Thai (2009) pointed out how IBM and other Fortune 500 companies go beyond the basics of grooming strong leaders—how they have come up with new ways to test their employees in the global marketplace. These top companies for leaders know that investing in their employees is not a luxury, it's a necessity. Randy MacDonald, IBM's vice president of human resources, says IBM is committed to "developing leaders from deep within our global organization. . . . As we enter our second century, leadership development will remain at the top of our agenda as we groom the next generation of leaders skilled at collaborating across teams, cultures, countries, and businesses" (IBM, 2011b).

Impact on Society

With other companies following IBM's lead in creating such global service-oriented employee leadership development opportunities, the program's greatest impact might just be outside the walls of IBM. Imagine the transformational effect on global economic development if every company used a similarly powerful leadership and social engagement approach. At IBM's THINK: a Forum on the Future of Leadership in 2012, part of the company's Centennial celebration, the possible larger impact was explored. If every company in the Fortune 500 adopted the CSC model and deployed just one hundred employees per year to work on teams in emerging markets, fifty thousand skilled people per year would be sent out to address serious problems in developing societies. Larger commitments would produce even larger effects. Such activities could improve relationships between the people of the developing world and those of the mature democracies. IBM's longtime leader, Thomas J. Watson, Sr., coined a motto: "World Peace Through World Trade" (Federal Union, 2011). The Corporate Service Corps offers a new promise: If businesses share their skills and knowledge with the governments and people of the developing world, we'll all be better off.

Starting a Global Service Program

A program like CSC evolves over time—it's "a living organism" that is continually adjusted and refined (IBM, 2011a). A variety of changes have been implemented as the CSC has matured. For example, the size and scope of the program were changed over time to meet demand (e.g., increasing the number of participants selected each year, expanding the target participants to include executives), and the focus of the engagements has become more strategic for IBM and clients. Also, management concerns were addressed related to top performers being out of the field (e.g., by increasing flexibility regarding timing of assignments, creating learning to help managers see how they can gain the most from their employee's experience), and local relationships were strengthened (e.g., building mentor relationships between participants and employees at IBM local offices in assignment countries).

Additional changes have focused, for example, on improving participant selection. Changes to the selection process focused on identification of individuals with personality or teamwork issues or personal commitments that might interfere with assignment performance. Also, increased collaboration across the business was emphasized to strengthen HR/talent and business unit support for the program so that high potential employees consider the program as a career or leadership opportunity.

Companies interested in starting a global service program should consider recommendations from Mirvis, Thompson, and Gohring (2012), which include aligning projects with business priorities, building diverse service teams, preparing and supporting employee volunteers, coordinating with NGO implementation partners, and customizing to best align with company strategy and objectives. Exhibit 10.3 presents some key areas to consider when

---

Exhibit 10.3. Program Design Considerations

Program Objectives and Scope
- How will the program focus align with the business strategy?
- What type of development work will be provided (e.g., educational, environmental, and/or economic)?

Governance Structure
- What management structure will best support the program?
- Who will provide oversight?

Funding Model
- What budget is needed?
- How will the program be paid for?

Implementation Partners
- What relationships are needed to most effectively engage in the target markets?
- Who brings the needed expertise to meet the program's business and logistic needs?

In-Country Organizations
- Who are the recipients/clients (e.g., business purpose, country location) ?
- How will clients be identified and selected?

Project Identification
- What types of projects will teams work on?
- How will projects be identified, prioritized, selected?
- How will potential projects be matched with employee expertise?

Program Elements
- What is the program experience for the participants?
- How will the program be structured to create the experience (e.g., pre, during, post)?

Team Size and Structure
- How many participants will be assigned to a team?
- How will the teams be structured?
- What activities will be built into the program to support team building?

Program Duration and Timeframe
- How long will participants be on assignment?
- When will assignments occur (e.g., year-round, quarterly, or other deployments)?

Preparation Activities/Curriculum
- What preparation is needed to support participants (e.g., in understanding the culture of host country, building a cohesive team)?
- How does the program fit within the existing workforce management process?
- Who will design the experience and maintain the curriculum?

Participant Selection Process
- Which employees are eligible for the program?
- What criteria will be used to select participants?
- When will potential participants be selected?
- Who will evaluate and identify participants?
- Who will oversee and coordinate the selection process?

Program Impact and Measurement
- What does program success look like?
- How will program success be evaluated?
- What data need to be collected?
- Who will be responsible for metrics and reporting?

developing a global service program, based on the information included in the Marquis and Kanter (2009) case study and areas where IBM focused on making enhancements after three years of program operation (IBM, 2011a).

In Hurst's (2012) interview with Stanley Litow, IBM's vice president of corporate citizenship and corporate affairs and president of IBM's International Foundation, Litow suggests that companies interested in creating a community volunteerism program "talk to your employees." He recommends that companies start by understanding the expertise they have and tap into what their employees know about their communities. Further, he acknowledges an idea shared by Rosabeth Moss Kanter: "When you give what differentiates you in the marketplace, you produce not only significant benefit in the community but also for yourself."

References

Aguinis, H. (2011). Organizational responsibility: Doing good and doing well. In S. Zedeck (Ed.), *APA handbook of industrial and organizational psychology* (Vol. 3). Washington, DC: American Psychological Association.

Chatman, J. A. (1989). Improving interactional organizational research: A model of person-organizational fit. *The Academy of Management Review, 14*, 333–349.

Federal Union. (2011, June 16). World peace through world trade. Blog retrieved from www.federalunion.org.uk/world-peace-through -world-trade/

Goodman, N. (2012). The value of cultural competence. *Diversity Executive, 5*(3), 18–21.

Greening, D. W., & Turban, D. B. (2000). Corporate social performance as a competitive advantage in attracting a qualified workforce. *Business and Society, 39*, 254–280.

Hewlett, S. A. (2012, February 1). Volunteer to juice your career. *Forbes.*

Hurst, A. (2012, January 20). IBM: Tapping top talent, for good. *Huffington Post.*

IBM Corporation. (2009a). IBM selects 200 new global leaders for the Corporate Service Corps to tackle socioeconomic problems in key emerging markets: "Corporate Peace Corps" heading for countries including Brazil, China, Malaysia, and South Africa. Retrieved from www-03.ibm.com/press/us/en/pressrelease/27012.wss

IBM Corporation. (2009b). IBM Corporate Service Corps external evaluation. Retrieved from www.ibm.com/ibm/responsibility/corporate servicecorps/press/2009_05.html.

IBM Corporation. (2011a, September). IBM's Corporate Service Corps: A new model for leadership development, market expansion and citizenship. Retrieved from www.ibm.com/ibm/responsibility/corporate servicecorps/pdf/IBM_Corporate_Service_Corps_Essay.pdf

IBM Corporation. (2011b, November). *Fortune* magazine names IBM #1 global company for leaders. Retrieved from: www.tradershuddle .com/20111103329361/PRNewswire/fortune-magazine-names -ibm-1-global-company-for-leaders.html.

Judge, T. A., & Cable, D. M. (1997). Applied personality, organizational culture, and organizational attraction. *Personnel Psychology, 50,* 359–394.

Kowitt, B., & Thai, K. (2009, November 19). Top companies for leaders. *Fortune.*

Marquis, C., & Kanter, R. M. (2009, March). IBM: The Corporate Service Corps. *Harvard Business Review Case Study*: 9–409–106.

McGill Murphy, R. (2011, November 3). How do great companies groom talent? *Fortune.*

Mirvis, P., Thompson, K., & Gohring, J. (2012). Toward next-generation leadership: Global service. *Leader to Leader, (64)*, 20–26.

Orlitzky, M., Schmidt, F. L., & Rynes, S. L. (2003). Corporate social and financial performance: A meta-analysis. *Organizational Studies, 24,* 403–441.

Palmisano, S. (2006, May/June). The globally integrated enterprise. *Foreign Affairs.*

Regester, M., & Larkin, J. (2008). *Risk issues and crisis management in public relations: A casebook of best practice.* London, UK: Kogan Page.

Tergesen, A. (2012, January 8). Doing good to do well: Corporate employees help and scope out opportunities in developing countries. *Wall Street Journal.*

Thompson, K. (2012). Personal communication.

Weiner, S. P. (2013). Corporate philanthropy and the role of industrial-organizational psychology. In J. B. Olson-Buchanan, L. L. Koppes-Bryan, & L. Foster Thompson (Eds.), *Using I-O psychology for the greater good: Helping those who help others* (pp. 148–175). New York, NY: Routledge.

CHAPTER ELEVEN

Using Part-Time Assignments to Broaden the Senior Leadership Pipeline at Genentech

Nisha Advani

Director Development Pathways (DDP) is an innovative, integrated talent development experiment launched at Genentech, the pioneer biotech company deeply focused on scientific excellence from its inception. In its early stages, Genentech had a clear purpose and strong leadership, and people, like ideas, flowed quite readily across one primary site company. As Genentech grew bigger and more complex, employees found it more challenging to cross the functional silos, formally or informally, to broaden their knowledge of the business. This strategic, end-to-end perspective, requiring cross-functional understanding of the business, is critical for success at higher levels of leadership. Furthermore, wide networks across the company are essential both for getting work done, as well as for enabling people to feel part of a community; yet increased size and time demands made it more difficult for leaders to build and maintain them, particularly across functions.

Note: The author warmly thanks Tanja Miller for partnering in the design, development, and implementation of DDP and for leading the creation of the valuable website. Without her, the experience would have been quite different and certainly not as much fun!

Figure 11.1. 70–20–10 Development Framework

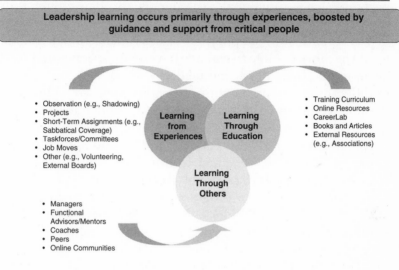

Leadership learning occurs primarily through experiences, boosted by guidance and support from critical people

- Observation (e.g., Shadowing)
- Projects
- Short-Term Assignments (e.g., Sabbatical Coverage)
- Taskforces/Committees
- Job Moves
- Other (e.g., Volunteering, External Boards)

Learning from Experiences

Learning Through Education

Learning Through Others

- Training Curriculum
- Online Resources
- CareerLab
- Books and Articles
- External Resources (e.g., Associations)

- Managers
- Functional Advisors/Mentors
- Coaches
- Peers
- Online Communities

DDP is designed to help director-level participants create customized learning opportunities for building cross-functional perspectives and business knowledge through part-time assignments supported by a targeted network. Participants are like "part-time exchange students" in a different "host" function, with a solid support group to help them navigate the host environment while using a systematic development process and tools. The pilot program leveraged the widely cited 70–20–10 development framework (see Figure 11.1). The primary development methods employed were learning from experiences and other people. Educational components were also used, but to a lesser extent, mainly in the intermittent group sessions and through online information, presentations, and other functional materials.

By design, the first year of DDP was positioned as a pilot, as it set expectations of experimentation, shared accountability, learning, and the intent to use multi-source feedback to enhance the solution. Deliverables included an experience-based pilot program for a closely shepherded, nominated cohort of participants, as well as a "self-service" methodology and toolset that put the cross-functional, experience-based approach in the hands of participants and their managers.

The pilot program was designed to test the DDP approach of part-time, cross-functional assignments for development of a director-level population. The thinking behind the pilot was that if participants were shepherded closely in the initial rollout, it would be more feasible to manage the user experience and receive meaningful observations and feedback to assess the effectiveness of different components of this new approach. We believed that a cohort would also create a core cross-functional network among these carefully selected directors, which would provide them support during the DDP experience and beyond in their business. Group sessions were designed to bring the cohort together on relevant business and personal development topics. We also believed that the group program would create greater visibility and increase key stakeholder buy-in, thereby increasing the likelihood of a successful development, even in the solution's infancy. This sponsorship was very important given that formal cross-functional development was largely counter-cultural and that this solution had an innovative design of part-time experiences.

This chapter will narrate the journey of DDP's creation and launch in a dynamic business environment. For this, the context and pilot experiment will be described in some detail, including the design, participants, and organizing framework. In this knowledge organization that places ultimate focus on deep technical expertise, DDP was an initiative of experimentation and change. Actions taken to influence stakeholder buy-in and support and lessons learned from this experiment are as instructive as the program design, content, and tools. In addition, the DDP website will be described, along with specific examples of tools and resources for enabling successful development outcomes for participants.

Context

The founding of Genentech in 1976 marked the founding of the biotech industry. From its birth, Genentech was entrepreneurial in spirit and passionately dedicated to finding cures for unmet medical needs, standing tall for its focus on excellence in science and dedication to patients. Correspondingly, people were hired and rewarded for deep technical expertise and grew in the company primarily through their technical contributions in their domain areas. While the company was mid-sized and growing, an individual's personal interest, initiative, and relationships seemed sufficient for creating broader interaction and learning opportunities. As the company expanded, however, it became more siloed, and crossing functional boundaries grew increasingly more challenging. In addition, given increased complexity and workload, it became harder for people with big jobs to find time and informal opportunities to build a perspective of the larger organization.

A rapid expansion period of over five years changed the landscape and significantly stretched the organization. As the growth rate started tapering off, senior executives reflected on consolidating and preparing the organization for its next chapter. External and internal workforce trends revealed shifts in the talent picture. Changes in the external environment indicated hiring shortages for critical talent in the biotech-pharmaceutical industry, particularly diverse senior talent. Internal data showed turnover starting to creep upward for directors, who were the mid-senior-level leaders comprising the feeder pool for executive leadership positions. Analysis also showed that internal development and promotion for critical senior leadership positions in this unique, intense culture had been a more successful strategy than hiring externals. Simultaneously, in-depth surveys indicated that directors felt stuck and were asking for clearer development paths, help with developing their careers and navigating the culture, all of which had become more challenging in the now more complex, much larger, dispersed firm.

Human resources (HR) had also identified other workforce realities and challenges, including for other segments of the population. One of the most significant challenges was the mindset that career advancement meant promotion. With slowing growth and decreased job creation, promotions were less likely. Development therefore needed to be incorporated into employees' existing jobs. The company also needed to better address the needs of an evolving workforce, for example, women's particular needs of flexibility and customizability, employees' desires to maximize their preferred learning styles and choose how to use their time, and the changing expectations of younger generations of workers, who were a growing proportion of the workforce. Most of these issues were director issues as well.

Directors at Genentech are generally managers of managers, have significant responsibility and large jobs. They are expected to have deep technical expertise and significant people leadership skills. In addition, they are expected to have a strategic mindset, with end-to-end perspective of the business so they can make effective decisions. HR recognized that in order to support these directors and help them with their needs, concerted efforts were needed, and quickly. The company wanted to show directors that it was committed to their continued development and would create concrete solutions to support them.

DDP was one element in a set of initiatives designed to address the interrelated challenges facing directors. Other solutions focused on broader workforce populations; however, given that the director segment is the critical feeder pool for executive positions, additional attention was focused on this population. DDP helps directors enhance performance and continue to grow in their current roles, that is, it is a solution that supports development in place and preparation for future opportunities. The premise underlying DDP is that career development occurs over a long period of time across an individual's work life and can be viewed as a unique combination of shorter duration development pathways, that is, customized sets of learning opportunities, primarily focusing on experiences across functions. Experiences include job shadowing, observation, special projects, committee or task force participation, informational interviews, entrée into decision-making meetings, and so forth.

We knew that a director's developmental path needed to include exposure to and first-hand experience in other functions to gain an understanding of how the other functions contributed to the business overall, and how they impacted decisions he or she had to make in his or her own area. And for this level of leaders, building cross-functional networks was just as important as understanding other functions. However, it was not feasible to provide first-hand, cross-functional experiences for directors primarily through job moves or even through temporary full-time assignments. Given that directors are mid-senior leaders, usually with deep expertise and with jobs of large scope, finding "back

fills" would have been hugely challenging. DDP was thus envisioned to address this need and was mindfully designed to be a
flexible, part-time solution.

Development of the Experiment

DDP was unique in its design of learning through part-time assignments. The larger objective of DDP was to provide a self-serve
development solution for all directors, with a centralized, online,
user-friendly repository housing the methodology and tools.

Prototype Design

The pilot was designed to test the approach and tools and, therefore, functions where directors would most readily benefit from
broader cross-functional perspective were considered. The entire
end-to-end business was examined and ultimately four functions
(product operations, product development, marketing, and
finance) were invited to participate. In order to support development in place, the jobs identified were director roles that were
broad enough to allow participants to see examples of within-role
progression in responsibilities, skills, knowledge, and perspectives. DDP participants were nominated from these identified
positions and were expected to spend about 10 percent of their
time over six to nine months in an assigned host function.

In addition to part-time assignments in different (host) functions, another unique feature of the design was the rich
structured support network, which included the participant's
manager, the HR partner, a functional advisor, and an external
coach (see Table 11.1). The role of the manager was pivotal to
guide the participant's development through the DDP experiment. Since participants were carefully selected high performing
talent, HR partners committed to supporting and shepherding
them through their experiences. Each participant was also paired
with a functional advisor (i.e., a local mentor), who helped the
participant navigate in the host function. In addition, each participant had an external coach. These external coaches were
selected on the basis of their company knowledge and understanding of the culture, and were briefed on their role for each

Table 11.1. Roles of Support Network

Role	Responsibility	Time Commitment
Participant: Nominated high-performing director who would benefit from and is motivated to gain cross-functional experience	Take initiative to create and execute a development plan based on cross-functional experiences and learning through others.	Approximately 10 percent of time over six to nine months
Participant's Manager: Manager of participant guides and supports participant through the developmental experience	Provide time and flexibility to guide and support participants in their development journey. Help participants extract lessons from experiences and drive toward successful outcomes.	One hour per week—more heavily front-loaded
Functional Advisor: Senior leader in the host function who knows the function well and will make time to guide the participant	Assist participant to understand the function, meet key people, and navigate the culture of the function.	Less than one hour per week—more heavily front-loaded
Coach: Development coach who can help participant in assessing developmental needs and aspirations, structuring key conversations, and extracting learning throughout the experience	Provide tools and coaching to participant on selecting experiences and maximizing learning.	One to three hours per month
HR and Training Partners: Key HR and training partners who steer program focus and support participants, their managers, and functional advisors	Guide and support participants and their support networks. Provide guidance for reflection and application of learning for participant's current role. Provide input for program tools.	Approximately one hour per week—more heavily front-loaded

stage in the journey. In addition to the direct network, executive sponsors and HR partners in home and host functions agreed to champion the initiative actively. In many cases, cross-functional peers and managers also played important roles as teachers and informal coaches.

Participants

Participants were nominated into the pilot program based on a set of clearly communicated criteria, which included factors such as demonstration of high performance, showing interest in and making time for development, and high likelihood of benefitting from a cross-functional opportunity. Although the primary participants were the nominated directors, in effect, DDP created interactive development experiences for other members of their network of support as well! As part of the high-touch design of the pilot, these secondary "participants" received significant guidance (for example, regarding the program and their roles at each stage of the process) and were invited to all of the group sessions. Orientation meetings and customized guidebooks were provided to each constituent in addition to engaging them with ongoing group updates; they clearly knew that they were critical for the success of the pilot.

Organizing Framework

The DDP methodology is a basic five-step process, which served as the organizing framework for a suite of resources and tools available on a new DDP website. This website was intended to be the key resource for the post-pilot extension of DDP to the larger director population. In addition, as an outcome of their involvement with DDP, we hoped that this simple intuitive process would enable systematic, ongoing development to become second nature for participants. The five steps in the DDP development process are

- Assess strengths, needs, interests, and aspirations.
- Investigate possible cross-functional opportunities.
- Create a detailed action plan.

- Execute action plan and modify with new relevant information and feedback.
- Debrief and reflect upon experiences and extract learning for application back on the job.

The concepts of reflection and feedback are important throughout DDP, as they lead the participants to determine more accurately how they are doing—what is working well, what refinements they can make along the way, and how to best apply what they have learned back to their current jobs. For each of the steps, participants make note of specific actions to help them maximize their development (more on this in a later section of the chapter). Key questions are provided to help the participant reflect and best apply what he or she has learned back to his or her current job. Emphasis is placed on individuals creating a customized structure that will work for their personal situations and ensuring that they leverage important conversations and interactions with their support networks and others to help make their development experiences relevant.

Program Development and Education

The pilot involved extensive program development activities, from development of tools to gaining buy-in to the business value of cross-functional development, which was not trivial in a company that had built-in silos of deep domain expertise. One tool that was developed was a comprehensive development profile for each of the job categories represented in the pilot cohort group. For each job category, this required working with a representative group of incumbents and their managers to articulate typical responsibilities and key success factors in that job. Also included were types of development opportunities that job incumbents would benefit from pursuing.

The profiling work itself served to help people understand the initiative and job-based development. Given that this was a new innovative offering, extra attention had to be paid to major aspects of leading change: to recruit and educate all constituents, guide nominations of participants, and match them with functional advisors. Repeated communication to all parties was necessary and tailored orientation sessions were offered to managers with their HR business partners, functional advisors, and coaches. Every effort was made for all involved to hear an overview of DDP, understand high-level expectations regarding their involvement, and have an opportunity to ask questions and to interact with others involved in DDP, thereby initiating other small cross-functional communities early.

The Pilot Program

Participants created their own development pathways that were anchored primarily in cross-functional experiences, with guidance from their managers and help from others. Cross-functional experiences included an orientation of the function, its core purpose and how it fit into the overall business, key interfaces, governance bodies, priorities, and challenges. In addition, directors were encouraged to tour labs or plants, attend key meetings (especially of decision-making bodies if possible), shadow people from different sub-functions to get a first-hand view of their challenges, join a task force or project team if time permitted, and ensure time to debrief and reflect on their experiences with their functional advisors.

Group Sessions

Group sessions, interspersed about quarterly in the nine-month pilot journey, created opportunities to learn from role models, peers, and experts on select topics relevant to directors (see Figure 11.2). These sessions also included a core interactive piece to facilitate community building for this director group. In addition, given that this was a pilot in part planned so that we could obtain comprehensive feedback on the various components of DDP, a multi-phased evaluation strategy was carefully implemented, including pulse surveys at each session, and mid-term and final feedback collection mechanisms.

The kick-off session featured one of the company's most-admired leaders. She discussed her personal journey, explicitly identifying decision points and non-linear moves, and candidly shared reflections and lessons learned. She also responded openly

Figure 11.2. Flow of the Pilot

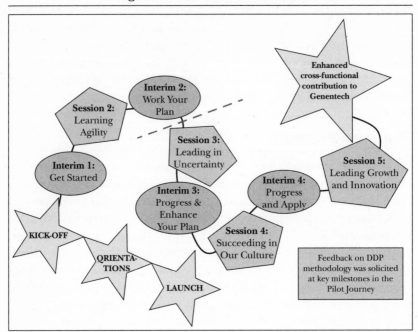

to direct questions about the tradeoffs in her several choices of lateral moves. Feedback after the session indicated that participants were greatly inspired by her story, and several commented that it moved them to think of new possibilities for themselves. Sponsorship of this kind reinforced the value of DDP and, with tools in hand and solid support, participants enthusiastically stepped forward to craft their own development pathways.

Business Events

Shortly after program development started, Roche of Basel, Switzerland, already the primary shareholder, bid to buy out all outstanding shares of Genentech. Merger distractions continued for almost eight months, but people tried to focus on "business as usual." Still, the timing was challenging, and the DDP pilot was developed and kicked off during this period of great ambiguity and angst. The keynote executive's presence and talk at the kickoff meeting were critical in visibly signaling the importance of broader knowledge and experience to be effective at the director level.

Given the positive feedback from the first session, participants enthusiastically looked forward to the second one, which featured the conversation with another highly regarded executive about his personal journey. Particularly interesting were his experiences outside his primary practice, even though he chose to maintain his expert edge. This session also included a discussion with Morgan McCall, from USC's Marshall School of Business, on his solid research and actionable ideas on learning from experiences.

The third session was planned to be on strategy, a broadly expressed need for this population. However, business circumstances cut short the pilot program at this point, leaving interested participants with the self-service website, which provided useful tools, resources, and guidance for part-time experience-based development.

The Self-Service DDP Website

The DDP website is the online repository for all tools and resources, organized according to the five-step development process, laid out by role to support the specific needs of participants, managers, and coaches (see Figure 11.3). In addition to housing DDP materials, the website linked to other relevant Genentech tools and processes to ensure the most streamlined and effective approach to director development. Of particular relevance were the learning and development resources for directors, including a mentoring guide and on-the-job toolkit. This toolkit provides a set of resources to accelerate everyday learning on the job, including descriptions of and tools for maximizing different kinds of development opportunities, such as stretch assignments, special projects, cross-functional teams, temporary assignments, and job shadowing. Other Links were also provided to Genentech's main development processes, such as performance review and feedback, 360-degree feedback, and development planning. Managers could also directly connect to the Genentech's manager toolkit,

Figure 11.3. Primary Tools Housed on DDP Website

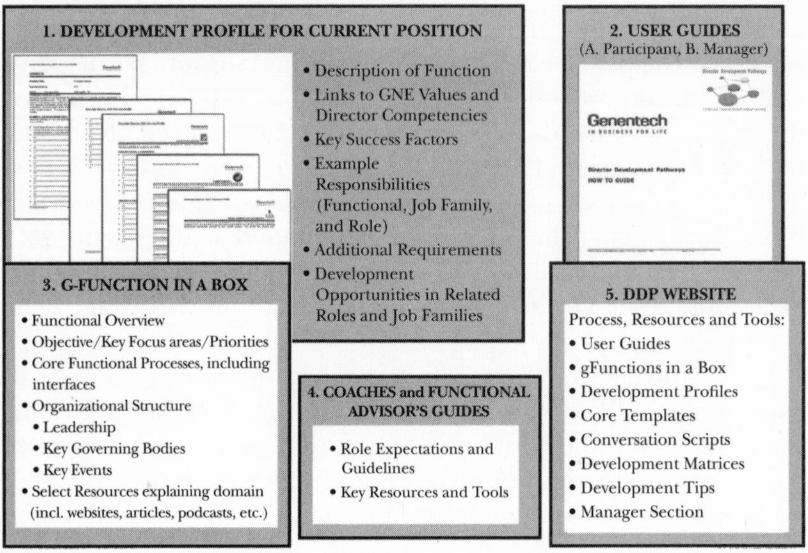

which contained a wealth of relevant people management information and tools.

DDP Development Methodology

The five-step DDP process guides participants to successful development outcomes and serves as the organizing framework for all the tools and other resources on the DDP website:

1. Assess strengths, needs, interests, and aspirations.
2. Investigate possible cross-functional opportunities.
3. Create a detailed action plan.
4. Execute action plan and modify with relevant information and feedback.
5. Debrief and reflect upon experiences, and extract learning for application back on the job.

Each process step is summarized on a single page, with summary tools including: short descriptions of the step;

suggestions for support people, including coach, manager, and functional advisor; key decisions and outcomes; relevant resources and tools, such as key questions for the director at this step, instructions for actions and templates to record them, and scripts to facilitate the needed conversations.

Step One: Assess

This first step involves the participant assessing his or her current skills, competencies, and development needs, and also interests and aspirations. DDP includes a number of tools to help participants effectively do a holistic assessment. A starting point for the assessment is for a director to understand how he or she is doing now, referencing the "development profile" for his or her current position. The development profile is a pivotal tool in DDP; it is similar to a job description and contains specific information that is helpful in creating targeted development plans. Each profile contains several elements, including key success factors that define how success in the role is typically measured, example job responsibilities that give a sense of the types of tasks typically performed by directors in each position, and developmental opportunities that outline specific types of development that would benefit job incumbents.

Development profiles can be used by directors, their managers, and the overall organization for other purposes as well, including to increase understanding of expectations in current role, development and career planning, recruitment and informational interviewing, on-boarding new staff members, performance planning and reviews, understanding promotion expectations, and selection for the job. Although this was a core tool used in multiple steps in DDP, even if a job had not been formally profiled, potential participants could leverage existing job descriptions and their own and colleagues' knowledge of positions to create relevant development pathways.

The core tool for this step is an assessment summary template that guides the participants to reflect on their developmental interests and aspirations, review recent performance and development feedback, list strengths and development areas, draft development goals, and list preliminary ideas on which functions might be valuable to gain exposure to. Having synthesized the assessment information, directors plan and structure their development conversations with their managers, leveraging the second tool for this step, an assessment discussion script. It is helpful to discuss their self-assessments and development interests with their managers and then together determine which cross-functional opportunities to explore. Although assessment is highlighted in this first step, regular reviews along the way and at the end of the process are important for both managers and employees to track progress. Key questions for the director in this step include: What are my strengths and development areas? What are my aspirations and interests? What do I want to focus on? Are increased cross-functional exposure or knowledge high priorities for my development? In what ways will broadening my knowledge and perspective be useful for me in this role?

Step Two: Investigate

This step involves determining the specific types of experiences that will benefit the participant in his or her development. Directors begin investigating targeted functions by reviewing job descriptions and development profiles websites, the DDP tool "Genentech Function in a Box" (described below), as well as by leveraging their managers and functional advisors' networks, conducting informational interviews to learn more about possibilities, and using their DDP coaches to assist them as needed. In this step, directors explore specific opportunities to meet their interests and accomplish their goals. Key questions include: What kinds of experiences and other activities will help me further my needs and interests? What specific development opportunities are available to me now in this or another function? The primary tool for this step is the investigation summary, which guides the director when planning which functions, activities, and people would be able to help them sharpen and accomplish their objectives (see Exhibit 11.1). The accompanying investigation discussion script is helpful for planning systematic discussions with their manager.

A unique tool on the website was the Genentech Function in a Box (gFIB), created for each function participating in the pilot. The purpose of this tool was to provide a synthesized, accessible overview of each host function to help participants make sense of it at a macro level and be able to navigate it more coherently. gFIBs

Exhibit 11.1. Tool for Step 2

Investigation Summary

Use the DDP Investigation Summary to explore possible functions, oportunities, and activities. With this information, revise your Learning Objectives and finalize your Development Goal.

1. List the functions (and departments or groups within each function) that would provide you the tartgeted perspectives, knowledge, etc., you would find valuable. (See gFIBs.)
2. List types of opportunities or potential activities that are availale in your function(s) of interest. (See Functional Development Opportunities.) If appropriate, note with whom and the approaches you would use to implement each activity.
3. Review and, as appropriate, revise your learning objectives, incorporating information related to potentially available opportunities and activities. Update your development goal if necessary.

were built by subject-matter experts in each area and included a functional overview, key focus areas and priorities, organizational structure, leadership and governing bodies, and a list of primary events (for example, annual conferences and summits) and select resources (such as websites, articles, and podcasts) that help explain the purpose and activities of the function. This tool was also created with the aspiration of being useable for other objectives, most readily for any new employee in a department.

Numerous additional development tools were linked in for use as needed, such as leveraging a mentor, working with a coach, and detailed matrices with tips for learning from experience, through others, and via educational activities.

Step Three: Create Action Plan

Having identified development goals and explored opportunities, directors need to select and link activities to create targeted and specific action plans. The critical tool to use in this step is the action plan template to capture specifics of their selected activities, events, dates, and names of people who will support their development. Guidance is provided to be realistic about the time these activities will take and obstacles they may encounter and proactively to identify some of the people they could leverage if needed. This plan is a useful map to help guide their DDP journey; undoubtedly it will be dynamic and evolve as they begin to execute it.

Participants are advised to review their plans regularly, listing new activities as they learn more, and to plan a systematic mid-term review of their plans; this will ensure that it is still relevant and has sufficient activities listed for the remainder of their time available. Key questions in this step include: How can I make the most of this activity? How will it help me achieve my development goals? Who can support me in my development activities? An additional tool, the action plan script, provides tips for conversations with their managers and functional advisors, so that they can enlist the support needed to enable success.

Step Four: Execute Plan

Directors will spend the majority of their time in this stage, actually learning about their target function. Activities initially identified and agreed to in the action plan are implemented during this time, including attending meetings with their functional advisors and coaches for guidance, assistance, and feedback as needed. An action plan is the directors' primary tool in this step. It serves as a map as they navigate, which they are encouraged to fine-tune and refine as they progress. Directors can leverage the gFIB as a starting point and are also advised to be flexible and seize unplanned learning opportunities that may present themselves. Key questions during implementation include: How am I doing? What can I do to fine-tune my action plan? What additional opportunities are available that I can target to enrich my understanding of this function and accomplish my development objectives?

Several other useful tools accompany the action plan, such as an ongoing discussion script that offers suggestions for discussing progress with their managers and functional advisors or others. In addition, meeting notes and journal templates are provided for directors to keep meeting and activity notes and to record observations, insights, and challenges, as well as ideas for applications back on their current jobs. These notes serve as useful memory logs for them to share and debrief with their managers, advisors, and coaches, enabling them to be specific and extract lessons from their experiences and to more coherently discuss applications. Genentech's on-the-job toolkit (mentioned earlier) is another particularly useful resource set during this implementation stage. It provides a rich set of general tools, templates, and guidance for learning from job experiences.

Step Five: Debrief, Reflect, and Apply

The final and crucial step is where participants solidify their insights and determine how to translate their lessons back to their day-to-day work. Self-reflection plays a large role here, with assistance from their functional advisors, managers, and coaches. As they complete the DDP activities, directors are advised to identify and record the perspectives they can apply to their current roles and responsibilities. Reflection and application may occur as they end activities and in conjunction with Step 4, as part of ongoing development discussions. In this DDP step, however, reflection and application are the main focus. Key questions for the director include: What was useful and what was not? How and where can I apply my new perspective and knowledge in my current role? What do I want to find out more about?

Directors are strongly encouraged to make time to reflect on their lessons learned and think through application ideas. The core tool for this step is the learning and insights summary (see Exhibit 11.2). This summary can incorporate reflections and insights from progress notes from the action plan and observations and ideas from the DDP journal. Recording these strengthens the commitment with self and increases the likelihood of follow-through. The accompanying tool of the learning and insights summary script can be helpful when planning their discussion with the manager or functional advisor.

Usage of Website

The website was an important repository for the pilot program. However, it is the essential tool for DDP as a self-serve solution

Exhibit 11.2. Tool for Step 5

Reflections and Insights Summary

Use this DDP Reflections and Insights Summary to record lessons learned and insights gained in your cross-functional experiences, opportunities to apply these, and new additions to your network.

1. Reflect and list key insights and learning from the DDP experiences.
2. Identify and list three to five opportunities to apply these insights and lessons back on the job.
3. Identify and list new cross-functional contacts to add to your network.

for a larger director population, which was the ultimate vision of DDP. When using the website for self-guided development, critical factors for successful outcomes include participants creating a customized and flexible development plan that fits their situations, identifying a support network that meets their needs, and ensuring that they hold and leverage important conversations and interactions with their managers and other key people.

Lessons Learned

Lessons learned were informed both by a formal evaluation that generated feedback and by our own observations and experiences with the initiative. A comprehensive evaluation strategy solicited feedback from all constituents on the multiple aspects of the DDP program. In addition, feedback was solicited on the fit of the approach of part-time, experience-based, cross-functional development for our company and particularly for the director-level leaders.

The use of good change management practices when introducing this new innovative solution ended up being highly impactful. The main practices included explicitly aligning the solution with business needs and ensuring that this linkage was articulated clearly; visible executive sponsorship across the enterprise, especially since this was a cross-functional solution; and repeated targeted communications to all involved parties. Another factor that impacted outcomes was careful selection of participants: directors were extra-committed because they knew they had been nominated; and executive stakeholders, direct managers, and functional advisors were also extra-committed because they had participated in selecting these special nominees.

Feedback on and observations of the components of the DDP solution were also instructive. Participants strongly endorsed the value of the development network, particularly the functional advisors or mentors, saying that without them navigation in the host function would have been much more challenging. Managers were critical for success, especially for supporting time away from their current roles. In general, coaches were most helpful in new and changing circumstances. Once they had traction in an area, director-level leaders did not turn to external support. The self-service website received strong accolades and clearly can be leveraged for any future experience-based self-service program.

Another novel component designed into DDP were tools and guidance to participants for reflecting systematically on their experiences and thinking through applications back to their jobs. Although leaders regularly have new experiences, this planful reflection and feedback to extract meaning from experiences was seen as a valuable practice.

Overall, the DDP approach was very well received and seen as relevant: the business need for directors to have solid business knowledge, cross-functional perspectives, and broad networks is recognized as being ever more critical in today's complex, fast-moving, global environment. However, multiple short-term sessions for an extended time seemed to be challenging for most directors. It is very clear that the size and complexity of directors' roles makes it difficult for them to leave their jobs for development, even for short durations. This lends support for a customized and flexible self-paced solution, enabled with online, accessible tools and support, rather than a cohort program. Given the demanding jobs of directors, on a case-by-case basis, they would need to determine whether it would be more realistic to take a short-term cross-functional assignment and find a back fill so that they could be away for a set period or sign up for a part-time project of short duration.

Important success factors identified were a customized and flexible structure and timeline and a network of support. Therefore, ready access to the self-serve website, with all the guidance and resources, will be critical as individual directors embark on cross-functional development experiences. As we reflect on our original objective of using part-time assignments to broaden a senior leadership pipeline, we believe that, with small modifications (e.g., regarding time options), this DDP approach would be a valuable inclusion in a suite of solutions.

In addition, we believe that this kind of part-time solution of assignments over a period of time (that requires some work realignment for participants) can yield strong outcomes and be more broadly implemented with a less-senior level of people managers or individual contributors. Furthermore, if a high-touch, high-resource cohort program were being considered, it would be beneficial to select areas of the business in which there are frequent interactions and hand-offs across functions, for example, early development into product development.

Despite business volatility during the pilot program, which cut short the pilot, there are many lessons that can be applied to future development solutions as companies continue to grow more global in mindset and operations. Increased efforts have to be made to help employees at all levels broaden their business knowledge and build cross-functional perspectives and networks. As, for a number of reasons, it is becoming more difficult and costly to move people around the globe, companies have to look creatively at work, both in how to break it down into manageable shorter-term assignments and projects, as well as how to leverage the work itself to develop their key people at every level. Knowing that experience-based development is one of the most effective ways for people to learn and change, it is sensible to consider such less costly and less disruptive, short-term opportunities for their best people, including at director levels. As they tailor these opportunities, the DDP approach, with its self-serve tools and support network, could provide a very useful methodology to achieve both project and development outcomes.

Resources

Charan, R., Drotter, S., & Noel, J. (2001). *The leadership pipeline: How to build the leadership-powered company.* San Francisco, CA: Jossey-Bass.

Corporate Leadership Council. (2001). *Maximizing on-the-job experiences for development during business downturns.* Washington, DC: Corporate Executive Board.

Corporate Leadership Council. (2008). *Key findings: Experience-based development.* Washington, DC: Corporate Executive Board.

McCall, M. W., Jr. (1998). *High flyers: Developing the next generation of leaders.* Boston, MA: Harvard Business School Press.

McCall, M. W., Jr., Lombardo, M. M., & Morrison, A. M. (1988). *Lessons of experience: How successful executives develop on the job.* New York, NY: The Free Press.

McCauley, C. D. (2006). *Development assignments: Creating learning experiences without changing jobs.* Greensboro, NC: Center for Creative Leadership.

CHAPTER TWELVE

An Indian Experience of Leader Development

The Fire of Experience and Krishna-Arjuna Coaching

P. V. Bhide, Meena Surie Wilson, Rajeev Kakkar, and Dilep Misra

Founded more than one hundred years ago, the JK Group (Eastern Zone) today is a multi-business, multi-product, and multi-location operation. With the Indian economy growing healthily at more than 8 percent GDP for the last five years, the group aspires to quantum growth by increasing turnover from the present USD$2 billion to USD$4 billion in the next four years and USD$8 billion by 2020. This quantum growth calls for enhanced financial resources and new strategic partnerships such as joint ventures, mergers and acquisitions, outsourcing, contract manufacturing, and technology tie-ups. To drive competitive advantage and achieve this vision, strategically identified positions must be manned by top performers.

Like other businesses, the JK Group is susceptible to dynamic changes in the global environment that bring uncertainty, complexity, and competition from unexpected quarters. We believe that companies do not compete in the market with just their products and services but, in the long run, with the quality of their leadership. CEOs and other top executives make crucial decisions on business strategy—where to play and how to grow and win. This entails developing a robust leadership pipeline to execute business strategy—based on developing tomorrow's leaders today.

The main human resource challenge is to manage talent strategically. Leadership development has to be dramatically accelerated to multiply the supply of leaders who can take on C-suite positions. The Fire of Experience program, strengthened by the Indian way of Krishna-Arjuna coaching, has been designed to meet this need. In this chapter, we share unique practical insights and proven processes integral to an Indian leader development initiative. We hope this will be useful to other organizations that would like to base leadership development on learning from experience.

The JK Group (Eastern Zone) Today

The JK Organisation was founded more than one hundred years ago and is a USD$2 billion plus industrial group in India. The president of JK Organisation, the late Shri Hari Shankar Singhania, a visionary entrepreneur and the guiding spirit of the organization, made significant, award-winning contributions to domestic economic activity and international trade. Under the leadership of Shri Singhania, and with the support of his family members, the organization has grown continually in diversified fields of industry. The companies in the group manufacture and market a range of products with strong brand names, with market leadership positions in their segments. These include automotive tires and tubes, paper and pulp, cement, V-belts, oil seals, power transmission systems, hybrid seeds, sugar, food and dairy products, clinical research, and insurance. With its nine businesses, the JK Group is recognized as a dynamic force playing a key role in resurgent India.

The group operates in almost every Indian state and employs more than twenty thousand people. Its nationwide sales and service network runs to more than eleven thousand distributors and a large number of retailers and service centers. The organization has a global presence with manufacturing activities in Mexico, outsourcing arrangements in China and different parts of the world, and exports spanning more than eighty countries across six continents.

The core values of the group are (1) caring for people; (2) integrity, including intellectual honesty, openness, fairness, and trust; and (3) commitment to excellence. Its ethos of care for people extends beyond the organization, with group leaders setting up and maintaining a number of educational, social, and health care institutions and supporting causes such as rural uplift, HIV and AIDs control, adult literacy, and population control. One manifestation of its commitment to excellence is exemplified by the highly reputed Harishankar Singhania Elastomer and Tyre Research Institute (HASETRI) that the group has established in India.

The challenge today is to escalate and diversify growth. Turnover has been going up at a compound annual rate of 16 percent for four years. Diversification into sectors such as thermal power and solar energy, defense, aerospace, and internal security is planned. The success of the group is based not only on more and highest quality leadership, but also on the use of the latest technology, continuous research and development, and innovation.

Finding and Developing Tomorrows' Top Leaders: A Fresh Approach

Historically, 5 percent of top performing managers, or approximately 120 future leaders, are identified. To avoid the subjective bias inherent in boss-subordinate performance appraisals, these high performing managers are screened through a three-day assessment and development center exercise. This creates a pool of talent drawn from all companies. To prepare them for taking up top leadership roles in the future, they are given additional opportunities to develop themselves.

In 2009, corporate HR (three of whom are authors of this chapter) decided to experiment with an alternate approach to developing their high potential managers. Our reasoning: We have tried the "develop competencies" approach; now we want to try the "learning from experiences" approach. There were several reasons for devising a different way.

For the previous five years, individual development plans (IDPs) had been used to develop competencies. But IDPs could not be tightly aligned to business strategy and growth. Several aspects of the IDPs focused on only short-term breakthrough performance on immediate project goals. Some aspects, such as reading books and participating in community assignments, were perceived by participants and their bosses as theoretical and impractical due to work pressures. Last, measuring improvement of leadership competencies was difficult and often subjective.

Job rotations were tried, but did not turn out to be feasible for applying across all the companies. More than 120 high potential leaders would have to be rotated through jobs lasting about three years. Although several individuals moved into top positions as a result, this system was not sustainable and could not produce the necessary quality and quantity of leaders quickly enough.

Fortuitously, corporate HR interest was piqued by the idea of creating learning experiences without changing jobs (McCauley, 2006). This seemed like an interesting way of getting around the limitations of job rotations. Corporate HR also decided to take a closer look at the 70–20–10 framework, which suggests that a ratio of 70 percent challenging assignments, 20 percent developmental relationships, and 10 percent coursework and training makes for efficacious leader development. Several possibilities emerged: perhaps challenging assignments could be aligned with business strategy and participants' career aspirations; perhaps developmental relationships could help future leaders to successfully negotiate the bends in their managerial careers (Charan, Drotter, & Noel, 2001); perhaps coursework on learning styles (Kolb, 1984) for participants and their mentors and coaches would increase their capacity to learn.

At this juncture, the JK Group was invited to participate in a study of the key developmental experiences of successful executives in India. Corporate HR signed up, hoping to use research insights on how Indian leaders learn, grow, and develop. In fact, the findings from this research (Wilson, 2010) became a central feature of the Fire of Experience program. Involving in-depth interviews with more than one hundred top and senior Indian leaders from eight home-grown multinational companies, the study generated a unique 7–11 Model of Development based on the seven experiences and eleven lessons that Indian business leaders described most often. Since senior leaders at the JK Group had participated in the research and the insights came from Indian business leaders, top management bought in. In collaboration with the business heads, corporate HR began to design the pilot program.

For the Fire of Experience pilot, senior executives from each business group reviewed the list of candidates already in the JK Group's leadership talent pool, narrowed that list to those who had secured an "A" performance and potential rating, and then short-listed that to three to five high potential managers from their own business group. Within each business group, these nominees' backgrounds were reviewed once again by the business head, unit/functional head, and unit HR head. Those perceived as capable leaders with high aspirations for advancing their company and themselves, strong commitment to personal growth, and highly positive attitudes toward their company and co-workers were selected as candidates for the program. With corporate HR aiming for equitable representation from all the companies, seventeen individuals from four businesses were chosen.

Each participant's progression through the program is linked to his overall career plan. Senior executives who take part in the selection process continue to be tapped to support participants' development in different ways. For its part, corporate HR ensures that there are multiple one-on-one and group-based interactions, which serve to monitor participants' progress and build collective rapport and trust.

The Fire of Experience Program: An Overview

The Fire of Experience program is designed to be a relatively safe environment in which future leaders are assessed, supported, and challenged. According to Carlos Ghosn (Ghosn & Reis, 2005), leaders are formed in the "fire of experience," when challenging and strategically important developmental assignments (without job rotation) are incorporated in existing jobs. The difficult part is to design experiences with the right kind of fire, customized to each potential leader—ensuring that they do not come out mildly singed, half-baked, or burned out (McCall, 2010). The program takes place over the short span of two years and unfolds in three major phases: (1) a preparation phase; (2) a six-month first assignment phase focused on becoming a better boss; and (3) a third phase in which participants are assigned two developmental experiences—their second and third assignments—each of which is four to six months long. All assignments are integrated with the participants' regular job responsibilities. The exercises introduced during the first phase—which are aimed at helping participants to become better bosses—continue throughout the program. The assignments that are part of the third and final phase are drawn from the seven types of experiences in the 7–11 Model (see Table 12.1).

This compact sequencing of assignments over a short time frame without a job rotation seems to be a practical way to develop junior, mid-level, and senior managers. At corporate HR, we think that up-and-coming managers can be cycled through the seven core experiences several times, such as during the early, middle, and late stages of their careers. First, the experience at each level will be different, with assignments progressively becoming broader and deeper (more complex). Second, the impact of the lessons learned (on the manager and the people whom he or she is leading) will evolve because leadership learning is cumulative. Developing leaders by immersing them in seven types of experiences promises to be a powerful way of speeding up leader development.

Table 12.1. Seven Fires of Experience

Seven Experiences	Description
Turnaround	Fixing and stabilizing a failing or underperforming unit or organization. Productivity and profitability are achieved by restructuring, downsizing, or closing down a unit, function, or operation, or by implementing an organizational culture change. These troublesome assignments often arouse turbulent thoughts and feelings in the manager. An example is handling chronic problems such as underperforming machinery or processes.
New Initiative	Building something from nothing by leveraging an opportunity to develop or launch a new product or service, adopt new technologies, craft a new policy or process, set up a plant or unit, enter a new market, embark on a new line of business, or create a new business entity. An example is substantially improving an existing operational process.

(*Continued*)

Table 12.1. Continued

Seven Experiences	*Description*
Horizontal Move	Transition or rotation to another function, business unit, organization, or industry sector where the work and work culture are different. The move does not involve a promotion and can be initiated by oneself or one's organization. Examples include line-to-staff and staff-to-line rotations.
Cultural Crossing	Regular, direct contact with co-workers whose values, motivations, language, life routines, and social customs are different. The manager may have to relocate to another region or country with different political, economic, and legal systems. An example is getting to know the views and practices of co-workers from a different region.
Increased Job Scope	A significant increase in budget, number of people to manage, access to resources, and complexity of tasks. Typically involving a promotion, an increase in job scope raises the manager's responsibilities and visibility. An example is a vertical rise to run a function about which one knows very little and with direct reports who are more expert.
Influence Without Authority	Influencing peers, higher management, or other key people over whom one has no direct authority, working across organizational boundaries, coordinating action across the organization, and handling internal politics. Examples include creating a cross-organizational network or representing the concerns of employees to higher management.
External Pressure	Managing the interface with important groups outside the organization, such as customers, vendors, partners, unions, and regulatory agencies. Requires representing the organization, negotiating with external groups, and building shared agendas among diverse groups. Examples include retaining an important but irate customer or handling media relations during a crisis.

In the next section, we describe the meticulous behind-the-scenes orchestration that takes place six to eight weeks preceding formal program launch. Integral to success, key aspects include framing boss-subordinate relationships as Krishna-Arjuna interactions; securing the buy-in of an array of stakeholders, each of whom has a clear and important role in the leadership development process; and aligning stakeholder commitment by providing in-depth orientation sessions.

Preparation: Creating a Safety Net of People and Relationships

Broad-based support from multiple stakeholders is woven into the fabric of the program. The Indian culture is collectivistic (Hofstede, 2001). This means that the needs of the group are typically placed before the needs of the individual. To ensure the future success of the organization, decisions about how to develop carefully selected managers are made collectively. This is followed by support for unlocking their leadership potential, which is enacted collectively. Finally, due to the collectivistic norms of Indian societal culture, stakeholders expect to be deeply involved in nurturing future talent. Recognizing these norms, corporate HR makes sure that all stakeholders are brought on board to the fullest extent. During the six to eight weeks in the preparation phase, several orientation activities are conducted so stakeholders become aware of how development occurs and their roles in the Fire of Experience program.

Broad-based involvement in leader development is culturally preferred in India (especially in family-based businesses); according to recent research, broad and deep relationships provide emerging leaders with the support they need to learn from experience (Yost & Plunkett, 2009). A related idea is that for sustainable behavior change, multiple stakeholders must become involved with guiding the leader (Goldsmith & Reiter, 2007). Finally, the naturally occurring bends in a managerial career—from technical specialist to manager of people to manager of managers to functional manager to business manager (Charan, Drotter, & Noel, 2001)—call on growth-oriented managers to become continual learners, and this is more easily achieved with social support for new learning. We propose that when emerging leaders are placed in a network of relationships, the necessary shifts in values, behaviors, attitudes, skills, and knowledge are more likely to occur because of social learning.

Given these insights about how relationships support development, even before the start of the first assignment, networks of relationships are put in place—primarily within the participants' business units or functions. Integral to the success of the program, the people involved at various points include the participant's boss (Krishna); the boss's boss, that is, the business unit or functional head (Super Krishna); an external executive coach; peers and subordinates; a family member at times; the unit HR head; and various members of the corporate HR team. As will be described momentarily, each plays a separate and differentiated role during the leadership journey of the participant (Arjuna). The relationship between participants (Arjunas), their boss (Krishnas), and boss's boss (Super-Krishnas) are foundational.

The Krishna-Arjuna Relationship

The boss-subordinate relationship is elevated by framing it as a Krishna-Arjuna interaction. Krishna and Arjuna are protagonists in the *Mahabharata,* a national epic of immense literary and cultural significance. A majority of Indians from all socioeconomic levels are familiar with the saga, which continues to have philosophical, mythological, spiritual, and practical relevance in their daily lives. (There is a separate initiative across the JK Group that uses the Krishna-Arjuna concept as the basis for boss-subordinate interactions; but the facets of the Krishna-Arjuna relationship are designed more precisely in the Fire of Experience program.)

At the center of the Mahabharata epic (written between 540 and 300 BC) is the rivalry of the Pandavas and Kauravas. These families, who are first cousins, battle over power and kingdom in a mighty war that is fought at Kurukshetra. The Pandavas are portrayed as righteous propagators of *dharma* or the ethical way. The Kauravas are regarded as deceitful and treacherous for the purpose of acquiring the mighty kingdom of Hastinapur.

Throughout the epic, and at various crucial times, Lord Krishna is a mentor, coach, and guru for Arjuna, a Pandava prince. Arjuna is renowned as the best archer of the time. To guide this ambitious and charming high potential leader on the battlefield, Krishna becomes Arjuna's charioteer. But just as the war commences, Arjuna becomes crestfallen and depressed and wants to lay down his bow and arrow and withdraw from the war. Not only his cousins, but his great-grandfather (Bhishma Pitama) and his gurus are lined up on the Kaurava side. Arjuna argues with Krishna that he does not want to stain his hands with their blood.

Krishna's counsel to Arjuna has been immortalized in the *Bhagavad Gita* or Song of the Lord, which is considered a sacred text by Hindus and used by people of many different faiths for spiritual guidance. Krishna's philosophy of life revolves around responsible action that is fearless, detached, and undertaken with a stable mind. This is *dharma* or duty or ethical action. To set oneself free from the limitations of egoism, one must follow the paths of *bhakti yoga*, *gyana yoga*, and *karma yoga*. This translates into yoking oneself (yoga) with higher powers through devotion (bhakti) that surrenders to a higher purpose, knowledge (gyan) that is discriminatory, and action (karma) that is brave and ethical, with the superordinate goal of uplifting society.

Arjuna regains self-confidence and wins the war for the Pandavas by performing his duty and killing the major warriors of the Kaurava army. Hence, Krishna is regarded by most Indians as the epitome of a mentor, coach, and guru or friend, philosopher, and guide.

The Stakeholders

Against the backdrop of the Mahabharata epic, stakeholders assume the roles described below. (Currently, stakeholders are predominantly men; and so we will use the pronoun "he.") The significance of the stakeholders' roles and role-related behaviors are discussed with them in the orientation sessions.

The boss (Krishna) plays a key part in his subordinate's development. At the outset, working in tandem with HR (business unit and corporate), bosses are asked to have conversations with the subordinates they nominated about their career aspirations. The question is whether the subordinate is willing to take up the career progression pathway the organization is charting for him.

The boss's boss (Super Krishna) is the business unit or functional head. He is tasked with working closely with Arjuna's boss to design the second and third assignments. The Super-Krishna's involvement ensures that the deliverables assigned to Arjuna are in sync with the unit's business plan and will have business impact. Super-Krishnas are also called on to become informal mentors and to review the development process and Arjuna's progress each quarter.

Executive coach. The JK Group has used a panel of six to seven experienced external coaches for a variety of initiatives. Over a period of time, these coaches have built up their own networks of in-company relationships and become familiar with the organization's business objectives and culture. In the Fire of Experience program, each coach is assigned to work with two or three participants or Arjunas. Their role is to enable their Arjunas to reflect and learn from their entire sequence of activities and experiences over the two-year duration of the program.

Peers and subordinates. Four to five peers or subordinates are identified as stakeholders for each of the developmental assignments. For example, during the first assignment to become a better boss, four to five subordinates are the stakeholders. In the second and third assignment, a different set of peers and subordinates may be chosen. Peers and subordinates provide critically important feedback, which helps Arjuna assess his progress toward the goals he set.

A family member is included at times as an informal stakeholder due to his or her day-in, day-out presence in the life of the participant. A family member is typically in the best position to observe behavior changes at close quarters. Families also benefit greatly from the participant adopting new positive behaviors and eliminating negative behaviors. So program participants are encouraged to ask a family member to be a stakeholder. This relationship is not monitored and the honest and valuable feedback that Arjuna receives from a family member remains private.

The *business unit HR head* links with the corporate HR team to ensure that processes and activities are not diluted or neglected.

As facilitators of the process, they play a central role in ensuring the success of the program.

Corporate HR and business unit HR co-own the process, although corporate HR is primarily responsible for the overall direction of the program. They work in tandem to facilitate and monitor the logistics of the multiple one-on-one and group meetings. Corporate HR calibrates expectations, perceptions, and performance by orchestrating the numerous interactions between stakeholders.

The participant (Arjuna) owns his relationships with all his stakeholders and is responsible for obtaining the guidance he needs for his learning, development, and performance. Even though superior performance on each assignment is expected, Arjuna's primary role is that of a learner.

Leadership development is not simple, nor a straight line. Not only must behavior changes occur, but others must *perceive* that changes have occurred. Not only must future top leaders become more competent, but their stakeholders must *perceive* that their competence is increasing. These possibilities are kick-started in the orientation sessions.

The Orientation Sessions

Corporate HR organizes two half-day face-to-face orientation meetings for stakeholders. These sessions take place before the Arjunas are convened for the first time. Information about the objectives, rationale, structure, and processes of the Fire of Experience program is shared. The roles that stakeholders will play and the knowledge and skills they will need are emphasized.

Orientation 1 is for executive coaches and the HR heads from the business units. The coaches are responsible for providing Arjunas with inputs that will produce behavior change, while the business unit HR heads make sure that process logistics are not compromised.

Orientation 2 is for the Krishnas (boss) and Super Krishnas (boss's boss). Their initial role was to help select program participants. With the program about to launch, their next task is to design the second and third assignments for their respective Arjunas. This requires ingenuity because the forthcoming assignments must meet two objectives: a business priority and the developmental needs of their nominees. By introducing this responsibility during orientation, corporate HR primes Krishnas and Super Krishnas to think ahead about assignments that will occur several months later. Corporate HR is a partner in this process.

Topics covered to help stakeholders grasp the objectives of the various components and processes of the Fire of Experience program include:

- Description of leadership capabilities desired by the JK Group for future leaders, so that all are on the same page regarding the intent of leadership development;
- Rationale for using developmental assignments, which has been validated by research at the Center for Creative Leadership (McCauley, 2006; Wilson, 2010) and the 70–20–10 guideline;
- Importance of involving multiple stakeholders to regularly observe, interact with, and provide feedback to Arjunas, in line with Marshall Goldsmith's (2007) coaching methodology;
- The "feed forward" coaching process so that stakeholders consistently focus on improving future behaviors and overlooking or pardoning past behaviors (Goldsmith, 2007);
- Honey and Mumford's (1982) Learning Styles model so that stakeholders can help future leaders to become better learners who can draw on all four styles of learning—activist, theorist, pragmatist, and reflector; and
- The 7–11 Model for developing Indian business executives, which is the framework for the program (Wilson, 2010).

Perhaps the most critical aspect of the orientation sessions is obtaining stakeholder commitment to the rigorous communication and review process that undergirds the Fire of Experience program. There are informal face-to-face communications for exchanging observations about intended and actual behavior changes. There is ongoing virtual communication for managing logistics and for assessing how the program is working. Finally, there are formal communications during quarterly stakeholder review meetings for planning for the Arjunas' progress. These activities will be described in the following section.

The Participants Prepare

While stakeholders are oriented to their roles and the components and process of the Fire of Experience program, the Arjunas, or future leaders, are also busy. They work with corporate HR to complete data sheets that include a full history of work experiences in the JK Group, including job rotations, work experiences prior to their joining the JK Group, the results of the Learning Style assessment, and their track record of performance appraisal ratings. The data sheets become an important baseline of personal information.

The Arjunas also complete pre-program "homework," which is central to their first assignment. They are asked to think about the total span of their careers (within and outside the JK Group) and bring to mind memorable bosses who have modeled either positive or negative behaviors. After reflecting on what they especially liked or disliked about each of these bosses, they write up short stories. A worksheet is provided for them to write the stories and other relevant information (see Exhibit 12.1).

Arjunas' recollections surface a wealth of information and insights about memorable relationships with bosses and superiors and what was tacitly learned from them. The stories dwell on the boss's words and actions related to managing, motivating, and developing subordinates. Using the stories as a starting point, each Arjuna does an inventory of the behaviors that he would want to emulate or eliminate.

The completed data sheets and homework become inputs for the launch workshop and first executive coaching session. With all the puzzle pieces of past and current relationships (with bosses and superiors) on the table, the program moves into its second phase and formal launch.

The First Assignment: Becoming a Better Boss

Bosses have an enormous impact, particularly in countries where status differences are prevalent and inequality between people—based on hierarchy, title, power, and influence—is expected and accepted. Moreover, almost half of all Indian executives participating in recent research (Wilson, 2010) confirmed that their

Exhibit 12.1. Learning from Bosses and Superiors Who Make a Difference: A Worksheet for Participants

Please narrate positive and negative stories based on behaviors experienced by you. Please do not mention the boss's name, but only the organization. While answering, please avoid generic statements and be specific in your examples.

Boss 1, Company Name: _____

- Period you worked with him (in years)
- Positive behaviors or lessons learned from boss about managing and motivating subordinates
- Describe in the form of a short story the specific incident that illustrates the above-mentioned positive behavior or lesson.
- List positive behaviors or lessons *you are using* in your leadership behavior for managing and motivating subordinates.
- List positive behaviors or lessons *you are not using* in your leadership behavior in managing and motivating subordinates, but given a chance would want to implement (and the reason why).
- List negative behaviors or lessons that you experienced from your boss related to managing and motivating subordinates.
- Describe in the form of a short story the specific incidents that illustrate the above-mentioned negative behavior or lesson.
- List negative behaviors that *you are not using* in your leadership behavior in managing and motivating subordinates.
- List negative behaviors that *you are using* in your leadership behavior, but given a chance would want to reduce or minimize in managing and motivating subordinates (and the reason why).

own behaviors as leaders were definitively influenced by one or more bosses or superiors. So the crucial first assignment, mandatory for all participants, focuses on helping Arjunas becoming better bosses so that their behaviors are in turn emulated by their subordinates.

This is achieved by using a structured process and activities, including a launch workshop, executive coaching sessions,

360-degree "dipstick" surveys, and formal quarterly reviews. Unfolding over six months, the first assignment creates a momentum for personal development that is expected to continue through the remaining eighteen months of the program and thereafter.

Launch Workshop and First Executive Coaching Session

Conducted by corporate HR, the launch workshop is about becoming a better boss. Two areas of changes are encouraged: managing and motivating subordinates and developing subordinates. Based on their earlier inventory of "good" and "bad" boss behaviors, participants identify one positive behavior that they wish to demonstrate and one negative behavior that they would like to eliminate for each of these two areas of change. Arjunas also uses the informal assessment exercises in their pre-reading (Wilson, 2010) as a resource. This stimulates their thinking about specific behaviors to work on.

The Arjunas and their executive coaches meet for the first time immediately after this workshop. Arjunas identify their strengths and weaknesses as a boss. Learning methodologies—for example, learning style and journaling—are discussed. Arjunas identity the high-impact behaviors they want to improve, develop action plans, and think through how to implement the plans. Coaches ensure that the behavioral change goals that are identified are sufficiently challenging and that meeting the goals will make a noticeable difference to Arjunas' effectiveness as bosses.

The 360-Degree Dipstick Survey

The 360 Dipstick is a five-to-seven-minute survey that uses six to ten questions to ask for anonymous feedback. "Dipstick" alludes to spoons that are dipped into a pot of cooking rice to sample a grain of rice and test whether the rice is cooking well. The dipstick surveys are customized for each Arjuna, focusing on specific areas of improvement identified by him.

A sample worksheet used with stakeholders is included (see Exhibit 12.2). The survey is sent out each quarter—after three coaching sessions and before the quarterly review session—to

Exhibit 12.2. 360-Degree Dipstick Survey: A Sample Worksheet

Commitment of the Coachee

Indicate your opinions by choosing from options provided.

1. Mr. ABC invited you to be his stakeholder on his own.	Yes No
2. Mr. ABC has shared with you the "high impact behaviors" being taken up by him for his improvement.	Yes No
3. Mr. ABC contacts you for meeting for taking feedback/feed-forward. (please note how often)	Weekly Fortnightly Monthly
4. Mr. ABC seeks your feedback on improvements made by him and takes suggestions from you for improvement during feed-forward.	Yes No
5. Mr. ABC is acting on your feedback and feed-forward.	Yes No

Interim Progress

Please give your ratings on a Scale of 1 to 10 (1 = low, 10 = high).

(*Note:* questions are customized for each participant)	Rating before coaching was started	Rating three months after coaching was started
1. Mr. ABC is taking interest in the hopes and dreams of subordinates.	_____	_____
2. Mr. ABC has stopped rebuking subordinates in public.	_____	_____
3. Mr. ABC is providing useful and timely negative feedback.	_____	_____

(*Note:* questions are customized for each participant)	Rating before coaching was started	Rating three months after coaching was started
4. Mr. ABC is developing a pool of employees instead of focusing on one.	_____	_____

Feed-Forward Suggestions from Stakeholders

Feed-forward suggestions for helping Mr. ABC's journey on chosen four behaviors.

1._____

2._____

3._____

4._____

participants, their coaches, and all other workplace stakeholders. An Arjuna's improvement on specific behaviors is rated on a scale of 1 to 10. The averaged responses are considered a reliable indicator of behavior changes and used during the quarterly review. The stakeholders also give feed-forward suggestions for future improvements.

This informal evaluation tool brings out important information, which is shared with Arujunas and their coaches. For example, the discrepancies between self and stakeholder ratings become a reality check for Arjunas. Similarly, the feed-forward section reveals different perspectives on desired behavior changes. These data help each Arjuna, his coach, and corporate and business unit HR to gain a sense of how the program is working and do some fine-tuning.

Quarterly Stakeholder Review

In the Indian cultural ethos, high power distance (Hofstede, 2001) is accepted and the hierarchy of positions is respected.

Figure 12.1. Quarterly Stakeholder Review

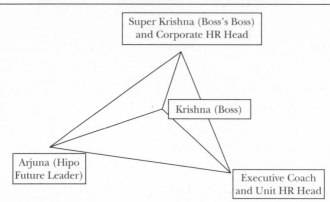

Stakeholder reviews are structured to leverage the dynamics of power-distance based relationships. The structure of these dynamics is best represented by a prism (see Figure 12.1).

The executive coach and Arjuna (high potential future leader) form a two-point line. The business unit HR head is considered part of this line because he coordinates and supports the interactions between Arjuna and his executive coach. When Krishna (boss) is added as a point, the single line converts to a triangle, representing a broader base of communication and relationships. The triangle becomes a prism, an even stronger structure, when Super Krishna (boss's boss) and corporate HR head are placed at the apex. In effect, rather than two-way communication between only two people (for example, between the executive coach and Arjuna), there are multi-direction communications among five people concerning the development of the emerging future leader.

About ninety minutes in length, the quarterly stakeholder reviews occur regularly, about every four to six months, over the two-year duration of the program. This prism-like structure of relationships, which is the core of the structured communication and review process, has proved to be very effective.

The quarterly review starts with the executive coach discussing Arjuna's progress on desired leadership learning. At this point, only the Super Krishna, Krishna, and corporate HR are present.

The executive coach's observations are based on his monthly coaching sessions with Arjuna, monthly telephone or video interactions with as many stakeholders as possible, and information from the 360-Degree Dipstick survey. The coach provides his own insights, and as evidence, narrates incidents described by Arjuna and other stakeholders.

Then Krishna enters the conversation, primarily addressing Super Krishna. He describes the ways in which he has mentored, coached, and supported Arjuna. This exchange serves to seal Krishna and Super Krishna's mutual commitment and interest in Arjuna's continuing progress.

Finally, Arjuna is brought in to join the meeting. To energize and motivate him, Super Krishna and others' opening remarks are compliments on his genuine improvements. Arjuna is asked to debrief the positive and negative aspects of his experience. Urged to have weekly talks with his stakeholders from the very beginning, he is now asked to be transparent in sharing how he has progressed or not, and to ask for guidance with humility. He summarizes his personal journey of learning and performing. When he is done, corporate HR asks him what additional support he would want from his stakeholders and the JK Group. The review ends with an action plan to give further momentum to Arjuna's development.

In the Indian context, these triangulated interactions have a lot of impact. For Arjuna, the presence of the higher level Super Krishna and Krishna is a great honor. Their compliments, advice, and encouragement are greatly motivating. In addition, the involvement of Super Krishna, and respect for hierarchy, forces and motivates both Krishna and Arjuna to make serious and sincere efforts to meet program objectives and put their best foot forward.

Becoming a Better Boss: Reported Behavior Changes

Concerning boss-subordinate relationships, it is the little things that matter. The behavior changes may be small, but they have to be observable by others and make managers more capable of managing, motivating, and developing their subordinates. During the pilot of the Fire of Experience program, after the first assignment was completed, corporate HR sent an informal email to program participants, their coaches, and all stakeholders. The short note asked for how participants had benefitted from the program. (Other information—about implementation challenges, obstacles to self-improvement, and further suggestions—was also collected and is integrated with the final sections of this chapter.)

We found that coaches, subordinates, superiors, and participants made similar remarks. The most frequently reported changes in participants' behaviors are increased patience, less impulsiveness, and more control of temper. Interactions with subordinates became calmer and more respectful and two-way communication improved. Here are typical comments:

- "In terms of controlling his short tempered-ness, which had caused a distance between him and his subordinate colleagues, he has since mellowed down and has, to a large extent, endeared himself and has increased his acceptability as an empathetic people manager."
- "He has reduced on admonishing his subordinates in front of their juniors, which has been highly appreciated by his subordinates. This change has also been highlighted by his Krishna and Super Krishna."
- "Not only some improvement, there has been significant improvement. Even with superiors, he would walk out and then come back. That has improved."

Another observed change was that participants began to proactively develop their subordinates. Some examples of new behaviors included delegating work, coaching a subordinate outside work hours to help him meet a personal goal, encouraging subordinates to attend training programs, and setting learning and performance goals that would challenge and energize one's team. Subordinates reported feeling very pleased by their boss's involvement because they believed they were being developed for higher responsibilities.

Interestingly, Arjunas readily acknowledged areas in which they had not been successful and where there was room for further improvement. The goal that was most often "not achieved" was that of keeping up with journaling. Other illustrative comments included:

- "I still need to improve my time management skills. I also have not been able to maintain a daily diary, which should have contained my daily reflections. I will try to do so regularly in the coming months."
- "I feel I can further improve upon empowering subordinates. But it is a thin line between giving the necessary space for the subordinates to work and improve and getting the desired results."

Final Phase: Two More Developmental Assignments

The second and third assignments are selected from seven possible types of experiences (see Table 12.1). As a result of ongoing multi-level conversations, each customized assignment meets strategically important business goals and the needs of the participant simultaneously. Individual progress is supported by the involvement of an entire cast of stakeholders at every step of the way.

Although the assignments vary a great deal, at their core, each is designed to be challenging enough to create mixed feelings of anticipation and anxiety. For example, one Arjuna was temporarily moved into managing the environmental impact of a plant, which was a new area for him. Another was assigned to increase product capacity for newly introduced concrete construction material. Yet another was asked to set up exclusive commercial tire care centers in western India to meet the needs of current shop owners and attract future entrepreneurs. Other Arjunas concentrated on developing new products, introducing products into new markets, or brown fielding new manufacturing sites. The following two examples illustrate the nature and learning from the final, third phase assignments.

Truck Wheels: Commercial Vehicle Total Tire Management

Mr. Kapoor was very pleased to be given responsibility for planning and setting up Truck Wheels centers across India for total tire management of commercial vehicles. This innovative service of "selling miles" (or cost per kilometer) was a new concept for his company and the country. In his words, "The very fact that I was chosen for this responsibility has been a great motivator. There was no existing work done on this activity. All aspects had to be thought out and designed. The name itself—Truck Wheels— had to be arrived at, along with the new logo to be used."

A major trigger for the Truck Wheels initiative was to counter competition, especially from multinational global players with products based on advanced tire technology. The concept of "selling miles" evolved from the need for JK Tyre to keep its competitive edge by bringing out an innovative service. The idea was to brand JK Tyre, already a market leader in the truck radial tires segment, as better equipped for keeping vehicles on the road. Top management wanted to offer a better business experience to its large fleet customers by changing the ground rules—that is, marketing their product on a "cost per kilometer" basis. They reasoned that their "total tire management" approach would help them to retain and lure large fleet customers, trumping the better technology, brand names, perceptions of quality, and lower tire pricing and discounts offered by competitors.

Mr. Kapoor worked on the concept, the budget, the revenue model, the cost/benefit analysis, and on selling the idea to his superiors. He traveled extensively to identify prospective partners and to persuade dealers and potential customers to sign on. Suppliers had to be contacted to work out machinery specifications. Within his own company, he had to partner with the purchasing department so that they were involved in the decision-making process. But his work did not end there.

The design and construction of Truck Wheels was also a part of his job. So he worked with architects, construction firms, and interior designers to develop a branded look for the centers. As he continued, Mr. Kapoor realized that "once all the basic requirements were finalized, the real work of identifying and finalizing the tie-ups with the partners had to be done. It required me to modify the basic concept already designed to suit the individual requirements of each partner. This led to further streamlining of the whole concept."

Then, working with his team, he planned and executed the inauguration of the first Truck Wheels by top management and turned his attention to ensuring that the centers would run smoothly and make profits. "This has been a great learning experience for me!" was Mr. Kapoor's enthusiastic comment about his assignment, which involved setting up a completely new business and generating a lot of positive buzz about Truck Wheels and the JK Group in the media and within the industry.

Transforming a Rural School into a Center of Excellence

Mr. Pattnaik was asked to take six months to develop a community school in rural India into a Center of Excellence. He had to immerse himself in journal, magazine, newspaper, and website articles on a variety of topics about school education. He also had to form relationships with school administrators, teachers, and the community. His aim was to work with the school principal to introduce all the necessary changes.

What made this assignment strategically critical? The largest manufacturing facility of JK Lakshmi Cement (with 5.2 million tons per year capacity) is located in a remote tribal area. But this makes it almost impossible to attract and retain top managerial talent. In India, as in many other countries, parents want the highest possible quality of education for their children. They are committed to investing in their children's long-term career prospects but are typically reluctant to send their children to boarding schools. Most are willing to sacrifice their own career growth for their offspring.

At the same time, rural schools are almost always poorly resourced, traditional, and backward in their educational approach, with the additional disadvantage of being staffed by professionals who are underpaid, under-motivated, and poorly qualified. Given the buoyant job market, the JK Group's top talent can easily seek other job opportunities that keep them in cities with a wealth of schooling options. This is the on-the-ground reality that made Mr. Pattnaik's assignment strategically invaluable.

Mr. Pattnaik's first contribution was to initiate parenting skills workshops. He wanted to bring about a mindset shift among teachers, parents, and students that would cause them to aspire to academic excellence. Due to his initiative, a comprehensive one-week training program was conducted for pre-primary and primary teachers. He thought of establishing an assessment and development center and identified officers who could guide this venture. This team began talking with various stakeholders to capture their expectations and ideas about what "assessment and development" could mean.

Mr. Pattnaik realized that this was a valuable learning opportunity. He was also aware of the obstacles that would have to be overcome. "Challenges are expected to come up as I move from the planning to execution stage. To meet the timelines will be a challenge, as a lot of synchronization of activities with various departments will be required."

These situational constraints were recognized by Mr. Pattnaik's coach, too. "He is working with multiple stakeholders over whom he has no formal authority. The assignment involves a lot of convincing and mindset change. He will need to enhance his ability to motivate and convince the teachers to move out of their comfort zones and proceed toward excellence, taking the school principal into confidence. In the assessment center project he will have to work to ensure a complete buy-in of the senior management team in finalizing the competencies to be assessed and the assessment center methodology to be adopted. He will have to balance his present responsibilities with his projects, which will test his time management and execution skills."

The coach's recommendation was that Mr. Pattnaik schedule fortnightly reviews with him so that he could receive the guidance he needed and complete all the steps that Mr. Pattnaik himself had outlined on a bar chart.

Although the point of the assignment is leadership learning, participants to date have delivered on business objectives. The strategic importance of their assignment means that Super Krishnas, Krishnas, and Arjunas work together to succeed at achieving the results they want.

Kudos and Watch-Outs: Lessons Learned by Program Designers

The chapter authors have contributed to the design and administration of the Fire of Experience program. We are pleased with the outcomes so far. We think many factors account for program success, such as:

- Complete buy-in from top management—the chairman, directors, CEOs and Super Krishnas, Krishnas, Arjunas, and other stakeholders;
- The background research, theoretical insights, and attention to detail brought to bear on the design of the program by corporate HR;
- Detailed briefings for Super Krishnas, Krishnas, Arjunas, executive coaches, and other stakeholders and business unit HR heads before the program was launched;
- Customization of design and processes to accord with Indian cultural norms and ethos and the JK Group's organizational culture and values; and
- Relentless follow-up by corporate HR to ensure all process steps were implemented in time, with rigor, and with the involvement of all stakeholders.

Setbacks occurred. Some features of the program were not implemented as planned. Some of the difficulties that were encountered include:

- The bi-monthly meeting of all Arjunas as a group could not take place. The first meeting was to be inaugurated by the CEO of one of the companies and facilitated by corporate HR. Arjunas were to share their experiences and progress by narrating incidents and lessons learned. All coaches would have attended. Given business priorities, and the difficulty of getting all the Arjunas together at one time, these meetings could not be held.
- Executive coaches were not able to contact Super Krishnas, Krishnas, and other stakeholders regularly to get their monthly feedback. Formative evaluation from coaches at the end of the second phase suggests that closer relationships between the coaches and the Krishnas and Super Krishnas would help the coaches to obtain more accurate information about Arjunas' behavior changes. In some cases, too much time goes by before an Arjuna checks in with a coach or Krishna or Super Krishna.

- The daily journal of personal reflections was completed regularly by only 50 percent of the Arjunas. Corporate HR believes that journaling about lessons learned, feelings of success, and emotions that go with setbacks are a powerful way for Arjunas to develop and grow. Reflection can strengthen personal resolve and insights on how to handle future challenges.

Future Incarnations of the Fire of Experience Program

Response to the Fire of Experience leader development pilot has been very positive, and a full-scale launch for 120 high potential leaders is planned. To give momentum and support to this organization-wide program, the launch will be attended by the group chairman, all directors, CEOs, Super Krishnas, Krishnas, executive coaches, and corporate HR and unit HR heads.

Primary responsibility for implementing the program will shift from corporate HR to the business units. Each business CEO and business HR team will be trained to lead the Fire of Experience program for his business unit. The role of corporate HR will be to monitor and ensure the quality of the training, progress and process integrity, and support the coordination of developmental assignments across companies.

Some refinements are necessary, such as greater clarity about the expected behavior changes and learning that each Arjuna needs. With corporate HR's involvement, this clarity can come from documenting the discussions between Super Krishnas, Krishnas, and executive coaches. The documentation can become the starting point for developing metrics to evaluate program outcomes annually. Other metrics could be identified from data about the success of the high potential leaders during the first year after they are promoted. In the long term, these data could be captured online.

Most of all, corporate HR would like to zero in on helping Arjunas become learners and grow into leadership positions that match their talents and potential. For this, a search is on to find instruments that measure the ability to learn and models that clarify how learning agility develops. Most of all, since Arjunas are the focal point of this initiative, they must understand how the Fire of Experience can help them to be better leaders and handle future higher level assignments. They need to grasp the big picture related to the valuable contribution that they are capable of making to the JK Group's future success. Upon completing the program, each Krishna-Arjuna pair truly deserves to be felicitated by their group chairman.

References

Charan, R., Drotter, S., & Noel, J. (2001). *The leadership pipeline: How to build the leadership-powered company.* San Francisco, CA: Jossey-Bass.

Ghosn, C., & Reis, P. (2005). *Shift: Inside Nissan's historic revival.* New York, NY: Random House.

Goldsmith, M., & Reiter, M. (2007). *What got you here won't get you there: How successful people become even more successful.* New York, NY: Hyperion.

Hofstede, G. (2001). *Culture's consequences* (2nd ed.). Thousand Oaks, CA: Sage.

Honey, P., & Mumford, A. (1982). *Manual of learning styles.* London, UK: P. Honey.

Kolb, D. A. (1984). *Experiential learning.* Englewood Cliffs, NJ: Prentice-Hall.

McCall, M. W., Jr. (2010). The experience conundrum. In N. Nohria & R. Khurana (Eds.), *Handbook of leadership theory and practice.* Boston, MA: Harvard Business School Press.

McCauley, C. D. (2006). *Developmental assignments: Creating learning experiences without changing jobs.* Greensboro, NC: Center for Creative Leadership

Wilson, M. S. (2010). *Developing tomorrow's leaders today: Insights from corporate India.* Singapore: John Wiley & Sons (Asia).

Yost, P. R., & Plunkett, M. M. (2009). *Real time leadership development.* Oxford, UK: Wiley-Blackwell.

CHAPTER THIRTEEN

Virtual Reality and Leadership Development
Randall W. Hill, Jr.

Leaders learn, grow, and develop their skills through experiences on the job, yet on-the-job learning has a number of pitfalls. First, it can take a long time to learn particular skills because the right experiences may not naturally occur. Second, even if the right experiences do occur, there is no guarantee that the right lessons will be learned, either because there is no time for reflection or because a mentor is not available to provide feedback and coaching. Third, just knowing a set of leadership principles does not adequately prepare a leader for the emotional intensity of the challenges that will be faced on the job. The stress of the working environment on a leader, compounded with situations where the people with whom the leader is interacting—subordinates, peers, and the boss—are in a highly agitated or irrational state, will stretch the leader well beyond theoretical knowledge and into the realm of practical intelligence (McCall, Lombardo, & Morrison, 1988; Sternberg, 2007). Finally, making a major mistake on the job can result in lost time and productivity, damage to personnel, and harm to one's own reputation in the organization. Wouldn't it be better to learn and practice a skill prior to walking into a live situation?

Note: The author of this chapter was sponsored by the U.S. Army Research Laboratory (ARL) and the content of the information does not necessarily reflect the position or the policy of the Government, and no official endorsement should be inferred.

Imagine sending a first-time supervisor through a boot camp for interpersonal skills, where the participant receives instructions on the basics of handling subordinates' personal problems and performance issues and then has the opportunity to practice these skills until proficient in a safe but emotionally intense environment. In the course of the practice, the learning is strengthened and focused by tailored feedback and coaching. And even after the initial training, when the new supervisor faces a novel situation, he or she can write a short description of a personnel situation that subsequently calls up a tutorial and practice environment that addresses a particular class of issues.

Advances in the learning sciences and simulation technologies now make it possible to acquire leadership experience by practicing virtually before meeting reality. Instead of facing a challenging interpersonal problem for the first time when a subordinate drops by the office, it is now possible to gain experience by practicing in a simulator, interacting with a virtual human—an animated character—in a real-world scenario. The virtual human will engage the leader in a lifelike conversation, complete with the emotional edge that often accompanies such encounters. Beyond one-on-one interactions, executives will use social simulators to gain a better understanding of the complex social environment of their organizations and the world beyond the one in which they are operating. These breakthroughs in technology will enable the leader to practice and learn in a safe environment where mistakes are not costly in human resource terms but are sources for reflection and learning.

This chapter describes an approach to experience-based learning that allows students to develop the mix of social skills leaders need, skills that span from one-on-one interpersonal situations to the complex dynamics of vibrant organizations. The use of virtual reality to realize such environments provides benefits over traditional techniques. To implement them requires advances in simulation technology to create the social environment in which leadership skills can be learned and practiced. The first part of this chapter will describe the technology enablers—virtual human technology and social simulation—that will make this vision possible. But technology alone is not the answer. The learning experience must be implemented using approaches to instructional design that research has shown are the most effective way to teach such skills.

The second part of the chapter will describe such a method, called Guided Experiential Learning (GEL), that has been put into practice for creating several simulation-based learning environments at the University of Southern California Institute for Creative Technologies (USC-ICT).

The third part of the chapter will focus on the final ingredient, the design and creation of compelling experiences for leader development. Going beyond traditional instructional design, this phase leverages the power of story, play, and empathy to create an experience that approximates the rich social fabric of the real world. The combination of technology, instructional design, and creative content will make possible a new era for learning.

Technology Enablers: Virtual Humans and Social Simulation

Simulation technology has long been used to provide highly effective training, beginning in the early days of aviation. One of the first widely used flight simulators was the Link Flight Trainer, which was developed in the late 1920s and consisted of a small physical model of a plane—a "blue box"—complete with instruments, controls, and actuators. The Link Trainer began to gain widespread use in 1934 when the Army Air Corps had to take radical steps to address the high fatality rate among pilots who were crashing when they had to fly by instruments in bad weather. The training was so effective that by World War II more than ten thousand Link Simulators were in use to shorten the training time and increase the safety for over 500,000 pilots (ASME, 2000). In more recent times, the military developed the SIMNET technology to model the modern battlefield, first to train armored tank crews and later commanders who engaged in large scale force-on-force engagements (Miller & Thorpe, 1995). What characterized all these simulations was that it was adequate for training purposes to model the physical and kinetic aspects of the world. All this changed beginning in the late 1990s when researchers began to go beyond modeling the physics of the world to developing models of human behavior—social physics, so to speak—both at the level of individual humans and at the group or population level.

Virtual Humans as Role Players

The early flight simulators enabled pilots to gain experience flying in a safe environment, where errors made in the course of gaining expertise would not cost the pilots their lives. By analogy, a simulator for leaders should provide an environment in which they can gain experience making decisions and interacting with people, but where they can make mistakes that won't result in a career-threatening crash and burn situation.

Many of the skills needed by a leader are social in nature and require a deep understanding of people and the processes that affect them. Leaders interact with individuals, ranging from the boss to peers and direct reports. Interpersonal skills are used in all of these relationships, whether for managing up, negotiating with or influencing others, or dealing with performance issues or personal problems among one's subordinates. Until recently the only two ways to gain this type of experience were on the job or in the classroom in role-playing exercises with peers or actors. Goldstein and Sorcher (1974) pioneered the use of human role players to teach interpersonal skills to the supervisors of difficult employees. The program proved to be effective, with marked changes in rates of absenteeism and turnover. It is now possible to gain the same type of experience with face-to-face counseling situations through conversational interactions with virtual humans.

A virtual human is an animated character that understands what is said to it and reacts with a spoken response, complete with facial expressions, gestures, and body language. This is made possible through the integration of a number of technologies: speech recognition, natural language processing, graphics, non-verbal behavior generation, animation, computer vision, and artificial intelligence algorithms.

One of the first demonstrations of the potential uses for virtual human technology was the Mission Rehearsal Exercise system (Swartout, Hill, Gratch, et al., 2001) developed at USC-ICT. The original demonstration scenario was set in Bosnia and involved an accident where an American military vehicle on the way to quell a disturbance in another part of town had crashed into a civilian vehicle and injured a young boy. The scene facing the participant was ominous. The boy lay motionless on the ground and his mother moaned and screamed as she rocked back and

forth on her knees next to him. A hostile crowd began to sur-
round the accident site and a television camera appeared on the
side. Playing the role of the platoon leader, the participant inter-
acted with the platoon sergeant and had to decide how to handle
the accident scene at the same time the platoon was supposed to
be accomplishing a time-critical mission down the street where a
riot was breaking out. The decisions involved conversations with
members of the team on the ground and over the radio, and the
pressure on the participant built as the situations collided. The
experience of watching this particular demonstration was visceral,
and on several occasions military officers who had been in similar
situations remarked how strongly they felt transported in space
and time and felt compelled to tell their own stories. The Mission
Rehearsal Exercise technology demonstration marked a new era
in training—it demonstrated that virtual humans could be used
to play roles in compelling interactive stories where the participant is faced with critical, time-sensitive decisions.

Until recently, interactive training scenarios of this type,
involving interpersonal or cultural situations, have required the
use of human role players. There are a couple of advantages to
using a virtual human for this type of role-playing exercise over
peer-based role playing. First, virtual humans are tireless and
always available. They do not need to be paid or coerced into role
playing and they have a consistent temperament. Second, virtual
humans can deliver a standardized experience to all the learners
in a cohort, which is important for large organizations where
there is a desire for consistent responses to certain categories of
behavior.

The idea of a standardized model for interacting with humans
is not new. Fifty years ago the medical community created an
innovative and highly regarded method for testing doctors' diag-
nostic skills using a human standardized patient (HSP) model
(Barrows & Abrahamson, 1964). Hired actors would portray a set
of symptoms carefully prescribed by a script, and the doctors
would diagnose the illness based on an interview with the HSP.
While this approach has been lauded as providing a superior way
of standardizing the training and assessment of medical skills, it
has not been widely adopted due to the cost of hiring actors
(Adamo, 2004; Collins & Harden, 1999). In addition, human role

players, especially when they are peers, are not necessarily going to provide a standardized experience. There will be variations in their performances due to differences in acting skills, in their understanding of the role, and so on. In addition, as shown by the medical community, human role players are not always available, which leads to a second advantage of using virtual humans as role players: they are tireless and they can repeat their performance again and again with consistency. While there is an up-front cost for creating a new character or scenario, once developed, it can be distributed and used throughout an organization.

The following dialogue is a short excerpt from the Immersive Naval Officer Training System (INOTS) being used to teach new supervisors how to handle performance issues and personal problems in their subordinates (Campbell, Core, Artstein, et al., 2011a). In the scenario the learner is a novice Navy officer who is confronting a subordinate, a sailor named Jacob Cabrillo, about a pushing incident that occurred in the workplace.

Navy officer: Okay, so Chief told me you pushed Thomas.
Cabrillo: Sir, I don't know why it is me who is in here.
Navy officer: It is pretty simple, you pushed Thomas. Why?
Cabrillo: He deserved it. If he didn't start talking trash about my wife none of this would have happened.
Navy officer: Thomas may have pissed you off, but next time, just walk away.
Cabrillo: I can't believe this. . . . You know what, sir, I get it. I shouldn't have pushed him. But walking away was not an option.
Navy officer: Cabrillo, you are a supervisor. You need to set the right example.
Cabrillo: I get that, sir, but what do you do when a guy acts like that?
Navy officer: Well, pushing him was definitely not the right answer.
Cabrillo: I know, sir, it won't happen again.

The preceding transcript does not represent an ideal interaction between a supervisor and a subordinate—more will be said about coaching and feedback later—but it does begin to convey the intensity of the encounter. The sailor is a life-size animated character sitting across the desk from the Navy officer. Initially the sailor sits upright, but when confronted by the officer, the sailor reacts defensively, gesturing outward with his hands and moving from an attentive, respectful posture to a position where he is leaning forward, with his elbows on his knees, no longer looking the officer in the eyes. As the dialogue progresses the sailor leans back, shrugs his shoulders, and slumps in the chair. His voice conveys first anger and later resignation. All of these signals, both verbal (words and prosody) and non-verbal (expressions, gestures, and posture), convey the emotional state of the sailor, and depending on what the leader says, the level of frustration and defiance can grow or diminish.

While using virtual humans instead of real ones has many advantages, there are some important limitations. One major difference between a virtual human and a real human is the level of intelligence and flexibility. Conversations that wander outside the bounds of the virtual human's knowledge will hit a wall. A variety of techniques can be employed to steer the conversation back on topic, but common sense knowledge may be found missing. Yet, in spite of the fact that the virtual human is not real—it is an animated character with limited knowledge—experiments have shown that people respond to virtual humans as though they are human. In one experiment with the Navy training system described above, a comparison was made between human role players and virtual humans to see how students responded. Hays, Campbell, Trimmer, Poore, Webb, Stark, and King (2012) found that interacting with virtual human role players was just as engaging as interacting with human role players. Several other studies have shown that people react to virtual humans as though they are real (Gratch & Wang, 2007). In one case real teachers were put in front of a virtual classroom; if the students were attentive, the teacher was more confident and poised, but when the virtual students were negative—sleeping, talking, and throwing paper airplanes—then the teacher tended to become anxious (Pertaub, Slater, & Barker, 2001). In another study on impression management, on a website where the participants could choose between watching a documentary on Einstein and watching a James Bond movie, when a virtual human was present on the same web page, the majority of the people chose the documentary over the action movie. Even though the virtual human was clearly not a real person, the human participant reacted as though it were real, seeking to create an impression of being interested in education over entertainment (Krämer, Bente, & Piesk, 2003). Likewise, it has been shown that men perform better on math problems when observed by a female virtual human (Hoyt, Blascovich, & Swinth, 2003). In each case, even though the people knew the characters were virtual, they reacted as though they were real.

Social Simulation

Leaders perform their duties within complex social situations and structures. They operate first in the context of their own organization, which has a life of its own, imbued with rich social dynamics, and their organizations are part of a bigger world of competitors, collaborators, and other forces. Organizations are composed of groups of people, and while there may be a clearly defined overarching mission, it is often the case that there are conflicting goals and subcultures among the groups. Communication is often a problem, as well as a host of other issues, such as the allocation of resources. In the same way that there have been very few options for practicing interpersonal skills outside of an on-the-job context, there have been even fewer options for learning about the social dynamics of organizations. Leaders develop their understanding of corporate culture and how things work through development assignments where they experience different parts of the organization, thereby gaining an understanding of how different groups relate to one another and how they work together.

One of the recent advances in simulation technology has been the development of a social simulator called PsychSim (Marsella, Pynadath, & Read, 2004; Pynadath & Marsella, 2005), which models the interactions of a diverse set of entities, both groups and individuals. Each entity has beliefs about the world, actions it can take, goals it wants to achieve, relationships with other entities, and mental models of others. Entities generate their behavior based on their expectations of how their actions will change the world, as well as how they will influence others' beliefs and future behavior. An entity can influence others, but that influence is modulated by the others' assessments of the entity's possible ulterior motives, their own self-interest, and relational factors such as trust and affinity.

To get an idea of how a social simulator would be useful for leader development, consider UrbanSim, a game-based simulation for military leaders (MacAlinden, Gordon, Lane, & Pynadath, 2009, Mockenhaupt, 2010; Peck, 2011). The UrbanSim learning environment is a turn-based strategy game comparable to commercial games such as Civilization® and Age of Empires®. The learning objectives of the game are centered on how to conduct a counterinsurgency and stability-focused mission in a sophisticated social-cultural context where there are rival factions with conflicting goals. To succeed in their mission in the game, the players must learn how to influence the actions of others in the world through every option available—rebuild the infrastructure of the city, provide security, use strategic communications with the population, and so on. In most cases the player is not in a position to directly command other entities to pursue a particular course of action. Rather, the player must take actions that block harmful behaviors, encourage positive actions, and work at changing the beliefs and goals of those who would do harm. It is common for a player to take an action that on the surface appears beneficial to the local population, but it may result in unintended consequences. For instance, in a scenario that was simulating a situation in Iraq, one participant thought he was doing good when he created high paying jobs in one district, but the unintended consequence was that it created a rush of workers from other districts. Not only did this move create an imbalance in the local economy, but it actually caused a shortage of doctors because they were leaving their practices to be paid more to perform an administrative function elsewhere. In the end, players gain an understanding of the second- and third-order effects of their own policies, communications, and actions, which have surprising results at times.

Virtual humans and social simulation are still in their early years of development, but these technologies are maturing rapidly. Just as flight simulators revolutionized the way pilots were trained, simulations of people and organizations have the potential to be game changers in the field of leader development. They are already being integrated into education and training packages that provide a safe practice environment and are providing leaders experience in handling a broad range of interpersonal matters, from negotiation and conflict resolution to dealing with performance issues and personal problems. Likewise, social simulation can help leaders to understand the dynamics of influence and complex social networks within and between organizations. But the tools alone are not sufficient to provide good development experiences to leaders—they are technology enablers. There are several other essential ingredients necessary for producing an effective learning experience with a virtual human or a social simulation, beginning with design.

Designing for Learning

Armed with the technologies to create a simulator for leader development, the next question is: What is the best way to teach leadership skills leveraging these emerging technologies? While it may be tempting to begin by implementing an immersive, game-based simulation, this approach could lead to a serious inefficiency in learning and even errors in what is learned. The approach that we have taken at USC-ICT builds on four pillars: (1) a theory of learning and instructional design called Guided Experiential Learning (GEL) (Clark, 2004; Clark & Feldon, 2008), (2) a creative design process that infuses the experience with emotionally evocative aesthetics, narrative, empathy, and game play, (3) the selective use of the simulation technologies to provide an appropriate practice environment, and (4) a mechanism to support feedback, coaching, and after-action review, to reinforce the lessons to be learned. What makes this approach to designing for learning unique is the integration of the analytical procedures of instructional design, the creative and conceptual design process normally associated with the art and entertainment world, and the knowledge engineering design derived from working with subject-matter experts to create a realistic simulation and an automated mentoring system.

Guided Experiential Learning

An educational psychologist, Richard Clark, and his colleagues at the University of Southern California Center for Cognitive Technology developed GEL, a method of design grounded in M. David Merrill's principles of instruction that has been used extensively in the development of training environments for leader development at USC-ICT. Merrill (2002) states that learning is promoted when learners are engaged in solving real-world problems; when existing knowledge is activated to serve as a foundation for new knowledge; when new knowledge is demonstrated; when it is practiced; and when it is integrated into the learner's world. GEL incorporates these principles and capitalizes on what has been learned over the past twenty years about the human cognitive architecture and how people acquire new knowledge and skill. Learning begins with concepts in the form of declarative knowledge, and this knowledge gradually becomes procedural and automated as the student puts it into practice. Once the concepts have been learned, students are provided step-by-step demonstrations of how to perform the task, where they learn the decisions and actions to take as well as the conditions under which to apply them. The student then practices the skill, beginning with simple sub-parts of the task, moving gradually to more challenging versions of the task as the steps are assembled and applied to integrated, realistic problems. By practicing on many variations of the problem, students not only automate the procedure, but their ability to apply the procedure in novel situations improves, moving them toward an expert level of performance (Clark & Feldon, 2008).

Cognitive Task Analysis

What do the experts know that the target audience needs to learn? This is the question that must be answered once a general instructional goal has been identified for a lesson or course. The challenge for a designer during this stage of the process is that expert knowledge is tacit. As scientist turned philosopher Michael Polanyi wrote in *The Tacit Dimension,* "We know more than we can tell." In other words, once knowledge becomes automated, which is what happens in the course of becoming an expert, it becomes very difficult for experts to articulate the decisions they made in the course of performing a procedure (Polanyi, 1966). It has been estimated that when experts are asked to explain their actions during a procedure, they leave out 70 percent of the decisions they made in determining when and how to perform the tasks to solve the problem (Feldon & Clark, 2006). They have automated the knowledge—it is chunked—and they are not consciously aware of what they are doing. Experts unconsciously recognize the situations where they should apply particular procedures. This is called control knowledge. The combination of control and automated knowledge is what one would want to learn from experts, but by its tacit nature is difficult for them to explain (van Merriënboer, Clark, & de Croock, 2002).

GEL goes beyond the standard task analysis techniques used in instructional design to identify how to perform a task to solve a problem and uses a technique called cognitive task analysis (CTA), which involves interviewing several bona fide subject-matter experts using a structured protocol for extracting implicit and explicit knowledge (Clark, Feldon, van Merriënboer, Yates, & Early, 2008; Crandall, Klein, & Hoffman, 2006; Schraagen, Chipman, & Shalin, 2000; Schraagen, Chipman, & Shute, 2000). The CTA elicits from an expert the integrated use of both control and automated knowledge over the course of hours or days. The knowledge elicited from the first expert is verified and expanded by additional experts. The product of the analysis is a description of how to act and decide in the environment, new concepts and processes that arose during the deep dive into the domain, a list of the equipment and material needed to perform the tasks, and a set of performance standards for the task. Performing a CTA is an intensive effort. It will increase the design time by 20 percent, but it pays off in the training time, decreasing how long the training must be performed by 20 to 50 percent (Clark, Feldon, van Merriënboer, Yates, & Early, 2008).

Learning Objectives and Instructional Frameworks

The CTA process is crucial for gathering essential domain and expert knowledge and distilling that information into measurable tasks. The CTA process also highlights important first principles that novices may be lacking for a variety of reasons. Additionally, there may be discrepancies between the presumed performance problem and the actual performance problem. Therefore, once the CTA has been completed, it is absolutely essential to cultivate, choose, focus, and refine the terminal and enabling learning objectives of the course or lesson. The terminal learning objective (TLO) states what the student should be able to do after completing the training, under what conditions, and how well he or she must perform (condition, task, standard). The enabling learning objectives (ELOs) describe the tasks required for successfully accomplishing the TLO, and they must be observable and measurable (Smith & Ragan, 2005). In addition to defining the TLOs and ELOs, the design team develops an instructional framework. These frameworks provide students with a roadmap for learning and remembering important information and procedures, as well as providing a structure for organizing effective after-action reviews (AARs).

The design team needs to master the domain knowledge to a point wherein there is a fluency that enables them to communicate the necessity and utility of the learning objectives and instructional framework to the client with certainty. The design team must come to full agreement with the client over the learning objectives and the instructional framework. This depends on effective channels of communication with the users and stakeholders so that there are good feedback loops and no misunderstandings about the final outcomes. Again, it is critical to ensure there is agreement over what is to be trained and how.

Evidence-Based Instructional Design

Once the domain knowledge and learning objectives have been established, the design team creates the instructional design for meeting the learning objectives. Clark's (2004) GEL model guides the process and products that support the instructional design to include a set of learning objectives; an instructional framework; goals and reasons for learning the content (providing a reason to learn the subject matter helps to motivate the learner by showing how it is important to the job or mission at hand as well as to the organization); overview information describing how each learning objective fits into the overall instructional framework; and the new conceptual content derived from the CTA. Some of the results of this process are described in the "Two Examples" section that follows. The instructional design must inform system design and incorporate learning theories regarding how people process information most efficiently (Paas, Renkl, & Sweller, 2003), as well as how to present that information. Knowing how to present the information to the training audience is just as important as the information itself.

Feedback and Coaching for Reflection (After-Action Review or AAR)

Feedback and reflection are essential for learning (Chi, Siler, Jeong, Yamauchi, & Hausman, 2001; Kirschner, Sweller, & Clark, 2006; McCall, Lombardo, & Morrison, 1988; Schön, 1983, 1987), thus the final ingredient of an effective training experience is to provide the feedback and coaching that support this process. According to Bloom (1984), one-on-one human tutoring leads to marked improvement in learning over conventional methods of teaching. Kurt VanLehn (2011) has shown that intelligent tutoring systems are nearly as effective as human tutoring. From a design perspective this means that serious consideration must be given to what feedback and coaching should be given and when.

During reflection, the leader reviews what happened in a challenging situation and considers what made the outcome a success or a failure. Even if the outcome is successful, improvement may be possible. With reflection, successful strategies are solidified and alternative courses of action considered. It is often more efficient when this process is stimulated and directed by a coach or tutor.

Referring back to the example given earlier of the interaction between the Navy officer and Cabrillo, there were several points in the conversation between the two that warranted feedback to the officer for the purpose of reflection and learning. For instance, when the Navy officer said, "It is pretty simple, you pushed Thomas. Why?" he did the right thing by stating the performance issue and asking for Cabrillo's side of the story. Likewise, when the Navy officer said, "Thomas may have pissed you off, but next time, just walk away," he did a nice job of describing the target behavior, but he didn't effectively summarize what Cabrillo had said in a neutral style, indicating he didn't effectively practice active listening. It would have been more ideal for him to say, "I understand you think Thomas is in the wrong, but you pushed him."

Feedback provides a snapshot and assessment of the learner's performance and can, in many cases, be automatically generated from a trace of the interactions in the simulation. When an instructor is not in the training loop, an automated coach or intelligent tutor can provide a learner with advice on how to improve performance and the motivation to make the needed changes. The learner's actions can be tracked and compared to an expert level of behavior, leading to a variety of possible methods for coaching. From a learning perspective, it is usually best to design the feedback so that it is especially frequent in the beginning as a skill is first being practiced and then begins to fade away as the learner progresses to higher levels of experience. Again, from a design perspective it is critical that opportunities for reflection and feedback are considered up front to reinforce the lesson.

Designing Compelling Experiences

Finally, there comes a point in the design process where a shift begins to take place, moving from the analytical work to the heavy lifting that will now be required of the creative team. While the instructional design process necessitates involvement from both perspectives through all the steps, the creative content developers apply a different set of skills. Content developers need to be as familiar with the domain knowledge as the instructional designers. They need to follow the instructional framework that provides the roadmap for teaching, practicing, and assessing the terminal learning objectives.

The instructional framework influences the type of media and technologies best suited for the given training. Furthermore, as the designers think about how to provide the learners with practice, they must identify compelling scenarios and narrative to introduce concrete examples that reinforce and ground the new knowledge. The practice environment, whether it is an immersive mixed reality simulation or game-based software application, must be engaging and able to track and assess student performance based on the learning objectives. Ideally, tasks will increase in complexity and learners will achieve mastery by solving problems under varying conditions.

Conceptualize and Create the System

While empirical research should drive the instructional design process, the conceptual design process must allow the freedom to explore a variety of creative solutions. One source of inspiration is Daniel Pink's book, *A Whole New Mind*, in which he makes the case that society is leaving the information age and entering the conceptual age, where success will no longer rely primarily on linear, analytical thinking. Rather, the conceptual age will be increasingly high concept and high touch, drawing also on creative and empathetic skills. Pink makes the case for combining analytical thinking with what he identifies as the six elements of the conceptual age: design, melding function with aesthetics; storytelling, communicating through narrative to appeal to our most ancient form of passing knowledge; empathy, creating a sense of emotional connection and identity with others; symphony, bringing all the pieces together to see the big picture; play, engaging through fun; and meaning, appealing to a desire to make a difference (Pink, 2005).

An Appeal to Emotion

While analytical thinking is rooted in logic and rationality, connections must also be made to emotion in some way, such as through a well-crafted story. Empathy is the ability to read and understand the emotions of another—a skill that is of great value to leaders. And play is normally associated with creating a sense of enjoyment, laughter, and recreation, and as we have seen with video games, it can create a high engagement level that can be nearly addictive in nature. Emotion is involved in all these elements, as well as in the others on Pink's list, and it plays a very important role in our lives that we need to understand and leverage as leaders.

Emotion is a powerful ally in learning and memory. Research has shown that people remember more emotional events than they do non-emotional or neutral events (Kensinger & Schacter, 2008). Emotions affect attention, prioritizing what stimuli will be encoded and, once encoded, emotional memories are more likely to be retained. There are a number of explanations for these phenomena, but probably the overarching reason is that one's ability to recall good and bad things that happen impacts the ability to adapt and thrive in an environment.

To translate what all this means for design for learning in a leadership context, let us elaborate a bit more on some of these elements and how they can be put to use in implementing the learning blueprint.

Conceptual Design

Design is a skill that produces "utility enhanced by significance" (Pink, 2005). What this means is that design does not merely produce a functional plan or an object that gets the job done. A good design also conveys a quality of elegance or beauty that adds value to the object through symbolism. Steve Jobs had a penchant for delightful design, and it is reasonable to believe that this is one of the sources of popularity of products from his company. It often makes the most complex concept or information accessible and intuitive. Edward Tufte is well known for his work on the visual portrayal of information and has shown that quantitative data can be brought to life with a well-designed visualization.

Likewise, in the realm of interpersonal relations, the design of a virtual environment and virtual human can radically change the experience. The design of the experience begins with the end in mind: What knowledge and skills does the learner need to acquire and master? During the analytical phase, the designer employs the best practices in instructional design and the learning sciences to identify the knowledge and skills underlying expert levels of behavior in the domain. The analysis produces an instructional framework for what needs to be learned and the order in which to learn it. But this is only the beginning. Designing an effective virtual experience also requires the ability to emotionally engage the learner in order to create an evocative and memorable event. Just as in real life, where experiences are often remembered because of their emotional impact, the virtual experience must be designed for the same sort of effect.

The conceptual design must therefore take into account the ambience of the environment where an interaction will take place; it should be similar to the office or work environment so that the skills will more readily transfer from the practice environment to the real world. The emotional-cognitive state of the virtual human also needs to be designed to capture the essence of interpersonal dynamics. This involves the artists who actually depict the character's appearance, and it also involves planning the gestures and body language of the character so that they change appropriately through the course of the dialogue.

Power of Story

Stories are the oldest form of communication for transferring experiences from one person to another. People are wired to enjoy stories—to listen to them, to form memories about them, and to recall in vivid detail the imaginary world that was encountered. A good story has the power to transport the reader to another place and another time, where emotional ties are formed with the characters and the reader is immersed in the dilemmas they face, all while the real world is put on hold (Green, Brock, & Kaufman, 2004). The entertainment industry understands this principle well, which is one of the reasons why good movies are so much more memorable than everyday reality. To test this idea, recall a movie you saw many years ago. Do you remember what else happened that day? Probably not, but you remember the movie. Why is that?

There are different theories about why stories are memorable. Stories can evoke strong emotions, which, as discussed earlier, help in the creation of memories. But others believe that our brains are hardwired to understand the world through a narrative structure (Bruner, 1991), and this ability is rooted in our social nature, where we are tracking other members of our group and their interactions with one another and the world, and these activities are best recalled by being encoded and represented as stories.

Three important takeaways about the power of story: First, stories are memorable and accessible. To demonstrate complex concepts, to make a particular lesson stick, we can leverage this fact when we think about how to create leadership experiences. Second, stories naturally lead to opportunities to exercise empathy, which is a social skill that leaders must master in many different contexts. Empathy is the ability to enter into and understand the emotions of others, to mentally walk in their shoes and see a situation from their perspectives. This parallels what happens when engaged with a story—the reader identifies with the characters, who have realistic emotions and face familiar situations. As cognitive psychologist Keith Oatley (2008) puts it, a story is the equivalent of a flight simulator of the mind, where social life skills can be practiced. Thus, a story can be the equivalent of a simulator that exercises a leader's empathetic responses.

The third point is that good stories are not easily written, and stories that help realize learning objectives are arguably even more difficult to write. The level of craftsmanship is easily detected by the reader and directly affects whether the reader feels transported. It takes special skills to construct a good narrative that includes a richness of detail that enables the reader to visualize and understand what is happening and why. The emotions of the characters must be psychologically realistic and the plot line cannot just be a sequence of events, but must contain elements of conflict, suspense, climax, and resolution. To achieve these effects, we have used professional writers to create engaging, well-written narratives. The added twist is that the writer must take into account the goals of the learning module in crafting an experience for the practice phase of the learning. In the end, the story provides a rich emotional context where learning can take place, so it must be crafted with care.

Power of Play

The emergence of video games as a dominant entertainment medium highlights the power of play. With the ability to attract people to devote tens to hundreds of hours in mastering a single game, it is clearer than ever that an element of play is at the core of who we are and how we interact with the world. Play is fun and brings joy, and it is often considered to be the opposite of work. But as Doug Thomas and John Seely Brown point out in their book, *A New Culture of Learning*, play is a natural way for humans to explore and interact with the world, understand concepts and boundaries, and use their imagination to solve problems (Thomas & Brown, 2011). Undoubtedly, the fun factor is what makes the difference between a game and just another simulation, so designing for *play* involves the art of transforming what would otherwise be a functional practice environment into an engaging interaction. Like story, a game with a sense of play will suspend the learner's sense of time and make the practice session seem like a real-life experience. And as with story writing, game design is a special skill set that can be found in the creative community.

Taken together, applying the elements of design, story, empathy, and play to the creation of a virtual experience results in a realistic, affective context for practicing leadership in situ—a flight simulator for mastering the practical social skills associated with leadership. The virtual practice environment, combined with informed reflection (feedback, coaching, and after-action review), is a potent combination that addresses many of the pitfalls of learning on the job by taking a systematic approach to education and training. The combination of technology, instructional design, and creative content will make possible a new era for learning.

Two Examples

Leadership Counseling Skills

The example given earlier of an interaction between a Naval officer and a virtual sailor was taken from a training system that was developed following the principles described in this chapter. The Navy version of the system is called the Immersive Naval Officer Training System (INOTS) and the Army version is called the Emergent Leader Immersive Training Environment (ELITE). The system itself has been integrated into a classroom environment that can handle more than fifty students at a time. The class begins with a brief lecture. The instructor is encouraged to share a personal narrative that helps explain the counseling principles for two basic situations: when there is a performance issue and when there is a personal problem.

The underlying skill to be practiced is active listening, but the difference is in applying it differentially to a performance issue versus a personal problem. In the case of a performance issue, the instructional framework is summarized as an acronym, I-CARE, which stands for (1) initiate communication, (2) check for underlying causes, (3) ask questions and verify information, (4) respond with a course of action, and (5) evaluate by following up. In the case of a personal problem, the students are taught the LiSA skills for active listening: (1) listen without interruption, (2) summarize in a neutral style, (3) ask for confirmation, and (4) then follow the steps of CARE above (Campbell, Hays, Core, Birch, Bosack, & Clark, 2011b).

Once the fundamental concepts have been taught, the instructor demonstrates the concepts in action using a series of animated videos with short vignettes. This enforces the learning principle of showing students how to perform a procedure before they actually perform it. Following the demonstration, the students have the opportunity to put their new knowledge into action. One student is selected to go to a separate room called the Digital Immersive Virtual Environment (DIVE) to have a face-to-face encounter with a human-size virtual subordinate, while the rest of the class participates by watching the interaction through a video feed. The classroom students participate in the virtual counseling session at each step by using a clicker to select what they would have said from a menu of choices. Everything about the session is recorded, both the video feed from the DIVE and all clicker responses made by the classroom students. This information is collected at the instructor's workstation. Based on a statistical compilation of the responses, the instructor can see which steps in the interaction were most troublesome, both at an individual level and for the class as a whole. The instructor can use these points as a launching pad for a facilitated discussion, analyzing the pros and cons of the approach to take in the situation at each step. In addition, the instructor can rewind the session and play the interactions of the student in the DIVE with the virtual character as a launching point for further discussion and feedback.

The approach just described closely parallels the work by Goldstein and Sorcher (1974), who developed a similar method for training supervisors on their interpersonal skills using human role players for the practice phase. The ELITE/INOTS system uses digital media to demonstrate concepts and virtual humans in place of real human role players. The resulting practice environment brings a new dimension to learning about interpersonal communication because the characters bring an emotional intensity to the situation that can be missing with a novice human role player or purely text-based or video-based situations. The emotions of the character come out in response to actions taken by the student, and they are conveyed not only by words but also by tone of voice, facial expression, gesture, and overall posture. In addition, the virtual human role players are tireless and are available at all hours of the day. The sessions are written as interactive stories and learning points are woven into the dialogue.

SimCity® for Commanders

The second example comes from the turn-based strategy game called UrbanSim described earlier. UrbanSim prepares Army commanders to conduct counterinsurgency and stability operations in an area of operations. The game is built on top of PsychSim social simulator, integrated with a story engine, which uses real-life events that have occurred in the past as a basis for picking out likely consequences to a commander's plan of action. The leader plays the game by first reading the mission brief and then developing a set of mission objectives. Next the commander identifies lines of effort (LOE), such as provide civil security, train the host nation security forces, stabilize local governance, reestablish essential services to the area, and stabilize and stimulate the local economy. There will be an associated set of measures of effectiveness (MOE) for evaluating whether progress is made in any of these areas.

Given these LOEs and MOEs, on each turn the commander formulates and executes plans within the area of operation. The system computes the effects of the mission by running the social simulation and the story engine. The social simulation computes the new beliefs, attitudes, goals, and actions of the various leaders and groups represented in the network. The results are graphically portrayed and messages updating the situation are communicated to the commander via a stream of reports, maps, and statistical displays of information. Feedback and explanations for trends along each of the LOEs provide the commander with an understanding of what worked, what did not work, and why. What often surprises students are the second- and third-order effects that take place in a scenario—efforts to improve one LOE can be counterproductive to other lines of effort.

Similar to ELITE and INOTS, a rigorous design process was used to develop UrbanSim. Both story and game play are key ingredients to the experience. Since the training is focused on populations of people and their behavior, UrbanSim does not use virtual humans in the interactions. While individual empathy is not as important as in an interpersonal counseling scenario, gaining an understanding of the mindset of diverse factions within a population is extremely valuable in helping commanders formulate plans that will achieve a mission in a complex cultural environment. Feedback is extremely important in this system; otherwise, the population would be a black box and the commander would not understand the causes and effects of particular lines of effort.

Lessons Learned

The approach described in this chapter was developed over the course of several years, beginning with the first demonstration of virtual human technology in the Mission Rehearsal Exercise system. MRE was purely a technology demonstration that wove together the elements of a social simulation and a story. It was not a training system, and the lessons that were subsequently learned took place as we came to grips with the elements of instructional and conceptual design discussed here. Here are a few of the lessons we learned that might be useful to others pursuing this approach.

Game changing technologies are here: be prepared to leverage them. Breakthroughs in virtual human and social simulation technology are going to change the way we educate and train the workforce, particularly those who have jobs requiring social skills. It is going to be possible to learn and practice certain leadership skills in a safe environment prior to walking onto the job. Virtual technologies are enabling us to build the modern equivalent of the flight simulator for social skills. Anyone who is in a position to make decisions about leader development for an organization needs to pay attention to these trends and what they portend for the future. But they are only one part of the equation for developing an effective learning experience.

Demand a systematic approach to educational design with virtual technologies. Leaders in organizations who commission an instructional program involving virtual or gaming technologies need to ask the development team key questions about their methodology: What is the goal of the training? What is the expert knowledge a novice needs to perform the tasks that meet the training goal? What decisions will the learner be making in the domain and how do experts perform? Is there an instructional design process in place to identify learning objectives and support system design that meet the training goal? As with any training intervention, it is not sufficient to develop training with virtual technologies if there is not a clear idea of what is to be learned and how it will be learned, both conceptually and experientially.

Require a feedback system. Strong provisions for feedback, coaching, and after-action review (AAR) must accompany the learning experience so that, as the student reflects on his or her performance; the right lessons will be learned from each experience. Without feedback, the lesson may be lost. An effective AAR highlights what happened, why it happened, and how it can be done better.

Technology alone is not the silver bullet for leader development. The emerging technologies described in this chapter are extremely alluring. They will enable a whole new generation of learning environments for leader and organization development. The cautionary note for organizations that choose to use these technologies is that they can also create completely useless experiences from a developmental perspective if the learning objectives are not well defined and intentionally baked into the design of the system. This chapter describes a holistic process that balances technology, instructional design, and compelling experiences to help leaders develop interpersonal and social skills in a safe and effective training environment.

References

Adamo, G. (2004). Simulated and standardised patients in OSCEs: Achievements and challenges 1992–2003. *Medical Teaching, 25*(3), 262–270.

ASME. (2000). The Link Flight Trainer: A historical mechanical engineering landmark. Retrieved from http://files.asme.org/asmeorg/Communities/History/Landmarks/5585.pdf

Barrows, H. S., & Abrahamson, S. (1964). The programmed patient: A technique for appraising student performance in clinical neurology. *Journal of Medical Education, 39*, 802–805.

Bloom, B. (1984). The search for methods of group instruction as effective as one-to-one tutoring. *Educational Leadership, 41*(8), 4–17.

Bruner, J. (1991). The narrative construction of reality. *Critical Inquiry, 18*, 1–21.

Campbell, J., Core, M., Artstein, R., and others (2011a). Developing INOTS to support interpersonal skills practice. *Proceedings of the*

Institute of Electrical and Electronics Engineers (IEEE) Aerospace Conference, AIAA, Big Sky, Montana.

Campbell, J., Hays, M., Core, M., Birch, M., Bosack, M., & Clark, R. E. (2011b). Interpersonal and leadership skills: Using virtual humans to teach new officers. *Proceedings of the 33rd Interservice/Industry Training, Simulation, and Education Conference* (I/ITSEC), Orlando, Florida.

Chi, M., Siler, S., Jeong, H., Yamauchi, T., & Hausman, R. (2001). Learning from human tutoring. *Cognitive Science,* (*25*), 471–533.

Clark, R. E. (2004). Design document for a guided experiential learning course. Retrieved from www.cogtech.usc.edu/publications/clark_gel.pdf

Clark, R. E., & Feldon, D. F. (2008). *GEL, adaptable expertise and transfer of training.* Report produced under contract sponsored by the U.S. Army Research, Development, and Engineering Command (RDECOM).

Clark, R. E., Feldon, D. F., Van Merriënboer, J.J.G., Yates, K., & Early, S. (2008). Cognitive task analysis. In J. M. Spector, M. D. Merrill, J.J.G. Van Merriënboer, & M. P. Driscoll (Eds.), *Handbook of research on educational communications and technology* (3rd ed.). Mahwah, NJ: Lawrence Erlbaum Associates.

Collins, J. P., & Harden, R. M. (1999). *The use of real patients, simulated patients and simulators in clinical examinations.* Association for Medical Education in Europe, AMEE Medical Education Guide No 13. Retrieved from www.medev.ac.uk/resources/features/AMEE_summaries/Guide13summaryMay04.pdf

Crandall, B., Klein, G., & Hoffman, R. (2006). *Working minds: A practitioner's guide to cognitive task analysis.* Cambridge, MA: MIT Press.

Feldon, D. F., & Clark, R. E. (2006). Instructional implications of cognitive task analysis as a method for improving the accuracy of experts' self-report. In G. Clarebout & J. Elen (Eds.), *Avoiding implicity, confronting complexity: Advances in studying and designing (computer-based) powerful learning environments.* Rotterdam, The Netherlands: Sense Publishers.

Goldstein, A., & Sorcher, M. (1974). *Changing supervisory behavior.* New York: Pergamon.

Gratch, J., & Wang, N. (2007). Creating rapport with virtual agents. *Proceedings of the 7th International Conference on Intelligent Virtual Agents*, Paris, France.

Green, M., Brock, T., & Kaufman, G. (2004). Understanding the role of transportation into narrative worlds. *Communication Theory, 14*(4), 311–327.

Hays, M., Campbell, J., Trimmer, M., Poore, J., Webb, A., Stark, C., & King, T. (2012). Can role-play with virtual humans teach interpersonal skills? *Proceedings of the 34th Interservice/Industry Training, Simulation, and Education Conference (I/ITSEC)*, Orlando, Florida.

Hoyt, C., Blascovich, J., & Swinth, K. R. (2003). Social inhibition in immersive virtual environments. *Presence: Teleoperators and Virtual Environments, 12*(2), 183–195.

Kensinger, E., & Schacter, D. (2008). Memory and emotion. In M. Lewis, J. M. Haviland-Jones, & L. F. Barrett (Eds.), *The handbook of emotion* (3rd ed.). New York, NY: Guilford.

Kirschner, P., Sweller, J., & Clark, R. E. (2006). Why minimal guidance during instruction does not work: An analysis of the failure of constructivist, discovery, problem-based, experiential, and inquiry-based teaching. *Educational Psychologist, 41*(2), 75–86.

Krämer, N., Bente, G., & Piesk, J. (2003). The ghost in the machine: The influence of embodied conversational agents on user expectations and user behaviour in a TV/VCR Application. In G. Bieber & T. Kirste (Eds), *Proceedings of the International Workshop on Mobile Computing, Assistance, Mobility, Applications*, Rostock, Germany.

MacAlinden, R., Gordon, A., Lane, H., & Pynadath, D. (2009). A game-based simulation for counterinsurgency and stability-focused operations. *Proceedings of the Workshop on Intelligent Educational Games*, 14th International Conference on Artificial Intelligence in Education, Brighton, UK.

Marsella, S., Pynadath, D., & Read, S. (2004). PsychSim: Agent based modeling of social interactions and influence. *Proceedings of the International Conference on Cognitive Modeling*, Pittsburgh, Pennsylvania.

McCall, M. W., Jr., Lombardo, M. M., & Morrison, A. M. (1988). *The lessons of experience.* New York, NY: The Free Press.

Merrill, M. D. (2002). First principles of instruction. *Educational Technology Research and Development, 50*(3), 43–59.

Miller, D. C., & Thorpe, J. (1995). SIMNET: The advent of simulator networking. *Proceedings of the IEEE, 83*(8), 1114–1123.

Mockenhaupt, B. (2010, Jan/Feb). SimCity Baghdad. *Atlantic Monthly.* Retrieved from www.theatlantic.com/magazine/archive/2010/01/simcity-baghdad/307830/

Oatley, K. (2008). The mind's flight simulator. *The Psychologist, 21,* 1030–1032.

Paas, F., Renkl, A., & Sweller, J. (2003). Cognitive load theory and instructional design: recent developments. *Educational Psychologist, 38*(1), 1–4.

Peck, M. (2011, September 28). Confessions of an X-box general. *Foreign Policy.* Retrieved from www.foreignpolicy.com/articles/2011/09/28/Xbox_general

Pertaub, D. P., Slater, M., & Barker, C. (2001). An experiment on public speaking anxiety in response to three different types of virtual audience. *Presence: Teleoperators and Virtual Environments, 11*(1), 68–78.

Pink, D, (2005). *A whole new mind: Why right-brainers will rule the future.* New York, NY: Riverhead Books.

Polanyi, M. (1966). *The tacit dimension.* New York, NY: Doubleday.

Pynadath, D., & Marsella, S. (2005). PsychSim: Modeling theory of mind with decision-theoretic agents. *Proceedings of the Nineteenth International Joint Conference on Artificial Intelligence,* Edinburgh, Scotland, UK.

Schön, D. (1983). *The reflective practitioner: How professionals think in action.* New York, NY: Basic Books.

Schön, D. (1987). *Educating the reflective practitioner: Toward a new design for teaching and learning in the professions.* San Francisco, CA: Jossey-Bass.

Schraagen, J., Chipman, S., & Shalin, V. (2000). *Cognitive task analysis.* Mahwah, NJ: Lawrence Erlbaum Associates.

Schraagen, J. M., Chipman, S. F., & Shute, V. J. (2000). State-of-the-art review of cognitive task analysis techniques. In J. M. Schraagen, S. F. Chipman, & V. J. Shute (Eds.), *Cognitive task analysis* (pp. 467–487). Mahwah, NJ: Lawrence Erlbaum Associates.

Smith, P. L., & Ragan, R. J. (2005). *Instructional design* (3rd ed.). Hoboken, NJ: John Wiley & Sons.

Sternberg, R. (2007). A systems model of leadership: WICS. *American Psychologist, 62*(1), 34–42.

Swartout, W., Hill, R., Gratch, J., and others (2001). Toward the Holodeck: Integrating graphics, sound, character, and story. *Proceedings of 5th International Conference on Autonomous Agents,* Montreal, Canada.

Thomas, D., & Brown, J. S. (2011). *A new culture of learning: Cultivating the imagination for a world of constant change.* Self-published.

VanLehn, K. (2011). The relative effectiveness of human tutoring, intelligent tutoring systems, and other tutoring systems. *Educational Psychologist, 46*(4), 197–221.

van Merriënboer, J.J.G., Clark, R. E., & de Croock, M.B.M. (2002). Blueprints for complex learning: The 4C/ID-Model. *Educational Technology Research Development, 50*(2), 39–64.

Maximizing Learning from Experience

CHAPTER FOURTEEN

Formal Development Enhances Learning from Experience at Microsoft

Lori Homer

Microsoft is a diversified technology, services, and devices company with more than $50 billion in annual revenue and 90,000 employees in 190 countries worldwide. In addition to Windows, its flagship computing platform, and the Office productivity suite, Microsoft supports a range of technology-mediated experiences, including customer relationship management (CRM) solutions, phones and related applications, entertainment, and gaming. Microsoft is committed to empowering people to be more effective and creative through affordable and widely available technology, offered through supporting software and services across various devices.

In the rapidly changing, technology-driven world that Microsoft helped create, organizations worldwide depend on innovation to generate strategic competitive advantage. Consequently, organizations, including Microsoft, hire smart, driven people who are motivated to tackle hard problems. As the *Lessons of Experience* (McCall, Lombardo, & Morrison, 1988) made clear, hard problems offer many opportunities for learning. If work is fundamentally organized around solving hard problems (and so, presumably, people are growing in role at all times), what is the necessity or value of "formal" development?

While the *Lessons of Experience* research highlighted that experience is the primary mechanism of leader development, it is also true that experience alone does not ensure leadership growth; certain interventions can increase the learning that comes from experience. Also, through the Waypoint project, Plunkett, Yost, and the research team (of which I was a member) replicated the Center for Creative Leadership (CCL) work of twenty years prior on the power of experience in developing leaders. This research taught that formal development makes unique contributions to leadership development—lessons that experience by itself does not always teach (Yost, Plunkett, McKenna, & Homer, 2001).

This chapter outlines principles for designing formal leadership development to enhance the unique value it can provide, while also catalyzing improved on-the-job learning. Examples and illustrative impacts from my work within the Leadership Development Group (LDG) at Microsoft are included. Note that "formal development" is also known as "classroom development," "training," or "program." "Formal development" is used throughout the chapter to encourage thinking more broadly than the classroom setting. It is also intended to focus specifically on experiences that are structured for the primary purpose of learning and development.

Value Differentiators and Design Principles

According to the *Lessons of Experience* research, formal development offers unique value that on-the-job experience typically does not. Specifically, it:

1. Connects peers and leaders;
2. Gives leaders new frameworks and perspectives on their challenges; and
3. Creates space for leaders to pause and make meaning of their experience.

These are *the* three differentiators of formal development; that is, differentiated from what on-the-job learning experiences typically provide. Building on the *Lessons of Experience* research and following the best practices of adult development, formal development should be both experiential and applied. These three differentiators are also *the primary objectives* of any formal

> **Exhibit 14.1. Five Design Principles to Optimize Formal Learning's Differentiated Value**
>
> 1. Address Live Business Challenges
> 2. Enroll the Right People
> 3. Flip the Classroom
> 4. Leverage Your Leaders
> 5. Provide Real-Time Support

development experience I design. When formal development is designed to optimize for these three differentiated outcomes, the investment translates into increased value for time, transfer to the job context, and learning agility (aka capacity for learning from experience).

Using the three unique differentiators as the primary objectives of any formal development will change the experience for both leaders and learning professionals. In designing for these outcomes, I engage five design principles (named in Exhibit 14.1) that are further described and illustrated with examples throughout the chapter.

Address Live Business Challenges

With the demands and pace of work at Microsoft, any amount of time that leaders spend in formal development must be relevant and directly applicable to leading the business. In LDG we align offerings to business needs in two different ways. First, every two to three years, we research, summarize, and frame our formal offerings within the context of the enterprise-wide business challenges. Then individual offerings are designed to make use of live business challenges—either using the participants' own scenarios or specific cases that are selected and prepared to illustrate the concepts and tools of the formal offering.

Frame the Offerings

The learning and development portfolio is designed around the business and leadership challenges that leaders are experiencing.

This is different than designing for competency development. We use an agile development approach (Larman, 2004; Waters, 2012) to understand the business challenges. Due to the typical rate of change in most businesses, we focus on getting it "right enough" to start rather than focusing on defining a complete and exhaustive list of challenges.

To use the agile development approach, we collect just enough information about what leaders struggle with now and what is anticipated that they will need to drive business growth within a two- to three-year timeframe. We use multiple sources—external analysts' commentary on company direction and leadership, customer input, competitors' successes, and senior leader input—to identify themes. Next, we validate those themes and obtain input from key stakeholders and iterate just until we are confident that the themes are directionally correct and key stakeholders have bought in to the top challenges.

In LDG we expect a framework to be valid for approximately two or three years. That expectation guides our depth of investment in defining the business challenge framework. For example, say you find the top business challenges are

1. Building strong leadership teams;
2. Helping leaders new-in-role to transition effectively;
3. Working more effectively across silos; and
4. Identifying new opportunities for profitable business growth.

You may find stakeholders agree with some but not all of the priorities. Or you may not have strong enough agreement across stakeholders to keep one of the challenges as a *top* priority. In such cases, the agreed-on challenges, not individual leader competencies, become the organizing framework for the formal leadership development offerings. Using the example above, if your stakeholders bought in on (1), (2), and (4), but not (3), you may design a formal offering for each of the three agreed-on top challenges. Depending on the stakeholder input and resource constraints, you may develop a fourth offering for clients who recognize that learning to work across silos is something their business growth depends on. When a specific skill or competency is addressed within the formal experience, we always frame it within the business context, providing both a roadmap and a rationale for learning and changing.

Work on Current, Real Problems

Another way we bring live business challenges into the formal development experience is through working on current, real problems. "Real" problems come from either:

- The participants' own challenges that they identify and scope in pre-work or
- Action learning problems that are compelling for the business.

Either way, we structure the formal experience so that real and current challenges are the focus.

Because the challenges are both current and real, participants are more likely to see the time spent in formal development as important, relevant, and applicable to their roles. When leaders tackle real problems on the job, there is always a time crunch and multiple competing demands. In contrast, a formal development experience gives leaders a "container" or dedicated time and space within which to reflect on the challenge more broadly and more deeply. When working through the challenges openly with peers, leaders are able to:

- Expand understanding of the challenge through surfacing multiple perspectives;
- Experiment with applying the principles or models; and
- Build working connections with other leaders.

With these additional benefits, leaders are more likely to carry the collaborative work forward and draw upon each other after the formal experience ends, increasing their capacity to learn from experience in the future.

Designing a formal experience around real and current challenges increases relevance, builds leader perspective, and, realistically, can also make things messy. Real and current challenges are not sanitized and edited to fit neatly into the frameworks being presented, and typically they also do not have a single solution.

Formal development programs are often held suspect by leaders with regard to their relevance or applicability. Designing formal experiences to address challenges being faced by the business increases relevance. Using the challenges being faced by the business also has the potential to broaden leaders' perspectives through framing the most critical company-wide issues. When formal development is designed to address current business challenges, it is also critical to the formal program's effectiveness to enroll the right people in the right experience.

Enroll the Right People

This design principle suggests that leaders need to be enrolled in formal development so as to optimize the outcome that will best serve each enrollee's needs. At Microsoft we rely on help from front-line HR representatives to identify and prioritize leaders for offerings based on the challenges they are facing. Grouping leaders who are facing similar kinds of challenges together increases application. Participants working with and on each other's similar challenges have multiple opportunities to try out the frameworks and apply the tools.

For example, say a leader, Ted, is challenged by developing his leadership team and has already experienced some painful interpersonal dynamics on the team. Through the formal development experience targeted at developing leadership teams, Ted is connected to a dozen other learners working to develop their teams. Everyone else's challenges are both salient and also distant enough that Ted can emotionally unhook from his own team's dynamics and help his colleagues. Further, as Ted's mind plays through the different scenarios, given time to think within or beyond the program, he identifies similarities and differences with others' situations, and is more likely to extract lessons and apply them to his team. Further, working on similar challenges strengthens the network benefit through creating a community of people with a shared purpose. Ted is more likely to learn *along with* his colleagues over time, even back on the job, as he and they work to develop higher functioning teams.

At this point, you may be wondering: Do leaders really make the time to connect beyond the formal program? Based on what our leaders tell us, sometimes they do. And when they do, they find it very, very useful. One way we support leaders connecting with each other is by pointing out to them the *potential value* of getting together to consult on the challenge that brought them together. Also, in one formal development experience, *we assign them the task of getting together* between modules of a two-part offering; we find this works better if they have practiced this behavior within the formal development experience.

Flip the Classroom

One of the most promising innovations in K–12 education of the past quarter century is the flipped classroom, also known as "reverse instruction," and "backwards classrooms" (http://en.wikipedia.org/wiki/Flip_teaching). While educators have experimented with and written about the idea since the 1990s, this notion has been made popular more recently through Sal Khan's attempt to help a cousin via Skype. Khan's Skype-based lessons led to videotapes posted on YouTube that went viral (Khan, 2012). In a more traditional education model, content delivery is done in the classroom and the practice—where most real learning takes place—is relegated to homework, usually done outside of the classroom. In the flipped classroom, content is consumed outside of the classroom, typically mediated by technology (for example, online videos or recordings, Internet research, or even assigned reading). The classroom, or formal development time, then, is dedicated to practice, experimentation, and coaching, whether from peers or an expert.

At Microsoft, we use the flipped classroom idea to enable leaders to work on business challenges with each other away from the frenetic and varied demands of the business. We ask leaders to read a book and scope a real business challenge before class starts. Once the formal development experience begins, the program iterates between reminding participants of an idea from the reading and having them work in peer consultation groups of four or five people to apply the idea or model to each other's challenges. Each small group is staffed with a coach to help manage the process and keep participants learning versus moving quickly to solutions.

Formal leadership development efforts have used variations of "flipping" for a long time, such as when leaders are assigned pre-work or pre-reading before arriving for a session, and then time in class is spent practicing a skill. Even so, there is often a tension between content and practice. The true test of whether a formal experience is taking full advantage of the flipped notion comes when the facilitator is faced with an in-the-moment time adjustment. Does he or she shorten the practice time in order to fit in one more concept, framework, or tool, or is he or she willing to sacrifice delivering the full complement of ideas or tools in the interest of giving leaders more time to practice and work together? Through consistently prioritizing practice and interaction over content delivery, leaders report better value for time in class and, as mentioned earlier, are even more likely to continue practicing with and learning from each other after the formal development offering ends.

Using the "flipped" model for leadership development is both rewarding and risky; it also demands a slightly different set of skills. The quality and scope of the pre-work is critical, as it equates to less time in class devoted to delivery or content explanation. The flipped classroom also requires facilitators to stay grounded in the service of the group. This may result in the leaders changing the agenda for part of a day in the interest of group or team learning. Unlike traditional math or English assignments from primary school, the practice problems in adult development do not typically have right answers. Holding space in the schedule for flexibility and tolerating the ambiguity associated with not having right answers can be uncomfortable for both facilitators and leaders. How this discomfort is handled by the facilitator is an indicator of whether the classroom is truly a practice space or a delivery vehicle. More flexibility leads to better awareness and ownership of the development, which leads to better transfer and learning on the job.

Leverage Your Leaders

While the rhetoric about "leaders building leaders" has been around for a while, how to implement the notion for the highest value impact while also maintaining good relations with the executives requires strategizing and stakeholder management. This design principle is more susceptible to organizational context than the others. What "leverage your leaders" looks like in your organization depends on the organization's culture, the behaviors you are introducing or fostering in the program, and the executives' existing skills and attitudes toward leadership development.

For example, at Microsoft, we do not have leaders who would choose to do front-of-room instruction, and we are unlikely to staff formal development that way. Further, in a formal development offering aimed directly at changing culture, leaders who show up as prime examples of the entrenched culture is a no-win scenario; it undermines the message, the development experience, and the leader.

Instead, we do extra work to provide instructors and leaders with opportunities they value that also align with the needs and objectives of the formal offering. For example, leaders who are very motivated to meet the company's young technical talent are more likely to help out when we invite them to participate in a formal offering targeted for that audience. In another example, for formal development experiences focused on designing and innovating business models, we invite leaders who are currently executing a business model shift as special guests.

We have also found that the dialogue is more engaging and learning-oriented when focused on *current* business challenges than when a leader speaks retrospectively. This seems to hinge on the leader representing an attitude of "I'm learning along with you," versus being the "sage on stage." To have an open conversation about current challenges, leaders must be prepared and they must be open to having their work, including their thinking and progress (or lack of progress), on display for others. We have found that offering "free help" to senior leaders from across the company who are invited to think along with executives can be attractive. Executives also have a chance to practice simplifying and communicating what are usually complex issues with a live audience.

How Participating Leaders May Benefit

For one formal offering, five senior executives were asked to bring forward a strategic challenge to which teams of the most senior high potential employees (HiPos) could apply new strategy frame-works. An invitation was also extended to a junior staff member of the executive's choosing. This junior staff member was asked to join and help support the HiPo experience as the subject-matter expert (SME) on the current strategy and the executive's liaison to the group. By enlisting the junior staff member, we were guaranteed higher-quality preparation and background materials and the junior staff member, in return, received a developmental opportunity through working with more senior high potential leaders from across the company. The SME/liaison was respon-sible for framing the strategy challenge and working with a member of the LDG team to meet the conditions for a workable case. For illustration, these conditions are listed in Exhibit 14.2.

Preparing each case included two thirty-minute meetings with both the executive and the SME/liaison. One was up front, to set expectations, and the other was just prior to the program, to brief the executive on how the case had been framed and would be used within the program. In between the two meetings, a member of LDG and the SME/liaison worked together to scope the strat-egy challenge and provide the right level of supporting analyses. This typically consisted of one or two additional in-person meet-

---

Exhibit 14.2. Necessary Conditions for a Strategy Case

1. The challenge is of significant scale, affecting one or more of our businesses or suite of products.
2. The market boundaries are being redefined by emerging or converging technology and consumer patterns.
3. A reevaluation of target customers and markets, the business model, and monetization approach are likely required.
4. The strategy questions are product and customer oriented versus functional or sales oriented, in order to align to core content of the program.
5. The challenge is both real and urgent for the sponsor, decisions on the challenge are not yet closed, and the sponsor is interested in, and open to, the input of a senior, cross-division, high potential team.

ings and several email iterations for shaping and editing the content. Through this work, we found the SME/liaison also needed coaching on being open to alternative interpretations and input from non-subject-matter experts. It was helpful to have a set of in-common talking points explaining our objectives (for example, "participants learn to apply new strategy analysis tools and learn about a business outside their direct area of expertise") and the conditions necessary for success (such as the problems needed to be real and current, and the sponsor needs to be interested in, and open to, the input of a senior, cross-division, high-potential team).

Preempt the Skeptics

In our company of deep technical expertise, there is a tremendous pull to treat exercises like this in one of two ways.

1. Participants may over-function, fully immersing themselves in order to "solve" the challenge for the executive sponsor, and thereby demonstrating to the executive sponsor and their peers that they are the smartest person in the room.
2. Participants may under-function, likely because the case is not solvable by a handful of smart but not expert people in the 2.5 days they have, or because the executive sponsor has other smart people working on the problem full-time.

With either option, learning is not optimized. Recognizing both of these scenarios as potential risks, I sought to mitigate the risks by bringing the executive sponsors into the program on the first day to set expectations. This gave the sponsors an opportunity to give context on the case, acknowledge the work that had been done to date, and state expectations for the HiPo participants assigned to their case. When asked why they would bring their key strategy challenges that already had smart people working on them into the artificial setting of the program, the executive sponsors said they hoped to think deeply about one thing with the participants for part of the week, and hoped to get fresh eyes on a problem that they and their people had been enmeshed in for a long time. They invited participants to bring both naiveté and renewed rigor to the challenge.

Set and Reinforce the Context

Thereafter, participants were reminded that the executive sponsors themselves had said they expected not answers but fresh perspectives and good questions about taken-for-granted assumptions. This framing gave the participants a problem to solve for and the opportunity to raise new awareness with executives, rather than the need to provide a single answer. When the executive sponsors returned at the end of two and a half days, they were also reminded of the desired outcomes, giving them an opportunity to listen and seek to understand, rather than critique, what was wrong or missing, or defend work already done by their teams.

In sharing concrete examples of how Microsoft engages its executives in formal development, we are mindful that these examples will not entirely align to other contexts and that other organizations may have different best practices for involving senior leaders in formal development. The broader message is that each organization has its own opportunities and constraints associated with engaging leaders in formal development. Success in leveraging leaders as a teaching asset requires understanding the leaders and what engages them. Microsoft has had some success engaging leaders in formal development opportunities: When we succeed, participants report getting higher value for the time they have invested. We are also more successful the clearer we are about the value proposition we have and the more we align the invitation to visiting executives' interests and needs.

Provide Real-Time Support

While understanding that most leadership development happens on the job, we also know that formal learning provides additional value that is not duplicated in direct experience. The four design principles already provided are essential to extracting unique value from formal development offerings. However, we are left wondering what, if anything, we know about the connection, real or ideal, between formal development and on-the-job experience. By making the fifth principle "provide real-time support," I am suggesting there is a critical and creative role that formal leadership development plays in supporting on-the-job application and ongoing learning.

By including a few well-designed follow-up interventions as part of formal development, the learning stimulated by the formal program has a much better chance of changing behavior on the job. Given what we know about training transfer, I argue that formal leadership development is not complete until it addresses how new models or skills will be supported within the existing job context. Sometimes our desire to fulfill this responsibility has us contemplating writing up contracts with receiving managers or changing an entire organization's culture. While these may be worthwhile, we have had success with a more modest approach of building follow-up support into formal development offerings. Support can come through formal coaching and the peer networks built during the formal development.

Coaching

Consultants or coaches, internal or external, who follow up with program participants can

- Remind participants of concepts, models, or tools learned in the formal program;
- Increase accountability for applying the learning;
- Surface and challenge taken-for-granted assumptions;
- Promote taking more creative, alternative approaches to a challenge;
- Validate the riskiness or anxiety associated with trying out new approaches; and
- Encourage ongoing reflection and meaning-making on the job.

Providing real-time coaching support for applying new skills or trying out new behaviors is one way of managing the formal development investment for greater return. As one participant reported: "The coaching made me make [the development] concrete; [I had to] own it and apply it . . . versus letting it wash over me."

Peer Network

Peers who learn about the similarities and differences related to their challenges, and practice coaching and problem solving with one another, become great resources to each other. We see the peer network provide value and support during formal development, but also outside of and well beyond the formal development. It is not uncommon for our participants to tell us that their coaching group continued to meet for weeks, or in some cases years, after the formal program. It is also quite typical to hear stories about how relationships forged across divisions during the formal development allowed leaders to make critical connections later that were absolutely necessary for making break-through progress.

We are most successful when we introduce the real-time support of either professional coaching or peer networking within the context of the classroom. If we expect leaders to be coached after the formal program, we provide opportunities during the program to be coached. If we expect the peer network to be instrumental in supporting the follow-on application, we empha-size peer consulting within the formal development experience. In other words, we use the "container" of formal development to provide leaders with the opportunity to "try on" the real-time support as they are "trying on" the new behaviors within the program.

Case Studies

The examples offered thus far have illustrated each design prin-ciple in isolation. In this section, two case studies are presented to illustrate end-to-end solutions that incorporate the five design principles—address live business challenges; enroll the right people; flip the classroom; leverage your leaders; and provide real-time support. These principles are employed to optimize the unique value differentiators of formal development—peers and leaders are connected to one another; leaders work with new frameworks and perspectives on their challenges; and leaders have the space to pause and make meaning of their experience. Each case illustrates a formal development program that has run for multiple years with consistently positive feedback about the high value of time spent in the classroom and increased effective-ness on the job.

Case Study 1. Shifting Leadership Culture

The increasing complexity of our businesses, our industries, and the global economy calls for our leaders to shift from the historic model of leader as "engineer, architect, and problem solver of known problems with knowable answers" to "political activist, mobilizer of people who tackle ambiguous problems with varied stakeholders and surface multiple, dynamic answers." With the ambition of shifting an entire leadership culture, LDG recognized that leaders would need different leadership models, an opportunity to step away from the on-the-job action to reflect and try out alternative behaviors, and access to a community or network of leaders with shared exposure to these different ways of thinking about and enacting leadership. So we developed a formal program to help bring about the shift in leadership culture.

Address Live Business Challenges

The greater business context (size and complexity of the business, rate of evolution, and disruptive innovation in the industry) framed the need for a formal development offering. In the course pre-work, participants were required to do the following:

> Identify a key challenge or opportunity that you are currently facing in your work (something you are actively concerned about in your role), that is important for you to make progress on. It should be something that you are willing to discuss openly and that will have a material impact on business performance or the success of your organization. It is important to select a challenge for which you are genuinely open to alternative possibilities— about what your role, and your organization's role or actions, should be.

Participants complete and submit this pre-work prior to the first class. If they come to class without having submitted their challenge, they are asked to outline and submit their challenge before joining the rest of the group. These business challenges serve as the basis for the application of content.

Enroll the Right People

Enrollment is limited to senior leaders operating in complex and ambiguous environments who need to lead differently to be effective (that is, acknowledging both the complexity and the ambiguity). We educate HR front-line partners on the requirements and objectives of the formal development session and rely on them to identify leaders in their organizations who fit the profile and who can benefit from the experience. Early sessions of the program also required participants to attend an intake meeting with a leadership development professional, to ensure parameters for the experience were being met.

We have actually turned people down and ruled some people out through this process. In other cases, participants who did not quite meet the criteria were still allowed to enroll in the program. Most of the time, we found that people who did not meet the criteria but we allowed in were not equipped to grapple with the content and fell short of the benefits achieved by those who met the selection criteria.

Flip the Classroom

In addition to identifying and submitting a business challenge, participants also need to read the first half of the book on which the content was based. The formal offering is structured as two three-day workshops spaced apart by eight to twelve weeks. About two-thirds of each workshop is dedicated to peer consultation and coaching (small group work), where participants apply concepts and ideas that they read prior to class and discuss in the large group setting.

Participants consistently say the small group consultation (practice) time was the most significant contributor to their learning. As suggested earlier, we repeatedly test our commitment to the flipped model; when a large group conversation runs long and a facilitator is faced with a just-in-time adjustment to the schedule, leaders receive better value from the experience when the peer consultation time is protected, even at the cost of eliminating a key concept or model.

Leverage Your Leaders

When LDG first rolled out this formal offering at Microsoft, we were subverting the historically dominant leadership culture.

Therefore, we did not start out inviting leaders to come in and speak to the value of the content. However, over time, as influential senior leaders felt the impact of and were changed by the experience, many of them approached us and wanted to sponsor a program for their teams or regions—and, of course, we were delighted to accommodate them. In populating these intact (team-based) sessions, we would again work with the HR front line, and the sponsors, to ensure the participants met the requirements and would benefit from the content at that particular time. Further, these sponsors were invited to attend the opening of their intact session and explain what they had experienced and speak to the changes they had made or were making in their leadership as a result. In some cases, the leaders participated in the full event a second time, because they wanted to try out new ideas within their teams, on their shared business challenges, in the relatively safe classroom environment.

Provide Real-Time Support

As indicated, the formal experience takes place in two three-day workshops separated by eight to twelve weeks. The interim period serves as a forcing function for application. Participants know when they sign up for the first workshop that they will be returning for the second session. They are assigned to continue meeting in their peer consulting groups. The stated goal is to meet twice during the interim period, or for enough time that each member of the peer consulting group receives an additional consultation beyond the initial three-day workshop. Each peer consulting group is also assigned a coach during the workshop. Coaches ensure the peer consultants follow the consultation process, are thoughtful and supportive of each other, and identify and apply relevant tools and concepts.

Early in the program rollout, coaches also met in the interim period with their assigned groups. As the new culture gained more currency, and more leaders evangelized the value of the experience, we were able to save costs by eliminating the coach as part of the interim experience. We found the peer consulting groups still met and found value. However, participants do report better value when they follow the prescribed coaching process. They also voluntarily report that they are more likely to follow the coaching process with the coach present. Perhaps most surprisingly, some particularly enthusiastic attendees report their peer consulting groups have continued to meet for many months, and in some cases years, beyond the second workshop.

Impact

As of this writing, this formal development program has been experienced by more than six hundred senior leaders and more than two dozen intact teams. This offering continues to receive strong, positive feedback on leaders' perceptions of value for time spent, and their likelihood of recommending it to others. Further, because this offering was designed to capitalize on the unique value a classroom can provide—such as exposure to new models, time to reflect and create new meaning, and connection to other leaders—the formal offering has had both staying power and enduring impact. The language and models used in this program are often referenced in other LDG-hosted programs, illustrating that it has made inroads on the original goal of shifting the leadership culture.

Case Study 2. Building Perspective on Emerging Markets

Thirty years ago, Microsoft was a small but fast-growing software start-up with just over $1 million in revenue and thirteen employees, all based in Redmond, Washington. As noted earlier, today Microsoft is a diversified technology, services, and devices company with more than $50 billion in annual revenue and ninety thousand employees in 190 countries worldwide. Our worldwide presence and the explosive growth potential in emerging markets necessitates that more of our leaders understand the opportunities and challenges associated with working and selling in emerging markets.

This case features a formal development offering called Front Lines that was designed to build leader savvy for doing business in emerging markets. Leaders who participate in Front Lines spend one week immersed in a single emerging market, learning culture and business context, and helping a strategic partner solve a business challenge. Participants also engage in eight weeks of follow-on team consultation with their strategic partners. Using Front Lines, I will again illustrate how the five design principles have been used to optimize the formal development experience.

Address Live Business Challenges

In addition to addressing the enterprise-wide need to grow our leader savvy for business in emerging markets, participating in Front Lines requires leaders to work with a strategic partner—one or more leaders from a non-governmental organization (NGO), government agency, or entrepreneurial endeavor—with interest and investment in emerging markets. The strategic partner brings a business challenge that is scoped and prepared with similar parameters to the leadership culture case. The challenge must be both urgent and real and represent something on which the partner is open to input and multiple possible solutions.

The partners must also hold a level of responsibility in their own organizations that allows them to make decisions about or materially influence the solution applied to the challenge. Typically, our partners are founders, C-level, or very senior officers. The strategic partners also participate in the formal development program, *along with* Microsoft leaders. Having strategic partners (in other words, customers and potential customers) both in attendance and as clients for the team output heightens the relevance and importance for the Microsoft participants.

Enroll the Right People

The first time we ran Front Lines, we invited a customer-facing audience that regularly interacts with customers as part of their day jobs. The translation from "field-facing" to "emerging market" was relatively straightforward. The second time we ran Front Lines, we increased our risk and the potential payoff by shifting the audience composition to include a majority of product or engineering leaders whose jobs typically exposed them to customer data, but rarely to actual customers, and even less frequently to emerging market conditions. In year two, the "field-facing" participants were in a distinct minority, but were still very present as teachers and facilitators. In both cases, participants reported the experience as being transformational.

Still not quite satisfied and very committed to our principle of enrolling the right people, the third time we ran Front Lines, we selectively balanced a group of engineering, product development, and field-facing participants, plus added Microsoft leaders located in the emerging market, so that each working team had a liaison who could translate local, regional, and business customs for the Microsoft participants and translate Microsoft culture for the strategic partners. Further, in the third year of Front Lines, we also offered briefing sessions for prospective participants with prior participants. This helped prospective participants decide how and whether they would benefit from participating and increased their focus on what they would gain from the experience.

Our own assessment of the leader and partner experience in year three indicates both high business and personal leadership impact. We learned that bringing together a diversity of global and business perspectives is required to truly build both global and business perspective.

Flip the Classroom

The formal Front Lines experience is a nine-week working session made up of one week in-country and eight weeks of follow-up consulting. The pre-reading is minimal, consisting of one or two articles on the business opportunities in emerging markets and a culture and safety briefing.

On the first day, we begin with an immersion-day field trip designed to acquaint participants with the entire socioeconomic range of the host country. For example, we typically visit a shanty town, a primary or vocational school, a profitable and growing corporation, and some of the strategic partners involved in the program, who are usually community or educational groups invested in improving conditions in the region. The entire group of approximately twenty participants experiences this immersion day and the evening gatherings together. Beyond immersion day, the formal program primarily consists of working sessions that bring together the smaller teams with their partners, focusing on their challenges. There is some social and networking time but almost no content delivery beyond the highly experiential immersion day.

Leverage Your Leaders

Microsoft leaders with responsibility for growing the company's interests across the world and in emerging markets (especially, for example, our chairman for emerging markets and the regional and country managers) are highly invested. They are very interested in increasing corporate leaders' education and awareness of the challenges, opportunities, and responsibilities of doing business in emerging markets. Our regional and emerging market leaders are willing sponsors and supporters who welcome the experience to work with both the Microsoft leaders and the strategic partners.

In Front Lines, our senior regional leaders are key stakeholders and partners in bringing the right strategic partners in and designing the event for maximum business and personal impact. Recognizing the power and value of our formal development experience, these global leaders have twice recognized and awarded Front Lines with highly visible, company-wide business impact awards.

Provide Real-Time Support

Each working team has a coach who introduces and manages the process for the group for the one-week session in-country. The process is designed to work for both simultaneous problem solving and group learning; each coach ensures that both are happening. The team continues consulting with the strategic partner for eight weeks after the in-country week. The coach also continues working with the group to facilitate learning (while working). Leaders tell us that the coaching structure used in Front Lines feels awkward at first but becomes easier over time. Leaders also begin to apply the learning technologies—asking questions, being curious, reflecting on "what could we have done better"—to their day jobs. These reports are what make us believe we are increasing learning agility on the job. However, leaders readily acknowledge that the awkward process is something they would not apply nor adapt to, on their own, without the structured and shared expectations set during the formal development program and the increased accountability to the coach.

Impact

Front Lines combines leadership development with Corporate Social Responsibility (CSR) and new business development to achieve a three-way win: for participants, partner organizations, and Microsoft. We are so committed to the three-way win that we ask constituents representing each perspective to evaluate the program. External partners leave the week in-country optimistic about their team's ability to help define an effective solution and grateful for the opportunity to participate. One participant noted: "The way Microsoft has designed its leadership program is fantastic. There is nothing better than learning from others. I have actually taken this back to our own organization and proposed that we take on something similar with our own partners."

Microsoft participants increase their understanding of the opportunities and challenges of the company doing business in emerging markets. Another participant reflected: "I learned how each country has its own agenda and about the value that a true customer and market focus can bring to business. In addition [the team process] was the best process I have experienced for team learning, storming and forming quickly and effectively."

Microsoft leaders who represent our global growth potential and client interests are pleased to help our future corporate leaders expand their understanding and awareness of the opportunities and challenges of doing business in emerging markets. A sponsor gave this feedback: "As a company, we have a global and inclusive mission statement around enabling opportunity for people and realizing potential. Getting our top talent to think about how our technology and people can make a tangible difference in people's lives is just incredible. I leave feeling even stronger about our prospects to make a tangible difference in people's lives and grow Microsoft business."

Front Lines clearly does not replace a global assignment for teaching about the complexities and nuances of global business. However, we are leveraging the unique value of a formal program to scale a taste of global experience to more, and in many cases different, leaders than those who would typically rotate through available global assignments.

Conclusion

I know well that no formal program can replace leaders' on-the-job experience. However, I also learned early in my career that formal development can provide unique value that on-the-job experience typically cannot.

Personally and professionally, I am frustrated by the rhetoric that makes experience "developmental" and formal development "a waste of investment." I wrote this chapter in an attempt to elevate the discussion and practice of leadership development from what I hear largely as "on the job, *not* classroom" to "on the job *for most growth* and formal, structured development *for some things.*"

One of my favorite roles is helping leaders learn from experience. When I coach senior leaders on their careers or their talent strategies, I advocate for job rotations, the importance of developmental assignments, and the necessity of being reflective about what experience is teaching. At the same time, in the thirty-plus years since the *Lessons of Experience* research was conducted by CCL, formal development programs may have become more experientially based, but they have not disappeared.

Further, I feel strongly that formal leadership development experiences should not go away entirely. Formal development experiences offer unique value that leaders typically do not get from their day-to-day experience. Based on my experience and relative success experimenting with formal development, these programs can increase a leader's ability to learn more from experience. Formal learning experiences can

1. Connect leaders with each other, increasing their empathy with and trust in one another, which benefits the business;
2. Give leaders new frameworks and perspectives on their experience; and
3. Create space away from the job, which gives leaders the opportunity to pause and make meaning from their experience.

While I am an advocate for learning from experience, I also design and implement offerings that are optimized for the unique value that formal development provides. I optimize formal development for its value-added outcomes by employing the five design principles described and illustrated throughout this chapter—address live business challenges; enroll the right people; flip the classroom (even sacrificing content for more practice or work time); leverage leaders where and as it makes sense; and provide follow-up support for leading differently.

Leaders value experience-based coaching; I have personally witnessed transformations stemming from such experience. At the same time, Microsoft program participants also value the time invested in formal development experiences. Formal development at Microsoft aims to help leaders be more attentive to the lessons experience holds for them, back on the job. We also regularly see leaders become more effective based on the insight, coaching, and connections made within a formal development program. Individual leaders and the organizations they lead are better off when both on-the-job and formal development investments are optimized for the unique value each provides.

References

Khan, S. (2012). *One world schoolhouse: Education reimagined.* London, UK: Hodder & Stoughton.

Larman, C. (2004). *Agile and iterative development: A manager's guide.* Boston, MA: Addison-Wesley Professional.

McCall, M. W., Jr. (1998). *High flyers: Developing the next generation of leaders.* Boston, MA: Harvard Business School Press.

McCall, M. W., Jr., Lombardo, M. M., & Morrison, A. M. (1988). *Lessons of experience: How successful executives develop on the job.* New York, NY: The Free Press.

Waters, K. (2012). *All about agile: The book.* Self-published. Available at www.allaboutagile.com.

Yost, P. R., Plunkett, M. M., McKenna, R. B., & Homer, L. (2001). Lessons of experience: Personal and situational factors that drive growth. In R. B. McKenna (Chair), *Leadership development: The strategic use of on-the-job assignments.* Symposium conducted at the Society for Industrial-Organizational Psychology, San Diego, California.

CHAPTER FIFTEEN

Experience-Based First-Line Manager Development at HEINEKEN

Mary Mannion Plunkett and
Dagmar Daubner

The role of the first-line manager is arguably one of the most important in any organization or business. Individuals in first-line management roles are held accountable for achieving the task (e.g., delivering the product or service), building and maintaining effective work teams, and serving as the bridge between line staff and senior management. First-line managers are responsible for communicating, delegating, mentoring, motivating, solving problems, influencing, dealing with complexity, conflict management, strategy and operations, time management, employee and management communications, resource planning, legal compliance, and achieving results. It is no wonder that new first-line managers report feeling overwhelmed (Hill, 2003).

In terms of leadership development, it is well documented—practically and theoretically—that experience is the best teacher. As early as 1988 one of the best leadership development research endeavors documented a framework of key experiences that stretch, challenge, and produce leadership learning (McCall, Lombardo, & Morrison, 1988). Subsequent researchers and practitioners have built upon this framework (for example, McCauley, Ruderman, Ohlott, & Morrow, 1994; Yost & Plunkett, 2009). It is no surprise that first-line management roles have been consistently identified as one of the fundamental key experiences in a leader's development. It is also not surprising that most organizations have adopted "70–20–10" learning philosophies acknowledging that an employee can expect at least 70 percent of his or her learning to occur on the job, through experiences; 20 percent to come from feedback, mentoring, and coaching; and 10 percent from more formal classroom-based or online training.

What is perhaps surprising is that, despite widespread support for the effectiveness of learning on the job and agreement that first-line management roles are key experiences, the first-line management experience is not leveraged to develop first-line managers. Organizations of all shapes and sizes and geographies do invest in first-line manager development. It was estimated that companies in the United States spent $13.6 billion on leadership development in 2012; trends suggest that first-line management development is gaining an even larger investment share than in past years (Bersin and Associates, 2012). Given cost and performance pressures in all organizations today, the business case for ensuring value for leadership development investment has never been more compelling.

This chapter will describe the design, implementation, impact, and lessons learned related to a systemic intervention that focuses on leveraging the experience of being a first-line manager. As with any leader development initiative, it is critical to first understand the business context and goals of the intervention prior to describing specific design and implementation elements.

Business Context

The intervention was designed for HEINEKEN,* a fast-moving consumer goods company (FMCG). The FMCG industry is responsible for the production, distribution, and marketing of consumer packaged goods normally consumed by customers at regular intervals. Some of the prime activities of FMCG businesses are operations, production, sales, marketing, distribution, financing, purchasing, and general management. Keeping pace with

---

* *Note:* When referring to the company rather than the brand, HEINEKEN is always capitalized.

consumer trends and competition are perpetual challenges of FMCG companies.

HEINEKEN is committed to the responsible marketing and consumption of its more than two hundred international premium, regional, local, and specialty beers and ciders. The company's aim is to be a leading brewer in each of the markets in which it operates and to have the world's most valuable brand portfolio in order to surprise and excite consumers with its brands and products everywhere. HEINEKEN is Europe's largest brewer and the world's third largest by volume. Heineken® is the most global beer brand, enjoyed in 178 countries around the world. The company has a unique, worldwide footprint with operations in seventy-two countries, more than 140 breweries, and beer sales in excess of two billion liters ensuring a broader brand reach than any other brewer. The organization has more than eighty thousand internationally diverse, committed, and entrepreneurial employees. The passion of the Heineken family remains as strong today as it was in 1864 when Heineken was first brewed.

Over the past five years, HEINEKEN has experienced significant growth in volume (74 percent), revenue (59 percent), employees (64 percent), and brands (55 percent). Further, HEINEKEN has transformed its emerging market presence in recent years through an acquisition strategy, strong organic growth, and joint venture partnerships. Overall, the beer market is competitive and challenging in terms of external economic, regulatory, and demographic trends (e.g., aging and increasingly female populations). Operating in developing countries adds further challenges such as underdeveloped infrastructures, weak distribution networks, and political instability. All of these factors contributed to the need to strengthen and refocus internal processes to leverage scope and scale of the business, while continuing to drive operational efficiency and increasing consumer orientation within a decentralized structure.

HEINEKEN's organizational matrix includes seventy-two independent operating units across five regions (Africa Middle East, Americas, Asia Pacific, Central and Eastern Europe, and Western Europe), global functions (Commerce, Supply Chain, Finance, Human Resources, Corporate Relations, Legal), and a newly created Global Business Services organization (Finance, Procurement, IT). Management teams within each operating company typically consist of a general manager and functional heads for commerce, supply chain, finance, and human resources (HR). A key pillar of the new HR strategy is to build functional and leadership capability to support business objectives. The present and future world requires different skills in HEINEKEN leaders including technical skills in off-trade, brand building, and innovation; competence to succeed in emerging as well as mature markets; and stronger relationship management capabilities due to increased partnerships and joint ventures.

Target Audience

Targeting a leadership development initiative for first-line managers was an intentional strategy to strengthen the leadership pipeline in a sustainable manner, both for short-term impact (e.g., improving skills and capabilities in first-line managers and HR professionals) and longer term (e.g., enhancing development of first-line managers' direct reports, ongoing development for HR professionals). The quality of first-line managers has well-documented impact on business performance; first-line managers also have direct influence on employee capability development, motivation, engagement, and retention (Corporate Leadership Council, 2006).

One of the first challenges was identifying a first-line manager in language that could be commonly understood, irrespective of whether the first-line manager was in production or marketing, in Nigeria or New York. Ultimately, the initial target audience was defined as individuals across the global organization who have accountability for managing two or more employees and are at the first step in a management career at HEINEKEN. This initial target audience numbered approximately six thousand individuals. Although the roles of these individuals were as diverse as the businesses they support, a series of focus groups surfaced consistent general needs that evolved into a global development framework.

Designing the Intervention

Designing the intervention unfolded in four phases: Discovery, Commitment, Anchoring, and Implementation (Daubner & Priestland, 2012).

Discovery Through Curiosity

Key elements of the discovery phase included building a core team, developing active sponsorship, and creating the initial case for change. In this phase, the core team interviewed HR professionals from various operating companies to validate the need for a global first-line manager program. The conversations highlighted that, although some countries offered a local program for this target audience, there was room for improvement and a need to create a common approach to leverage design costs for a large target audience. At the same time, it was confirmed that a "one size fits all" program structure, applied to all subsidiaries, would not be effective. There were large variations in the development offers for the target audience. Some operating companies offered a number of training programs for first-line managers; others provided very little support for this management level. Furthermore, local business requirements could not permit large numbers of first-line managers to leave the operations to attend development programs. Therefore, the new intervention had to offer flexibility in terms of delivery and local responsibility for implementation in order not to disrupt operations.

Commitment Through Engagement

Key activities of the second phase included repeated cycles of involving key stakeholder groups in the diagnosis, design planning, and piloting ideas and actions. Concrete actions during this stage involved engagement sessions in operating companies with first-line managers, their line managers, and their direct reports, as well as HR professionals. By bringing representatives of the whole system together, it became clear that the expectations of first-line managers varied widely. Although those who manage first-line managers identified translation of departmental mission, strategies, and deliverables into daily operations as a key requirement, first-line manager direct reports expected support to overcome challenges that kept them from their daily routine. During these meetings, the term "sandwich manager" was established. This metaphor describes the way the first-line managers saw themselves, that is, being in the middle of various demands, expectations, and forces. They saw their main challenge as balancing different expectations. As a result of these engagement sessions, the core team identified more than fifty relevant skills for first-line managers. Through an iterative process with key stakeholders, the most important skills were prioritized and translated into a program framework, which was presented and tested in the third project stage.

Anchoring Through Testing

This phase focused on the identification of structures that would be needed to deliver and sustain a high-quality experience-based intervention over time and resulted in pilot programs in selected countries. During this phase, the project team proposed three main structural design elements, which were approved by the HR leadership team:

1. Develop comprehensive training materials for the prioritized content elements,
2. Include action learning as a comprehensive part of the program, and
3. Develop a unique logo and layout for the program that could be recognized globally within HEINEKEN.

This was the time when the term FLM-DP (First-Line Manager Development Program) was born and became the widely communicated abbreviation for the new intervention. FLM-DP will continually be used in this chapter to refer to the program. As part of this project phase, the FLM-DP was piloted in seven operating companies spread over four different regions. These early programs provided the opportunity to test assumptions and to make required adjustments prior to wider deployment.

Implementing Through Learning

The final phase in designing the intervention was characterized by the identification of global deployment principles and ingredients for successful deployment, which were derived from evaluations of the pilots. In this phase, the program was approved for wider implementation, leading to the integration of the program within regional and local development curricula, and the identification of concrete deployment objectives in the subsidiaries.

Program Description

A common global first-line manager development framework was developed, with the objective to implement the program locally in the operating companies. In line with HEINEKEN's Learning Philosophy, the program was designed in the 70–20–10 approach. The 70 percent leverages the first-line job, including daily experiences and challenges, the 20 percent represents peer coaching under the name "Continuous Learning Groups," and the 10 percent is formal classroom training in the form of workshops. All these elements were integrated into a sustainable and consistent modular framework that provided flexibility for local adjustments (see Figure 15.1). The modules can be delivered individually or grouped together into the three core components outlined below. The workshop content was developed drawing from existing internal training materials. All businesses providing some form of first-line management development were encouraged and acknowledged for sharing their content with the core design team. The materials were modified and packaged into a consistent look and feel. Regardless in which market the FLM-DP is implemented in, this standardized program design provides a development experience for twelve to sixteen first-line managers over approximately nine months.

Kick-Off

The kick-off session introduces the program to the first-line managers, and also provides an opportunity for the first-line managers to meet each other. First-line managers are asked to attend with their line managers. This way both parties are introduced to the purpose and objectives of the FLM-DP and learn about the expectations and commitments that the first-line managers will need to make over the course of the next few months. During the kick-off workshop, participants define learning goals and agree on the focus for their learning during the program with their line

Figure 15.1. HEINEKEN'S FLM-DP Framework

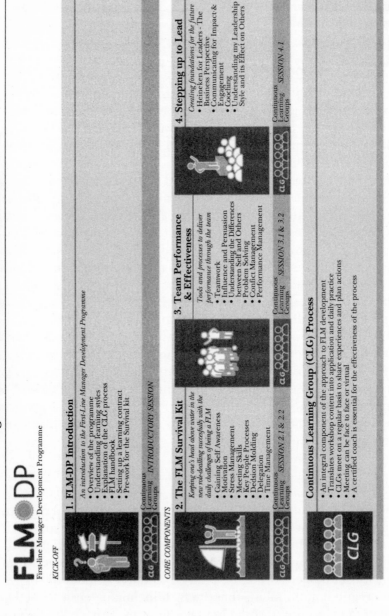

FLM●DP
First-line Manager Development Programme

KICK-OFF

1. FLM-DP Introduction

An introduction to the First-Line Manager Development Programme
- Overview of the programme
- Understanding learning styles
- Explanation of the CLG process
- FLM handbook
- Setting up a learning contract
- Pre-work for the Survival kit

Continuous Learning Groups   *INTRODUCTORY SESSION*

CORE COMPONENTS

2. The FLM Survival Kit

Keeping one's head above water in the new role-dealing succesfully with the daily challenges of being a FLM
- Gaining Self Awareness
- Motivation
- Stress Management
- Meeting Skills
- Key People Processes
- Decision Molding
- Delegation
- Time Management

Continuous Learning Groups   *SESSION 2.1 & 2.2*

3. Team Performance & Effectiveness

Tools and processes to deliver performance through the team
- Teamwork
- Influence and Persuasion
- Understanding the Differences between Self and Others
- Problem Solving
- Conflict Management
- Performance Management

Continuous Learning Groups   *SESSION 3.1 & 3.2*

4. Stepping up to Lead

Creating foundations for the future
- Heineken for Leaders - The Business Perspective
- Communicating for Impact & Engagement
- Coaching
- Understanding my Leadership Style and its Effect on Others

Continuous Learning Groups   *SESSION 4.1*

Continuous Learning Group (CLG) Process

- An integral component of the approach to FLM development
- Translates workshop content into application and daily practice
- CLGs meet on a regular basis to share experiences and plan actions
- Meeting can be face to face or virtual
- A certified coach is essential for the effectiveness of the process

CLG

HEINEKEN

managers. This kick-off session creates the foundation for ongoing conversations related to challenges and learning among first-line manager peers and between a first-line manager and his or her manager.

Workshops

In total, the development program consists of three formal classroom sessions. First, the Survival Kit workshop provides first-line managers with some key skills and processes needed to adapt to a new managerial role and to effectively perform the job as quickly as possible. During this formal training session, participants are introduced to topics such as delegation, meeting skills, time management, and motivation. While the Survival Kit is about helping the first-line managers adapt to their roles, the focus of the Team Performance and Effectiveness workshop is on the line manager's team. Knowing how teams operate and understanding how to get the best from team members is essential to a first-line manager's performance. This workshop supports first-line managers in harnessing individual strengths and differences to enhance team results and provides tools and processes to deliver great performance as a team. Covered topics include teamwork, conflict management, problem solving, and performance management. The third workshop, Stepping up to Lead, focuses on creating the foundations for the future in terms of leading others. This final set of modules builds on the earlier ones and introduces various skills and knowledge that help first-line managers shape a better future, rather than just react to what is going on around them. It consists of modules such as coaching and impactful communication.

The FLM-DP is designed in a flexible way so that the program can be locally implemented as a whole with all nineteen content modules or in a modular approach, where only specific modules are added to existing local programs. All globally designed workshop modules are delivered in the operating companies by local trainers. The objective of this program is not to provide in-depth training in nineteen content themes. Instead, it aims to introduce the first-line managers to these themes by providing basic tools and information that can be applied effectively in their daily work.

Multiple learning methods are included in the workshop design, such as formal instruction, sub-group activities, role plays, feedback sessions, as well as individual reflection phases.

Continuous Learning Groups

In an ever busier world, the ability to reflect on personal and organizational experience is critical for first-line managers in order to recognize successes and mistakes and to embed that learning in their future activities. Therefore, the third component of the FLM-DP aims to enhance learning application through coaching, feedback, and networking.

The development framework includes action learning, under the name "continuous learning groups." A new name was used because the term "action learning" was already used in HEINEKEN in various forms, and individuals held different connotations about the term. Furthermore, the new name suggests that learning occurs frequently, not only during classroom settings, and thus would foster the application of the 70–20–10 learning philosophy.

To help anchor the formal learning into day-to-day practice and to encourage additional skills development in peer coaching, problem solving, and working together, continuous learning groups run at regular intervals throughout the program. Continuous learning groups consist of six to eight first-line managers who meet on a regular basis. One FLM-DP cohort is usually divided into two learning groups. This part of the development framework is grounded in Reg Revan's approach of action learning (Revans, 1972, 1983), which makes use of the current job as the learning laboratory.

Two models underpin the approach so that continuous learning supports the first-line managers' thinking and decision making. The first model is the "action learning equation," which states that learning (L) comes from programmed knowledge (P) and questioning insight (Q) and can be summarized in the formula: $L = P + Q$. This equation highlights that action learning is based on the idea that people have an unlimited capacity to learn from experience but a limited capacity to learn from being taught. The first-line managers in the program learn from their own situations and challenges rather than through exclusively taught knowledge and skills.

The second theoretical basis for action learning is Kolb's learning cycle in combination with the adult learning styles, which have been defined by Honey and Mumford (2006). This theory states that adults have different preferences in how they approach new situations. In order for effective learning to occur, they ideally follow four stages: (1) having an experience, (2) reviewing and reflecting on the experience, (3) concluding from the experience, and (4) planning the next steps. Assuming that phases 1 and 4 mainly take place on the job, the continuous learning groups aim to support the first-line managers in their reflection process and in the development of solutions to difficult problems at work.

For all involved members, these groups provide peer learning, good practice sharing, and reflections. During the sessions, members receive support and challenges from their peers through the central techniques of asking open questions, careful listening, and thoughtful feedback. In order to create a supportive and challenging learning environment, a certified coach facilitates the group meetings. The role of the coach is to introduce the members to the process, to enable trust through good listening, timing, and sensitivity—and perhaps most of all—the ability to allow silence, hold back, and give real space to the group members who present their challenges. Furthermore, the coach demonstrates open questions and fosters honest exchange of constructive feedback.

The role of each learning group member is multi-dimensional. Each member's task during the sessions is to relate to the problems under review and to look for underlying causes. If he or she presents a challenge, the member's role is to take ownership of the issue and to remain open to new perspectives. For all members, it is crucial to use open and curious questions and to apply active listening and high concentration throughout the sessions. Furthermore, all group members agree to follow some simple ground rules. These include respecting the confidentiality of the group members, being present at agreed-on group meetings, and having high commitment to participate actively in the process. Each meeting follows a similar structure and various phases, which the continuous learning coach introduces at the beginning of the first meeting.

The first phase is the Arriving Round. The learning coach asks all members to quickly introduce themselves and to give a short update since the last meeting.

The second stage is called Bidding. Each group member presents issues or a challenging situation at work. At the end of the round, the members decide between them who is going to present to the group on that day. The topics that are brought up during the bidding phase might vary, as they are not bound to a specific topic. Although they do not necessarily have to be related to the topics that have been covered in the classroom workshops, they often are. Examples of topics that have been brought up by group members include personal work-life challenges, difficulties with under-performing team members, creating a team spirit in their teams, and dealing with high pressure and multiple stakeholders.

Once the session topic and presenter are identified, the meeting moves to the Presenting stage. Here, the presenting first-line manager describes the situation, without being interrupted by the group members or the coach.

Once the experience is fully described, the learning coach checks in with the presenter and opens the Questioning phase. This is the core stage of the continuous learning process, as all group members help the presenter to explore his or her issue from different perspectives through open, curious questions. The questions aim to help the presenter to explore his or her own thoughts, experiences, and underlying feelings. In this stage the main challenge for the group members is to avoid giving advice indirectly via leading questions.

During this phase the learning coach checks regularly with the presenter and, when appropriate, announces the next phase, Formulating Actions. In this part, the presenter formulates concrete actions as an outcome of the many questions that have been asked and answered.

After this step, no more questions are asked and the group moves to the Reflection stage. Members reflect back to the presenter what they have heard and talk about their own individual learning and feelings. After listening to each group member, the presenter speaks last and reflects on the experience. The meeting cycle ends with a group Process Review, where the members review how they have worked together and agree on actions in order to make the continuous learning group session more effective.

On average, a full cycle takes approximately ninety minutes. Depending on the scheduled meeting time, a second or third presentation can take place during one session. Throughout the sessions, the learning coach monitors the time and offers observations when appropriate. As this process was a new element of the first-line manager program, the coaches had to be identified and certified prior to piloting the program. Selected HR professionals from the pilot subsidiaries were invited to a global coaching certification workshop in Amsterdam, where HEINEKEN's head office is located. In total, eighteen participants were initially certified as learning coaches, whereby they formed three action learning sets of six individuals each. For this process, HEINEKEN cooperated with Action Learning Associates Limited, a UK-based provider offering in-house training to run action learning sets. The certification included a blended approach of three days of face-to-face classroom training, four virtual coaching sessions, as well as individual reflections captured in a reflective learning log. Once completed, the learning log was submitted to the external coach and the participants shared main learning points in their learning sets. As a result, the participants received an internal HEINEKEN certificate, as well as a certificate from the Institute of Leadership and Management (ILM) in the UK. After the successful first workshop, this certification process was integrated into the overall deployment plan, which assured regular certification events to up-skill HR coaching capabilities for selected learning coaches.

Pilots and Deployment

In its first year, the FLM-DP was piloted in seven operating companies spread over four regions. These subsidiaries were located in Nigeria and Egypt (Region Africa Middle East), in Switzerland and the U.K. (Region Western Europe), in Greece and Austria (Region Central and Eastern Europe) and in the United States (Region Americas). While most markets deployed the framework as explained above, a few subsidiaries chose a modular approach and blended the FLM-DP content with local workshop content. The concept of running continuous learning sessions between classroom workshops remained throughout all pilots.

The choice of local trainers who delivered the program also varied. Some subsidiaries chose to run the program by internal trainers (i.e., learning and development professionals in their respective location). Other subsidiaries chose to cooperate with external trainers to deliver the workshops. These experienced individuals had previous relationships with the operating companies based on prior delivery of leadership training. All trainers received the bank of participant and facilitator materials in advance and had the opportunity to contact the core project team members in case of specific questions or required coaching. In some subsidiaries, such as Nigeria, Austria, and Egypt, the project managers joined the kick-off sessions and supported the trainers with the preparations to run the workshops. In addition, the trainers as well as local HR professionals received access to an online e-room, which captured the training materials and additional information. Due to various language requirements, some markets translated the training materials to their local languages.

In the first year of the program, all pilots were deployed successfully, and quantitative and qualitative evaluations were conducted. Once the seven pilot programs were completed, the operating companies proceeded with the deployment of the FLM-DP for a wider group. Beyond introducing the FLM-DP to the pilot markets, the core team cooperated closely with the regional learning and development managers to promote wider deployment in the organization. The cooperation included presentations at regional HR meetings as well as regular phone conversations and meetings with the regional teams. At the end of its first year, the FLM-DP was introduced to the wider organization. Within the four pilot regions, more than twenty-five subsidiaries had signed up for FLM-DP deployment. In addition, Region Asia Pacific planned an FLM-DP introduction workshop with the core team to introduce the initiative to their subsidiaries. Furthermore, the program was piloted for fourteen first-line managers for a global function in the head office. The experiences from these events supported the global rollout of the program, leading to more than thirty-five subsidiaries deploying the program by mid-2012. Throughout the implementation of the initiative, evaluations have been conducted to analyze the intervention's impact.

Impact

To assess the impact of the program, quantitative and qualitative evaluations have been conducted in the pilot markets, and best practices around successful deployment have been captured and shared for future application.

Quantitative scores indicate that the first-line managers themselves have been highly satisfied with the workshops. On a 6-point scale, the average score for all pilot workshops was 5. Main points addressed in the evaluation forms were relevance of the covered content, satisfaction with the trainer, preparation prior to the workshops, as well as the alignment and support from the line managers. Although satisfaction with the trainers and covered content were always scored high, the first-line managers' satisfaction with their line managers varied. In some operating companies, first-line managers reported a lack of their managers' interest and support in the FLM-DP. This made it more difficult for them to apply the new lessons effectively on the job. Information meetings with the line managers were held to bridge this gap.

In addition, qualitative evaluations have been conducted with first-line managers themselves, their line managers, continuous learning group coaches, and HR professionals. Overall, the evaluations reflected the high impact of the program and the high satisfaction of those involved. The first-line managers themselves were committed to the program and reported a change in their behavior and a sense of unity, which developed during their participation in the program. Their ideas for improvement included a more structured process to review the learning contract progress with their managers at regular intervals throughout the program, as well as an outline of a long-term development curriculum.

The line managers of the first-line managers also observed a positive change in the first-line managers' behavior, such as increased listening skills. To improve their understanding of the FLM-DP, the line managers suggested providing better understanding of the operation and purpose of the continuous learning groups.

The third group who contributed to the qualitative evaluations consisted of local HR managers in the pilot markets, who recognized that the program impacted the organization positively and valued a global investment in this initiative. While local HR reported overall that the workshop modules were well received, some HR professionals thought that the content could be perceived as too intense (i.e., in Austria) or too light (i.e., in the UK).

The continuous learning group coaches made up the final group providing feedback about the FLM-DP. Similar to the first-line managers, the coaches confirmed the relevance of the continuous learning groups to the overall FLM-DP architecture. This group also highlighted another aspect: their own development and the fact that the continuous learning groups build HR capability within HEINEKEN. Asked for suggestions to improve the program, some coaches mentioned the need to better understand the FLM-DP, for example, by experiencing selected modules themselves.

Evaluating the pilots and the active involvement of the core project team resulted in a bank of experiences and best practices around the successful deployment that were shared with regional representatives and other markets that planned to deploy the program. One important role of the global team was to analyze successful program deployments in order to identify ingredients for success and to communicate these more broadly. Ultimately, seven main areas were highlighted (see Figure 15.2).

1. *Program Architecture:* Delegates quickly realize that the program is more of a development journey than a one-off workshop, and they appreciate the mix of elements. Although the program framework was developed centrally, it leaves flexibility for the operating companies to adjust it to their local needs.

2. *Flexibility in Relevant Content:* Participants and trainers of the pilots reported a demanding workshop agenda, but at the same time doable. Therefore, the local training team is required to adjust the content covered and the pace of delivery to suit the local group composition and needs.

3. *Delivery Style:* Trainers might need to adjust their training styles, especially in those regions or operating companies where more lecture is predominant, such as in Nigeria. For the FLM-DP, an active, participative delivery of the content is essential for success. The core team pointed these differences out to the trainer

Figure 15.2. FLM-DP's Seven Ingredients for Success

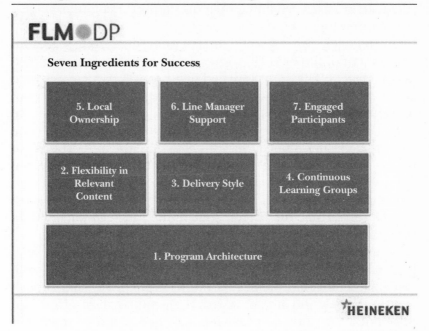

teams and supported their first delivery through role modeling, coaching, and feedback.

4. *Continuous Learning Group Process:* This element is seen to be a positive and innovative addition to classroom training, which supports the implementation of the 70–20–10 learning philosophy. With this action-oriented element of the FLM-DP, individuals have a clear example of how on-the-job learning and peer coaching can contribute to a successful change in behavior.

5. *Local Ownership:* Accountability by the local operating company is critical to the success of the program. Where the local HR team has made extra effort, the benefit is seen in terms of clarity of expectations, pre-work completion, engagement of attendees, and sponsorship through senior management.

6. *Line Manager Support:* The line managers are essential for the success of the FLM-DP. In the pilot programs, the majority of supervisors of the first-line managers attended the kick-off session.

Prior to the program, as well as during this session, they received adequate briefings, enabling them to support first-line managers in their development.

7. *Engaged Participants:* The last ingredient for successful deployment of the FLM-DP addresses the target audience of first-line managers. The pilots revealed that, overall, participants were active, motivated, and eager to learn. Since this initiative includes first-line managers of all functions, there were diverse levels of experience and capability of attendees across the operating companies. Delegates valued this diversity and the opportunity to receive insights about other areas in the business, which created a sense of unity. At the same time it was clear that the challenges of being a first-line manager are similar, irrespective of the function or role. Thus, the overall conclusion and recommendation from the center was to run the FLM-DP cross-functionally.

Another aspect for success relates to the selection of the first-line manager participants. Since the FLM-DP targeted a wide audience of first-line managers within HEINEKEN, the project team purposely did not issue strict selection criteria. However, since not all six thousand first-line managers could be trained at the same time, they recommended choosing high performers and learning-motivated, development-oriented employees for the pilots or first training batches in the subsidiaries. While the initially inclusive program became exclusive in terms of immediate participation, this had the positive effect that the chosen participants felt rewarded and they appreciated being selected for this initiative (Daubner & Vinkenburg, 2012).

In conclusion, the FLM-DP proved to be successful on three levels: (1) the program architecture that sets the foundation for the intervention, (2) the three structural program features that have to be considered and realized in cooperation with the regional and local HR professionals and the local trainers: flexibility in relevant content, delivery style, and the continuous learning groups, and (3) local HR responsibility for local ownership, line manager support, and engaged participants.

The positive feedback and experiences from the pilots resulted in a continued pull from the wider organization and thus an extended rollout to more subsidiaries in all regions. In the summer of 2012, the FLM-DP initiative was awarded with the International HEINEKEN HR Star Award in recognition for outstanding accomplishments. To date, the FLM-DP stands as a best practice to create a sustainable, experienced-based development offer for first-line managers in HEINEKEN.

Looking Forward

Following the experiences and feedback from the pilots, a set of deployment principles was created, as shown in Table 15.1. In short, the deployment principles aim to assure the high quality and sustainable application of the program worldwide. While they are derived from the observed and aggregated ingredients for success, these principles are future-oriented. They illustrate room for local modifications and boundaries for operating companies.

As the program continues to take root in businesses around the world, it will be imperative to review and clarify roles for the center and regional staff. Many operational tasks such as scheduling and program evaluation should shift to the regions to allow the center to focus on content enhancements, continuing education of the learning coaches, and facilitating the sharing of lessons learned and best practices across regions. In addition, the center must begin to systemically address the learning needs of managers of first-line managers in order to continue developing the leadership pipeline.

Insights and Inquiry

This section originally began as "lessons learned"; however, the design team put into practice lessons they and others had learned, captured them as Ingredients for Success (Figure 15.2), and created sustaining mechanisms for ensuring relevance, utility, and broad deployment of these ingredients. Hence, this section will leverage the FLM-DP intervention as a catalyst for insights and further inquiry related to experience-based leadership development interventions.

People Want Programs

The very successful FLM-DP described in this chapter contains more program elements than were originally envisioned. The vision and essential guiding principle for the design and

Table 15.1. FLM-DP Deployment Principles

Deployment Principle	Description
Local Delivery	• Ownership by the local operating company is critical to the success of the program. • Where extra effort has been made by the local HR team, the benefit is seen in terms of clarity of expectations, pre-work completion, and engagement of attendees.
Common Framework with Flexible Modular Approach	• The first-line managers appreciate that they can draw on similar development wherever they are in HEINEKEN. • The local training team must adjust the content covered and the pace of delivery to suit the local group composition and need.
70–20–10 Learning Philosophy: Core Content and Continuous Learning Groups	• Delegates quickly pick up that this program is different—more of a development journey. • They appreciate the mix of elements, inputs, activities, reflection, and continuous learning groups. • The continuous learning group process has been very well received and seen to be a positive and innovative addition to the classroom training.
Efficiency and Sustainability	• Operating companies integrate existing programs into the FLM-DP framework over time.
Consistent High Quality	• Banks of resources are developed with flexibility of application in mind. • Operating companies source trainers from locally known and trusted providers they have worked with in the past. • Continuous learning group coaches take on the role only after having been through a global training and certification process.
Regional Prioritization	• Regions decide on nomination criteria and rollout plans together with their operating companies.

implementation of an intervention to develop first-line managers (and serve as a catalyst for system-wide development) was to focus on the 70 percent on-the-job, experience-based learning, not the 10 percent formal training. So why has it been necessary to package and position the FLM-DP as a training program? The intervention is launched via kick-off workshops, followed by fairly typical training sessions covering multiple content modules prior to initiating continuous learning group activities.

First, there is an inherent comfort level in providing training programs to targeted audiences. This is the paradigm current line and HR executives have grown up with (and possibly experienced themselves); it suits the capabilities of many learning professionals; and it matches the expectations of those who invest in their own development. Further, we have structures associated with formal training, not with experience-based learning. Consider aspects of formal training such as defined course length, existing budget structures, benchmarks for costs and participant satisfaction, criteria for trainer selection (including facilitation skills and subject-matter expertise)—all very controllable variables. Development that places an individual's experience in the forefront doesn't have many controllable aspects to it: What is the experience? What content will be useful? How long will it take? Who has expertise (other than the trainer)? and How will success be measured? The fundamental question associated with the insight that "people want programs" is: Will we need to continue leveraging training containers to target real-time development?

Ongoing Investment Required

Real-time, experience-based development requires ongoing investment. This insight will certainly sound alarms in any organization, given the economic uncertainty coupled with a necessary focus on cost management. The challenge is to define the investment, as well as to attach a value to building leadership capacity and instilling collaborative, real-time learning throughout an organizational system. It is true that experience-based development programs, like the FLM-DP, should not conclude in the same way as training programs that have a defined beginning and end. In fact, it is still common practice for participants to receive certificates of completion at the conclusion of training programs.

Will the continuous learning groups garner enough momentum and return enough value to carry on as first-line managers continue to tackle new challenges in constantly evolving organizations? Will the organization continue investing in current and new continuous learning group coaches, providing additional support for new coaches and deeper development of capability among existing coaches? Will organizational culture and processes support the institutionalization of good practice transfer and lessons learned? Will the organization replicate the experience-based learning approach for other groups of leaders? Affirmative answers to any of the above questions will require ongoing investment. However, this doesn't have to mean additional investment. It will require shifting mindsets and resources from a more traditional, individual leader development model (e.g., distinct offers for segmented populations) to collective development (e.g., streamlined offers increasing capability across multiple populations).

Existing Structures Will Be Upset

By its very nature, experience-based development has greater potential to impact defined career paths, job families, role descriptions, and performance management than do more traditional management development approaches. For example, one could consider the continuous learning coach's role as a next step progression for a first-line manager. Perhaps not a full-time role, but building in time and expectation that a first-line manager should master the learning coach role prior to being considered for promotion to a next level management role expands career options and builds a stronger bench of mid-level managers with necessary coaching capabilities and the ability to learn from experience.

Unfortunately, roles that include requirements related to coaching, facilitating, or convening groups (in the case of FLM-DP groups of peers) are generally associated with HR, not with line management. Managers are rewarded for delivering results, not for developing themselves or others. The specific challenges highlighted during a leader's participation in an experience-based development intervention could be built into performance management objectives (as opposed to often broad and vague development objectives related to leadership), but will highlighting specific challenges be viewed as a weakness? Learning professionals in an HR function could be required to gain additional organization development expertise prior to contributing to an experience-based development intervention, thus raising the bar on requirements for those who design and facilitate leader development initiatives.

The questions and challenges raised above regarding experience-based development, while not an exhaustive list, remain to be answered. However, we do know the pace of change and the complexity of challenges facing leaders at all levels in organizations today is quickly surpassing traditional leadership and management development approaches. The example of FLM-DP detailed in this chapter describes the start of an experience journey for HEINEKEN and its leaders—its substantial success is yet to unfold.

References

Bersin and Associates. (2012). *Learning leaders 2012: Lessons from the best.* Oakland, CA: Author.

Corporate Leadership Council. (2006). *Making the transition to first-line management: Frameworks, tools, and templates for managing a smooth transition process.* Washington, DC: Corporate Executive Board.

Daubner, D., & Priestland, A. (2012). Walk slow to go fast: How HEINEKEN uses the SEARCH Approach. *OD Practitioner, 44*(4), 53–60.

Daubner, D., & Vinkenburg, C. J. (2012, April). *Does inclusive employee development become exclusive talent management? A case study of how HEINEKEN develops first-line managers.* Presentation at EIASM Workshop on Talent Management, Brussels, Belgium.

Hill, L. (2003). *Becoming a manager: How new managers master the challenge of leadership.* Boston, MA: Harvard Business School Press.

Honey, P., & Mumford, A. (2006). *The Learning Styles helper's guide.* Maidenhead, UK: Peter Honey Publications.

McCall, M. W., Jr., Lombardo, M. M., & Morrison, A. M. (1988). *The lessons of experience: How successful executives develop on the job.* New York, NY: The Free Press.

McCauley, C. D., Ruderman, M. N., Ohlott, P. J., & Morrow, J. E. (1994). Assessing the developmental components of managerial jobs. *Journal of Applied Psychology, 79,* 544–560.

Revans, R. W. (1972). Action learning: A management development programme. *Personnel Review, 1*(4), 36–44.

Revans, R. W. (1983). The validation of action learning programmes. *Management Learning, 14*(3), 208–211.

Yost, P. R., & Plunkett, M .M. (2009). *Real time leadership development.* Cambridge, MA: Wiley-Blackwell.

CHAPTER SIXTEEN

Turning Experience into Expertise
The Everyday Learning Disciplines for Leaders

Jeffrey J. McHenry and D. Douglas McKenna

Richard was a young manager on the move. From a slate of candidates, the worldwide operations VP had selected him for promotion to the operations director position on her team. Here's how he earned this assignment . . . and a warning from his new manager.

In seven years, Richard had moved up four levels in his division. He started out as an individual contributor before stepping up to front-line manager. Two years later, he advanced to site manager. And now, as operations director, he was taking on responsibility for more than one thousand employees and contractors at sites across the United States.

Richard had made his mark by turning around struggling teams. He was confident that he knew how to be a leader: immerse yourself in the details of the business, tell people exactly how you want things done, and push, push, push for results.

When he moved from managing a team to managing a site, Richard continued to spend 60 percent of his time with front-line employees, watching them in action, and instructing them on how to do their work. He urged them to text him any time they had an operations or customer problem.

They accepted his invitation—in droves. Richard boasted to a peer that his operations employees were sending him more than one thousand texts every month.

Now, as his VP informed him of his promotion to operations director, she expressed confidence that he could handle this assignment. But she also warned that this job would be a big step up. "You will have to change your style," the VP said. "You have a strong team of managers. You can count on them to run the operation. Customer satisfaction and employee morale are among the best in the business."

"Let me be clear, Richard: this is not a turnaround. What this business needs is a technology strategy. Focus your enthusiasm on that and you'll do well."

This job had the right stuff to spur Richard's growth as a leader. He would have to deal with the scrutiny of the executive leadership team. He would have to learn to lead an already successful organization. He would have to figure out how to manage through a team of capable managers, each of whom had earned the right to run his or her own piece of the business. Most important, given his track record, Richard would have to work against the grain of the approach that had worked so well for him in turnaround situations.

Now, just for a moment, imagine you are Richard's coach, mentor, or HR business partner. What if Richard had come to you, asking for your advice on how to tackle this job and learn as much as possible from the experience? What guidance would you have given him?

Unfortunately, Richard didn't ask anyone for help. He dove into the job with determination and a turnaround mindset. Despite his VP's warning, Richard focused on his organization's operations and saw problems everywhere. He disagreed with the way business processes were defined and executed. When his site managers attempted to explain how and why things were working, Richard refused to listen. He told them they weren't deep enough into the details to see the problems. Richard decided half the leadership team needed to be replaced. But before he could fire them, they started leaving on their own. Over the course of Richard's first year in the director job, four of his six managers left, and the organization's performance slid downhill.

Sadly, Richard never realized that his mindset would not scale. Rather than stretching to understand his new job and its context, he managed from within his comfort zone. He threw all his energy into doing more of what had worked for him before. As a result, he broke the organization. Things did not go well for his VP in the wake of this disaster. And HR spent months cleaning up after Richard.

Stories like Richard's occur too often. By force-fitting reality to their style or strength, a leader steers his organization off course. Performance and morale problems sprout like weeds and spread throughout the group's ecosystem. The job of pulling them usually falls to others (e.g., the boss, peers, other groups), who are forced to spend their time interrupting decline rather than cultivating growth.

But equally important in the long run, the manager who fails to learn from experience wastes a precious development resource—the job itself. Not only does the manager miss out on an opportunity to expand his abilities and prepare for bigger jobs, but so do others in the organization who need that assignment to build their portfolios of leadership experience and capability. The organization squanders a precious stretch job experience that could have been invested in another high potential leader.

Leaders grow primarily through experience, but if the way they go about it is more incidental than deliberate, then we are all leaving money and performance on the table. It's time to get serious about doing more than just guiding leaders into jobs that will expose them to the experiences they need to grow. Organizations—and people like us who spend our days trying to help managers and executives improve their performance and expand their capacity—need to do a better job of systematically helping them make the most of their experiences in stretch assignments.

But here's the good news: over the past twenty years, a new field of research has emerged. It is the science of expertise. Its groundbreaking investigators are discovering principles and practices that stand ready to be capitalized on by organizations, leadership development professionals, and leaders themselves.

In this chapter, we invite you to join us in exploring this new science, which investigates how experts—elite performers in their fields—break through barrier after barrier in their quest for the kind of learning that drives great, not just good, performance (Ericsson, 2009; Feltovich, Prietula, & Ericsson, 2006).

First, we will explain the key principles of expertise and consider their generalizability to the nature and development of leadership.

Second, we will present a set of practices based on these principles and designed to help leaders squeeze as much learning as possible out of the curriculum of situations they face every day. We call these practices the Everyday Learning Disciplines. For managers like Richard who need to relax their grip on a favored style or previously successful mindset, the Everyday Learning Disciplines give them a way to step back and take a more objective view of their circumstances, their understanding of what's happening, and how their actions are contributing to the sequence of events they are experiencing. From that new vantage point, they are able to try out fresh ways of conceptualizing their challenges and experiment with different patterns of action.

Third, we will conclude this chapter with thoughts about how you, as a manager or leadership development professional, can put the Everyday Learning Disciplines to work with your leaders to help them gain the most from their experience and move toward mastery.

Principles of Expertise

Expertise Is Extreme Adaptation to Context

Experts "extremely adapt" their responses to the unique characteristics, conditions, and constraints—the context—of the task at hand (Ericsson, 2009; Salas & Rosen, 2010). This definition holds for experts in any domain, whether that domain is deep, like quantum physics, or wide, like general management. Musician David Byrne speaks of extreme adaptation in his definition of genius: "Genius, the emergence of a truly remarkable and memorable work," he writes, "seems to appear when a thing is perfectly suited to its context" (Byrne, 2012, p. 30).

An expert dives deep into the tasks and context of her work. She is determined to understand how things happen so she can pull the right levers to get extraordinary results. She strives to be as reality based as possible, consciously and unconsciously looking for and taking into account facts, features, and patterns that less expert performers might overlook or misinterpret. She watches for signs that important factors have changed because reality is a moving target. This helps her avoid the mistake of force-fitting an obsolete, inadequate, or wrong-headed mindset onto an evolving circumstance.

In essence, an expert is constantly refining his ability to do the right thing at the right time in the right way to achieve superior results.

But what happens when a road-tested expert in one context moves into a new job in a different context? For example, what should we expect when a three-star Air Force general, an expert in a well-funded military bureaucracy, becomes a senior executive in a corporation selling military aircraft to foreign governments in a climate of stiff competition? Or when Richard, an expert in turning around unsuccessful small groups, takes charge of a successful large organization needing a strategic intervention?

Elite Performance Is Non-Transferable

The answer from the science of expertise is that superior performance does not transfer from one domain or context to another. But hold on, you say. Wouldn't an Air Force general be able to put his hard-earned insights, skills, and character strength to work as an aerospace executive? Wouldn't Richard's ability to troubleshoot operational problems and deliver tough feedback give him a leg up in his new job?

Of course. But for the general or Richard to achieve an *expert* level of performance, these abilities will have to be re-tuned to their new context. A superstar in one industry, company, or function must shift into high learning gear to achieve the same level of performance in a different context. This is true "even when the domains seem, intuitively, very similar" (Feltovich, Prietula, & Ericsson, 2006, p. 47).

Competent performance may transfer, but superior performance must be earned over and over as the work and the context change.

We watched many leaders grapple with this challenge during our years in leadership development at Microsoft. Senior executives with sterling records and diverse experience at other companies, even those who had worked at other successful software companies, floundered or failed if they did not take or were not given the time to adjust to Microsoft's unique culture and context.

What does this mean for leader development? It means that leaders must maintain a perpetual learning mindset to realize superior performance. It means that subtle differences in context are a big deal when you aspire to play at the highest levels of your field. It means leaders in new assignments—and their managers— must manage their expectations during the time it takes to adjust to a new context.

Expertise Takes Time and Experience to Develop

Studies of elite performers across many fields (e.g., science, fine and performing arts, athletics) show that it takes a minimum of ten years of experience in a domain to perform at a world-class level (Ericsson, 1996). It takes a long time because expertise develops through repeated exposure to and practice in handling the important situations that arise in a performance context.

But in many contexts, getting the repetitions you need to refine your skills can be difficult. In organizations, some important situations may only occur once a year (e.g., annual business reviews), others even less frequently (e.g., a product reliability debacle). So an aspiring expert who moves on to her next job too quickly may get only one round of practice—or no practice at all—in handling a type of event that is key to superior performance in that job or context. She misses the opportunity to apply lessons learned from the first experience to improve her performance the second and third times around.

It also takes time to develop a deep, functional understanding of a job or domain. Whether it's patterns of pieces on a chessboard or competitors in a market space, an aspiring expert needs experience to begin to see how elements and events in her field of play are organized and how they affect each other.

For executives, these insights into how things work in their jobs and business contexts allow them to see through complexity and focus their attention on the most precise, efficient, and powerful levers of action. Where others would be confused or paralyzed by too much or too little information, an expert leader has learned to look for key bits of information that signal the operation of an underlying pattern, a pattern she's seen and handled before. As a result, she can narrow down her alternatives for action to those that have worked when that pattern has appeared before. This enables her to focus on tuning her response to the nuances of this particular situation, adapting her action to the context.

If you've worked closely with developing leaders, you understand the time it takes for them to experience the rhythm and challenges of a particular job or context. You've probably watched a number of fast-track leaders move in and out of jobs so quickly that they missed an important phase of a business cycle. Or you've stood by and witnessed a rising star launch a giant reorganization, then leave before having to deal with the consequences of his decisions.

There are fast tracks to the top, but shortcuts exact a price. Critical experiences are missed or go undigested. Too many bright young executives arrive at top-level jobs without the breadth and depth of experience they need to lead. They've moved up too quickly to achieve mastery of the context at each step on their career paths.

Experience ≠ Excellence

But experience does not guarantee excellence. We have all failed at times to learn from our experience. Or we've learned the wrong thing. So a long resume recounting years of experience—even potent, diverse experience—is not a good predictor of how a person will perform in a new job (McDaniel, Schmidt, & Hunter, 1988). And you don't have to be a scientist to appreciate this fact. Community organizer Saul Alinsky described the problem well in *Rules for Radicals*: "Most people go through life undergoing a series of happenings, which pass through undigested" (Alinsky, 1971, p. 47).

In some fields, however, experience is related to performance—but in the wrong direction. Studies of physicians and nurses show that experience beyond the first two years of practice is associated with declining performance (Ericsson, Whyte, & Ward, 2007). Anders Ericsson (2009), a trailblazer in the study of expertise, observes that even with ten or more years of experience, "most professionals reach a stable, pedestrian level of performance and stay there *for the rest of their careers*" (p. 405) [emphasis added].

So now we have a puzzle to solve. Learners need time and experience in a domain to achieve proficiency and improve their performance. But time and experience do not guarantee proficiency, let alone mastery. There must be another factor in the equation that interacts with experience to produce improved performance. But before we reveal that factor, let's take a closer look at the role of experience in learning.

Experience Builds Flexibility and Automaticity

To perform competently and independently, a learner must be able to handle the problems and situations that arise in a given job or activity. With conscious effort, practice, and feedback, the individual learns to recognize differences between situations and adjust her response accordingly. With additional practice, her adjustments become automatic and habitual; she is able to perform competently without conscious effort or strain.

When it comes to complex tasks, we learn gradually, progressively—step-by-step. For a beginner, the first step is to apply rules or procedures to situations, giving minimal consideration to contextual nuance or complication. As long as the rules generally fit the situation, the beginner can avoid gross mistakes (Dreyfus, 1983). But to move past the beginner stage, the learner needs experience *in situ*. Through experience in different situations, the beginner learns when to bend the rules and how to adjust his response to take account of situation-specific features and conditions. When he can do this effectively, his performance improves and he moves up and out of the beginner stage. But this higher level of capability can only develop when he wrestles with the experience of different situations.

As the learner makes these adjustments repeatedly (i.e., he practices), his brain begins to process task-related information and performance differently as well. In the early stages of learning, when the learner must maintain a high level of conscious effort and attention to achieve an acceptable level of performance, functional magnetic resonance images (fMRI) show high levels of activity in domain general control areas or networks of the brain (Hill & Schneider, 2006). But with continuing practice, these general-purpose networks quiet down, turning over processing to domain-specific representation areas that support automatic, unconscious, effortless performance. As these psychological and neurological changes occur, the learner is able to perform at an acceptable level without even thinking consciously about it.

This is where the real challenge of developing expertise begins. Once an acceptable level of performance becomes automatic and effortless, most learners become comfortable and satisfied. They've worked hard, developed some good habits, and experienced some success. They relax and coast. But what if they are determined to improve?

Or what if an individual discovers that the nature of his situation has changed in an important way, making his automatic approach ineffective or even detrimental? Will he persist—like Richard—in doing what comes naturally or will he figure out how to adapt?

The Expert Paradox: Automaticity Interrupted

To adapt in real time, a performer must be able to see what's happening, know what to do, and know how to do it. This level of capability develops only with repeated exposure to and practice in a performance context. It is critical to competent performance.

But to *extremely adapt* to the reality of a novel or changing situation, the aspiring expert must interrupt her well-practiced instincts and make adjustments for features of the situation that are unexpected, unfamiliar, or previously unnoticed.

Efforts to improve performance require this same process of interrupting automaticity. As Ericsson (2009, p. 417) says, "Experts never allow their performance to become completely automated." This is the Expert Paradox: Experts build good habits, and then they break them. They interrupt their good habits and upgrade their performance by editing out weaknesses, refining useful elements, and adding new capabilities.

A senior executive needs the speed and efficiency of thought and action that comes with repetition. There is not enough time or energy available to consciously process the volume of information that constantly bombards a senior leader. Her automated understanding of a situation will never be perfect, but without it she will be swamped with data and paralyzed by uncertainty. Her working memory will be maxed out with details, leaving no open lanes in her brain available to attend to and make sense of features of situations that she has not seen or handled before (Kahneman, 2011).

However, these essential, but limiting, habits of thought and action resist interruption once they are neurologically inscribed. In a very physical way, practice makes permanent. Years of repetitive experience strengthen ways of thinking and acting that yield satisfactory performance. But then those habits become barriers to adaptation that leads to higher levels of performance. As we will see, breaking good habits is hard work, which is why most professionals stop improving soon after they reach an acceptable level of performance—the "OK Plateau," as Lemov, Woolway, and Yezzi (2012) so memorably put it.

These automatic patterns, built from experience and practice, must be interrupted and upgraded into more sophisticated mental models that detect situational nuance and direct attention to the most critical elements of performance in a particular context. Those who continue on the path of expertise, who continue to try to improve their performance, have found a way to do this. They have learned how to practice—how to work with experience—in ways that interrupt old habits and build new, more refined ones. This special kind of practice resolves the Expert Paradox and turns experience into expertise.

How Experts Practice

Experts resolve the Expert Paradox through deliberate practice (Ericsson, 2009). It involves a concentrated effort to interrupt automatic habits of thought and action and then rebuild them to facilitate a higher level of performance and/or adaptation to changes in context.

Deliberate practice is hard work that demands more than most professionals are willing to undertake once they have reached an acceptable level of proficiency in their domains (Ericsson, 2009). It focuses on identifying, eliminating, or changing any factor (i.e., cognitive, emotional, behavioral, contextual) that is limiting performance. It's not about playing to your strengths. It's about working on your weaknesses (Deakin & Cobley, 2003).

Deliberate practice begins when the learner recognizes that automated habits of thought and action won't allow him to achieve his goals. Practice tasks are then designed to interrupt those habits and develop a new approach. The problem could be an element of a golf stroke, an obsolete business plan, or how to respond to a sabotaging peer. Concentration distinguishes deliberate practice from mindless routine performance and playful engagement, both of which merely strengthen existing habits. Other key identifiers of deliberate practice include (Ericsson, 2009; Shadrick & Lussier, 2009):

- Focus on areas of weakness or limitation
- Emphasis on the more difficult aspects of performance
- Design and practice of tasks that interrupt automatic patterns
- Limiting the scope and duration of practice to avoid cognitive and emotional depletion and allow mastery to be achieved
- Immediate, focused, evaluative feedback on practice performance (e.g., from a coach, from objective performance measures)
- Repetition of practice performance as soon after feedback as possible
- Repetition of a new, more adaptive element until it becomes automatic and can be reintegrated with whole performance

Deliberate practice is a never-ending, iterative process for the elite performer. But it is also the path that must be taken by anyone with aspirations beyond basic competence.

The Everyday Learning Disciplines for Leaders

Just like other professionals, leaders need deliberate practice to adapt to new jobs and contexts and to enhance their performance. But how can executives, already working more than fifty hours per week, find time for this kind of intensive practice?

There's barely enough time to prepare for each meeting, let alone take time out to practice. It's always show time for busy executives, or as Miles Davis told a new member of his band, "We rehearse on the bandstand."

What if, rather than accepting the conventional argument that there's no time to practice, a leader could think of all the events, meetings, emails, and hallway conversations that keep her running from morning to night as opportunities for deliberate practice? What if she thought about each conference call as a chance to learn and improve, not just as a chance to move forward on her business goals? What if she had a simple methodology for putting the principles of deliberate practice to work with her day-to-day challenges?

In our teaching and executive coaching work, we have begun using an approach we call the "Everyday Learning Disciplines." These disciplines are designed to help leaders do deliberate practice in "the ongoing stream of experience" (McCall & Hollenbeck, 2008). The Everyday Learning Disciplines are a set of eight practices that any leader can use to interrupt old habits and build new ones, and in so doing, improve his performance and expand his ability to adapt to new and changing contexts. The Everyday Learning Disciplines take time, and we've already conceded that leaders' calendars are packed. But the leaders we've worked with say that the efficiencies gained from practicing these disciplines more than make up for the time invested. Our evidence is anecdotal, but what we've seen is promising.

Figure 16.1 shows the eight disciplines and how they work together to support a leader's learning from everyday experience.

In the following section, we will describe each discipline and trace its roots back to the principles of deliberate practice. We will also use Richard's story to show how he could have used the Everyday Learning Disciplines to grow into his new job.

Discipline 1: Position for Stretch

An aspiring leader must position herself for stretch at the career, job, and task levels of performance. First, at the career level, she must define the domain or context in which she will specialize and work toward expertise. As we have seen, experts understand

Figure 16.1. Everyday Learning Disciplines for Leaders

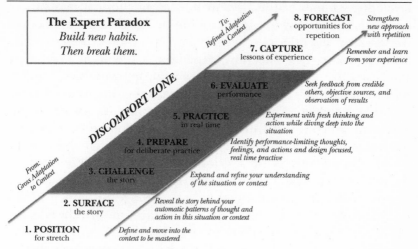

The Expert Paradox
Build new habits.
Then break them.

To: Refined Adaptation to Context

8. FORECAST
opportunities for
repetition

Strengthen new approach with repetition

7. CAPTURE
lessons of experience

Remember and learn from your experience

DISCOMFORT ZONE

6. EVALUATE
performance

Seek feedback from credible others, objective sources, and observation of results

5. PRACTICE
in real time

Experiment with fresh thinking and action while diving deep into the situation

4. PREPARE
for deliberate practice

Identify performance-limiting thoughts, feelings, and actions and design focused, real time practive

3. CHALLENGE
the story

Expand and refine your understanding of the situation or context

From: Gross Adaptation to Context

2. SURFACE
the story

Reveal the story behind your automatic patterns of thought and action in this situation or context

1. POSITION
for stretch

Define and move into the context to be mastered

that deep understanding and fine-tuned adjustments of action in a context develop slowly and progressively, even for the most gifted person.

A young leader has no time for dabbling on the road to excellence. She must focus on and specialize in a domain. That domain may be a function (e.g., sales, R&D, HR) or general management, but circumscribing the area in which she wants to develop expertise is essential to having repeated exposure, practice, and feedback across the range of important situations that must be mastered.

In making this choice of domain, it is critical that the leader define a domain (or a mission) that she is passionate about. On the road to expertise, she will persevere only if her determination to excel is strong enough to carry her through situations in which uncertainty, discomfort, risk, and resistance run high. Without a deep, driving desire to learn from and lean into tension-packed situations, the leader is likely to settle for competence versus mastery.

Second, a leader must position herself for stretch at the job level. Stretch jobs put leaders in hot seats. The seat may be hot because an organization is in trouble or because the challenges that await the leader are beyond her range of experience and understanding. One executive explained it this way: "Every time I'm ready for a new job and have several opportunities, I always pick the one that's scariest, because that's the one where I know I'll learn the most." This steady diet of complex, risky assignments is not for everyone, but for those whose goal is superior performance, it's the diet of choice.

Finally, a leader must position herself for stretch by tackling the job with a learning mindset. This is the mindset that will cause her, for example, to volunteer to go on stage to launch a new product at a major industry convention stage, specifically because she is anxious about speaking to large groups.

So how does this first Everyday Learning Discipline apply to Richard? We think he's chosen well in defining the context he wants to master (i.e., Operations). He loves the work and tackles its challenges with zest. And he has taken a job that will push him way beyond the limits of his well-developed first-line manager mentality. He has positioned himself very well for learning and growth.

But we would have liked to explore several positioning questions with Richard's VP before she bumped him up to operations director. First, given Richard's deeply ingrained hands-on style, is it possible that the operations director job may be too big a stretch for him? Before leaping into this big job, should she have insisted that he demonstrate the ability to delegate at least some decision-making authority to the managers working for him?

Second, is she prepared to invest *significant* time in coaching Richard on how to handle specific situations and relationships in a different way? What other support is she prepared to provide for what surely will be a challenging transition for him?

As McCall and McHenry note in the next chapter in this book, executives who are great talent developers think carefully about giving their direct reports just the right amount of "stretch." When the stretch is just right, the young leader can only succeed by rethinking her approach and exploring alternative paths of action. As a result, she breaks through the Expert Paradox and moves up to a new level of capability.

Discipline 2: Surface the Story

We know that experts improve their performance by bringing their understanding into closer and closer alignment with the realities of their work and its context (Argyris, 1999; Ericsson, 2009; Klein, 1999, 2002, 2009). They do this by observing the landscape, the people, and the forces that shape events and produce results. From these observations, the leader creates a story that, when carefully examined, reveals her theory about what is happening, how it's happening, why it's happening, and where things are going.

Most of the time, leaders aren't aware that they are continually rewriting their stories or remodeling their theories in response to new information. To surface this hidden process, we encourage leaders to write in a notebook daily. We ask them to make notes on interesting, important, surprising, or difficult situations that come up at work. Essentially, they are recording and gathering critical incidents from their own experience. These incidents, or "happenings" as we call them, surface and capture the story of a situation, a story that the leader herself is always composing.

We also ask leaders to draw organization diagrams showing key characters and their interactions in the story. These drawings often reveal characters that are operating outside the center ring of the narrative, but are important to understanding what is happening. In this way, diagramming situations helps leaders expand and clarify their views of the ecosystem or context of their challenges.

Finally, to sharpen their awareness of how situations are actually moving sequences of events and interactions, we encourage them to build timelines of key events that mark the history of an evolving situation.

These simple practices yield the leader's own story of a situation—a story that is then available for reflection. This process of reflection invites the leader to articulate her theory of what's happening and why. She asks herself: Who are the key characters in the action? What are they doing or not doing that is affecting the stream of events? Are there patterns operating that I've seen before? Where and when can I intervene to influence the situation most powerfully and constructively?

With regard to Richard, our advice as he transitions into his new job would be to take time to observe and record what's happening in his new organization before he decides on priorities or make big changes. Richard should think of himself as a journalist or scientist rather than a knight riding in to rescue an organization in distress. In fact, this is precisely what his VP told him to do.

We would encourage Richard to keep a log and record three to five happenings each week—events or situations that he finds interesting, important, surprising, or difficult. Once he has at least three or four weeks of stories compiled, he can identify the top priority issues to be addressed, how they evolved, where they seem to be going, and why. He would also benefit from drawing a diagram of key characters involved in each situation and thinking about how they are interacting with each other.

These observations, captured in a notebook, will change his angle of approach and his perspective on his new job. He will naturally gravitate toward a more objective, less embedded point of view. Having taken the time to step back and think, he will have a better chance of developing a more reality-based theory of what's really going on and what he can do to influence people and events in a positive direction.

Discipline 3: Challenge the Story

As a leader surfaces his story and theory of the situation, he has already begun to interrupt his automatic, intuitive sense of what's happening. This simple, reflective pause creates mental space for the leader to examine his assumptions and consider alternative ways of conceptualizing the situation. In this discipline, we invite the leader to use that pause to challenge his thinking further by asking credible colleagues what they think about the situation, his story, and his theory.

Dreyfus (1983) and others have found that the elite performers understand that their stories and theories are biased by their own subjectivity and experience. They are aware that even subtle misinterpretations or oversights can lead to poor decisions and misguided action. Nike CEO Mark Parker recognizes this as a core problem of leadership: "The notion that the way we've done things is a formula for success creates the trouble. That can be death" (Safian, 2012, p. 105). Leaders who are committed to excellence and their own development lean into the expert paradox to slow down their automaticity. They stop and ask themselves unsettling questions: Is it possible that what I think I know is wrong? This question takes the leader directly into her discomfort zone, which we have shown on the Everyday Learning Disciplines diagram (Figure 16.1) as beginning with discipline of challenging the story. From here, the path to expertise is steeper and bumpier.

When a leader challenges her story, she entertains alternative views of the reality she faces. Her goal is to identify gaps, fuzzy thinking, and questionable assumptions in her own story and theory. There are many ways to do this, but one of the most effective is to ask colleagues what they think. Those who have a different perspective are most helpful. They may have deeper expertise, a contrary point of view on key issues, or a different vantage point on the situation (e.g., industry analyst, peer, or customer). The leader who is determined to upgrade her thinking builds a network of such people who can be tapped for their insights as different situations arise.

Another way for a leader to challenge her story is to engage a coach. The coach might be the leader's manager, a mentor, the HR business partner, or an executive coach. The coach doesn't have to be a deep expert on the situation the leader is facing. But he or she must be able to surface and comprehend how a leader is thinking about a situation and how that thinking is contributing to the results that the leader is (or is not) achieving. The coach must be able to explain these insights to the leader in a way that causes her to step back, seriously examine her thinking, and push toward a higher level of refinement and adaptation.

Richard could have benefitted from such a coach when he transitioned into his new job. Perhaps a coach could have persuaded Richard to slow down, interrupt his impulse to micromanage, study his new situation, and practice giving his managers more breathing room to run their own groups. This would have put Richard in his discomfort zone, but a good coach would have come alongside Richard, assuring him that tension is normal and necessary when you take on a stretch assignment. Given Richard's fixation on a turnaround mindset and his bias toward invasive action, we think Richard could have used weekly meetings with a coach during his first ninety days on the job.

Discipline 4: Prepare for Deliberate Practice

The leader's goal in this step is to interrupt automatic response patterns and test out new, more adaptive approaches by identifying exercises or activities that she can practice during upcoming events.

The starting point is for the leader to do an honest diagnosis of the factors that might be limiting her performance. Deliberate practice focuses on eliminating weaknesses in performance—not building on existing strengths (Ericsson, 2009). It's easier to work from strength, of course, but practicing strengths may simply reinforce the leader's inclination to do what comes naturally, rather than what the situation requires.

After surfacing and challenging her story, the leader should have a better understanding of the situation—an understanding that should begin to reveal weaknesses that are limiting her performance. Here are three examples of weaknesses that could limit performance:

- *An inaccurate diagnosis of the problem.* We worked with an exceptionally bright leader who was frustrated with her team's lack of strategic thinking. The problem was, in her view, that she needed more strategic thinkers on her team. But when we watched her in action, we saw her dominate meetings and denigrate anyone whose opinion differed from her own. Confronted with these observations, the leader realized that she would have to learn how to encourage her directs to express their ideas on strategy, without sacrificing her commitment to rigorous thinking.
- *Weak connections with key players.* When asked to map the ecosystem of their situation, many managers realize that they

have fallen into a reactive pattern of interacting with those who are most cooperative, most resistant, or most demanding of attention. In so doing, the leader fails to take the time to invest proactively in other relationships that may have a more strategic impact on results. Although strengthening such weak relationships takes time, attention, and discipline, most leaders see immediate improvement in performance across the board when they cultivate key relationships.

- *Physical and emotional depletion.* Many of the leaders we work with are oblivious to the effects of physical and emotional stress on their behavior and decision making. When a manager reports an incident in which a meeting lost focus or went off the rails, we will challenge him to think about how physically or emotionally depleted he was going into the meeting (cf., Baumeister & Tierney, 2012). Chronic self-depletion due to decision overload, travel fatigue, or an unhealthy lifestyle is endemic among executives. It compromises their ability to think clearly, regulate their emotional reactions, and respond flexibly to changing circumstances.

Performance-limiting factors like these become the focus for designing deliberate practice that can be done back on the job. True to the principles of deliberate practice, we advise "portion control" when it comes to trying out new ways of thinking and acting. Leaders should avoid trying to fix too many weaknesses at once. It is important to tackle the most important limitations first, breaking them down into manageable parts, and taking every opportunity to practice a new, more effective approach before moving on to work on less critical weaknesses.

To qualify as deliberate practice, a practice plan should include three elements. First, it should target a specific weakness and describe what the leader will try to do differently. Second, the plan should identify a stretch goal for practice—a goal that will pull the leader out of his comfort zone. Third, the plan must specify when, where, with whom, and what to practice (e.g., "During my staff's planning offsite next Tuesday, I will focus on listening and asking questions in the morning, and wait until the afternoon to add my opinions to the conversation").

For bonus points, some leaders add hypothesis testing to their plans. They try to predict what will happen as they change their approach. This helps the leader build a new story based on her evolving theory about the situation (e.g., "When I speak less, others speak more"). This evolving theory can then be evaluated as deliberate practice takes place.

One of the big challenges the leader may face is how to avoid slipping into old, bad habits during deliberate practice. For example, the leader we described above who had the habit of critiquing every "bad" idea she heard during team meetings knew it would be hard to control her verbal and non-verbal reactions. So we encouraged her to prime herself for success with an "implementation intention" (Hassin, Uleman, & Bargh, 2005). She decided to watch for those moments when she felt the impulse to jump in and criticize, and when they occurred, she would replace her old habit of criticizing with a new one. Specifically, she decided that she would silently nod and smile whenever she heard an idea she thought was stupid. With practice, she was able to create more space for her direct reports to practice their strategic thinking in a relatively safe forum.

Richard would have benefited from taking time to prepare for real-time practice in his new position as operations director. He would have pondered his VP's warning, "You'll have to change your style," and put a plan in place to prevent himself from slipping into his old habits. And if his boss had monitored Richard's transition more closely, she would have seen that he was staying in his comfort zone, spending his time dealing with day-to-day operations issues, and working around rather than through his direct reports.

Here are some deliberate practice ideas we might have offered Richard:

- He could ride shotgun with his directs on visits to the front lines. His task would be to eavesdrop on conversations, not participate. We'd encourage him to save all his questions and ideas for a private conversation with his direct report after the front line tour. The goal of the practice would be to limit his anxiety about not having on-the-ground operations information, while preventing him from going around his managers.

- Richard could give his cell phone number only to his manager, peers, and direct reports. He could refer all messages from front-line employees to one of his directs.
- Richard could dedicate the best two hours of his day—the time when he has high focus and concentration—to the technology strategy task. He could build and tap into a diverse network of experts to help him take on this challenging assignment.

These practices would help Richard interrupt his default pattern of diving into front-line problems where he's most comfortable, working around his direct reports, and procrastinating on complex, abstract projects like the technology strategy. Notice also that each practice is easy to understand, but hard for a guy like Richard to do.

Discipline 5: Practice in Real Time

Now it's time for practice. While many other professionals have the luxury of practicing behind closed doors, leaders practice in the spotlight, under pressure to get it right the first time. As a result, even a leader with a well-designed practice plan can slip back into doing what comes naturally—good old habits. So as a leader dives back into work with the intention to practice a specific, new approach, here are some things she can do to stay on the path of deliberate practice.

First, if she's really doing something different, she will feel uncomfortable and self-conscious. This tension is normal, a sign that old habits are being interrupted and new ones being built. It often helps leaders to remember the saying coined by World War II pilots: "If you're not taking flak, you're not over the target."

Second, when she feels herself getting caught up in the work itself (not a bad thing unless she has stopped thinking), she can take a breath, step back, and get curious about what's happening. Deliberate practice requires conscious attention and curiosity about how things are working, or not working, in the practice situation. A curious mind is more open to learning than a driven mind.

Third, she should practice as planned. Deliberate practice requires the leader to concentrate her attention on and tolerate the tension of trying something new. She must hold herself accountable for trying the new approach, even if she feels like it's not working. There are times, of course, when the risk of trying something new is too high; then she'll have to go with what she knows. But to improve, she must be willing to make mistakes. As Samuel Beckett said, "Fail. Fail again. Fail better." Mistakes open the way to a deeper understanding of the underlying mechanics of a situation, a richer way of conceptualizing what's happening and how things work.

Fourth, she should practice as unplanned. She knows from her planning what she needs to work on. So she can be alert for unplanned opportunities to practice her new approach as situations arise. An experience is a terrible thing to waste. A leader on the path to mastery sees the possibility for practice and learning—for refining her understanding and skill—in every interaction.

Fifth, during the initial stages of practice, the leader should focus on mechanics rather than results. It is tempting for leaders to conclude that their new approach is not working well after one or two practice attempts and then go back to what they are comfortable with. It takes repetition to break neurologically inscribed habits and to build new ways of thinking and acting. Leaders need patience and persistence to push through this uncomfortable stage to a new level of understanding and performance.

We recently worked with a leader who was demoralizing his team with his complaints about resources, senior leadership, etc. He had slipped into this habit of negativity and blame over time. He understood its effect on his team, yet couldn't control himself. He decided that, in his next staff meeting, he would fold his hands in his lap and squeeze them every time he felt the urge to complain. He emerged from the next staff meeting with sore hands, but he was proud that he had kept his rants in check. He had even encouraged a constructive conversation about resource limitations. This is the kind of planning, effort, and determination it takes to practice in your discomfort zone.

As Richard shifts from planning to real-time practice, our advice to him would be to give his new approach time to work. He should commit in advance to working on and refining his new approach for at least two or three months before judging it a success or failure. Richard will hear about customer or operations problems that have not gone well and be tempted to return to his old, invasive ways of managing. Or he will run into unforeseen complications with his technology strategy and be tempted to find something more comfortable to do. In any case, he will need to remember that tension and uncertainty are constant companions for those who are truly on the path to leadership expertise. He will make mistakes; the big question is whether he will learn from them or just suffer from them.

Discipline 6: Evaluate Performance

Feedback, particularly negative feedback, is a *sine qua non* of deliberate practice and the development of expertise. It grabs, orients, and focuses the expert's attention on factors that are limiting his ability to perform at a higher level. It tells him whether he has hit the target in his practice. It confirms or disconfirms his hypotheses (based on his story/theory about the situation), and points him toward further refinements and adjustments he can make to improve his performance. Consequently, a leader who aspires to mastery welcomes all feedback. Even biased, incredible, or harsh feedback enriches the leader's view of what's actually operating in the ecosystem of his work. He places a higher value on information than on self-protection.

It is important for the leader to use feedback from real-time practice to deepen his understanding—his theory—of the situation or context. This deepened understanding is one of the most important products of deliberate practice. Recall that in planning for deliberate practice (Discipline 4), the leader prepared a story about key variables she should attend to and predicted how events would unfold. Was the story accurate? Feedback helps answer this question.

All feedback contains signal and noise. So obtaining feedback from imperfect, relatively independent sources gives the leader a chance to sort through and discern the validity of each input. In so doing, he builds a more accurate view of his performance and its evolving context.

First, the leader should obtain qualitative and quantitative feedback from the work itself. The meaning of such feedback must be put in context and interpreted by the leader. Although scorecards, financial reports, and employee surveys may appear to be objective, an expert leader knows that the discipline of evaluating feedback hinges on his ability to turn signs and numbers into information that tells him how he is doing and how he can do better.

Second, feedback should be obtained from credible others. As leaders rise through the ranks of management, honest, expert feedback becomes more difficult to obtain. Subordinates may not have the expertise or the objectivity to give useful feedback. Or they may spin the picture to protect themselves or their managers. Peers may have little visibility to the work the leader is actually doing. In our coaching, we commonly ask, "Who can you count on to tell you the truth as they see it?" Some of these people may be in the intelligence network that the leader builds in "Challenge the Story" (Discipline 3).

Third, and perhaps most important, the leader has to evaluate his own practice performance. Self-evaluation is critical because it is most immediately and readily available. The best feedback is immediate. But we say this with an important caveat: during practice, the leader should focus on observing situational cues and trying a new approach. He should not think about evaluating his performance until after practice. Questions like: "How am I doing? Is this going OK? Why am I so nervous?" are distracting and inhibiting when asked during practice. For optimal learning and performance, it's better to practice at full speed and evaluate afterward.

Self-evaluation is also important because, as the leader becomes more and more expert, there are fewer and fewer people who are qualified to judge her performance. Although elite performers often work with master coaches and mentors, they eventually find themselves in a place where they are the only ones who are qualified to judge their understanding, their mechanics, or their performance. This ability and inclination to evaluate one's own work—with an attitude that leads to self-improvement rather than self-flagellation—is useful at every stage in the development of expertise. So the earlier it can be cultivated in a leader's career, the more it will benefit her and become an enduring performance asset.

When practicing this discipline of evaluating performance, there is always the risk that leaders will discount feedback, especially if they are anxious about giving up the habits that have worked for them in the past. Anyone who has delivered a 360 feedback report knows this risk. Some leaders lock onto shortcomings in the data and in the people who provided it. Chinn and Brewer (1993) identified six strategies people use to deal with feedback that contradicts their beliefs:

- They ignore the data.
- They find something wrong with the data.
- They find a reason why the data didn't apply in their situation.
- They find a reason to shelve the data for future retrieval.
- They reinterpret the data in such a way as to reduce the contradiction.
- They make a small change in their thinking, but avoid a major overhaul.

Reminding a leader of these discounting strategies is often enough to get him back on a more objective, constructive tack. One angle we have used to do this is to suggest that the leader "prize surprise" as he considers feedback received. We experience surprise when our assumptions—many of which are unconsciously held—are violated by what we are seeing or hearing. Consequently, surprise is an alarm that alerts us that our current story or theory of the situation is flawed. It interrupts automaticity and, when carefully considered, can lead to a more accurate, reality-based understanding of the situation and what to do about it.

In Richard's case, he held firm to the belief that the world would implode if he did not personally handle every difficult customer or operations problem. Consequently, we suspect that he used his high IQ to contort incoming feedback to fit that conceptualization. But we also know that he took pride in his ability to produce results. So we would have worked with him to identify metrics on his organization's scorecard that would be more objective indicators of whether he was spending his time on the responsibilities that were most important at his new level. We would also have pointed out that since his metrics had been trending negative during the past year, even a halt to that trend would be an improvement. Finally, we would have reminded him that his primary job was to pay attention to his scorecard, not to isolated operational incidents.

Discipline 7: Capture Lessons of Experience

Leaders take their learning to another level when they document their experiences in writing. Writing is key to capturing, extracting, and consolidating the insights that come from deliberate practice.

Memory is subject to all kinds of self-serving distortions of reality. This is particularly true when a learner has developed strong habits that have served her well in the past. Of course, these same biases can contaminate a written account of an experience. But for most of the managers we work with, writing about happenings changes their angle of view just enough to put a new, more objective light on their experiences.

Although writing things down may seem archaic and unnecessary to time-pressed executives, even a cursory glance at great leaders in history reveals journals, diaries, and letters detailing their experiences and the lessons they learned from them. If one aspires to be an elite leader, the writing habits and documents of extraordinary people warrant close attention.

Few leaders in history exemplify this aspect of deliberate practice better than the brilliant German Field Marshall Erwin Rommel. He painstakingly recorded his experiences and lessons learned from World War I in what would become the book *Attacks*.

When published in 1940, its wisdom was devoured and promoted by Allied generals such as George Patton. Beyond the content of its lessons, this book is a template for leaders who are motivated to capture their experience in writing. Of course, Rommel's genius was due to more than just his ability to reflect and write. Military biographer David Fraser (1994, p. 77) describes Rommel in this way:

> "He leapt at every experience of battle, but he turned experience into military wisdom by his shrewdness and his objectivity. It was this gift of Rommel's for distilling experience, for translating individual achievement, recollected, into the language of enduring—and universal—operational and tactical lessons that made him remarkable and lay at the heart of his success. He could, throughout life, decide fast, act boldly, remember clearly, narrate vividly, ponder and deduce wisely."

So what are the practical steps in the everyday discipline of capturing the lessons of experience? To practice this discipline, a leader must record her experiences, reflect on what they mean, and then extract insights learned from the experiences.

First, we ask leaders to record in writing what happens when they practice in real time. Getting these things down on paper is important because, as every reporter knows, and as research clearly demonstrates, memory "undergo(es) continual change with time" and is "susceptible to disruption" (Kandel, 2012, p. 575). Recording thoughts and events helps reduce such changes, losses, and distortions. It also lightens the load in the leader's working memory, allowing him to think more freely about what experiences mean, rather than struggling to remember what happened.

Second, we ask leaders to reflect on the meaning of their documented experiences—at a regular time at the end of each week. Our goal is to get them into a steady rhythm of reflection. If they can do this for at least a month, they begin to establish and then stabilize an everyday learning mindset. In our coaching practice, we reinforce this into a habit by scheduling weekly phone conversations with them for the first three months of the engagement. Even twenty to thirty minutes of written review plus a coaching conversation produces tangible, practical value that motivates leaders to keep doing the exercise. We ask them to reflect on simple questions like the following:

- "What happened last week that was important, interesting, surprising, or difficult?"
- "How did your real-time practice [planned the week before] go this week?"

The third step in this discipline is for leaders to extract insights and lessons from these recorded happenings and practices. We ask them simply, "What did you learn from these experiences last week? Has your thinking changed as result of what you learned?" One of the most powerful ways of doing this is to write an updated story of their leadership challenge and compare it to the story they prepared at the outset of their learning work (see Discipline 2: Surface the Story). The differences in the stories will highlight how the leader's theory of the situation has changed and the skills she is gaining as a result of deliberate practice.

In addition to a regular reflection on the events of the week, we also encourage leaders and their managers to do after-action reviews immediately following a key event or milestone. One of our executive colleagues used after-action reviews masterfully to develop the people working for her. After any of her direct reports made a presentation to company executives, she would pull that individual into a conference room, then ask him to reflect on what had gone well, what had not gone well, and what he would try to do better next time. Time and again, these immediate, brief reviews resulted in better thinking and performance during the individual's next executive presentation.

The primary benefit of this discipline for Richard would have been to slow down his impulse to habitual action, provide a pulse-like interruption of his limited thinking about his job, and introduce him to a process whereby he would hold himself accountable for seeing and adapting to the unfamiliar territory of his big new job. As we've said before, Richard needed a mentor or coach who was willing to invest time and energy in teaching him how to learn and adapt like an expert. We doubt he could have done this on his own, even if he had read this chapter.

Discipline 8: Forecast Opportunities for Repetition

We know that experts perform automatically, unconsciously, and effortlessly. This level of performance requires regular repetition of practice. If newly acquired insights and skills are not put to immediate use, they will quickly erode. Lessons captured have to be reinforced with more practice as soon as possible.

In coaching leaders, we include time in every conversation to look ahead on their calendars for important meetings, conversations, communications, or tasks. Then we ask them to identify situations coming up in the next few weeks in which they will be able to practice the new thinking and skills that they worked on the previous week. After just a few coaching sessions, most leaders get into the habit of looking for practice opportunities in their calendars.

With this forecasting step, the leader cycles back naturally to the beginning of the Everyday Learning Disciplines process. She thinks about how to position herself for stretch during the upcoming week. She considers how her story of the situation has changed as a result of her experience, practice, and reflection. And finally, she thinks about how she will use upcoming events to practice her new learning and gain repetitions of new skills.

Here's an example: a senior manager was being held back for promotion because the members of the company's leadership team did not see the results of his work. The manager claimed he was terrible at schmoozing and uncomfortable scheduling meetings with executives "just to brag about myself." He wanted to find an approach to sharing his work with executives that was comfortable for him. He had business issues to discuss with two senior leaders, so he scheduled meetings to catch the executives up on his progress and recent business successes in a way that felt genuine.

This worked, but still left many on the senior leadership team unfamiliar with his recent work. So he scheduled meetings with two more executives, but struggled with how to explain to them why he needed to meet with them. "I wish I could tell them that I'm interested in continuing to have new job opportunities. I know they are part of the team making those decisions, and I haven't done a good job letting them know what I've been doing lately. At least that would be honest!" He said this in jest, but instantly realized that it was a good approach for him to take. He adapted his practice plan. The conversations went well. He scheduled meetings with several of the remaining senior execs. With each conversation, he became more confident and practiced in his skills. Within six months, he had a new internal job offer. Just as important, the repetitions expanded his understanding of how senior executives get to know key talent in their organization.

Now let's go back to Richard. His habit of intervening directly in every customer problem is deeply engrained. Fortunately, given the nature of his work, he will have almost daily opportunities to learn how to delegate customer problems and escalations back to his direct reports and hold them accountable for achieving great customer metrics. Our advice to Richard, in addition to practicing the first seven Everyday Learning Disciplines, would be to review his calendar *daily* so he can anticipate and be ready to resist and redirect those first-line customer problems that draw him like a moth to a flame. This could help him focus on learning how to do his own job.

How Leadership Development Professionals Can Enhance Learning from Experience

In the previous section, we described Everyday Learning Disciplines that leaders can use to develop their own expertise. We also touched on several ways that bosses and others involved in coaching and mentoring relationships can help enhance leaders learning from experience. In this section, we turn to ways that those in two other leadership development roles can leverage the principles of expertise to help leaders maximize their learning from experience: talent professionals and learning and development professionals.

Talent Professionals

Talent professionals are involved in leader assessment, succession planning, staffing leadership positions, and leadership career models (e.g., critical leadership capabilities and competencies, leadership career paths, job experiences that help build leadership capability). Many organizations base their leadership talent practices on the principle that experience is the key to learning and development (cf. McCall, 1998). Talent professionals in these organizations help ensure that leaders gain the experiences they need to grow their skills (see Silzer & Dowell, 2009). Here we offer three recommendations to talent professionals, some of which may be familiar to those who are steeped in experience-based development, although we hope you'll find a few new twists.

First, talent professionals should ensure that talent programs and processes enable the organization to develop *all* the various types of leadership expertise the organization requires. Most research and writing on talent management has focused on development of general manager leaders. As a result, we have a reasonably clear understanding of the types of experiences that are instrumental in developing expert general managers.

But organizations also need leaders who are deep experts at marketing, engineering, operations, finance, human resources, and so on. Recall our first principle of expertise: expertise is extreme adaptation to context. As a result, the job experiences and assignments that build expert functional leaders are different from those that develop general managers. To ensure that their organizations have the broad array of leadership talent they need, talent professionals should identify all the key types of leadership expertise their organizations require and document the experiences and job assignments (i.e., career paths) that are most powerful developmentally for each type of leader. Their talent practices should help ensure that general managers receive the experiences they need to become expert general managers and that functional leaders receive the experiences they need to become expert functional leaders.

Second, talent professionals should make certain that leaders spend adequate time in each job assignment to master the lessons of that assignment. This follows from our third principle of expertise: expertise takes time and experience to develop. Leaders need repetitions in order to build mastery. They also must spend enough time in an assignment to experience the consequences of their actions; otherwise, they will not gain the insights they need to refine their understanding of the situation and adjust their actions as needed. In their zeal to develop leaders quickly and fill key leadership positions with high potentials, organizations may try to move developing leaders too quickly through job assignments. Talent professionals occasionally may need to apply the brakes.

Third, talent professionals should help ensure that high potentials and future leaders receive job experiences and assignments that provide the right degree of stretch. We noted this previously in our discussion of the first Everyday Learning Disciple: Position for Stretch. Ideally, each new job assignment should provide one or perhaps two big new challenges that the leader has never faced previously (e.g., working in a new division, working in a new function, working in a new geography, managing a turnaround for the first time, taking on a larger organization size, working in a staff role for the first time), but not more than that. Part of Richard's challenge may have been that the director job was more of a stretch than he could handle.

A subtle situation in which stretch matters occurs when hiring external candidates into leadership positions. Consider the case of a marketing executive who has run creative, successful marketing campaigns. He has applied for a senior marketing position in another company in his industry. The stories he tells about the work he has done and the success he has achieved dazzle everyone on the interview loop.

As the talent professional prepares to interview the candidate, she is aware of the principle that expertise is *extreme adaptation to context*. During the interview, she digs deep to understand the environment the marketing executive has worked in and adapted to. It turns out that the candidate has spent his entire career working for an organization in which marketing plays a key leadership role in business strategy and product planning. "If we can't market it, Engineering and Manufacturing both tell us there's no sense building it," he says proudly. He gives examples of products that have been reshaped as a result of his marketing advice.

In the hiring organization, engineering and manufacturing jointly decide strategy and develop product plans. The role of marketing is to figure out how to create demand for the products that engineering and manufacturing have decided to build. The talent professional realizes that, despite the candidate's outstanding track record, it may be a big stretch for him to figure out how to be a successful marketing executive in this different context. She asks whether he's ever led a successful marketing campaign for a product he didn't help design. He seems perplexed by the question. "That would just never happen," he says. "It would be a disaster."

At the end of the day, the talent professional meets with the other interviewers to discuss the candidate. They are all very enthusiastic. They talk about how smart the candidate is, what great results he's achieved, his professionalism, and so forth. When it's her turn to speak, she lists four ways that the job is significantly different from any job that the candidate has previously held. "These are four big stretches for this candidate," she tells the other interviewers. "Typically, it's difficult for someone to be successful when a new job provides two new stretches. It requires lots of coaching, lots of support, lots of patience." She then turns to the hiring manager: "You've been telling me that you need a candidate who can hit the ground running, who can take total charge of marketing because you need to focus your attention elsewhere. I feel pretty certain he'll fail if he doesn't get *a lot* of guidance and support. So how much coaching and support are you prepared to provide this candidate if you hire him?"

A savvy talent professional helps ensure that developing leaders are placed into jobs that represent the right degree of stretch for them. She can also help ensure that the leader's boss and other key stakeholders are prepared to provide the developing leader with the support needed to be successful into his new assignment.

Learning and Development Professionals

Learning and development (L&D) professionals develop and deliver formal leadership programs (e.g., classroom learning, action learning) and other learning interventions. One of the greatest challenges L&D development professionals face is "stickiness"—that is, ensuring that the concepts and skills taught in leadership development programs stick with participants and are put into action. The expertise principles we've outlined in this chapter point to several concrete ways that leadership development professionals can deliver stickier learning experiences.

First and foremost, leaders should be taught how to learn more effectively. Research indicates that the capacity to learn from experience is one of the best predictors of leader effectiveness (see McCall, 1998). Most people have a very primitive understanding of how to learn effectively, but they can learn how to become better learners. Perhaps the most valuable training class that an L&D group can offer is one that teaches leaders the Everyday Learning Disciplines.

Second, L&D professionals should focus their attention on leaders in transition (e.g., leaders who are scaling up from functional leader to general manager; leaders trying to solve a business challenge they have never faced before, such as how to turn around a business with sagging revenues and earnings). Leaders in transition are positioned for stretch (the first Everyday Learning Discipline), so they are perfectly situated to embark on the next leg of their journey to leadership mastery. To support leaders in transition, the L&D organization must have a process in place to track which leaders are experiencing big, new challenges. This is an outstanding opportunity for L&D professionals to partner with talent professionals, who are involved in placing leaders in new job assignments and who know the challenges these leaders in transition will most likely encounter in their new roles.

Third, L&D professionals should design their learning interventions in a manner that helps leaders step through the first four Everyday Learning Disciplines:

- *Position for Stretch.* Help leaders clarify the challenges they are facing and what they must learn in order to be successful on their jobs.
- *Surface Your Story.* Prompt leaders to describe the situations they are facing, critical variables to which they must attend, assumptions they have about cause-effect relationships, and alternative courses of action available.

- *Challenge Your Story.* Expose leaders to new models and frameworks to help them make better sense of their job challenges; suggest alternative courses of action for consideration.
- *Prepare for Deliberate Practice.* Require leaders to develop a specific action that describes what they will do differently, the results they will attempt to achieve, and the setting in which they intend to practice (when, where, with whom, etc.).

These four disciplines can be readily incorporated into classroom or online training programs. We have not seen any online learning tools explicitly designed with the Everyday Learning Disciplines in mind, but it's easy to envision how this could be accomplished.

Learning circles (or their close cousins, peer coaching groups and mentoring rings) are another learning intervention that is very consistent with the Everyday Learning Disciplines. In a typical learning circle, a small group of six to eight leaders meets regularly (either face-to-face or virtually) to discuss the top challenges they are facing, how they are approaching these challenges, and what they are learning from their experience. They obtain feedback and coaching suggestions from other learning circle participants. Learning circles require leaders to articulate how they are thinking about their toughest problems, describe the approaches they have tried, reflect on what worked and what didn't, and explore ways they can refine their approach. The reflection and after-action review that takes place in learning circles significantly enhances learning (cf. Ellis, Mendel, & Nir, 2006).

Learning circles can be formed in a variety of ways. We have worked with successful learning circles comprised of high potentials at similar job levels from across the enterprise, peers in very similar jobs in different geographies or business units (e.g., country managing directors responsible for mid-size geographies), or leaders from a range of job levels within a job function (e.g., finance leaders learning circle). L&D professionals can play a valuable role by organizing learning circles and by helping them use the Everyday Learning Disciplines to maximize what participants learn.

Conclusion

*Nothing is a waste of time if you use the experience
wisely.*

AUGUSTE RODIN

As we have noted throughout this chapter, challenging experiences are the basic raw ingredient in leadership development. What's wonderful about this is that leaders almost never have to go looking for challenging experiences. Leaders face problems from the moment they step out of bed, as they commute to work, as they move from meeting to meeting, as they make decisions and give direction, as they deal with conflict, as they celebrate good times, as they rally themselves and their followers during the bad times. The question is not whether leaders will be presented with the challenges they need to learn and grow as leaders. Rather, as Rodin has noted, the question is what they will do with those experiences.

In this chapter, we have described Everyday Learning Disciplines that promote learning from experience. Leaders who practice the disciplines will learn more, and learn more quickly, than those who don't. They will have more impact and advance further in their careers.

Managers who apply the Everyday Learning Disciplines to developing their up-and-coming leaders will achieve better results because their teams will be more capable, and they will enjoy their jobs more because they'll be able to focus their attention on activities that are more interesting and rewarding. Organizations will benefit because they will have a larger supply of leaders equipped with a technology for scaling up and ready to move into executive positions in which they can tackle bigger business challenges.

All of the practices that make up the Everyday Learning Discipline are important; all contribute in important ways to learning. But if you, our reader, were to remember and apply just one concept from this chapter, we hope it will be *deliberate practice.*

In his Pulitzer Prize–winning biography of George Washington, Ron Chernow notes that Washington was not the most brilliant or original thinker or the most charismatic leader, but he excelled at deliberate practice. In Chernow's words, "George Washington always demonstrated a capacity to learn from missteps. 'Errors once discovered are more than half amended,' Washington liked to say. 'Some men will gain as much experience in the course of three or four years as some will in ten or a dozen.' It was this process of subtle, silent, unrelenting self-criticism that enabled him to rise above his early defeats" (Chernow, 2010, pp. 49–50). Washington took full advantage of deliberate practice to continuously enhance his leadership effectiveness.

In biographies of other great leaders—Churchill (Manchester, 1983, 1988), Mandela (1995), Gandhi (Easwaran, 1972)—we read similar stories of deliberate practice in action. These individuals were able to put aside the arrogance, overreliance on strengths, and failure to acknowledge blind spots that have caused so many other leaders to derail and fail (McCall & Lombardo, 1983).

So we return to the story of Richard. His key metrics were in decline, he had high turnover on his team, he was receiving tough feedback from his VP; yet he persisted in micromanaging his organization.

At the end of three years, he applied for a bigger, global operations job. He was disappointed when his VP instead selected one of his peers. But she gave him an opportunity to move to a high-growth emerging market where he would have some operational responsibilities and also the opportunity to create business processes that would be implemented worldwide. "This is your chance to show that you can lead differently and contribute at a strategic level," she told him.

Richard got off to a good start. But soon he was deep into the details of his operations organization. With each passing month, he paid less and less attention to his responsibilities for creating global business processes. His VP warned him that he was displaying his old, bad habits. She noted that he was not making sufficient progress on his global responsibilities and that the managers on his emerging market operations team were not capable of making any important decisions without his involvement. But Richard opted not to change his behavior.

After two years, Richard was ready to return to his home country. He fully expected a promotion and bigger job upon his return. He explained to his VP, "I've been at my current level for five years and successfully completed both assignments you gave me." She offered to find a role for him, but told him that he still did not lead like a director needed to lead, so his next job assignment would be at his current job level. Richard rejected her offer. He was given twelve weeks to find a new job. That search was unsuccessful.

About three weeks before the end of his search, Richard met with his VP to talk about his (lack of) progress. He swallowed his pride and asked whether her offer to find him a role at his current level was still on the table. This surprised her. After a long pause, she asked Richard what he had learned from his experiences of the past five years. He told her he had learned how to lead large organizations and how to live in another country. Then he said that the main thing he had learned was that you have to be responsible for your own career; you can't assume anyone else will look out for you. His VP told him she did not have a job available for him. Two weeks later, Richard left the company.

Alas, as Douglas Adams has noted, "Human beings, who are almost unique in having the ability to learn from the experience of others, are also remarkable for their apparent disinclination to do so" (Adams & Carwardine, 1990).

Richard's sad story illustrates the huge cost of missed development opportunities. The organization lost a talented manager with great potential who could not overcome his blind spot. The total cost of his expatriate assignment was in the neighborhood of $250,000. His VP felt that she had wasted her investment of two plum job assignments and hours of coaching in Richard. She also was deeply saddened by the outcome because she liked and cared about Richard personally. And, of course, Richard himself paid a steep price—the embarrassment of seeing his career derail and losing his job, lost income, friendships and business relationships left behind, and finally the need to uproot and relocate his family for a new job with a different company.

We believe the Everyday Learning Disciplines outlined in this chapter, and in particular the concept of deliberate practice, are key to making the most of development opportunities. The disciplines provide a path to enhanced learning and effectiveness for aspiring leaders and better business results for the teams and organizations they lead.

References

Adams, D., & Carwardine, M. (1990). *Last chance to see*. London, UK: Pan Books.

Alinsky, S. (1971). *Rules for radicals*. New York, NY: Vintage Books.

Argyris, C. (1999). *On organizational learning* (2nd ed.). Malden, MA: Blackwell.

Baumeister, R. F., & Tierney, J. (2012). *Willpower: Rediscovering the greatest human strength*. New York, NY: Penguin.

Byrne, D. (2012). *How music works*. San Francisco, CA: McSweeney's.

Chernow, R. (2010). *Washington: A life*. New York, NY: Penguin.

Chinn, C. A., & Brewer, W. F. (1993). The role of anomalous data in knowledge acquisition: A theoretical framework and implications for science instruction. *Review of Educational Research, 63*, 1–49.

Deakin, J., & Cobley, S. (2003). A search for deliberate practice in figure skating and volleyball. In K. A. Ericsson & J. Starkes (Eds.), *Expert performance in sport: Advances in research on sport expertise* (pp. 115–136). Champaign, IL: Human Kinetics.

Dreyfus, S. (1983). Beyond reasoned analysis: How experienced managers tend to let the gut lead the brain. *Management Review, 72*(9), p. 56–71.

Easwaran, E. (1972). *Gandhi the man: How one man changed himself to change the world*. Tomales, CA: Nilgiri Press.

Ellis, S., Mendel, R., & Nir, M. (2006). Learning from successful and failed experience: The moderating role of after-event review. *Journal of Applied Psychology, 91*, 669–680.

Ericsson, K. A. (1996). The acquisition of expert performance: An introduction to some of the issues. In K. A. Ericsson (Ed.), *The road to expert performance: Empirical evidence from the arts and sciences, sports, and games* (pp. 1–50). Mahwah, NJ: Lawrence Erlbaum Associates.

Ericsson, K. A. (2009). Discovering deliberate practice activities that overcome plateaus and limits on improvement of performance. In A. Willamon, S. Pretty, & R. Buck (Eds.), *Proceedings of the International Symposium on Performance Science 2009* (pp. 11–21). Utrecht, The Netherlands: Association Europienne des Conservatoires Academies de Musique et Musikhochschulen (AEC).

Ericsson, K. A., Whyte, J., & Ward, P. (2007). Expert performance in nursing: Reviewing research on expertise in nursing within the framework of the expert-performance approach. *Advances in Nursing Science, 30*, E58-E71.

Feltovich, P. J., Prietula, M. J., & Ericsson, K. A. (2006). Studies of expertise from psychological perspectives. In K. A. Ericsson, N. Charness,
P. Feltovich, & R. R. Hoffman, (Eds.), *Cambridge handbook of expertise
and expert performance* (pp. 39–68). Cambridge, UK: Cambridge
University Press.

Fraser, D. (1994). *Knight's cross: A life of Field Marshal Erwin Rommel.* New
York, NY: HarperCollins.

Hassin, R. R., Uleman, J. S., & Bargh, J. A. (Eds._. (2005). *The new unconscious.* New York, NY: Oxford University Press.

Hill, N. M., & Schneider, W. (2006). Brain changes in the development
of expertise: Neuroanatomical and neurophysiological evidence
about skill-based adaptations. In K. A. Ericsson, N. Charness, P.
Feltovich, & R. R. Hoffman (Eds.), *Cambridge handbook of expertise
and expert performance* (pp. 683–704). Cambridge, UK: Cambridge
University Press.

Kahneman, D. (2011). *Thinking, fast and slow.* New York, NY: Farrar,
Straus and Giroux.

Kandel, E. R. (2012). *The age of insight: The quest to understand the unconscious in art, mind, and brain, from Vienna 1900 to the present.* New
York, NY: Random House.

Klein, G. A. (1999). *Sources of power: How people make decisions.* Cambridge,
MA: MIT Press.

Klein, G. A. (2002). *Intuition at work: Why developing your gut instincts will
make you better at what you do.* New York, NY: Doubleday.

Klein, G. A. (2009). *Streetlights and shadows: Searching for the keys to adaptive
decision making.* Cambridge, MA: Bradford Books.

Lemov, D., Woolway, E., & Yezzi, K. (2012, September 18). Put your
shoulders down the mountain: Why mastering a skill means falling
with precision. *Fast Company.* Retrieved from www.fastcompany
.com/3001376/put-your-shoulders-down-mountain-why-mastering
-skill-means-falling-precision.

Manchester, W. (1983). *The last lion. Winston Spencer Churchill. Visions of
glory: 1874–1932.* New York, NY: Dell Publishing.

Manchester, W. (1988). *The last lion. Winston Spencer Churchill. Alone:
1932–1940.* New York, NY: Dell Publishing.

Mandela, N. (1995). *Long walk to freedom.* Boston, MA: Little Brown & Company.

McCall, M. W., Jr. (1998). *High flyers: Developing the next generation of
leaders.* Boston, MA: Harvard Business School Press.

McCall, M. W., Jr., & Hollenbeck, G. P. (2008). Developing the expert
leader. *People & Strategy, 31,* 20–28.

McCall, M. W., Jr., & Lombardo, M. M. (1983). *Off the track: Why and how
successful executives get derailed* (Technical Report 21). Greensboro,
NC: Center for Creative Leadership.

McDaniel, M. A., Schmidt, F. L., & Hunter, J. E. (1988). Job experience correlates of job performance. *Journal of Applied Psychology, 73,* 327–330.

Rommel, E. (2011). *Attack.* Translated by L. Allen & J. R. Driscoll. Vienna, VA: Athena Press.

Safian, R. (2012, October 15). The secrets of Generation Flux. *Fast Company.* Retrieved from www.fastcompany.com/node/58002/print

Salas, E., & Rosen, M. (2010). Experts at work: Principles for developing expertise in organizations. In S. Kozlowski & E. Salas (Eds.), *Learning, training, and development in organizations.* New York, NY: Routledge.

Shadrick, S. B., & Lussier, J. W. (2009). Training complex cognitive skills: A theme-based approach to the development of battlefield skills. In K. A. Ericsson (Ed.), *Development of professional expertise: Toward measurement of expert performance and design of optimal learning environments.* New York, NY: Cambridge University Press.

Silzer, R., & Dowell, B. E. (Eds.). (2009). *Strategy-driven talent management: A leadership imperative.* San Francisco, CA: Jossey-Bass.

CHAPTER SEVENTEEN

Catalytic Converters
How Exceptional Bosses Develop Leaders

Morgan W. McCall, Jr., and
Jeffrey J. McHenry

In the opening chapter of this book the case was made that experience is at the heart of leadership development. To say that experience is at the heart is not to say that experience in and of itself is sufficient to develop leadership talent. As the chapters of this book have shown, all experiences are not created equal, nor are they equally relevant to the business, nor are they available for everyone, nor is it automatic that the lessons they offer will be learned. While one possible conclusion from the research reported in *Lessons of Experience* (McCall, Lombardo, & Morrison, 1988) and *Developing Global Executives* (McCall & Hollenbeck, 2002) is that "whoever controls who gets what job controls development," logic dictates that "who controls what happens on the job" is just as important. One of the most important factors in what happens in a job experience, and therefore what is learned from it, is the immediate boss. In a sense, the boss can be a catalyst that converts experience into learning.

Research on leadership development documents the importance to learning of timely and accurate feedback (Kluger & DeNisi, 1996), coaching and mentoring (Allen, Finkelstein, & Poteet, 2009; Hollenbeck, 2002), job challenge (McCauley, Ruderman, Ohlott, & Morrow, 1994), after-action review (Ellis & Davidi, 2005; Ellis, Mendel, & Nir, 2006), learning orientation (DeRue & Wellman, 2009), and openness to learning (Spreitzer, McCall, & Mahoney, 1997), and other factors, but strangely enough has little to say directly about a primary instigator (or inhibitor) of such things—the boss. And while many (or even most) bosses may themselves be mediocre leaders, they still impact the experiences of those who report to them. More importantly, we know that the very good and the very bad ones can have a profound impact on the development of leadership talent (McCall, Lombardo, & Morrison, 1988). Bad bosses can be an experience in and of themselves and by their nature teach lessons about how to survive and what not to do. With the possible exception of truly extraordinary bosses, most "good" bosses do not teach a particular lesson, but they do serve in numerous ways as catalysts to learning (e.g., by providing experiences, by giving feedback, and by making it OK to experiment). Our focus is not on "boss as experience" but on "boss as catalyst." We want to explore exactly how and why these exceptional bosses have the impact that they do and what, if anything, can be done to increase the positive impact of bosses on the development of leadership talent.

To explore these issues we took the simplest approach—we asked exceptional bosses how they thought about development and what they did to develop talent. We also asked selected people they had developed for their perspectives on what their bosses did that helped them develop as leaders. Five prominent multinational organizations, four U.S.-based and one India-based, each identified ten senior managers (the vast majority within two or three reporting layers of the CEO) they considered among their very best developers of talent based on input from HR and senior leaders as well as available metrics (360 feedback, leader surveys, number of high potentials nurtured and passed along). For each of them, at least one person he or she had developed was also identified (we called them protégés), yielding a sample of about one hundred people we interviewed.

We asked the developers questions ranging from their philosophy and motivation to how they chose whom to develop to concrete examples of actions they took. In the protégé interviews, we asked about the specific boss identified as a developer as well as other bosses and factors that had influenced their development over the course of their careers. We begin this chapter by looking at the variety of ways these bosses influenced the development of their protégés.

Good Bosses and Developmental Experiences

Often the objective of an exercise like this is to catalog everything that people do, thereby generating a list of "best practices" to guide bosses in developing leaders (e.g., Axelrod & Coyle, 2011). But the bosses we talked to, while all identified as the best developers of talent, varied considerably in their leader development philosophy, motivation, and practices. Some provided opportunities for growth, some made connections with mentors or senior management, some provided career guidance, some worked to correct flaws or build specific skills, and some focused on setting high standards and holding people accountable. Some did two or three of these things. Almost no one did them all. In other words, there is no simple "to do" list for developing talent, but rather a variety of approaches, each of which is valuable in its own way. As tempting as it is to make generalizations like "all great developers of talent give candid, timely feedback," it simply is not the case that all of them do. There were perhaps just two things that all of these developers had in common. First, developing leaders was a priority for them personally. Almost every great talent developer indicated that he or she had come to this realization as a youth or early in his or her career. They could point to specific incidents and experiences that shaped them—a role model parent who was frequently called upon for coaching and advice, a teacher in school, a coach on a sports team, a manager who took a keen personal interest in them early in their careers, an experience they had when they themselves became front-line managers for the first time. Second, they all provided a lot of leeway for their protégés to figure out how to meet their leadership challenges, to take risks and make mistakes, and to learn through trial and error; none of our great talent developers was a micromanager. So instead of a bullet list of practices, we look at the different ways exceptional talent developers go about this work.

Providing Opportunities for Growth

> He took a couple of big risks with me, first recruiting me to move into a marketing role, and then, even more daringly, tapped me to be the product manager based in Singapore. What made this

assignment unconventional and controversial was that I was responsible for sales and I had no sales background or experience. In addition I was going to a location where I didn't have much of a safety net—my manager was not down the hall and there was no one around who could really guide me or act as a sounding board. To top it off, a month after I moved to Singapore he was tapped to take on a new role. But to his credit, he continued to be available to me when I had questions. He was a classic leader with big shoulders who gives you a lot of space but is there for you to ensure that you don't drive off a cliff.

At first glance it looks like this boss was throwing his protégé to the wolves, testing him to see if he had the "right stuff." Indeed, many of our developers enticed (or sometimes forced) their talented people to take on bigger or unconventional assignments, understanding that people learn the most when they are stretched and that staying with what you know is not the path to leadership. But unlike selection-oriented managers, who use challenging assignments as a test, these bosses had various strategies for seeing to it that the protégé was successful. In the example above, notice that this boss was careful about sequencing ("first recruiting me to move into a marketing role"), kept an eye on what was happening ("is there for you to ensure you don't drive off a cliff"), and did not desert the protégé when he was promoted ("he continued to be available to me").

Other bosses, when giving their people challenging assignments or tasks, gave a clear account of how the assignment would stretch the protégé and what the protégé could expect (or should attempt) to learn, set very clear expectations and held the protégé accountable, scheduled regular one-on-one sessions to monitor progress and provide opportunities for discussion, gave guidance and/or useful feedback, or made sure that the protégé had coaching or mentoring or other kinds of support.

Often these developmental assignments violated norms or traditional career paths and the protégé was not fully qualified for the position, so the boss was taking a risk not only with the protégé but with his own standing. In many cases the boss provided "air cover" for the protégé or kept the assignment low profile so that mistakes along the learning curve would not prove fatal. Clearly, bosses did not want their protégés to fail and carefully weighed the possibilities before throwing them in and did what they could to ensure success, often behind the scenes and without the protégé even being aware.

Providing Exposure to Senior Executives; Making Connections and Opening Doors

> Two skills my boss helped me build were executive communications and business insight. When my skip-level manager, who was a senior vice president, visited my district, the feedback from him was that I was too casual. I was stunned by the feedback because I always prided myself on being well prepared. My boss told me, "This feedback is a gift." This helped me accept the feedback and then reflect on what happened. I finally went to my boss and told her I needed help presenting in situations like that and demonstrating business insight. She told me how she had learned to handle situations like this ten+ years ago and described the process she followed in similar situations. We practiced ten times for an upcoming business review, where she offered to give me another opportunity to make a positive impression. Every practice session, she would critique me—I felt like I was back in grade school and getting assignments from my teacher marked in a red pen. But when the moment came, I was well prepared.

Whether with senior executives, customers, technical gurus, or some other significant group, some of the developmental bosses were focused on exposing their protégés to the "right" people. Most often the point was to build valuable relationships, that essential glue that holds organizations together. From a developmental perspective, these contacts could be gatekeepers who provided access to certain jobs, coaches or mentors who could provide guidance in ways the boss could not, or more simply, people who would be helpful in achieving business objectives.

In some cases the objective was to get the protégé known or showcased so that more opportunities would be available. When this was the goal, sometimes a boss just made sure that senior executives were aware of a person's accomplishments without actually engineering a personal appearance. Less frequently, bosses tried to overcome a tarnished image of the protégé among senior management or tempered senior managers' expectations when they seemed to overestimate a person's readiness.

Like challenging assignments, exposing a protégé to powerful people could put both boss and protégé at risk, so making these connections was not done lightly. As in the example opening this section, some bosses would see to it that the protégé was fully prepared for the meeting by having rehearsals, providing insight into the preferences of the audience, or reviewing materials beforehand. One example stands out:

> Mechanically he was really good, but he was weak managing up and influencing senior leaders. My mission was to teach him how to influence this company to go for a breakthrough. I helped him on strategy, positioning, and influence by putting him into situations where he had to influence senior leaders. I didn't throw him into the fire, but coached him along the way and did a good debrief after each encounter. I take risks that others won't take. He needed $350 million for a business idea and rather than do it for him I told him to invite the CEO here and convince him to support the idea!

Sometimes the protégé was on his or her own, but the boss briefed the senior executives that the person was just learning and even coached them on how to respond to the protégé's presentation. "If I'm asking someone to present to senior leaders for the first time, I might send the leaders a note ahead of time explaining that the person is inexperienced and I may 'coach the boss.' They [the protégé] may never know until later that we did that."

Bosses can play a critical role in making connections that will benefit their protégés' future development, both in building protégés' skills in presenting to and understanding executives and in helping them build their networks.

Developing Skills and Mitigating Flaws

Many of the bosses we interviewed played a traditional coaching role, using their own expertise (or drafting others with the needed expertise) to help their protégés develop needed skills or, conversely, to better manage their flaws. Given the seniority of the group, their collective knowledge and experience spanned an enormous territory and allowed for coaching on a vast array of skills.

Sometimes the focus of the coaching was on new skills the protégé needed to develop. Examples include:

- How to be a strong decision maker and present a point of view
- How to collaborate and make a matrix work
- How to create a business plan

In other instances, the boss coached the protégé to repair bad behaviors and relationships that threatened to derail the protégé's career, such as:

- Driving for results in a way that burned out staff, hurt morale, and created a lot of baggage:
  - "Her people skills were atrocious."
  - "He is a micromanager and his team is frustrated but won't tell him."
  - "He was very smart, technically brilliant, but he had a chip on his shoulder—he was brusque with his peers and they hated him."
- Confusing personal chemistry/"un-likability" with performance issues
- Trying to do too much themselves instead of figuring out how to get things done through others

The list of topics goes on (and on and on), but the boss's expertise was not sufficient to create change; the boss had to deliver feedback, offer suggestions and guidance, and stick with it long enough to see the results. The story told us by one managing director captures the challenge of coaching to mitigate a flaw:

> One of my employees was curious why, in spite of delivering good results, he was never promoted or given a bigger job. I discovered that he was always looking for opportunities to show off. He took pride in publicly getting recognized for his personal accomplishments. I gave him some direct feedback on this and told

him he needed to show more humility. In addition, I told him he needed to think more about the legacy he was leaving—not just what he himself was achieving, but how he was setting the organization up for future success. I met with him regularly, at least monthly and often weekly. He came to trust me and took my advice to heart, and we had more open conversations. He had the will to change, and was open to receiving strong feedback. He changed his behavior and senior leaders noticed. He was promoted.

Notice in this example that the boss began by doing his homework to understand the issue. He then gave direct feedback to the protégé (along with specific examples not included in the quote above) and framed it in a larger business context (his "legacy"). He engaged the protégé regularly, building trust, and over time succeeded in changing the behavior. It's worth noting that in our interview with the protégé he commented, "My boss consistently gave me direct, honest feedback. It's not always happy feedback, but it's valuable. The focus is always on what I should do to improve myself and my business. It hurts a little bit, but I start thinking after a few hours about the truth of what he is saying and look for ways to improve."

Sometimes a boss's good intentions misfire. In an effort to make a protégé successful, rather than coaching, this boss surrounded him with "people who could fill his deficits" and "made sure he kept at least one such person." Later, when the protégé was promoted to run a different division under a different boss, he lost his cover and quickly derailed.

Inspiring; Raising the Bar; Demanding Excellence

According to Walter Isaacson (2011), Steve Jobs' biographer, Jobs was particularly gifted in inspiring and driving people beyond what they thought was possible. One result of pursuing the "insanely great" is the development of innovative products like the Mac, iPod, iPad, and iPhone. But another possible result is personal development, as individuals venture into new territory and learn, if nothing else, that they can do it. "He had the most impact on me," his protégé said, "because he set a high bar of excellence and had a clear vision of what he wanted the organization to do."

That sentiment was echoed by a protégé in a different company whose boss (and champion) quickly intervened when the protégé tried to set a low bar for his organization after he was moved into a very challenging new assignment:

> We missed plan the first quarter I was there, which was OK because I was new and just getting settled. We seemed well on our way to hitting our numbers in the second quarter. In fact, I was so sure we had hit our Q2 numbers that I had promised my boss and had done a webcast to my entire organization just before the end of the quarter thanking them for their great work. But sales collapsed during the last two weeks of the quarter and we came up just short. Right after that, I submitted a pretty conservative forecast for Q3 because I didn't want to disappoint my boss and the organization again. Usually at this point, my boss would schedule a phone call with me to sign off on the numbers—this was typically a formality–but instead my finance director and I got summoned to company headquarters to meet with my boss. He took a strip out of me about 4 inches wide. He told me that he hadn't sent me to this job just to explain bad results—there were one hundred other people he could have chosen for the job who could have done that just fine—he sent me to the job to deliver. Not only did he expect us to achieve our original objectives for Q3, he also expected us to deliver the $1M we had missed during Q2. It was very stressful and scary. My boss didn't tell me how I should get these results, he just told me to deliver. At this point, we were almost halfway thru Q3, so we were running out of time. I did the only thing I could think about doing—I went back and lit fires under people! I told people what I expected, and I stayed after them to deliver, just like my boss was doing to me. We not only made our Q3 numbers plus the $1M shortfall from Q2, we also beat our target by $1M. In the four years since then, I have never missed my quarterly results. After that talk from my boss, I just refuse to let that happen. It really clarified for me that my job was to get results, no matter what it took. I know I now have a bit of a reputation as a hard ass, which is so counter to how I see myself or how people like my wife see me. But it's because I am so determined to produce results.

So it was with many of the bosses we interviewed. Their central focus was improving the performance of the team or the business or the organization, and doing so by inspiring or driving people forward. "He forced me to overcome my shyness and take the stage," said one protégé, describing a boss who literally forced him to go on stage to speak to groups. "She valued me and encouraged me to be myself," said another protégé. "She saw things in me that I didn't." Yet another said about his boss, "She was hands off and trusting. She held me accountable but had faith in me." Seeming to sum it up, a protégé observed, "She always finds something in people and pushes them."

One boss described his role this way:

> My role is to challenge the employees to operate beyond their comfort zone, to have a dream, and make that dream a reality . . . . You have to invest first in building credibility, a sense that we're in this together, that I will support you and you will support me . . . . Once you have credibility you have the right to ask more from people, to ask them to achieve the dream. You don't tell them the way; you help them figure it out. You support them. And you're always asking them to do more and helping to show them the way to their dream.

From the other side it looked the same. That boss's protégé described it this way:

> He continually raised the bar. He constantly challenged me to look at new ways of growing the business and supported me when I came up with creative ideas.

"He inspired more than taught," is the bottom line for bosses who develop leaders this way.

Watch Me, Listen to Me

If you've ever had a chance to watch a master practice a craft, you know you can learn a lot simply by paying attention. By watching how their bosses went about doing business, many protégés learned valuable lessons. It makes sense that those in a leadership role are examples because they are watched by their people and conclusions are drawn about what they do—for better or for worse. It surprised us a bit, though, to hear that setting the example and leading by example was, for some bosses (especially senior executives), a conscious developmental strategy. As one boss put it:

> I learned that it is incredibly important to lead by example. Every time I go into a room with my directs or with a large group from my organization I am very thoughtful about how I present myself and the behavior I model. I know that people will be paying attention and will imitate me. If I come across as unstructured or undisciplined, if they don't sense that I care and am passionate and paying attention, they will think it's okay to be that way. You can do this and be genuine; you shouldn't pretend to be someone else. As a leader you are always on.

Many of the executives were aware that they were always on and tried to be consistent in a variety of ways that supported development (for instance, taking the time to really listen to what their people have to say). They made a special effort to recognize both outstanding performance and growth, they modeled giving credit, they spent time on activities that developed others, and some even expected their highest performers to build the team rather than "score points." One was adamant about "getting rid of bullies" because, he said, people won't think you are serious if you let them remain. Another reinforced the point by saying "You have to deal with performance issues—they are obvious to everyone."

Many bosses combined role modeling with teaching in developing their protégés. For example, in an effort to get people to take more risks one boss not only takes risks himself but "tells stories about things I screwed up." When people do take a risk and fail, the boss "provides air cover" by absorbing the business loss and/or taking steps to prevent the mistake from destroying the person's reputation. Others make sure to explain why they make the decisions they make, aren't afraid to go into the trenches, don't make people feel stupid for asking questions, follow up and deliver on promises . . . and on and on, modeling what they believe is important for leaders to do. One protégé described learning how to facilitate a meeting from an exceptional boss: "She was a master at running meetings—she framed issues, got everyone involved, listened, asked questions. It caused people to think better over time."

Some executives took role modeling and teaching a step further by inviting their protégés to shadow them as they attended business reviews or traveled to field locations. The executives took advantage of the intense time together to teach and educate their protégés about the business, company culture, and how to have a successful career. The protégés benefited by gaining a much broader perspective on both the business and what it takes to be a successful executive. One protégé recalled what a rich learning experience this was:

> He hired me into my first international role. He would take me on trips with him. He'd coach me along the way on what was going to happen. He'd have me sit right next to him at key meetings. He'd provide color commentary during the meetings. 'That was a mistake. Watch what our CEO is going to do next.' And as we were leaving sites and traveling to the next location, he would sit next to me on the plane and debrief with me. He was constantly teaching, especially about context issues that were beyond where I was in my career at the time.

Offering Career Advice and Guidance

Talented people who achieve results also get many opportunities. Deciding which ones to take or to seek out can be a challenge, and some bosses play an important role by offering career advice. "He had an offer to take a position in HR and wanted to know if he should go. I had him talk to the right people who could help him decide. He got a temporary position and liked it, so I helped him become permanent." In another case a protégé was torn between two career opportunities, so the boss arranged for her to take temporary assignments on projects, one in each of the domains of interest.

Giving career advice, particularly when it involves crossing organizational boundaries or consideration of future leadership roles, requires extensive knowledge of both the organization and the person. One vice president might have summarized all of the interviews with executives who emphasize this aspect of development when he said:

> The most critical thing is to get to know everyone who works directly for you as an individual. Each has a different personal situation, different family situation, a spouse with different needs and expectations. You can't limit yourself to job talk; you have to get to know the people, their personal situations, and their career expectations. Then I can give guidance based on my thirty-one years of experience in the company regarding what is and is not realistic.

What this executive highlights is that giving meaningful career advice requires understanding people's situations well beyond the job. His experience has taught him that mobility, a key to making career moves, is deeply impacted by the family situation. If a person accepts relocation despite family concerns, unhappiness in the family can lead to work problems (especially in international assignments).

This executive was exemplary too in his knowledge of the company. In those thirty-one years he had moved between functions and geographies, typically staying in a role no more than a couple of years. He began in finance, shifted to logistics, moved into sales and marketing supporting Italy initially and then the entire European Union. He moved to the U.S. for four years in global roles where he was responsible for Latin America and Asia, was promoted to director in Norway, and from there went to Brussels as he took over as leader of a large business unit operating in twelve European countries. After that and two years leading marketing for Western Europe, he was promoted to vice president for Central and Eastern Europe. He has tremendous insights into how the organization works, how careers unfold, and which jobs offer the best career development versus which jobs are career dead-ends. Needless to say, many bosses have neither sufficient knowledge of their people nor of their organization to offer meaningful career guidance beyond the immediate circumstances.

In structuring the chapter around these six foci we've made things appear more segmented than they actually are. The executives we talked with, boss and protégé alike, confirmed that developmentally robust bosses come with various combinations of these perspectives. For example, one boss might be a role model and provide challenging assignments while another might provide career guidance and make connections.

Further, the approach can shift over time and with protégés of differing maturity. Some bosses, for example, dramatically increased their time spent developing talent later in their careers, while others were always attuned to it but did not have the experience and exposure to do more sophisticated interventions until later in their careers. Some bosses also made it clear that the maturity of their protégés affected how they approached development, with skills/flaws coaching more likely for younger protégés and challenging assignments with autonomy and accountability for the more experienced ones.

Exceptional Bosses in Action

In our interviews, we were interested not just in what great bosses did to develop their protégés, but also in how they approached the relationship and how they leveraged formal HR tools and processes.

The Boss-Protégé Relationship

While it is clear that to develop someone effectively you must know him or her pretty well—strengths and weaknesses, aspirations, prior experience—the bosses we studied varied considerably in the degree of closeness they developed with their protégés.

In many instances, bosses and protégés became personally close. Relationships were variously described as uncle, brother, mother lion, parent, with whatever connotation those kinds of relationships inspire. Some were friends but did not socialize outside of work. In several instances, they became so close that their families would get together regularly outside of work. But even in these instances, several protégés commented that they were subordinate to their boss at work. One protégé who was close friends and a bridge partner with her boss outside of work summarized it well: "I know my place. She's an executive vice president and I'm not."

Many other bosses maintained a professional distance between themselves and their subordinates. One protégé commented, "I would not use any family terms to describe my relationship with my boss. He definitely does not act like an uncle or big brother. He is the boss. He is very comfortable with hierarchy."

But whether the relationship was very close or professionally distant or somewhere in between, we were struck by the consistency with which protégés used certain terms to describe their bosses: respects me, trusts me, trustworthy, genuine, authentic, transparent, candid, cares about me, clear about expectations, available. In other words, while differences in style, motivation, approach, and closeness abound, there is a common core that makes the development relationship work. From the bosses' perspectives their commitment was rarely driven by self-interest. It was the right thing to do, or part of the job, or necessary to make the team or the business successful. Because protégés understood that the motivation of their bosses was not purely self-serving, they were more open to negative and sometimes harsh feedback and the coaching or guidance that accompanied it.

The Added Value of Formal HR Processes

Perhaps one of our most surprising findings was how seldom these folks referred to the human resource practices aimed at talent development, including annual performance reviews, succession planning, high potential identification, and training programs.

Each of the five companies that participated in the study has a formal performance review process that includes documentation of formal development goals. This was almost never mentioned by either the bosses or the protégés unless we explicitly asked about it during the interview. Virtually all bosses and protégés said they complied and submitted formal development goals, but these typically reflected work that the boss and protégé were already doing together, and neither had any qualms about abandoning these formal development goals if job conditions changed. One boss commented, "I generally take a pretty organic approach to development. I think about assignments that will be both challenging and interesting and motivating for the employee. But I don't worry a lot about formally documenting development goals." A protégé added, "We did not set formal development goals. It was more trial by fire. As long as I kept figuring out how to get the job done, he kept betting on me."

Similarly, we heard very few direct references to succession planning or high potential identification, except that many bosses and protégés commented that there were several critical assignments and job experiences that people needed over the course of their careers to advance into senior leadership roles, and this was something that either they explicitly discussed together or it was something they both knew and so guided the development work they did together (e.g., special assignments and projects, introductions provided to senior executives, coaching). Training was mentioned very rarely, except in one participating company, where many protégés with engineering degrees said they were encouraged by their boss to obtain an MBA, and this had been a valuable part of their development.

Development is deeply embedded in the culture of these organizations, and processes, systems, and programs have evolved to support it. Perhaps the reason that so few executives and protégés mentioned formal HR processes is because they are so embedded and taken for granted. But more likely it's because these exceptional bosses tend to see development as something that happens in real time, day to day, as events unfold. To wait for an annual review or to restrict a developmental conversation to whatever is on the competency list would not cross their minds. Indeed, some of the executives even felt that the formal review system worked against development because it determined promotions and raises and therefore led people to avoid taking risks or assignments that might hurt their ratings! "He had my back" takes on even more meaning in that environment.

In the Larger Context

This study was focused on bosses viewed as exceptional developers of leadership talent and the leaders they had developed. But some of the questions asked of the protégés took a larger perspective and explored other bosses in their careers. Not surprisingly, they came in all shapes and sizes. There were bosses who were essentially mediocre but who contributed to their development in a relatively minor way. And there were memorable bad bosses who contributed in negative ways by micromanaging, yelling at people, making people feel stupid, lying, and so forth. There was even one protégé who reported having two "crazy" bosses, one who was "good crazy" and included her and gave her exposure, and one who was downright mean, a "stress monkey," who taught her how not to treat people. But as significant as each boss might have been, what struck us was how important it was to have a contrast—other bosses against whom to compare the exceptional one. There is some truth to the notion that it's only when we've been exposed to a variety of good and bad that we can recognize the extraordinary.

The larger picture also highlights differences among the five organizations based on their talent strategy. In some of the organizations, the talent strategy is to hire large numbers of college graduates, invest heavily in their development, and promote the best from within, with the expectation that the vast majority of executives will be individuals who have spent almost their entire careers with the organization. In these organizations, where talent development was an organizational imperative, many protégés reported that they had worked for two or more exceptional talent developers over the course of their careers—although interestingly, even in these organizations, almost every protégé also had the experience of working for a very bad manager. Bosses reported little to no conflict between achieving business objectives and developing talent; rather, they saw the two goals as tightly linked. There was virtually no resistance to sending people across organizational boundaries for job assignments, and there was solid cooperation among executives in creating developmental opportunities.

Executives in these organizations know each other well and could readily talk about talent as well as share it. Typically, the executives had held a wide variety of positions themselves, so they knew what assignments were potentially most powerful developmentally and why. Several executives reported that they had managed the same protégé two or more times over their careers and had continued to track and influence the protégé's progress over time. These are not trivial advantages if the goal is to develop leadership talent through experience, although it carries with it the disadvantage of individuals being pigeon-holed by senior managers (perhaps based on an early event that no longer defines the person).

Almost every executive could identify an occasion on which he or she had bet on the wrong protégé, and the solution was typically to restore the protégé to a smaller-scale role within the organization where the protégé could contribute effectively. One boss told us, "We have a culture of trying to save everybody. A person may be great but in a job exceeding his readiness. We work hard not to do that, so I try to temper the expectations of senior leadership that often wants to move people too fast. One person I put in a job with a lot of corporate visibility, followed by a larger organization to polish that. [His] development took two steps instead of putting both together." Another reported, "I give people a second chance. For example, one of my directs was in trouble in a plant and I was ready to fire him. Instead I found a spot for him in a different plant, and it worked out. When there is a problem, we deal with it."

While there were few direct, tangible rewards for bosses who developed talent—even in the organizations we studied where development was embedded in the culture–bosses still made development a priority, they knew it was expected of them, and they spoke of the indirect rewards of better business performance and a network of close relationships.

In other organizations, internal talent development and promotion from within were lower priorities than hiring the best possible person for the job, regardless of whether this was an insider or outsider, and there was a strong belief that significant external hiring—even into senior level positions—helps bring fresh perspectives to the business and supports a culture of innovation. Talent development often took a back seat to other considerations in staffing management and leadership positions, so, not surprisingly, it was rare for protégés to report that they had worked for more than one exceptional talent developer, and they seemed extremely grateful for the opportunity and the benefits they had derived when they worked for a great boss.

Fewer of our great talent developer bosses in these organizations helped their protégés plot out their careers or identify a developmentally useful next job assignment, perhaps because the boss himself had spent his entire career in a single business unit or function and had limited connections to senior executives in other parts of the business. If they happened to place a protégé in a stretch assignment that was beyond the protégé's competence, their most typical solution was to exit the protégé from the company. One boss based in a European country where it's hard to terminate employees told us, "I was very optimistic about one employee I promoted, but I have now started having conversations with him about whether our company is the right place for him. In general, I try to be very thoughtful when I make the decision about whether to exit someone or move him out of the company. But you can't just replant someone if you can't identify a job where you're very confident he can be successful. You have to test the waters—are there others in the company who know him well and are interested in hiring him?"

One might imagine the differing outcomes if equally talented managers were to spend their careers in the two different environments. It suggests that if an organization is serious about developing leadership talent, it must be serious about whom it promotes into leadership roles.

Implications

Over the past several years, there has been renewed interest in leadership development circles in how to engage leaders more effectively in building the next generation of leaders. This follows on the heels of the War for Talent research, showing that a talent mindset is key to leadership development inside organizations (Michaels, Handfield-Jones, & Axelrod, 2001), and books by very effective CEOs who attributed much of their success to deep, personal investments in leadership development (Bossidy & Charan, 2002; Lafley, 2011; Welch & Byrne, 2001). As a result, many organizations, including those participating in our study, have committed to the principle of "leaders building leaders" and have tried various approaches. Books and articles have been written suggesting that the secret is to turn all leaders into teachers (Tichy, 1997; Tichy & Cardwell, 2002) or to teach leaders the five steps to developing the people who work for them. It would make life easier for leadership development professionals if there were a simple, single solution. But our interviews demonstrate that this is not the case. There are a variety of different ways that executives who are great talent developers approach leadership development. Each of these approaches has strengths and limitations. Each helps contribute in important ways to the development of emerging leaders. So what should a leadership development professional do to grow more great talent developers inside her organization?

First, begin nurturing great talent developers early in their careers. As noted, most of the great talent developers interviewed indicated that their passion for this activity resulted from something that happened to them early in life or early in their careers. Most commonly, a boss made a special investment in them that they were determined to pay forward, or they learned in a first management experience that the best way to get work done was by empowering and developing the people working for them. What might happen if eagle-eyed bosses and HR professionals were on the lookout for early career high potentials who were learning first-hand about the power and benefit of talent development? With a little prompting and coaching, we suspect that many more of these individuals could be turned into great talent developers.

Second, don't over-invest in trying to incent bosses to become great talent developers. None of the bosses we interviewed indicated they invested in people in order to earn a bigger bonus or because they saw it as a way to be promoted (although they did not say they would object to it). Rather, they became great talent developers because helping and developing others is a strong personal value and/or because they believe that developing others is the only sustainable way to achieve outstanding business results as a leader. For example, one female executive we interviewed, who is currently a vice president in charge of a major product line, studied chemical engineering in college and, at twenty-one, began her managerial career in charge of fifty-four men at a manufacturing plant. She succeeded there and went on to achieve outstanding results in a succession of extremely challenging jobs. Despite all of her personal sacrifices and the sterling bottom-line results she has delivered, she confessed that "What makes me proudest in my twenty-two years with the company is the capability I have developed in others."

Another executive said, "I've had people invest in me—at least four or five spent a significant amount of time on my development. I have an obligation to pay that back." He went on to say, "I want to make this company as good as it can be. If I don't develop and train and coach, it won't be the best it can be." Another senior executive noted in a similar vein that talent development is simply a business imperative: "People will only stay with a company if you're making them more valuable faster than any other company."

Companies that value people and development create the conditions for great talent developers and motivated protégés to flourish. But we have no evidence from our interviews that incentives directed solely at development of talent were necessary to motivate these exceptional talent developers. That said, we believe that to promote and reward managers who do not develop their people sends a message that works against embedding development in the culture. Perhaps the lesson here is that developing leadership talent should be an expectation and as such a sine qua non for progressing in the managerial ranks. Incentives might better serve the business attached to the outcome of effective talent development: improved performance. What they need most are resources (such as an adequate budget) and, especially, support (such as top management commitment and clarity, freedom to give people developmental opportunities and tolerate their mistakes, support for cross-boundary moves) that help them in their efforts to develop others. We were surprised that systems and processes intended to help development, things such as performance ratings and succession planning, sometimes got in the way by inhibiting risk taking or by branding people in ways that worked against them.

Third, recognize that it's valuable for different leaders to take different approaches to developing their employees. Every organization can benefit from a mix of performance coaches, career coaches, role models, and task masters who continually elevate performance expectations. Resist the temptation to train all leaders and managers in a single step-by-step approach to developing their people. Instead, encourage each leader to find her "development voice"—that is, an approach (or combination of approaches) that she feels comfortable, confident, and expert at using. Expose them to the six approaches described here, as well as others that leaders have successfully adopted inside the organization. Encourage leaders employing similar approaches to share best practices and build their expertise. We suspect that differences in approach may be related to leader temperament and style, but we are optimistic that leaders can build their expertise in their preferred approaches through training and deliberate practice.

Fourth, insofar as possible, match emerging leaders with talent developers whose approach can best aid their development. Is there a high potential who could benefit from a higher-level perspective on the business and from learning more about how executives manage themselves? Assign her to a boss who is a great role model and teacher. Is there a high potential who has spent most of his career in a single organizational silo and has limited exposure to corporate-level politics and executives across the company? Match him to a boss who understands how to get things done across organizational boundaries and excels at exposing his team members to key leaders in different parts of the business. Different bosses are catalysts for different types of development, just as different job experiences teach different leadership lessons. So matching a high potential employee to the right boss might be almost as potent developmentally as matching that employee to the right job assignment.

Fifth, organizations need to examine their talent strategy to determine how successfully they can lean on "leaders building leaders" to provide them with a deep leadership talent bench. In general, organizations focused on development and promotion from within will have a larger supply of great talent developers and plentiful good talent developers, and these individuals will have more knowledge and tools at their disposal to help develop their protégés. For example, they typically will have a more complete network of executive contacts across the organization and thus be better able to make connections for their protégés. They typically will have a wider range of job experiences inside the organization so will be better able to offer their protégés more complete guidance on career possibilities. The consequences for "failure" tend to be less severe in organizations that depend almost exclusively on promotion from within—demotion or lateral reassignment with the possibility of eventual rehabilitation versus termination—so they can encourage their protégés to take more risks.

This is not to say that bosses can only be great talent developers in organizations with a promote-from-within talent strategy; that is far from the truth. But we did find that protégés in organizations that make a significant percentage of external hires into mid-level and senior positions typically had a narrower range of job experiences (e.g., all within one function and/or one business unit and/or one geography), had more questions about how to grow their careers outside the business unit and function where they were working, and were a bit more anxious about their careers because they had seen so many colleagues crash and burn. These organizations should consider how they provide exposure to alternative career paths to their high potentials (e.g., include a module on career management in their formal high potential development programs, run internal career fairs to help high potentials learn about jobs and career opportunities in different parts of the organization) and also how they can encourage these individuals to take the career risks that we know are required in order to become competent broad business leaders.

Finally, don't expect that investment in formal HR programs and processes such as competency models and formal career development conversations will yield significant growth in the number of great talent developers. The bosses we interviewed paid little to no attention to these. We are not asserting that formal HR career development processes have no value. We know from research that organizations with good people processes outperform those that don't on a wide array of organizational effectiveness metrics (Huselid, Becker, & Beatty, 2005). But we suspect the primary value of "process and program" investments is that they make mediocre and average managers somewhat more effective at talent development by giving them a language to use, a discipline to follow, and a process that they must comply with. However, if the organization's goal is to increase the number of truly outstanding talent developers, the organization would do better to identify those with potential to be great talent developers, help them find their "development voice" and adopt a talent strategy centered on development, as described above.

Epilogue

> *Before you become a leader, success is all about growing yourself. After you become a leader, success is all about growing others.*
>
> JACK WELCH

We went into these interviews suspecting that the immediate boss could determine whether and what a protégé learns from experience; it is hardly surprising that these suspicions were confirmed by both our boss and protégé interviews. There were, however, some surprises. First, we had not expected to find the rich variety of approaches that exceptional bosses take in developing the people who work for them and the unique contributions each approach makes to leadership development.

Second, while we expected bosses to have a significant role in the development of their protégés, we knew that other factors play important catalytic roles as well. So it was surprising to hear from protégés just how valuable their exceptional bosses were to their development. In an informal survey at the conclusion of our protégé interviews, the protégés overwhelmingly rated their special bosses significantly higher than "any other factor that influenced your development." These bosses made a lasting difference in the lives of their protégés and to the future leadership of their organizations.

Last but not least, we were struck by the integrity, selflessness, and outstanding personal values of the people we interviewed. We live in an age where newspapers and the Internet are filled with stories of corporate and individual greed, so it is easy to become cynical about the values of corporate leaders. The kinds of bosses we interviewed are often the unsung heroes in the corporate world who invest in the development of others because they care passionately about people, are passionately committed to helping their organizations achieve great results, and believe these two passions are simply sides of the same coin. Often they receive no special recognition or rewards for their work, but they develop others anyway because they believe it's the right thing to do. In many organizations bosses such as these are underappreciated and underutilized resources when it comes to developing leadership talent. The wise corporation will find them, recognize them, and support their efforts by creating a fertile context for growth.

References

Allen, T. D., Finkelstein, L. M., & Poteet, M. L. (2009). *Designing workplace mentoring programs: An evidence-based approach*. Malden, MA: Wiley-Blackwell.

Axelrod, W., & Coyle, J. (2011). *Make talent your business: How exceptional managers develop people while getting results*. San Francisco, CA: Berrett-Koehler.

Bossidy, L., & Charan, R. (2002). *Execution: The discipline of getting things done*. New York, NY: Crown Business.

DeRue, D. S., & Wellman, N. (2009). Developing leaders via experience: The role of developmental challenge, learning orientation, and feedback availability. *Journal of Applied Psychology, 94*, 859–875.

Ellis, S., & Davidi, I. (2005). After-event reviews: Drawing lessons from successful and failed experience. *Journal of Applied Psychology, 90*, 857–871.

Ellis, S., Mendel, R., & Nir, M. (2006). Learning from successful and failed experience: The moderating role of kind of after-event review. *Journal of Applied Psychology, 91*, 669–680.

Hollenbeck, G. P. (2002). Coaching executives: Individual leader development. In R. Silzer (Ed.), *The 21st century executive*. San Francisco, CA: Jossey-Bass.

Huselid, M. A., Becker, B. E., & Beatty, R. W. (2005). *The workforce scorecard: Managing human capital to execute strategy*. Boston, MA: Harvard Business School Publishing.

Isaacson, W. (2011). *Steve Jobs*. New York, NY: Simon and Schuster.

Kluger, A. N., & DeNisi, A. (1996). The effects of feedback interventions on performance: A historical review, a meta-analysis, and a preliminary feedback intervention theory. *Psychological Bulletin, 119*, 254–284.

Lafley, A. G. (2011). The art and science of finding the right CEO. *Harvard Business Review, 89*(10), 67–74.

McCall, M. W., Jr., & Hollenbeck, G. P. (2002). *Developing global executives: The lessons of international experience*. Boston, MA: Harvard Business School Press.

McCall, M. W., Jr., Lombardo, M. M., & Morrison, A. M. (1988). *The lessons of experience.* New York, NY: The Free Press.

McCauley, C. D., Ruderman, M. N., Ohlott, P. J., & Morrow, J. E. (1994). Assessing the developmental components of managerial jobs. *Journal of Applied Psychology, 79,* 544–560.

Michaels, E., Handfield-Jones, H., & Axelrod, B. (2001). *The war for talent.* Boston, MA: Harvard Business School Press.

Spreitzer, G. M., McCall, M. W., Jr., & Mahoney, J. (1997). Early identification of international executives. *Journal of Applied Psychology, 82,* 6–29.

Tichy, N. M. (1997). *The leadership engine.* New York, NY: HarperCollins.

Tichy, N. M., & Cardwell, N. (2002). *The cycle of leadership: How great leaders teach their companies to win.* New York, NY: HarperCollins.

Welch, J., & Byrne, J. A. (2001). *Jack: Straight from the gut.* New York, NY: Warner.

Section Five

Conclusion

CHAPTER EIGHTEEN

Putting Experience at the Heart of Leader Development
Concluding Thoughts

Cynthia D. McCauley and Morgan W. McCall, Jr.

A general framework for experience-driven leader development like the one described in Chapter 1 can be useful, but it's a long way from generalities to practice. Although several of the organizations in this book were aware of and even used the framework, many were not, and it was not a criterion for invitations to contribute to the book. Nor did we start with a list of topics from the framework that we thought were important to include in a book about experience-driven leader development. Instead, and partly as a test of the robustness of the framework, we sought out practitioners who were working to put experience at the heart of leader development. We let their efforts suggest exactly what that looks like. We asked them to describe how experience-driven leader development can be brought to life in an organization. Each of the resulting chapters is unique, yet from this collection of practices a clearer picture emerges of what "putting experience at the heart of leader development" is all about. Certainly it's about practical ways to support the business strategy through a talent management system based on experience. But perhaps more importantly, it's about embedding learning from experience as a core organizational value.

Experience at the Center of the Talent Management System

For a number of years, competency models have been portrayed as a central, integrating element for the various components of talent management systems (e.g., staffing, performance management, and succession planning). The logic is that if each component is designed to reinforce the same set of competencies, then the components will work in unison to develop higher levels of competency. The organizations represented in this book, in contrast, emphasize *experience as the driver of leadership competence*. Competency models don't go away; they are viewed as simply another element of the leadership talent management system, and experience moves to center stage (see Figure 18.1). Each component in the system is recast to strengthen experience-driven development:

- Individuals are assessed not just in terms of their leadership behaviors and capabilities ("competencies"), but in terms of their ability to learn from experience, the variety of leadership challenges they've experienced, and what they have learned from these experiences.

Figure 18.1. Experience at the Center of the Talent Management System

- Placing individuals into new positions or staffing project teams is not just a matter of finding the best talent to do the work, but rather finding who can bring strengths to the assignment while also being stretched in ways that will provide an opportunity to develop. With this approach, line managers and their HR partners have to hone their ability to find the right balance between business requirements and individual development while considering the cost of failure. To counteract the tendency to err too much on the side of business requirements, some organizations designate certain roles to be staffed as developmental assignments. Others create special panels of line and HR executives with the authority to make staffing decisions with development in mind.

- On-boarding is no longer simply a process for getting the new job incumbent up to speed. It's also a time to identify how the job will challenge the individual and to put in place a plan to master that challenge. It's not just a time to develop connections with new stakeholders but to create learning partnerships that will deliver feedback and reflection—important catalysts for learning from experience.

- Performance appraisals aren't just about whether business goals have been met or not, but about how leaders have grown over the year and how they will leverage new learning.

- Development planning is a must-do rather than a nice-to-do. And it's not a list of courses to take, but rather emphasizes challenging experiences as the major vehicle for learning. Development is not an add-on; it is woven into the work. And planning for and evaluating it is ongoing—not a once-a-year event.

- In succession management sessions, open positions are examined not just in terms of the capabilities they demand but the capabilities they could sharpen. Top talent is assessed in terms of how much they have grown in their current assignments and what their next experiences should be to continue their development.

- Career planning is guided by delineated experience paths for building the skills and expertise needed for targeted leadership positions (e.g., general manager or head of a specific corporate function). These paths are not always moving upward, but include cross-boundary moves, special assignments, and perhaps even roles in the community or a nonprofit organization.

- Formal development programs are turned inside out. Instead of being cast as the source of learning that then is transferred (or not) to the job, development programs play a support role to enhance on-the-job development. This can take a variety of forms: programs focused on enhancing a participant's ability to learn from experience; just-in-time content available to leaders as they navigate new experiences; peer learning groups made up of leaders facing similar challenges—a setting that invites closer examination of one's experience and the sharing of insights and advice; and realistic simulations during which skills can be practiced and expertise developed. Action learning projects—a popular experience-based element of formal development programs— are embedded in the real work of the organization with consequences for the business.
- The purpose of mentoring and coaching is to challenge leaders to step into the discomfort of stretch experiences and experiment with new approaches, to provoke reflection and facilitate the articulation of new insights and perspectives, and to increase accountability for learning. Such relationships are seen as particularly critical during times of transition. Key relationships in an assignment (e.g., the boss, a project champion) factor into assessments of its learning potential for an individual. The 70 (experience) and 20 (other people) in the 70–20–10 catchphrase are seen as entwined rather than distinct sources of development.
- Competencies are positioned as one of the possible outcomes of experience. They describe the skills and expertise developed over time through practice—taking action and seeing the consequences of those actions. Knowing which jobs or assignments within the organization provide the best opportunities to develop different competencies is essential.

To make these types of changes in the components of a talent management system requires a new set of tools and processes specifically geared to the experience-centric perspective. Although this book has shared system-based perspectives on experience-driven leader development, McCauley, DeRue, Yost, and Taylor (2013) document numerous efforts to develop the tools and tactics to implement them.

Learning from Experience as a Shared Responsibility

Recasting the components of the talent management system to better reflect an experience-driven development strategy highlights how important it is for a lot of different people at various levels and with various responsibilities to work together toward a common goal. The default option that leader development is solely or even primarily a human resources responsibility is misleading, as is passing the buck by leaving it entirely up to individuals to develop themselves. Neither human resources, with limited control over who gets what job, nor individuals, with limited perspective on experiences that might develop them and even less control over access to those experiences, controls enough of the context to effectively drive leader development throughout the organization. Beginning with the chief executive and the senior management team, an effective leader development process based in experience requires participation from the general management population, human resources, immediate bosses, and, ultimately, the developing individuals themselves. At some level, even the board has an important role to play. But the roles that these different entities must play vary considerably, and collectively the chapters in this book suggest some specific responsibilities for each of them.

The potential contribution of the CEO cannot be overstated. We've seen how important the chief executive is in making leader development a fundamental part of the business strategy, in modeling expected behavior in developing others, and in holding managers accountable for the development of their people. Of course, the CEO can't do it alone—the senior management team must tailor the strategy to their businesses and functions, see to it that their people are held accountable, identify people with leadership potential, and make sure that the boundaries among their parts of the business can be crossed for developmental as well as business reasons. Along with the CEO, the senior team shares responsibility for the design and implementation of the system and for succession planning that ensures its preservation and refinement over time.

As we look across the chapters, it is clear that for experience-driven development to work managers at all levels must participate. They are frequently asked to serve, usually with human resource staff, on forums, panels, or committees that assess talent, choose people for particular experiences, and provide feedback and resources. Frequently, managers are asked to serve as mentors or coaches, to participate in programs as teachers, experts, or sponsors, or to bring in their business problems for developing leaders to work on.

Although human resources should not be *the* driving force behind development through experience, the function has a very important role to play in helping line management design and execute the systems. Their expertise is a crucial factor in balancing the business knowledge and performance orientation of busy line managers with the understanding of people, how they develop, and the tools and processes needed to make it work. In some organizations there is even a special breed of human resource professional called "business partners" who serve as advisors and coaches to line management to help them make wise developmental decisions. Business partners are uniquely valued for the knowledge of the business, jobs, and people and bring a cross-business perspective that is extremely important in experience-driven development.

There is no question that the potentially most influential force in using experience for development is the immediate manager, who has day-to-day control over work assignments, feedback, performance criteria and assessment, and who, in most organizations, decides or at least recommends who has leadership potential and should receive developmental opportunities. McCall and McHenry in this volume describe in detail the ways that exceptional developmental bosses do their thing.

Similarly, McHenry and McKenna, also in this volume, describe in detail ways that individuals can develop themselves, much like experts in any other field. Ultimately, individuals are responsible for those aspects of development that they can influence, most immediately taking developmental opportunities when they arise and proactively seeking them when they don't, being open to learning from these opportunities, and taking actions (such as seeking out feedback and building in accountability) that increase the likelihood of learning.

There is no perfect world, so it would be rare indeed for all these pieces to come together to optimize leader development through experience. Fortunately, there is overlap among the roles, and a strength in one domain can compensate to some degree for weaknesses in another. For example, working for a bad boss, individuals can sometimes do for themselves what the boss might otherwise have done—they can find other sources for feedback, hold themselves accountable, and seek coaching elsewhere. Human resource professionals can sometimes work developmental miracles, even without top management support. Individual managers who believe in development can create islands of growth, even in hostile environments.

As important as developing leadership talent is, it is unlikely to be an organization's first priority. This means that, even in developmentally oriented organizations, there will always be a tradeoff between what is best for developing talent and what is best for obtaining business results—and often a balancing act between long-term and short-term perspectives. The good news is that the nature of the beast is such that challenging experiences abound, so that opportunity is there if the culture of the organization reflects a priority for developing talent.

Learning from Experience as a Core Organizational Value

I came to see, in my time at IBM, that culture isn't just one aspect of the game—it is the game. . . . Vision, strategy, marketing, financial management—any management system, in fact—can see you on the right path and carry you for a while. But no enterprise—whether in business, government, education, health care, or any area of human endeavor—will succeed over the long haul if those elements aren't part of its DNA.

LOU GERSTNER (2002, p. 182)

Like the other systems mentioned by Gerstner, a talent management system can't keep experience at the heart of leader development unless it becomes part of the culture, the DNA of the organization. But how would you know if experience-driven development is in the organization's DNA? Ben Schneider, our colleague and a thought leader in this arena (and who acknowledges borrowing heavily from Schein, 2010), has advised us to focus on six aspects of organizations: the priorities of senior management, what is recognized and rewarded, what is measured and tracked, what people communicate about, what is supported by organizational processes and resources, and what employees are skilled at. Using this template, we see evidence in the cases in this book of organizations working to make learning from experience a core organizational value. Here are just a few examples:

1. *Priority of senior leaders.* Senior leaders are visible and involved in the project-based development initiatives at Tata Group, JK Organisation, and GSK as project guides, stakeholders, and sponsors. The CEO at 3M reviews more than one hundred executive positions, discussing with his team what additional experience each individual needs to be prepared for future roles. The CEO at Yum! Brands leads a program on motivating and aligning teams based on thirteen principles derived not from some theory or research, but *from his own experience.*

2. *Recognition and rewards.* Getting a spot in IBM's Corporate Service Corps is highly competitive, its attractiveness fueled by the benefits that participants say they gain: growth as leaders, a more global network, a sense of contributing to others, and renewed vigor and clarity in their work. The executives in the McCall and McHenry study were motivated as people-developers because of the impact their efforts had on individuals and the business. Perhaps it is not just what is rewarded that points to core organizational values, but what feels intrinsically rewarding to employees. On the other hand, it's important not to de-incentivize experience-based development. For example, organizations in the Intelligence Community found that they needed to modify practices so that individuals who take on

joint duty assignments are not penalized in terms of salary increases and bonuses.

3. *Measurement and tracking.* At Kelly Services, they measure leadership experiences as part of their assessment of managers. In a number of the organizations, such as Eaton and 3M, developmental assignments and their outcomes are tracked as part of succession management. Progress made by participants in Tata Administrative Services and in JK Organisation's Fire of Experience is scrutinized several times a year by multiple stakeholders, and feedback is provided so that course corrections can be made. Employees are expected to measure and track, too. For example, employees at Yum! Brands use four tactics to hold themselves accountable for follow-through on their development plans, including creating a metric to assess whether goals have been reached and a monthly progress review with their boss.

4. *Communication.* Efforts are made to embed a common language in the organization for talking about experience-based development, for example, the PARR model at Kelly Services and Eaton's profiles of key experiences. As the authors from Kelly Services point out, shared frameworks encourage leaders to leverage opportunities in their daily interactions to make learning part of their work. Kelly Services also uses social media to engage the whole organization in common experiences and in sharing their learning with one another. Randall Hill pointed out the power of story for transferring experiences from one person to another, and sharing personal learning-from-experience stories is alive and well in a number of the organizations represented here. And the peer learning groups at HEINEKEN and Microsoft are forums for real-time conversations about learning from experience.

5. *Processes and resources.* All the talent management processes noted earlier in this chapter are in support of experience-driven development. In his chapter, Paul Yost also makes the case for designing resources and tools that can "go viral" in the organization, promoting experience-driven development throughout the organization. The web-based resources for designing and learning from cross-functional assignments at

Genentech are one example of putting easy-to-use tools in the hands of individual employees.

6. *Employee skills.* Microsoft's approach to formal development is designed to better equip employees to learn from experience—by connecting them with peers, giving them new perspectives on their challenges and space to pause and make meaning of their experience. One of the criteria for advancement into leadership roles at Eaton is a commitment to personal development, which is demonstrated through continuous learning, sharing learning with others, and growing beyond the current requirements of one's role. Likewise, a high level of learning agility and strong development focus is one of the key criteria for selection into GSK's Future Strategy Group.

Clearly, there are a wide variety of ways in which organizations reinforce the belief that learning from experience is an important pursuit.

Looking Forward

Leaders have always learned from their experiences, and they will continue to do so even without organizational intervention. However, as the authors in this book demonstrate, line managers and HR professionals can create the conditions for more learning by more leaders and for learning focused in arenas that will advance the business strategy and the health of the organization. And they can deflect or dampen the forces that thwart learning from experience.

Clearly, efforts to be more intentional and systematic about experience-driven development have multiplied and matured in the last decade. Progress has been especially apparent in terms of integrating learning into the real work of the organization. For example, in some of the development initiatives for high potential managers, participants are assigned to strategic projects of importance to senior leaders (rather than nice-to-do projects that managers are willing for an action learning team to muck around in as part of a development program). And there's a clear recognition of job transitions as a critical learning juncture, with more developmental resources being intentionally applied at that point in time.

Yet it seems that the field is early in its journey. There is still a need for fresh, creative approaches to identifying leadership talent and for a more systematic look at catalysts for learning— Which ones work the best in what situations? One trend that caught our attention was the expansion of the boundaries of "on-the-job" development to include community service work, realistic simulations, and bosses as experiences themselves (not just catalysts for learning). And in many organizations, there are still obstacles to overcome. The authors of the HEINEKEN case point to two pervasive issues: the engrained paradigm that development equals formal training and the view that coaching and facilitating is an HR rather than line management responsibility.

It was particularly instructive to see how practitioners customize their approach to experience-driven development depending on their business context, the ethos of the organization, and broader societal influences—perhaps most clearly illustrated in JK Organisation's use of a culturally significant Indian epic in crafting stakeholder roles that support experience-driven development.

Finally, seeing leadership as a craft to be mastered rather than a set of competencies to be developed resonated with us. Two chapters informed by disciplines rarely drawn on by leader development practitioners illustrate the promise of this lens. Drawing from the expertise literature, McHenry and McKenna make the case for daily deliberate practice (over one's whole career) as the route to elite performance as a leader. And the work of Hill and his colleagues at the Institute for Creative Technologies illustrates how organizations might speed up the acquisition of expertise using cognitive task analysis to better capture expert knowledge that is then more readily acquired by less experienced leaders via simulations based on principles of guided experiential learning.

We are incredibly indebted to the practitioners who took the time to share their perspectives, their work, and their advice for others. We know that their words will spark ideas and launch experiments, and we hope will inspire others to share their own efforts to use experience to develop leadership talent. We are optimistic about the continued advancement of experience-driven leader development.

References

Gerstner, L. (2002). *Who says elephants can't dance?* New York, NY: HarperBusiness.

McCauley, C. D., DeRue, D. S., Yost, P. R., & Taylor, S. (2013). *Experience-driven leader development: Models, tools, best practices, and advice.* Hoboken, NJ: John Wiley & Sons.

Schein, E. H. (2010). *Organizational culture and leadership* (4th ed.). San Francisco, CA: Jossey-Bass.

Name Index

Subject Index

Page reference followed by *fig* indicate an illustrated figure; followed by *t* indicate a table; followed by *e* indicate an exhibit.